Advertising
in
America

Charles Goodrum and Helen Dalrymple

ADVERTISING

IN

AMERICA

The First 200 Years

Harry N. Abrams, Inc., *Publishers*, New York

Editor: Edith M. Pavese
Designer: Dirk Luykx
Photo Research: Neil Ryder Hoos

Frontispiece: Detail of a 1930 Sunkist California Lemons
advertisement that appears on page 131

Library of Congress Cataloging-in-Publication Data
Goodrum, Charles A.
    Advertising in America: the first two hundred years/Charles
Goodrum and Helen Dalrymple.
       p.   cm.
    Includes bibliographical references.
    ISBN 0–8109–1187–6
    1. Advertising—United States—History.   I. Dalrymple, Helen.
II. Title.
HF5813.U6G64   1990
659.1′0973—dc20   90–130
                                                              CIP

Published in 1990 by Harry N. Abrams, Incorporated, New York
A Times Mirror Company

Contents

Introduction

WE ARE ABOUT TO LOOK at two hundred years of American advertising.

There are few things we see more often or feel more strongly about than the endless stream of ads sprayed at us night and day. We are indignant every evening when our meal and news are interrupted by pitches about human ills we wouldn't discuss in a locker room, much less at our dinner tables. We are insulted by slice-of-life vignettes on the whiteness of towels or the wonders of a breakfast food that seem to assume we are childish idiots on our first day out of the cave. Yet we carefully examine the ads' hints on the latest in women's clothing fashion, about men's shaving gadgets, and everybody's electronic equipment, new housing, travel, and books. It's hard to generalize. When we're looking for an apartment, we're grateful for the want ads, but

This is typical patent medicine advertising. Today we sell drugs for slimming; in Grove's day healthy equalled plump. Since there was as yet no way to get color register in mass-produced newspapers or magazines, colored ads came from hand-fed lithograph and job presses. Thus advertising in color was limited to trade cards, multi-sheet posters, and counter cards like this one.

when we open our magazines we're furious at the sheaves of cardboard that must be dealt with before we can read the words we paid our money for. In this book, we're going to examine what's behind all of these ironies, but with such a controversial topic, it's only fair to declare the rules by which we're going to play right at the start.

First off, the above is about all the time we're going to spend viewing with alarm. It is foolish to act as if advertising is some kind of a threat to Western civilization and if only we would face up to it we could get it under control, maybe even make it go away. That's nonsense, and we have neither the time nor the space to belabor it. In this book we're going to look at how advertising got the way it is today, and how it works. We're not going to worry about whether it's good or bad.

Admittedly it is filled with paradox and anomaly. At one point in our research we had a chapter entitled, "They Must Think We're Stupid" into which we accumulated examples of assaults on our intelligence, taste, credulity, and good sense. In no time at all it was so filled with examples that we abandoned it; it was overwhelming all the other aspects we were trying to explore. But it did force us to ask, What is there about this endeavor that seems to strain so many expected givens? Why are there so many ironies? And from this exercise came the various areas we will explore in the coming chapters. Note some of the oddities:

Many of Us Are Threatened by Advertising

We are suspicious of it, even frightened. Why? We're afraid

A good example of "advertising as cultural history." The costume is clearly stated, the layout shows the influence of the then-recent Art Nouveau style, and the overall design of the ad seems "modern" albeit it is eighty years old. The slogan "That Highest Expectations meet Fulfilment," is, however, a long way from "Coke is it."

"Onyx"

Trade Mark

Hosiery

Lord & Taylor

Wholesale Distributers

New York

"Onyx" stamped on a hose means "That Highest Expectations meet Fulfilment."

c.1907

the advertisers know too much about us for our own good. Do they really? They certainly have spent a vast amount of time, money, and energy counting us and filing what we do. They've found such items as:

Forty percent of housewives do not put the spread on the bed in the morning when they make it.

Women will look at a picture of a nude woman longer than a man will. (Gloria Steinem says they are seeking comparison.)

Twenty-five percent of all food is eaten between meals.

Women in New York City use nearly 30 times as much makeup as those living in Vermont.

Eighty percent of all beer is drunk by 20 percent of the beer drinkers.

Women buy 45 percent of all Chevrolets.

The average person spends 3.2 seconds reading a magazine page.

Shoppers will pick up a package with a picture on it faster than if it simply has a design.

Shoppers will buy a round package faster than a square one.

Teenage girls now spend an annual average of $1,500 each in grocery stores (because 70 percent of teenage girls have working mothers who have their daughters do the shopping while the mothers are at work).

1913

This is advertising as the educator of new technology. Here, thirty years before the ordinary citizen had heard of air conditioning, General Electric is promoting a new appliance which proved to be a godsend to urban man.

Note the assurance that the fan is "readily attached to any lamp socket." When existing houses or apartments were first wired, only the drop light wire was installed; wall outlets did not come for another decade or more. The ad contains the copywriters' traditional line, "gives a lifetime of satisfactory service." Little did they know. There are still thousands of these actual fans working without difficulties seventy-five years later.

Our fear that the advertisers can make us think and buy anything they want proves to be somewhat excessive. Studies made outside the advertising world showed that 75 percent of all advertising is either ignored or forgotten. The first full year after tobacco advertising was taken off TV, the sales of cigarettes went up 3 percent and the manufacturers were able to save $70 million that they'd spent on commercials just two years before.

We Don't Believe What We See in Ads

The Victorian lady said, "It must be good; the advertisement spoke so highly of it." A contemporary ad director is shaken when his son shows him a picture in the latest magazine and asks, "Is this true or is it an ad, Dad?" In 1974 a major poll revealed that 59 percent of the public regarded advertising as dishonest; in 1986 the Ogilvy & Mather agency tried it again and found that 70 percent now believed

that ads, in general, do not "present an honest picture of the products advertised." Yet another poll asked what kinds of ads had led them astray, and the answer was overwhelmingly, "Not me. I've never been taken in, but they're dangerous to other people."

Who then? "Elderly people." Your mother or father? "Heavens no. They're more cynical than I am." Children? "Hardly. Saturday morning television commercials have conditioned them never to believe anything they see in ads." How so? "No toy is ever as big, or as dramatic, or does such wonderful things as they're promised. Once they've been disappointed three times, they discount anything they hear on the tube forever." Then who is being taken in? "Well, people on farms and in the ghetto."

So Why Is There So Much Appalling Advertising?

Mainly, we are convinced, because no one knows what a really good advertisement looks like. Once the violin and the bicycle were invented, there wasn't too much more you could do to improve them. But with an advertisement, there is an endless, almost metaphysical number of ways it can be created but no way of knowing which one is best—or even which one works at all.

This seems impossible to believe, but it is so. One of the classic quotes in advertising (it has been attributed to John Wanamaker in this country and Lord Leverhulme in England) is: "I am certain that half of the money I spend on advertising is completely wasted. The trouble is, I don't know which half." If this was bad in Wanamaker's time, think what it is like when you spend $1.3 billion a year as Procter & Gamble does. If the half that is wasted out of this could be put in the stockholders' pockets, it would make a nice start toward a vacation in Cannes.

Consider this catechism: Why do you advertise? To sell your product. What should a good advertisement do? According to Daniel Pope, an ad should provide "informational clues" regarding such matters as price, value, packaging, taste, safety, benefit to the buyer or provide new ideas for the use of the product. So we examine some television commercials:

> Jf it plese ony man spirituel or temporel to bye ony pyes of two and thre comemoracios of Salisburi use enpryntid after the forme of this preset lettre whiche ben wel and truly correct, late hym come to Westmonester in to the almonestrye at the reed pale and he shal habe them good chepe .·.·
>
> **Supplico stet cedula.**

1477

This is the first ad in English; it was written by William Caxton, and tells us that he is offering a volume of Easter rules. The books are for sale at his printshop under the sign of the red shield in the Westminster building where welfare payments are passed out. There the books can be had "good cheap."

One of the most famous advertising campaigns of all time is "Coke is it." That's all; that's it. It ran for years and that is all that was ever said. When General Motors was under its greatest pressure by Japanese carmakers to explain why its cars drove better, lasted longer, were safer, and got better mileage than the imports, it threw massive resources into a saturation campaign based on the single, repeated statement: "Listen to the heartbeat, Listen to the heartbeat, Listen to the heartbeat . . . of America." Many of the television commercials in the series showed only a single, one-second silhouette of the product, in this case, a Chevrolet. (In a recent year, by the way, Chevrolet spent over $150 million on advertising, which worked out to $71 per car sold. Not too bad considering the competition, but was it the advertising that sold the car or . . . ?)

The early soap manufacturers would have said that "Coke is it" was plenty. Pears' soap, promptly copied by Ivory, believed that the idea was simply to put the word Pears' (and then Ivory) in front of the reader again and again and again. You didn't have to tell what Ivory was or what it did just so it was in every magazine and every paper at least once a month—or week—forever. "Keep the Name before the People."

The N.W. Ayer ad agency's motto was, "Keeping everlastingly at it brings success." Bell Telephone believed this for almost a century even when the product it was selling was a monopoly, but they hoped to make Ma Bell so much a part of our consciousness that we would never challenge its role. Scholars presently studying what led to the painful break-up of AT&T lay much of the blame on the house advertising which, for example, Steve Coll charges against the flood of words which "impressed a lot of people in Washington with a kind of arrogance, [so] that nobody believed them." If this is so, Ma Bell should have followed William A. Shryer's advice from the 1920s: "The law of diminishing returns . . . is the real law of advertising." He said that you gradually convinced the customer "until the buying threshold was crossed"—then you stopped the campaign. After that your ad money was simply going down the drain. How could you tell when the threshold had been reached for the greatest number of customers? He finally concluded that a good manager could "just feel it in his bones."

But Can't Research and Polling Tell Which Ads "Worked" and Which Didn't?

No, unfortunately, they can't. There is still no way to determine whether it was the current campaign that got the product sold, or residue from previous campaigns. Was it the innovative presentation that got the customer out of his chair, or the economic situation, his colleagues' advice, his wife's impatience, or simply that the old one wore out right now and he "always" buys that brand. (Seventy percent of owners of anything re-buy another one just like the last one. Either satisfaction or habit.)

Well, at least the famous ads that we know and remember worked. Recall Alka-Seltzer's "I can't believe I ate the whole

"They said father didn't keep his Life Insurance paid up!"

THE PRUDENTIAL INSURANCE COMPANY *of* AMERICA
EDWARD D. DUFFIELD, *President*   HOME OFFICE, *Newark, N.J.*

1926

A typical ad of the 1920s–1930s. The panel tells a story, a "slice-of-life vignette." The sales message goes straight to the throat to get your attention, load your guilt, and get you to send in your payment. This was before Social Security, however, and a lapsed policy could indeed have tragic consequences—though not necessarily the orphan asylum.

thing!" series? Sorry. Not a good example. The more those ads ran, the more Pepto-Bismol was sold. We all laughed at the miserable victim, but when we became miserable ourselves we thought, "Alka-Seltzer thinks it's all a big joke and doesn't take my symptoms seriously. I feel awful. I want something serious to fix me up. Better buy Pepto-Bismol. All it ever promises is to coat and soothe my stomach walls, and boy, do my stomach walls need soothing." Remember how surprised we were when the Alka-Seltzer series was abruptly cancelled? (The lying Joe Isuzu car salesman was the most remembered of all television commercials two years running with the highest "sympathetic" response from the viewers researched. During the same two years, the number of Isuzu cars actually sold sagged steadily downward.)

It is enough to make an ad director weep. David Ogilvy, one of the most powerful of these himself, was bemused by Harry McMahan's analysis of the winners of the prestigious Clio Awards. The Clios identify the finest television commercials each year, and Ogilvy reports: "Agencies that won four of the Clios had lost the accounts. Another Clio winner was out of business. Another Clio winner had taken its budget out of TV. Another Clio winner had given half his account to another agency. Another refused to put his winning entry on the air. Of 81 television classics picked by the Clio festival in previous years, 36 of the agencies involved had either lost the account or gone out of business."

Well Then How Should a Perfect Ad Look?

People have been trying to design the perfect advertisement for centuries. The earliest advertisement in English was written by William Caxton in 1477 to sell a prayer book he'd published on his new press in Westminster Abbey. A facsimile of the ad appears on page 8.

Fine copywriting skills turn up early in the American story. Here's one written by Paul Revere in 1768 to sell his own brand of false teeth:

> Whereas many Persons are so unfortunate as to lose their fore-teeth by Accident, and otherways, to their great detriment not only in looks, but speaking both in Public and Private:—This is to inform all such, that they may have them re-placed with artificial Ones that look as well as the Natural, and answers the End of Speaking to all Intents, by PAUL REVERE, Goldsmith, near the Head of Dr. Clarke's Wharf, Boston.

As James Playsted Wood used to say, note the "modern" technique of his copy: He stresses the improvement of the buyer's "looks" first, how it will improve his public and private speaking second, and avoids the unglamorous gnawing of food altogether.

In the coming chapters, we'll see examples of really fine, honest, innovative ads through all the two hundred years, but as we searched the rows of magazines, what struck us most forcibly was the amount of repetition that occurred within any time period. In any decade, "they all seem to look alike" and from this comes a fundamental discovery: Since no one knows how a good advertisement really should look, whenever anybody thinks of one that appears to work, everyone copies it constantly—until the readers become first numb and then resentful. (But note that we customers are equally to blame for this endless duplication. Nowadays with so much money at stake, all ads and commercials are tested ad nauseum. Soap commercials, for example, are screened before club groups, church organizations, and faculty wives. At every showing, at least three possible ads are shown ranging from the "arty" to the hard sell, and time after time the review groups vote for those "hidden camera" routines showing the woman astonished that the whitest

stack of towels was washed with New and Improved Bubbly. We too expect an ad to look like all the other ads we know.)

As we will see, the ubiquitous Benjamin Franklin and a man by the name of George P. Rowell invented the way an ad looked in the early days of the Republic. A couple of generations later P.T. Barnum revolutionized the pioneer image. Two generations more and the patent medicine kings F.G. Kinsman and J.C. Ayer did it again. Then with the twentieth century the imitating comes faster. All automobile ads looked alike in the Twenties, Depression advertising looks like it was rubber stamped (among other things, refrigerators are always examined by men in tuxedos and women in evening gowns). In our day, innovators like William Bernbach with his Volkswagen ads, Calvin Klein with his perfume and blue jeans, and Claymation with its dancing raisins make a creative breakthrough, and then everyone else mirrors that one image until somebody gets a new idea and the profession stampedes to copy the new approach. Why does this happen? Three reasons at least: 1) Advertising now costs so much everyone wants to go with a sure thing; 2) The man paying the bill says, "I want an ad just like X; it looks great and my wife likes it"; and 3) There aren't that many Bernbachs and Kleins and Della Feminas to go around.

Enough of This for the Moment

The above ironies and paradoxes are simply samples of the kinds of things we will discover in the following chapters. What are we looking for in this book? Primarily how advertising got to be what it is in America. We're trying to find out how it has influenced our taste, the way we live, the places and clothes we live in. We will try to discover these matters in the following steps:

Bill Bernbach's famous Volkswagen campaign began in 1959 and soon symbolized the "creative advertising" approach of the 1960s. It embraced humor, single-point sales emphasis, dramatic layout, and honesty. Not only did it chalk up one of the highest readerships of any ad campaign ever, but it sold cars.

1963

JUST BECAUSE YOU'RE A NICE GIRL DOESN'T MEAN YOU CAN'T HAVE EVIL LEGS.

NIKE
APPAREL

1988

We'll start with a short, fast history of the whole topic so that we have established a timeline on which to hang more detailed examinations of parts of it. (The most astonishing thing we'll discover about the historical aspect of the subject is that almost everything that's used in today's advertising—all the ways the seller tries to get our attention and tries to convince us to buy his product—had been tried, perfected, and locked into the national perception of "how an advertisement looks" well over a hundred years ago. The ideas that were tried, failed, discarded, and haven't been used again, are as interesting as what seems to have worked.)

We will then examine some of the original shakedown experiments. Cereals, soap, and sex. And then exhume the first advertisements for some of the remarkably ancient products we still see advertised on tonight's television. Is there some great truth in the fact that a good majority of these started out designed for a completely different purpose from what we use them for today?

We will next note how ads for different kinds of products each have a theme and a tempo of their own—ways to change our appearance, travel, nudity or the lack of it, and special devices whose selling techniques have been refined and repeated through the years until they've become as ritualized as a religious litany. We meet these ancient protocols in the way we're sold cosmetics, automobiles, cigarettes, and underwear.

The ad makers have gotten very good at telling us their various stories, but occasionally they've overshot. We will look at some of their excesses at which we flinch and say, Oh no! They wouldn't dare. But they did. A gallery of shudders.

We will be looking at print images, not television. The printed ad spans the full two hundred years, the video only the last forty but it represents a whole world of its own and deserves a separate book to examine its techniques and idiosyncrasies. For comparison purposes, what TV sells and how it does it will be noted in the text but not in the images.

We must remember throughout our two-hundred-year sweep that the people who saw these ads were just as smart as we are, and just as unlikely to be taken in as we think we are. We must also recall throughout that the sole purpose of the ads from 1789 to date has been to sell us something. They want 1) to get our attention; 2) to convince us that what they're selling is desirable; and 3) to get us to go out—rise from our chair or couch—and *do* something. Half the fun is to ask, Did it work? Did they do it fairly? Would we have been convinced when they first appeared—indeed were we convinced in our own time? (And did the product work out the way they promised?)

For these reasons, scattered in among the intriguing examples of two hundred years of style and invention are some examinations of the reality of it all: how advertising functions, how it uses the skills of the artists and the creative writer, and how it seizes onto devices of each generation to hold our attention.

And having been bemused by the occasionally frivolous and superficial, we will end by looking at how advertising has changed our thinking about some things truly fundamental and significant.

What *isn't* here? As we have noted, television is given too short a shrift. The other element that is missing is the life stories of the great figures of the trade: the Albert Laskers and George Washington Hills and the many innovative minds of our own time. Examples of their work and the significance of what they did are here, but we have not done justice to their interesting and often colorful personalities. Again, the product seemed more important than the person when there wasn't room to do both. Our apologies to the people who did these creations, but the choice was ours. Don't blame the publisher.

Except for these admittedly major omissions, we hope there follows a fair examination of the first two hundred years of American advertising. Please join us. Lean back and enjoy.

James Walker,

At the Sign of the PIECE of LINEN, No. 14, WILLIAM-STREET,

Is now Selling off by the Piece or at Retail,

A variety of SEASONABLE and FASHIONABLE

DRY GOODS,

Many of them are bought at Public Vendue for less than prime cost, which he is enabled to sell from 1 to 25 per cent. CHEAPER than they are in general sold for;

VIZ.

SUPERFINE Broad, second and elastic cloths,

Buff, white and coloured cassimeres,

Double milled drab cloths,

Plain frizes, German serges, coatings flannels and baizes of different widths and colours,

Rose and striped blankets,

Milled and other swanskins,

Red, blue, green and white serges,

Ladies superfine coating,

Moreens, rattinets and shalloons,

A fashionable assortment of coat and vest buttons,

Taborets, durants, wildbores and tammies,

Camblets, callimancoes and bird-eye stuffs,

Silk and worsted crapes,

Sattinets, lastings and florentines,

Princess stuff and princetta,

Hair and worsted plushes,

Gentlemen's patent silk, cotton and worsted hosiery,

Twilled velvets, corduroys and thicksets,

Cotton-denim and royal rib.

Silk florentines and sattins of different colours, Nankeens

Pealongs, modes, and farsnets,

China and mode ribbons,

India taffaties and lutestrings of different colours,

Ladies black, white and coloured silk, gloves and mitts,

Kid, dog, lambskin and worsted do.

An assortment of gentlemens buckskin woodstock, beaver and kid gloves,

Black silk and washleather do.

Striped, check, jaconet and book muslins,

Do. Handkerchiefs,

Muslinets and dimities,

Marseilles and mock marseilles quilting and drawboys,

Chintzes, callicoes and cottons of various patterns, furniture do.

3 1-2, 4, and 4 1-2 pins,

Shawls and cotton handkerchiefs,

Pocket   do.

Printed linens,

Linen from 9d to 8s 6d per yard,

Cambricks and lawn,

Lenau and Scotch nets,

Scotch and coloured threads,

Bedticks by the yard or in patterns,

Silk cotton, cap, ribbon and skeleton wires,

Gentlemens fancy, velvet, and toilanet vest patterns,

Mens youths and childrens beaver, castor and wool hats, of different colours,

Ladies, sattinet, callimanco and lasting shoes. &c. &c.

NEW-YORK: Printed by HARRISSON & PURDY, No. 3, Peck-Slip, where Printing in general is performed with neatness, accuracy and dispatch, and on the most reasonable terms.

1790

At the Sign of the Piece of Linen in New York, James Walker tells his customers he has colored cashmeres, green serges, worsted plushes, and beaver skin gloves. He also has "Taborets, durants, wildbores, and tammies" with "camblets, callimancoes and bird-eye stuffs." This is a typical broadside ad used to escape the cramped space of contemporary newspapers. Note the variety of readable type styles and intricate borders.

A Short History of Advertising in America— From the Founding of the Republic to World War I

WE PICK UP THE STORY of American advertising in 1789—the year of the founding of the Republic. By the time we start, advertising is already here and remarkably well developed, having been imported from England where it is already a major, thriving business. Shop signs, the earliest billboards, have been in use in the colonies since the 1600s. The word "advertisement" has headed posters and broadsides nailed to post office and court house walls since 1660. By the end of the Revolution there are some 43 weekly newspapers in existence, and in 1784 the first daily has begun. But we have to be careful of the scene we paint, because it has some oddities in it. It is not today's commercial scene simply in period costume.

First, what are they advertising? Three things will cover 80 percent of the copy: land, runaways (slaves and indentured servants), and transportation—the latter announcing stagecoach schedules and the arrival and departure of ships with descriptions of their cargoes. The remaining 20 percent of the ads will be lists of goods offered for sale by local merchants and descriptions of books newly published. The point: these are simply announcements essentially answering the reader's two questions—where and when? Does anyone in the community have thread for sale? Has anybody got any cheese? When will there be a ship going to Charleston? Apparently the thirst for this kind of advertising was enormous. The first daily newspaper had 10 columns of advertising in a paper of 16 columns. That was in Philadelphia. The first New York daily in 1785 was overwhelmingly advertising with a thin film of news; it had pictures of furniture and cuts of three-masted sailing ships. This ratio of ads to news continued without change right into the 1800s.

This gets to the second element we should remember. *Where* you made your announcement governed what your advertising looked like. There were fully developed type fonts up to 36-points, but there was very little paper to print them on. All paper was 100-percent rag—marvelous stuff that was flexible, durable, and took ink beautifully—but was very hard to come by. Even before the Revolution, when most of the rags for paper came from England, they were always in short supply because rags were perpetually recycled by the consumers. They went from shirts and dresses into quilts and coverlets and then braided into rugs so it was years before they were sufficiently deteriorated to be sold by the pound for paper. Even then there wasn't much money to be made in it. It took three men a whole day to make enough paper for that day's newspaper, but you couldn't charge more than a few pennies for the edition, leaving very little for the paper it was printed on. The largest paper mill in New England was run by the *Hartford Courant* which could produce a bit over a thousand sheets a day, but the sheets (folded once to make four pages) produced a newspaper no larger than a present-day *Time* magazine page. Hartford was at the top of the scale. Many major urban papers had to get by on 300 to 400 sheets a day.

When the British were here and paper was more plentiful, creative publishers like Benjamin Franklin could produce beautiful newspapers—and very appealing advertisements. Franklin had been the first to use pictures to break up blocks of text; he used lots of white space around centered headlines, and made special engravings of spectacles and gloved hands for special customers. But by our 1789 date these aesthetics were disappearing fast. Paper was so scarce that

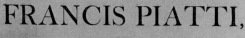

1788

1809

LEFT:

The New-York Journal and Weekly Register as it appeared in the final days before the paper shortage forced shrunken pages and tiny type.

BELOW LEFT:

Francis Piatti, trading in Richmond, Virginia, at the corner of the Street leading to Coutt's Ferry, offers West Indies and New England rum, salt by the sack or the bushel, powder and shot, and fish by the barrel. Doing business in a time of very little money, he concludes his broadside ad with: "He will sell low for CASH, or Country Produce . . . N.B. The highest Price given for every description of Country Produce."

OPPOSITE ABOVE LEFT:

Notices of runaway indentured servants, apprentices, and slaves were among the commonest form of advertisement from the beginnings of newspapers in this country. (The oldest known ad is on a Babylonian tablet requesting the return of a slave some 3,000 years ago.) This is an 1824 note from the Raleigh, North Carolina, Register seeking the future President, Andrew Johnson, who had run away from his tailor's apprenticeship. (This ad was a favorite discovery of Frank Presbrey, a leading advertising historian of the 1920s.)

OPPOSITE ABOVE RIGHT:

A graceful broadside with at least seven type fonts in evidence. Mr. Boyd, in Boston, notes: "It is known to all who have had any care of horses, that their standing on dry litter, or on a dry floor is unnatural to their feet—so much so, that from this cause alone, great numbers of them soon become [afflicted with] contracted heels, sand cracks, running thrushes, false quarters, &c." Mr. Boyd's sponge boots will solve all.

OPPOSITE BELOW LEFT:

A chilling broadside of the time, which would have been tacked to tree trunks at local crossroads, and on the courthouse and post office walls.

OPPOSITE BELOW RIGHT:

By the 1830s, shortage of paper had shrunk the type size to 6-point, and squeezed 6 columns on to the traditional 9 × 12 page. Thumbnail cuts sorted out the real estate and transportation ads. At least half of the paper was given over to advertising. Publishers believed that it was more prestigious to run many short ads than fewer long ones.

Ten Dollars Reward.

RAN AWAY from the Subscriber, on the night of the 15th instant, two apprentice boys, legally bound, named WILLIAM and ANDREW JOHNSON The former is of a dark complexion, black hair, eyes, and habits. They are much of a height, about 5 feet 4 or 5 inches The latter is very fleshy freckled face, light hair, and fair complexion. They went off with two other apprentices, advertised by Messrs Wm. & Chas. Fowler When they went away, they were well clad—blue cloth coats, light colored homespun coats, and new hats, the maker's name in the crown of the hats, is Theodore Clark. I will pay the above Reward to any person who will deliver said apprentices to me in Raleigh, or I will give the above Reward for Andrew Johnson alone

All persons are cautioned against harboring or employing said apprentices, on pain of being prosecuted.

JAMES J. SELBY, Tailor.

Raleigh, N. C. June 24, 1824   26 3t

1824

PATENT
SPONGE BOOTS,
FOR HORSES FEET.

THE subscriber respectfully informs the public, that he is manufacturing and has for sale, the above article, the utility of which, in preserving Horses' Feet from the many diseases to which they are liable, is appreciated on first sight, by all who have seen them.

It is known to all who have had any care of horses, that their standing on dry litter, or on a dry floor, is unnatural to their feet—so much so, that from this cause alone, great numbers of them soon become unsound.—Some of these diseases of the feet are known by the names of contracted heels, sand cracks, running thrushes, false quarters, &c. all of which can be prevented if the hoof can only be kept moist. To communicate this necessary moisture is the object of the

Patent Sponge Boots.

There is no trouble or inconvenience attending the use of these Boots. They may be kept on all the time the horse stands in the stable, only taking care to wet the sponge afresh, with soft water, every 12 hours.

Gentlemen who keep valuable horses, are respectfully invited to call and examine this article. They may find that by spending a *few* dollars they will save a great many, besides contributing vastly to the comfort of their animals; for it is believed that a dry, hard hoof, on a horse, produces a similar sensation to what a tight, hard boot or shoe produces on a human being. It is expected that the use of these Boots will entirely restore hoofs that have already become so brittle as to be incapable of holding the shoe.

Orders for the above, from any part of the country, will be attended to with punctuality.

JAMES BOYD.

Boston, June 1, 1825.   24, Merchants' Row.

TRUE AND GREENE, PRINTERS, BOSTON.

1825

LAND, NEGROES,
Stock, &c.
FOR SALE.

Being about to move my residence, I shall offer for sale, on the premises, on Monday the 21st of Jan next, to the highest bidder, on a credit of 1, 2 and 3 years, the Plantation on which I reside, in the county of Amelia, 40 miles from Richmond, 45 from Petersburg, and 8 from Amelia courthouse.

This tract is bounded by the Genito Road on the North, and by Flat Creek on the South; and contains between 1800 and 2000 acres of land, 250 of which are low grounds, partly reclaimed. There are 200 bushels of wheat sown on the land in good order, and some work done in next year's corn field. There is a large and comfortable dwelling house on the land, built within the last 9 years; houses for domestic purposes; good stables; a barn with a threshing machine attached (entirely new;) 6 large tobacco barns, all in good repair. The tract, if required, may be advantageously divided into two parts, allotting to each division a fair proportion of wood land, and houses necessary for farming purposes

At the same time and place, I shall sell to the highest bidder, for cash, 120 negroes, all of them born and raised on the plantation. The stock of all kinds, horses, cattle, hogs, sheep, household and kitchen furniture, plantation utensils, corn, fodder, shucks, straw— then remaining on the place will be sold.

Terms—for the land, bonds with approved security and a deed of trust on the property, and credit of 12 months, bearing interest from the date, if not punctually paid, on all sums over $20—under that sum, cash will be required.   W. J. BARKSDALE.

Haw-Branch, Amelia, Nov. 6, 1827.

N. B. The sale of the Negroes and the personal property, will certainly be made on the day appointed, whether the land is sold or no.   W. J. B.

1827

1831

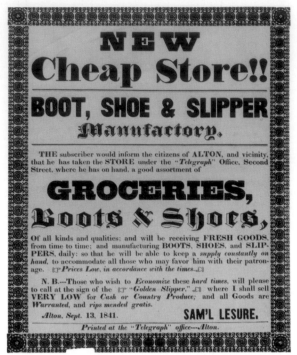

1841

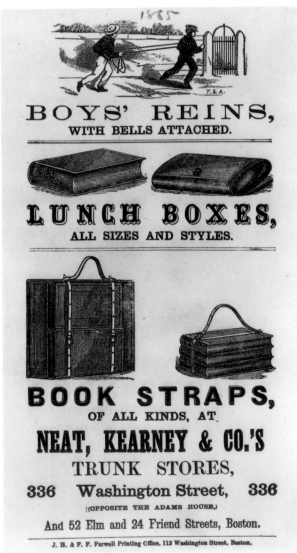

1865

the type size went from standard 12-point Caslon down to 6-point throughout the newspaper and this norm held for nearly 70 years. The New York papers crowded more and more type into less and less space so that all white space disappeared, pictures were eliminated, columns were increased from three to five then six per page; rules between columns were dropped, and from the beginning of the Republic until nearly the Civil War every page—ads or news—looked like our present want ad or legal announcement pages. This had two effects on advertising. It limited newspaper ads to abbreviated statements of product lists, and it moved "creative advertising"—display advertising—to handbills, broadsides, and trade cards.

Broadsides were usually the width of a newspaper page, but twice the length, and thus provided plenty of space in which to play around with elaborated copy and fancy type. Once printed they would be tacked up in public places, hung in bunches by the doors of stagecoaches and river packets where they were suspended by string driven through the top of the paper. Travelers would snap off copies and read them in their seats.

Broadsides were one-shot advertisements very similar to magazine ads today; newspaper ads were either announcements of the receipt of sale products or a listing of what a store sold. By the end of the 1700s, there was a set price of $30 a year for the running newspaper ads, and once set, the standing type would be used over and over again; the copy was seldom changed.

Finally, in thinking about where advertising all started, we must remember what the customers were like. For the first half century of the Republic, there was very little money to be spent. Ninety percent of the country lived on farms and the householders sold what small surplus there was after providing for themselves and their families. This surplus was the money the ads were appealing to, and most of it went for coffee and salt, hardware, clothes, and tools. Practically everything else was grown on the farm itself or traded with the neighbors. Oddly enough there was very little need to "advertise" to get customers. There was too little of *every-*

The advertising historian Frank Rowsome (who found this ad in a New York newspaper of the day) says that Barnum hated white space. Barnum believed that if you've paid for space you should fill it with everything you know; but to prevent an ad from simply being dense gray type, he would slant the lines, vary the typefaces, and slip in woodcuts with abandon. His prose style set a standard for generations of copywriters to come.

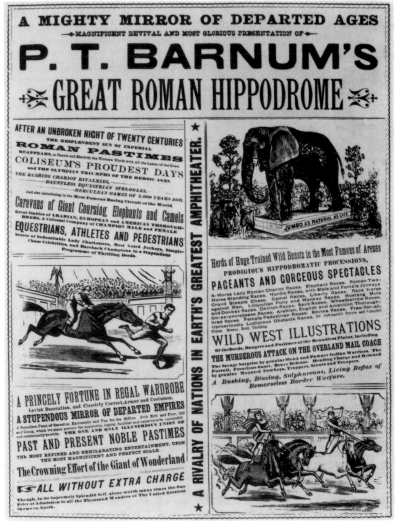

c. 1855

thing; anything you could make could be sold—wagons, shoes, flour, houses—for the first fifty years of the nation. The problem was rarely to find a market (and word of mouth took care of most of the exchange); the problem was finding someone with money to pay for it. The stock line at the bottom of the ads and broadsides read: "We will sell low for cash or country produce." Very few of the customers worked *for* anyone, and the few who did were paid in room, board, and a tiny amount of cash. As the economists say, they did not *earn* a living, they *made* a living. When this condition changed, advertising as we think of it, began in earnest.

1800 to the Civil War

When the 1800s started, most advertising was by local merchants selling to their own communities. As the communities grew larger and got richer, the merchants could sell more products to more people, but what they sold was what they sought out within a day's travel from their store. Very little was made at a distance and shipped to the market. Moving and storing things was extraordinarily difficult getting from the source to the shop via wagons for many years, and then by railroads. (The tracks reached the Mississippi in 1853.) Thus the earliest produce brought in from the outside was mainly sugar, coffee, liquor, and patent medicines. The first were generic—one sugar loaf was as good as the next—but the specific patent medicines were one of a kind. They became one of the earliest sources of national advertising.

The "patent" did not refer to having a patent on the ingredient, but was left over from colonial days when the bottles (small, easy to ship, and producing a lot of money for a small object) referred to the fact that they carried the crest of the king. As with Elizabeth II who still has certain tailors and food providers as special purveyors to the Crown, certain elixirs sold in the mid-1700s were granted a "patent of royal favor": patent medicine. Local merchants took out ads announcing that they were carrying specific patent medicines, and thus began what were essentially trademarks for specific products. From this thin edge of the wedge came the growth of patent medicine advertising which by the end of the 1800s provided one-third of all the profits made by the American press. We will return to this phenomenon.

As the 1800s developed, more and more goods were made in distant places and spread beyond their home communities to be sold: plows, stoves, textiles, hats, tobacco. By the 1830s the inventors began to produce specific gadgets made in a single shop and sold a long way from home: Cyrus McCormick's reaper in 1831, Elias Howe's sewing machine in 1846, and the like. In the middle of the decade, the French sent over a new papermaking machine that produced an endless sheet of paper made from all colors of rags. Until then rags for paper had to be light-colored to make light paper, but in the 1830s the chemical chlorine was discovered, and this permitted the bleaching of used rope and dark stockings, and with it the supply of rags for papermaking doubled and trebled. With more and cheaper paper available, newspapers started up everywhere and the first advertising agencies appeared, ready to exploit the added space available for ads.

G. P. Rowell & Co.'s Advertising Agency,
No. 40 Park Row, New York.
Send for a Circular giving lists of 1000 leading Newspapers and advertising rates.
THE LIST SYSTEM.

1868

George P. Rowell opened one of the very first advertising agencies in America, and he himself was certainly the most famous of the early agents. As soon as he found an advertising device that worked, he told all his competitors about it "for the benefit of the new profession." In 1888, he founded Printers' Ink, *one of the original advertising magazines.*

1875

The Chicago Daily Tribune, *January 3, 1875. By now, wood pulp newsprint has made paper cheap and plentiful. Large, display type shouts for attention, and white space is fashionable again. There are seven columns each on sixteen pages, but pictures in ads are still rare.*

The First of Many Philosophical Anomalies about Advertising

Advertising has long bothered the economists because it seems to be irrational in the substantial amounts of money it takes out of possible profit to be made on a product. A box of breakfast food has about four cents' worth of grain, 40 cents' worth of packaging and shipping, and the rest of the dollar and a half to two dollars is about equally divided between advertising and profit. A bottle of bourbon costs less than 50 cents to make, bottle, and ship; $5 goes for taxes, and the rest of the $10 is evenly split between profit and advertising. [How many cans of Pepsi must the company sell to recoup the cost of the latest Michael Jackson commercial? Answer: 192,307,692.]

The economists used to believe that the progress of advertising and sales went like this: Up to the Civil War, anyone who made something either made just enough to anticipate his buyers' needs, or he collected orders from his buyers and made the product after he had their orders in hand. With the invention of interchangeable parts, assembly lines, and factories to make things, goods flowed in streams rather than one at a time, and the manufacturers soon had too much invested in plants, tools, and employees to sit around waiting for orders; they could no longer even tolerate an "off season." They had to keep the plant running and the staff employed all the time, so they had to generate more and more sales, increasingly distant from the plant.

It used to be believed that at this point the manufacturer began to advertise beyond his neighboring customers. More newspapers in more towns gave him a place for his advertisements; more railroads permitted him to send his product farther from the factory; and more people with more money permitted him to sell ever more pieces of his product so his factory could run full speed, efficiently, the year around.

This theory has been the traditional understanding for many years. However, like the doctors and the nutritionists who reverse the conventional wisdom at endless intervals, the economists now tell us that this explanation misses the point. Mass, national advertising came about for a different reason, it is now believed: we are now told that the steady increase of inventions and factories and customers in the period up to the Civil War did indeed increase the number of goods flowing out; it was not, however, the need to sell more products that led to advertising but the need to get control of the price the manufacturer charged for his goods.

In the beginning, if a man needed a new wagon, he went to the two or three shops that made wagons in his community and asked how much they were wanted for a wagon, and then presumably bought the cheapest one from the man who could be trusted to make a good product. When the food jobber wanted to buy chocolate to re-sell to the grocers on his route, he went to the various chocolate packagers and found the cheapest price available. This left the manufacturer or the packager at the mercy of the buyer. The buyer told them what he would pay and they had to meet his demand at his price. *But* if the wagon maker could set a standard of quality, and set a specific trademark on his product, he could then say "If you want to buy a Studebaker wagon you must pay $100, take it or leave it. We don't care if you can get somebody else's for $75, it won't be a Studebaker." Similarly, "If you want Baker's chocolate, you'll pay a quarter; you can get other people's chocolate for 15 cents, but it won't be Baker's."

The challenge then, was to convince the citizens that they wanted Studebaker wagons so badly they would pay the extra amount of money to get them; to get the customer to want Baker's chocolate so badly that the grocers had to stock it and demand that their wholesaler-jobber sell it even if he didn't make nearly as much profit on Baker's as the special deal he could work with the 15-cents man.

Oddly enough, this parable seems to hold true at both ends of the timeline: Baker's chocolate was indeed one of the few brand names said to sit on the shelves in Abraham Lincoln's store in Old Salem, Illinois, and Studebaker wagons began to appear as a branded item (made many hundreds of miles away from where they were sold) as early as 1852. Similarly, today, many breakfast food and detergent manufacturers say the main reason they advertise is to bring the customer to a point that she *demands* that her local supermarket carries their brand. There are only x number of feet of shelving given over to cereals and soaps; the supermarket would much prefer to sell its own brands and dozens of new competitors are eagerly trying to muscle on to those limited shelves, but in order to keep Post and Kellogg's and Procter & Gamble products sitting there—and taking up all the space—they must keep the customers demanding them by name. If the supermarket does not stock them, the customer will go to a supermarket that does. Thus the present thought: the reason national advertisers advertise is not primarily to sell more of their products as individual units to individual customers, but to make the products so appealing that they can set their price in their factory (not in the marketplace) and see to it that the jobbers and wholesalers and supermarkets must stock them regardless of what price they set on them. Thus advertising permits higher profits, not just more sales. That is the current accepted wisdom; the period in which it set its roots was from 1830 to the Civil War.

The Look of Advertising in 1850

By 1850, the nation was booming; anyone who wanted a job could find one, and the swelling floods of immigrants did not begin to fill the need for workers. Industrial production was expanding exponentially, and the need for advertising the new products grew with it. How did an ad look by 1850? Newspaper ads were more repellent than ever. Most major papers required that no ad could be longer than two or three lines. All ads had to be in small type and in the same type style throughout the paper. No cuts or headlines could be

1888

Land has been advertised from the advent of American newspapers. Sometimes it has been by an individual owner, sometimes a developer, often the Federal Government. In this case The Kansas City, Lawrence & Southern R.R. is publicizing land that it merely hopes *will become available if Congress will only take it away from the Indians and open it to public homestead and pre-emption.*

POSTMASTER:
If not called for by the party to whom this is addressed, please hand to some unmarried person over 16 years of age.
DON'T DESTROY IT.

c. 1870

These instructions were traditionally printed on the envelopes of patent medicine direct-mail advertisements.

Late nineteenth century

Bitters were usually used to calm the stomach and involved various root drugs in a solution of 19 percent alcohol. Northern Army doctors used them in great quantities during the Civil War, and introduced the troops to their comfort in the way "take two aspirins" and "let these fizz in a glass of water" are prescribed today. Proprietary medicines were addicted to alliterations: Radway's Ready Relief; Swift's Syphilitic Specific; Cascarets Candy Catharitic.

used, and nothing could be wider than one column. Why? Because it was believed that to do otherwise would be unfair to the small advertiser. Everybody's dollar was worth the same, and it wasn't fair that just because some sellers could afford more, their ads should be permitted to detract from the little advertiser who couldn't afford as much. James Gordon Bennett with his huge *New York Herald* stated this repeatedly, but he also insisted that no ad could run longer

than two weeks without changing the copy. You could buy an ad by the day for 50 cents or for two weeks for $2.50 (two days' pay for a working man).

The deadly dull, half-inch ad had an odd side-effect. People who had a one-shot specific item to sell used it to describe their offering. But people who were selling the same kind of goods over and over, and were simply reminding the reader of its existence, devised slogans or catchwords that would just fill a line of type; they would repeat the line three times to make the block look different from adjacent ads, and get two or three variations to meet the new-copy-every-two-weeks rule. From this came the "Use Sapolio" and "Have You Used Pears' Today?" which grew into "Ivory—It Floats" and "Royal Baking Powder is Absolutely Pure." This so-called "iteration advertising" started the idea of slogans, and resulted in the ultimate breakdown of the every-ad-the-same-size rule.

While the dull page lasted, however, the result was that newspapers sold enormous amounts of space in one-inch chunks but at the same time forced any form of imaginative design into broadsides, handbills, and posters. And the famous P.T. Barnum created the image—the prototype to be copied—for these larger and more imaginative formats. Barnum started as a patent medicine salesman, shouting the benefits of his concoctions by the use of wild, typographic displays to attract attention. He filled these ads with agonizing testimonials describing the painful symptoms his medicines would cure, and followed all of the above with dignified endorsements from crowned heads and members of the U.S. Senate attesting to the effectiveness of his cures. Hyperbole was expected, and the customers learned to discount everything they read by whatever degree experience had taught them.

All of Barnum's techniques for advertising proprietary medicine moved into the general stream of product advertising, and by the outbreak of the Civil War, handbill and broadside ads featured marvelous displays of oversized type and fancy borders. Testimonials had become small, slice-of-life vignettes, and endorsements gradually worked their way across the full spectrum of products. Obviously, we have all these techniques with us today, right up to last night's TV commercials. The fact that so many of advertising's ways of getting our attention started with patent medicines and then moved with Barnum into circus and theater advertising, has caused what must be an unfair association in many generations' minds.

The Invention of the Advertising Agent

In the final years before the Civil War, newspapers not only proliferated, but their readership pressed deeper into the community. Richard Hoe's new rotary press could turn out 18,000 impressions an hour instead of the traditional 3,000 on a flat-bed; the paper supply was adequate (though still 100-percent rag), and the increasingly prosperous merchants were eager to advertise. But it wasn't easy. No one knew which all the papers were or where they were located. No one (including the major papers themselves) knew how many readers they had, and there were no set rates for commercial accounts—these were bargained over at each submission. It will come as no surprise then that this vacuum of unknowns produced the first advertising agents.

The first ones were really newspaper space salesmen. They provided no help in preparing the advertisement—just finding places to run it—but they got very rich very fast. The two usually credited with getting the idea first were Volney B. Palmer, who started in Boston in 1841 and soon opened offices in New York and Philadelphia, and John L. Hooper, who set up shop in New York alone. Their approach was fairly obvious. They each wrote to every paper they had ever heard of, and sent letters all over the country simply addressed to postmasters asking that they deliver the envelopes to any newspaper in their local communities. The letters offered to buy a certain number of column inches a certain number of times a month. The agents guaranteed cash payment at the outset, and this got the publishers' attention since 25 percent of all advertising receipts had traditionally gone uncollected. Once they'd agreed on a price with the publishers, the agents went to the merchants and patent medicine companies and offered to see that their ads were run in x number of papers x number of times for x amount of money. The idea caught on quickly and after a few years Hooper's agency was absorbed into a new George P. Rowell Company in Boston, and Palmer was bought out by N.W. Ayer in Philadelphia. (The venerable N.W. Ayer company is still in business.)

These start-up efforts sound so obvious one wonders why it all began so slowly and by so few—there were barely a half dozen such agencies as late as 1865—but the fact was that no one really seemed to have any idea about the five unknowns in the formula: what papers existed, where, how frequently they published, for how much, to what size audience. These variables were not fully sorted out until 1914 when the participants grudgingly agreed to the formation of the Audit Bureau of Circulation.

What is significant here, however, is that advertising agencies started as independent brokers standing half way between the newspapers and the advertisers. As the relationship developed, increasingly new agents started up by working for the papers, holding newspaper space, and trying to sell it to someone for money. The papers gave them discounts, they sold the space at full retail, and the agents found it very profitable. They saw their loyalty tied to the newspapers.

But by the last part of the century, the newly opened agencies began to offer their services to advertisers, promising help with writing the ads, seeing that they were placed in the best possible locations, and so on, and soon presented themselves as allies of the advertisers trying to get the best possible deals from the papers. This confusion over just whose side an advertising agency was on is still rocking

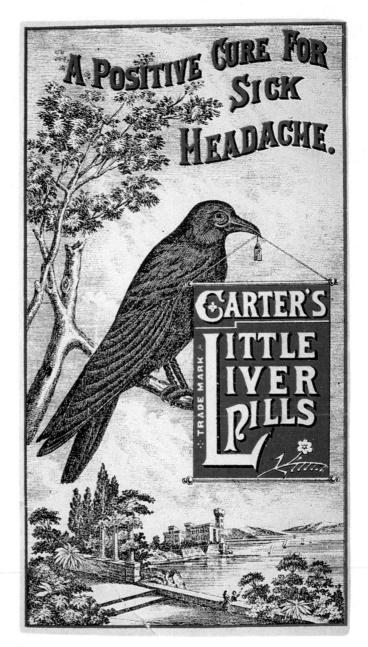

Late nineteenth century

It took the Federal Trade Commission sixteen years and 149 hearings to get the word "Liver" removed from the trademark, but this product is still selling well, a hundred years past its creation. Through the radio years, the slogans "Does the work of calomel without the dangers of calomel" and "Gets the vital digestive juices flowing at the rate of two pints a day" were so recognizable that they were used in numerous vaudeville acts and popular songs.

back and forth right up to the present. Even today an advertising agency works with the advertiser to create the best possible ad to sell the product and tells the advertiser where he should place the ad—the agency is paid not by the advertiser for whom he developed the campaign, but by the newspaper, or magazine, or television company to whom he sells it. And he is paid on commission, so the more ads he places or the more commercials he runs, the larger the cost of

Post-Civil War

the advertising campaign becomes—thereby getting more money for the paper and television company which bills the advertiser at retail. The advertising agency collects the money for the bill from the advertiser, lifts out 15 percent for itself, and passes what is left on to the newspaper or magazine or media station. The more time or space the agency uses, the more the paper or media pays him, yet the agency is hired by the firm who is advertising and has chosen the agency to get the greatest benefit for the least amount of money. [One of the classic parables in advertising is the story of the young media man who comes to his agency boss and says, "I took x company out of prime time television and put him in local newspapers for half the cost." The boss replies, "Great. He should be grateful. You're fired." The media man had cut the ad agency's income—its "billing"—in half.] In any other part of the current world, this would be called conflict of interest. Thanks to the hoary traditions begun by Palmer and Hooper, it is understood as being the way it is and should be, and is rarely challenged.

Before we leave the founding fathers of advertising, we should note a credo left for all their successors by the above-mentioned George P. Rowell. In his autobiography, written in 1871, he looked back on *Forty Years in the Advertising Business* and told us forthrightly how all advertising should be done:

Come right down with the facts, boldly, firmly, un-flinchingly. Say directly what it is, what it has done, what it will do. Leave out all ifs. Do not claim too much, but what you do claim must be without the smallest shadow of weakness. Do not say, "We are convinced that," "We believe that" or "Ours is among the best" or "Equal to any" or "Surpassed by none." Say flatly "the best," or say nothing. Do not refer to rivals, ignore every person, place, or thing except yourself, your address, and your article.

From the Civil War to World War I

It seems odd to parcel the history of advertising by military conflicts, but nothing seems to create such dramatic changes in the style and manner of this trade as does a truly savage war. After the Civil War, it was a whole new world for the advertising profession and the advertisers who used it. War-time shortages had forced the invention of wood pulp news-print, so paper was cheaper and more plentiful than ever. Wartime pictures from the battlefront spawned new ways of printing illustrations; the curved stereotype page on the presses permitted economies and innovations in publishing.

The need to produce hundreds of thousands of uniforms, underwear, and shoes stimulated mass production of clothing—and created a whole new generation of customers who had never bought any of these ready-made from a store before. With the men gone to war, the women got out of the house and went to work in the clothing factories to earn a money wage. They were permitted to buy bread in bakeries, soap at the grocers, and clothes off racks without being shamed as inadequate homemakers. Advertising thrived on every change; the only ground it lost was the front pages of

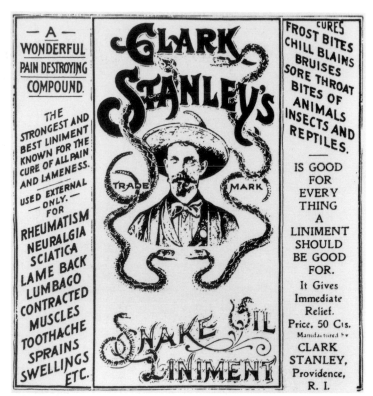

Post-Civil War

---

the papers. War news shoved the ads to the back of the book.

The manufacturers of soap and typewriters were the first to put pictures in their ads, but this innovation was quickly embraced by New York's Macy's and Lord & Taylor in 1867, and with the daily advertising clout of these (plus Wanamaker's in Philadelphia) the single-column-no-display-type rule was broken, and the techniques that had been perfected for handbills and broadsides moved onto the newspaper pages at last. The over-stuffed, over-elaborated look of Victorian design turned up in the typical ads of the period.

The Package

Advertising played a major role in two different aspects of the post-war citizen's day. First, the grocery scene went from the cracker barrel to the trademark on everything he had known all his life. When he entered the war, everything was shipped, stored, and sold in bulk—generically. Crackers actually did come in barrels, hard and tough so they didn't crumble en route, and they actually were sold from the barrel near the counter or the stove with the barrel lid off. Serve yourself. Peanut butter was in crocks, scoop it out and put it in your own jar at retail, or in the grocer's paper tubs for an extra fee. Bacon was in slabs, cut on order. Flour was in bins—the grocer would fill a paper sack for you. Peas and beans were dry in boxes; pickles in huge jars and sold one at a time.

Trademarking and packaging hit this area first. Crackers disappeared into wax paper–lined cartons and carried the

Uneeda Biscuit symbol on the side. Henry J. Heinz put 57 different foods into jars with their Pennsylvania keystone on the label. (From the very beginning, there were more than 57, but he liked the sound of that particular number.) Dr. Kellogg and C.W. Post ground up grain and sold it more as a medicine than a food, while Henry Crowell bought a milling machine and mashed oats into the Quaker Brand with a Quaker trademark on the side. (Was it made by Quakers? No, Crowell had found a picture of one in an encyclopedia and he looked "earnest, hard-working, and virtuous" just like the cereal.)

From there on the names popped up like dandelions in the Spring. Not just canned milk, Borden's Eagle Brand Condensed Milk, 1866. Not just soup, Campbell's Soup, 1869. Levi Strauss's Overalls, 1873. Eagle Pencils, 1877. Plain white soap, Ivory Soap! 1879. Adams' Black Jack Chewing Gum, 1884. Galoshes? Goodyear Rubber Galoshes, 1884. Not just coffee, Chase & Sanborn Coffee, 1886.

There is little doubt that the customer came out ahead on this. In every case, the trademarked product cost more than the traditional one that had come from the nearby community, but the product was cleaner, kept better, and of a more consistent quality. Nationwide advertising waved the trademark before the readers, and the copy told why the product was better. The customer knew the brand she wanted before she entered the store.

The other role that advertising played was in the introduction of new products—explaining what they were and how they were to be used. During this period the phonograph,

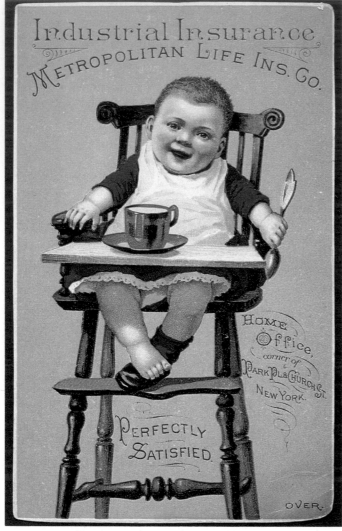

Late nineteenth century

It was early established that pictures of little children could sell anything—here, industrial insurance by a life insurance company that is still with us.

telephone, electric light bulb appeared. (Block-long bill-boards using these bulbs had made Broadway the Great White Way by 1891.) Eastman's Kodak appeared in 1888. Daimler and Benz started producing automobiles in 1885. Marconi's radio appeared in 1896. In every case, the manufacturers spent a great deal of money on advertising to get enough customers to justify the "mass production" needed to make a profit. In almost every case, they were offering a product without which the citizen had gotten along very well. The advertisement had to explain the benefits, and the copywriters became very skilled at justifying the money it was going to cost the reader to make life brighter, easier, and more fun.

The Unusual Role of Patent Medicines

We must return to the strange world of patent medicines for a moment, because of the many threads it built into the tapes-

try of today's advertising. There had been lots of patent medicine advertising before the Civil War (even Benjamin Franklin's *Pennsylvania Gazette* would have a half-dozen tonics in every issue, along with "a few hair growers, a cattle powder, and a patent arm and leg") but the military experience plus the opening of the western lands exploded the use of tablespoonfuls from a bottle.

Immediately before the war, approximately one half of all advertising would have been for drugs. The biggest name in the business was J.C. Ayer of Lowell, Massachusetts, whose "Cherry Pectoral" was known everywhere. Everywhere? Yes. Ayer was the first to see to it that his ads appeared in every newspaper, no matter how small, and in a rural society with few doctors and western pioneering with no doctors at all, every household had a shelf of home remedies. Some were "granny recipes" like sassafras, sulfur and molasses, rhubarb pastes, and fennel teas, and the rest were the advertised tonics and purges and liniments. Ayer and his Pectoral began big and got bigger. He soon branched out into pills, sarsaparillas, and a whole catalog of bottles of all shapes and sizes. He became so successful that a small Massachusetts town offered to change its name if he would bring his bottling works to their community and he embraced the idea with delight—thus starting Ayer, Massachusetts, the station to which Fort Devens was later attached and the portal through which a million New England soldiers entered World War II.

English patent medicines were imported by the case and bottles for Turlington's Balsam of Life, a "Remedy for Every Malady," have been found along the Santa Fe and Oregon trails. When the Civil War came, any able-bodied male who had not yet heard of patent medicines was introduced to them by the United States Government. It is said that the War Department bought Hostetter's Bitters by the railroad carload and soothed the Northern military stomach with it for four years. (When Col. Hostetter died, his estate amounted to $18 million in cash, back when $18 million was real money.) Similar to the stomach bitters treatment, anyone who went to the company aid tent with anything short of broken bones was equally liable to be given any of a dozen patent medicines based on calomel, a mercury compound that cleaned out the system.

The concept of "the system" was important in this, because both the Army and then the advertising industry picked up the idea of analogizing the human body to a smoothly running machine. Anything that was not in fine tune called for patent lubricants. This worked remarkably well for the druggists and the advertisers, since the majority of us could find an ache, a "taste," a "loss of our usual sense of well-being," which called for one of the tonics. The Army medical system agreed and one of the most popular brands it distributed was Peruna (invented by Dr. Samuel B. Hartman of Columbus, Ohio). Peruna was pleasantly flavored and averaged about 19 percent drinking alcohol, making it a bit stronger than wine. The soldiers consumed enormous

1896

Procter & Gamble was one of the earliest advertisers to use color and hire nationally-known artists to do its pictures. This one is notable as an early premium offer, and an example of the art work of Maud Humphrey, the mother of actor Humphrey Bogart.

Late nineteenth century

c. 1890

c. 1910

1888

Late nineteenth century

THOS. BRETT GEN'L. AGENT. CLEVELAND, O.
103 SUPERIOR ST.
DIEBOLD SAFE & LOCK COMPANY.

1879

OPPOSITE ABOVE LEFT:

Peruna made millions for Dr. Samuel B. Hartman of Columbus, Ohio. It was sold nationwide in great quantity, and its alcohol content exceeded that of wine. Although its bosomy models would seem to have been directed toward a male market, it was purchased mostly by women.

OPPOSITE ABOVE MIDDLE:

"Female weakness" seemed to have had class and geographic boundaries. Aristocratic eastern ladies and southern belles were supposed to have the vapors, feel giddy, and faint under stress. The eastern and southern servant girl was supposed to be strong, stoic, and healthy. The western pioneer woman of all classes was perceived as steel-willed and impervious to all ills. Dr. Pierce's market was presumably the urban woman, east of the Mississippi.

OPPOSITE ABOVE RIGHT:

Alfred E. Newman's vacuous smile, immortalized by Mad Magazine *in the 1960s, first appeared at the turn of the century on numerous brands of patent medicines. "What, me worry?" was "It didn't hurt a bit!" at this point. This is the earliest form of the grin so far found in the Library of Congress' copyright collection.*

ABOVE:

Clearly all the devils in Hell couldn't breach this Diebold safe. An unusually graphic, hand-drawn, stone lithographed ad. Note the delicacy of the printing, which would have been drawn (backward) directly on the stone with the lithographer's crayon.

OPPOSITE BELOW LEFT:

The owner of Pears' soap paid the distinguished English painter Sir John E. Millais £2,300 for his classic Victorian painting Bubbles. *Pears' used its image in its ads with great accuracy, and the sale (and probably the price) then made it acceptable for salon painters to do advertising art on the side. By the end of the century, such recognized American painters as Frederic Remington, Maxfield Parrish, Will Bradley, and Edward Penfield were doing ads. Note here the early celebrity endorsements of a trade product—in this case recommendations by Lily Langtry and Madame Patti.*

OPPOSITE BELOW RIGHT:

Challenge to the design department: How do you romanticize a wholesale coal company? Solution: trace the lump of coal from mine face, down railroad tracks to storage sheds, into the hearth that lights and warms two lovers. Complete with miniature dramatic scene. Surely the advertiser got his money's worth.

1896

1897

1905

ABOVE LEFT:

Celebrity testimonials have been with us since the eighteenth century—starting with artificial teeth and patent medicines. By the twentieth century, royalty had been supplanted by entertainers and sports figures. Here Sarah Bernhardt in a creatively styled hat endorses a chocolate bonbon whose name is on every piece.

ABOVE RIGHT:

Advertising for gold started in the newspapers in 1850 and appeared in the magazines in the 1880s. They sold stakes, claims, bars, and, as here in Collier's, shares. "We have the best-known men in America as Directors in this Company. Therefore your money is as safe with us as with your bank." How could you lose?

LEFT:

Ivory Soap was heavily advertised by Procter & Gamble in the early years of the twentieth century. Purpose: to keep the name of the product perpetually in the mind of the buying public. To this end, P & G "owned" the back of the title page of most of the major popular magazines, and ran copy in every issue. Note the custom of the time revealed in this frame. The leading families of the community were visited in their homes by the grocer. As we will discover, up to the appearance of the first supermarkets in the 1930s, even if you went to the grocery store, the grocer took the goods from the shelves, not the customer.

amounts of it, and proved to their satisfaction that it did indeed improve their sense of well being and reduced many of their aches as advertised. One of General Grant's friends maintained that Peruna was a "catarrhal tonic especially adapted to the declining powers of old age." When the war was over, the military thirst for Peruna was introduced to the general public, and although its advertisements suggested its primary effect was to enlarge the female bust, the main reason that it sold four or five times more effectively to

women than to men was that women were not permitted to go to the corner saloon, while a few tablespoons of tonic each day was acceptable in the home. The alcohol, the bottlers maintained, was necessary to preserve the roots and medicinal bitters.

What was actually in the post-war patent medicines? Almost always anywhere from 20 to 40 percent of the bottle was flavored ethyl alcohol. Floating in the alcohol could be anything from innocuous roots and herbs to laudanum, cocaine, and opium. Mrs. Winslow's Soothing Syrup was based on morphine. Lydia E. Pinkham's Vegetable Compound, on the other hand, had only the most gentle ingredients and not too many of them (a federal analysis found that in every 100 ccs of the famous compound, there were 17.9 ccs of alcohol and a total of 0.56 grains of Jamaica Dogwood, Pleurisy Root, Black Cohosh, Life Root, Licorice, Dandelion, and Gentian). Lydia promised the ethyl alcohol was "used solely as a solvent and preservative." (No one ever claimed the compound was harmful; only worthless.)

Mrs. Pinkham, like all the proprietary producers, advertised everywhere. She would send lead printers' casts of her face to be set at the top of her ads in local papers, which thus left the likeness in hundreds of type galleys across the land, and in the absence of expensive line drawings, her generic face was frequently used to head news stories. Gerald Carson has found her portrait variously identified as Sarah Bernhardt, Lily Langtry, Queen Victoria, and President Cleveland's new bride. Mrs. Pinkham herself was an early feminist and employed young women to answer letters about "female problems," which she solicited by material enclosed in the packing cartons. Resulting endorsements were used, but dutifully paid for. (Feminism apparently was in the air in Lynn, Massachusetts, where Mrs. Pinkham boiled and bottled the formula in her kitchen: Susan B. Anthony and Mary Baker Eddy lived within blocks of her house at the time. Mrs. Pinkham later built a huge factory nearby to produce the product, and the plant was run almost entirely by local girls both in the front office and on her production lines.)

How does all this patent medicine activity relate to the history of advertising? Four ways: 1) It was the urge of the druggist/bottlers to get their ads into every community that drove the first advertising agents to identify places to advertise and to regularize rates. For the first forty years of the advertising agencies' lives, over half of their revenues came from the patent medicine trade. 2) It was the increasingly outrageous claims of the patent medicine companies that forced legitimate advertisers to recognize that the omnipresent proprietary advertising was "giving advertising a bad name." People knew that a bottle of brown liquid could not simultaneously cure cancer, alleviate blindness, and straighten curvature of the spine. If the medicine ads were lies, how true were the clothing and real estate ads? This led to the national advertising industry beginning to police its own members for truth in advertising, and the business community beginning to police its local advertising via Better Business Bureaus. 3) Increasing revelations about the most extreme of the patent medicines showed that many of the liquids were genuine threats to the health of the community, which by the end of the century led to federal and state laws about truth-in-labeling, and governmental pure food and drug inspection and control. And finally, 4) patent medicines led to the invention of the *magazine* in America.

1903

Coca-Cola associated its product with fashionable, beautiful women from the very first. The wholesome American look became so tied to the Coca-Cola woman's image that scholars are still trying to decide whether the mid-century woman worked to look like the Coca-Cola girl, or the Coca-Cola image was simply the perfect reflection of the ideal "mid-American" woman.

From 1903 to 1905, the favorite Coca-Cola model was Lillian Nordica, then reigning queen of the Metropolitan Opera; she appeared on the company's metal serving trays, thermometer stands, posters, calendars, and in its magazine ads.

Magazines

It is hard to realize that at the end of the Civil War, you could count the commonly recognized magazines published in this country on the fingers of two hands. You had *Harper's Illustrated Weekly* and *Frank Leslie's Illustrated Newspaper* for the news, *Peterson's* and *Godey's Lady's Book* for clothing fashions, and *Graham's Magazine* for general "culture." All

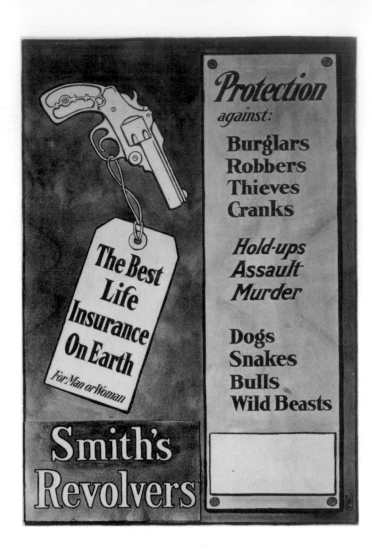

Protection against:

Burglars
Robbers
Thieves
Cranks

Hold-ups
Assault
Murder

Dogs
Snakes
Bulls
Wild Beasts

The Best Life Insurance On Earth
For Man or Woman

Smith's Revolvers

Stop!

AIMS EASY AS POINTING YOUR FINGER

THE burglar knows *he's far outmatched* when he looks down the black muzzle of a Savage. The thought of its ten ready shots flashes over him. He knows that even a woman points it straight in the dark.

The woman *does not fear* the Savage, as she fears other firearms, because she can see and feel when *this* Automatic is loaded and cocked.

You can't say you didn't know the *Savage* was loaded. Shoots one shot to each trigger pull—fast or slow—just as you want them.

Send 6c in stamps for book "If You Hear a Burglar."

THE 10 Shots Quick **SAVAGE** AUTOMATIC

Savage Arms Co., 710 Savage Ave., Utica, N. Y.
Makers of the Famous Savage 22 Hi Power and other Rifles

1903–1913

We assume that our current concern with handguns in the possession of ordinary citizens is something new. Only the fact that we are concerned is new. Ordinary household magazines at the turn of the century were filled with ads urging women in particular to arm themselves both in bedrooms and on the street. Here is a small sample drawn from the Saturday Evening Post of the time which frequently ran a dozen such images in every issue.

Hammer the Hammer

or Drive a Nail with an

Iver Johnson
SAFETY AUTOMATIC
Revolver

Hammer, $5
Hammerless, $6

but don't try it with *any* other. The Iver Johnson is equipped with our automatic safety lever that *must be in place before the hammer can touch the firing pin* and the lever cannot be in place unless you purposely pull the trigger all the way back.

Pull the trigger and an Iver Johnson is just as sure to fire as it's sure *not* to go off any other way.

For absolute reliability, accuracy, finished protection in every detail of material and workmanship, the Iver Johnson has few rivals and no superiors. It is made and guaranteed by the largest manufacturer of revolvers in the world. We make and sell almost as many revolvers as all other American makers combined. The quality of our goods is the reason.

Send for Our Booklet "Shots"

It's full of firearm lore; gives important facts that every owner of firearms should know, and goes into the details and illustrates by sectional views the peculiar construction of the Iver Johnson.

Iver Johnson Safety Hammer Revolver	These revolvers can be fitted, at extra prices, as follows: blued finish, 50c.; 2-in. barrels, no extra charge; 4-in. barrel, 50c.; 5-in. barrel, $1.00; 6-in. barrel, $1.50; Pearl stocks, 22-32 caliber, $1.25; 38 caliber, $1.50; Ivory stocks, 22-32 caliber, $2.50; 38 caliber, $3.	Iver Johnson Safety Hammerless Revolver
3-inch barrel, nickel-plated finish, 22 rim fire cartridge, 32-38 center fire cartridge - $5.00		3-inch barrel, nickel-plated finish, 32-38 center fire cartridge - $6.00

For sale by Hardware and Sporting Goods dealers everywhere, or will be sent prepaid on receipt of price if your dealer will not supply. Look for the *owl's head* on the grip and our name on the barrel.

Hammer the Hammer

IVER JOHNSON'S ARMS & CYCLE WORKS
147 River Street, Fitchburg, Mass.
NEW YORK OFFICE: 99 Chambers Street
PACIFIC COAST BRANCH: P. B. Bekeart Co., 2330 Alameda Avenue, Alameda, Cal.
EUROPEAN OFFICE: Pickhuben 4, Hamburg, Germany
Makers of Iver Johnson Bicycles and Single Barrel Shotguns

Accidental Discharge Impossible

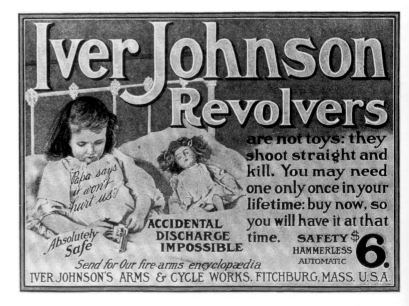

Iver Johnson Revolvers

are not toys: they shoot straight and kill. You may need one only once in your lifetime: buy now, so you will have it at that time.

Papa says it won't hurt us

Absolutely Safe

ACCIDENTAL DISCHARGE IMPOSSIBLE

SAFETY $6.
HAMMERLESS AUTOMATIC

Send for Our fire-arms encyclopædia

IVER JOHNSON'S ARMS & CYCLE WORKS. FITCHBURG, MASS. U.S.A.

the rest were literary magazines, priding themselves on their dignity, and mostly filled with serialized versions of books the publishing houses that owned them were about to print. Other than a list of forthcoming titles, there was no advertising in these magazines at all.

The patent medicine companies, desperate for places to advertise their products, recognized that here were blank sheets of paper that, if they could only break down the aristocratic distaste and resistance, would be a fertile field for planting their trademarks. F.G. Kinsman, the proprietary bottler of Augusta, Maine, decided the way to achieve this breakthrough was not by direct assault but through a flanking movement. He would not try to invade the respectable literary titles of his time, but he would start new magazines of his own and come at his market by linking them to religion. Kinsman became the largest publisher of Sunday School monthlies and weeklies in the country—all of which had patent medicines advertised at the back of the book.

He was phenomenally successful. Every family felt it had to have an inspirational magazine in the house, and soon each of the church denominations felt it should have its own Sunday School journal emphasizing its own denominational tenets. Kinsman was happy to supply all of these (each with his own medical ads discreetly in the back), and the N.W. Ayer company began to specialize in religious advertising to help other advertisers find their outlets more efficiently. (In 1898 one-sixth of all manufacturers advertising in this country were proprietary drug companies.) The combination of religion and paid space became extraordinarily profitable for both Kinsman and the agents.

Having their eyes opened to this new source of income, in the 1870s *Harper's Monthly*, *Atlantic Monthly*, *Scribner's*, *Century*, and the *North American Review* started "Proprietary Articles" and "Advertisers" departments in the back of their magazines. Their ads came overwhelmingly from only four sources: patent medicines, insurance, transportation (railroads and steamship lines), and the traditional announcements of their own new books.

With the Sunday School weeklies having shown the way, other publishers began to create whole new magazines—not for the literary elite, but for the common man. The stories were more dramatic, and the first of the "ideas for the home and housewife" began to appear. In the 1880s *Ladies Home Journal*, *Cosmopolitan*, *Munsey's*, and *McClure's* began, and all attempts to segregate advertising vanished with ads spread from one end of the issues to the other. At this point, as the economists say, the role of the publisher changed from being a seller of a product to consumers to being a gatherer of consumers for the advertisers.

Collier's, Saturday Evening Post, American Magazine, Woman's Home Companion, and *The Delineator* were candidly promoted in the business world as being created primarily as a vehicle to advertise in. In 1890, one of these publishers said in print, "If I can get a circulation of 400,000, I can afford to give my magazine away to anyone

who'll pay the postage." He did it, of course, on the money brought in by his advertising fees.

How Did an Advertisement Look at the Turn of the Century?

We all know that no one would confuse an ad of 1865 with one of 1900 (only 35 years later). Why? What did an ad look like in 1900? It looked very much like an ad does today.

First it had pictures, and we owe this, surprisingly enough, to Montgomery Ward and his imitators. In 1872, A. Montgomery Ward was a traveling salesman for a Chicago dry-goods store. He was convinced that if he could get catalogs into the hands of private individuals on his route (versus jobbers and store buyers), they would order their goods directly through the mail. He borrowed $2,400 from his friend George Thorne, and brought out the first mail order catalog; it was three and a half inches wide and seven inches tall with a hundred pages. It listed several hundred items for sale, with their prices, and it worked fine.

Very quickly Ward discovered that if he included a carefully drawn woodcut with the text, the item sold better, and from this came his greatest contribution. He did a full-dress research and development job on fine illustration in mass-produced, printed publications. Once he had that solved, he moved to color reproduction and devised the first mass-produced color pictures; this paid off handsomely. An early test run produced the discovery that four pages in color sold as many goods as twelve pages in black and white. The catalog techniques of color reproduction were embraced by the magazine designers and by 1900 four-color front and back covers were as stunning as anything printed up to World War II. Interior ads tended to be done with only one or two colors plus black, but they, too, were very attractive.

Museum-class art had also come to advertising by the turn of the century. Baker's Chocolate had been using black-and-white drawings of *La Belle Chocolataire* by Jean Etienne Liotard as a trademark (the original was in a museum in Dresden) since the 1870s. When color came, the lady with the tray appeared in full glory.

In 1886, Pears' soap bought an oil painting by Sir John Millais for £2300 and converted it to their trademark, black-and-white first, then full-palette. This (and the fee) seemed to make it acceptable for recognized, professional artists to do advertisements, and in the final years of the nineteenth century we have ads by Frederick Remington, Maxfield Parrish, Will Bradley, and Edward Penfield. Some of the finest work was done on high-quality color presses and individual sheets were tipped into the better magazines by hand; also in the 1890s, large copies of magazine covers were printed as posters in the manner of Beardsley and Lautrec, further making fine design acceptable for commercial projects. Having art work done outside the agency by contract stayed the norm for advertising design up until the Depression when the agencies began to do their own layouts, in-house, to save money.

1915. The Food and Drug Act of 1906 has been passed, most of the traditional patent medicines are gone, and a new generation of over-the-counter names are being introduced. But Listerine has been around since 1882, and in this ad The Voice of Authority (Trained Nurse) is enumerating the ways Listerine should be used: mouthwash, after-shave, scalp rub, gargle, antiseptic, and baby wash.

So a 1900 ad had pictures; what did the words say? Daniel Pope notes that the successful ad men of the time were only too happy to tell their peers what made a good ad: "Large headlines, white space surrounding the copy, and prominent illustrations." Edwin Dexter said, "The modern advertisment is not intended for the man who wants the thing already. It is for the one who don't in order to make him." Dexter said make it as big as you can afford—but Seymour Eaton was telling his friends, "an advertisement should be big enough to make an impression but not any bigger than the thing advertised." George P. Rowell warned, "Mention the name of a competitor and you advertise him; slander him and you do yourself no end of harm. Let your rivals pay their own advertising bills." John E. Powers said that "fine writing" and hyperbole were offensive, and that honesty and "the common-place is the proper level for writing in business." The print copy had to talk to two audiences: you had to convince the customer that he should buy the product and you had to convince the merchant that he would make money stocking it. In short, at the turn of the century the copy style was straightforward and direct. It stated firmly what the product did and even more firmly how it would benefit the buyer.

What the product was was looking more and more familiar to us. In 1890, the big advertisers were Quaker Oats, Cudahy meats, Remington Typewriters, Procter & Gamble, and two tobacco companies—American and P. Lorillard. From 1898 to 1902, American business went through a convulsion of mergers and combinations, and 2,653 individual firms combined into 269 consolidated companies. These, obviously, had much more capital and fewer trademarked brands, and the list of advertisers in a 1903 *Saturday Evening Post* begins to look remarkably like *Time* and *Newsweek* today.

The other result of the great consolidation spasm was that old-line companies—many of whom started as purveyors of drugs and health foods—shifted their pitch to match what the market had decided to use their product for. As Pope points out, Coca-Cola had started as a medicinal "tonic," Welch's Grape Juice was created by a congregation of Methodists as a substitute for wine; C.W. Post was allergic to coffee and created cereal-based Postum to correct stomach problems; while Dr. Kellogg of the Battle Creek Sanitarium was designing food products for patients with digestive problems. All of these firms abandoned their original *raisons d'être* and repositioned themselves to embrace the larger custom.

1915

Speaking of Positioning

As is apparent, by 1900 we begin to see the first segmenting of the reading audience so the advertisers can focus on a particular target. By the turn of the century, there were women's magazines, farm magazines, religious magazines, and even sports titles. What there was not was any way for an advertiser to have any confidence in how many copies of his ad would be printed, much less an estimate of how many would be read. The advertising agents guessed at the circulation of the newspapers and magazines, but the publishers maintained that the real truth was privileged information. Only one newspaper in four was willing to tell what its circulation was, and frequently this figure was grossly inflated by sending bundles of papers to clubs and institutions, continuing to send copies to subscribers who had dropped the publication or moved away, plus the expected amount of padding to cover any statistical slippage.

John Luther Mott tells about the newspaper editor in 1885 who was dying,

but when the doctor placed his ear to the patient's heart and muttered sadly, "Poor fellow—circulation almost gone!" he raised himself up and gasped, "'Tis false! We have the largest circulation in the country!" Then he sank back on his pillow and died, consistent to the end—lying about his circulation.

By 1900, this circulation was running in the hundreds of thousands of actual subscribers (although the "quality magazines" claimed that their readers were of a higher quality, too, and therefore should count for more) and the advertisers insisted they had the right to know what they were paying for. The publishers reluctantly agreed to a certified Audit Bureau of Circulation which finally came into being in 1914. (It worked even better than anyone had hoped, and of course is still with us, familiarly referred to as the ABC.)

So Where Did Advertising Stand in 1900?

Strangely enough, almost everything that we know as the profession today was in place. Except for the media carrying the messages—radio, television, and the like—what advertising is, how it is used, how it "operates" has only been elaborations of a theme already set.

By the turn of the century, the newspaper space brokers had become a dignified profession of advertising agents. Standards of ethics and uniform rules had been hammered out by industry cooperation, and regular organizations had been set up to oversee them. The Advertising Federation of America, the American Association of Advertising Agencies, the Association of National Advertisers were meeting regularly, and the inevitable fragmentation of specialization had started with the Direct Mail Advertising Association, the Outdoor Advertising Association, and the like.

Advertising was running the publishing business. Sixty-five percent of all the income received by magazines came from national advertising, and a comparable percentage of the income of local newspapers was from advertising revenues, although here more than two-thirds of that was from local sources. The confusion we are still struggling with comes from this national/local dichotomy, because today the great majority of criticism about the effects of advertising on the land refers almost totally to our distress over television commercials for *national* brands, magazines saturated with *national* advertising, and single-theme *national* advertising coming from billboards, bus cards, occupant junk mail, and what have you. There seems very little distress with the want ads and the supermarket ads and the local furniture store. This division was there at the turn of the century when the muckrakers were assaulting the "trusts and the fat cats." Ida Tarbell, Upton Sinclair, and Lincoln Steffens were about as outraged over the advertising campaigns of the tobacco industry and the meat packers and the oil barons as they were over their manufacturing practices. The Progressive Era struggled with the fear that the print publishers were in the pockets of the advertisers in the same way our generation is concerned that radio and television—which were created and paid for by the advertisers—now control what we see and hear.

In short, by World War I, all the foundation for the best and worst of American advertising was laid. But the edifice they've built on it has some fascinating furbeloes and embellishments.

Southern California

THE MOTORISTS' · PARADISE ·

3,736 Miles of New Highways

Most Perfect Roads in the World

IN SOUTHERN CALIFORNIA, "The Motorists' Paradise," are found advantages that do not exist elsewhere in the world—wonderful climate, beautiful scenery and sunsets, in combination with a system of the most perfect highways in the world, developed so that unobstructed travel between all points of interest is a delight.

Permit your fancy full play and let us take an imaginary "spin" over a portion of this wonderful boulevard system, in bright sunshine and balmy air.

We are motoring on a boulevard 3,736 miles in length, long enough to reach from Maine to California, and as smooth as New York's Fifth Avenue. It cost an average of $10,000 a mile.

We glide along for hours with a smoothness of motion hitherto undreamed of, for long stretches. It might be France. But the road is better than the French highway, because it is largely built of cement with asphalt surface, and there is no dust. There are mountains of asphalt in California.

We wind through a country of varied beauty and grandeur. Its gardens suggest England and Japan; the mountains Switzerland; and the seashores the south of France.

We are always within easy reach of one of the world's best hotels. We pass through a city of beautiful homes, "midst oceans of flowers," and in a few minutes are climbing a snow-capped mountain. Near its summit are beautiful lakes teeming with trout. We are on the "Rim of the World," thousands of feet up, and can motor for scores of miles along the sky line.

Below, like a great topographical map, lies a magnificent valley, growing almost every variety of vegetation known. We descend to a fragrant, rose-bordered orange grove—we drive through it—then among acres of lemons, grapefruit, figs, apricots, peaches, plums, California walnuts, great patches of strawberries—which yield luscious fruit every day in the year—next through a vineyard suggesting Italy, enclosed by stately palms which remind one of Egypt and the Nile—then past a vast tract bearing olives.

We swing to the right and twist and turn through a remarkable canyon. We emerge by the sea. A glorious spectacle opens out before us! Is it the Riviera? Surely Mediterranean's shores could be no more beautiful. We travel scores of miles to the music of the surf, drinking in the refreshing semi-tropical sea breeze.

1916

After World War I, ads in popular magazines like the Saturday Evening Post *were selling cities as vigorously as cars and breakfast foods. These were not for vacations, but for relocation and living. New towns in Florida asked why you wouldn't want to work in Heaven on Earth; and Southern California, trying to choose its most enticing feature, offered the country 3,736 miles of new highways. "Permit your fancy full play and let us take an imaginary 'spin' over a portion of this wonderful boulevard system in bright sunshine and balmy air.... We glide along for hours with a smoothness of motion hitherto undreamed of...." The automobile was barely fifteen years old, but the area was already "The Motorists' Paradise."*

A Short History—
From World War I to the Present

TWO UNLIKELY INVENTIONS changed the appearance of American advertising just before World War I: The invention of aspirin coupled with the passage of the Pure Food and Drug Act shrunk the patent medicine ads to the space traditionally given to canned soup and tennis shoes. Most proprietary medicines had relied on the placebo effect to stimulate the body's repair devices plus alcohol to dull the symptoms. Aspirin actually worked on the kinds of symptoms the proprietaries claimed they could affect (though no one knew why) but its effects were so clear that the old roots and herbs simply could not stand the competition; and right at the same time the federal government clamped down on the really threatening concoctions which contained dangerous and habit-forming drugs. The patent medicine craze was over, and its ads almost disappeared from the pages.

The other invention was the automobile. It burst on the scene in the first decade of the century, and you would assume that it would gradually grow into a generally advertised product. Not so. Almost within months of its birth, it was everywhere—completely dominating both national and local advertising. At the beginning there were literally dozens of different companies fighting for the buyer's attention, and we forget that in the early years, the car company only made the engine. The chassis, the bodies and the wheels, the light system and the brakes were made by different companies who advertised furiously either to get the engine manufacturer to use their products or the owner to put the products on the car himself. As the invention shook itself out, there were savage ad campaigns fighting over the

advantages of solid wheels over spoke wheels over wooden wheels. Solid tires over pneumatic. Solid glass over isinglass. And, of course, steam power over electric power over gasoline. Then as the idea developed, the battery companies and starters and curtains and chains got into the act.

We forget how many peripherals had to be developed to support the new invention. The *Saturday Evening Post* had ads for brick highways, macadam highways, petroleum product highways, and cement highways. "House and home magazines" had ads extolling chain link drives versus transmission/differential drives. (The ads claiming that wood chassises were safer than metal because wood flexed while iron snapped recall the slogan of one firm: "Wooden wheels, wooden frame" with the customers claiming "Wooden run.") The contending forces fought for survival on the pages of the national magazines, and automobile advertising was everywhere, more than offsetting the shrinkage of patent medicine space.

During the war, two other changes appeared in the advertising world. First, the federal government began to buy space in large quantities for the first time. It had used paid advertising to sell war bonds during the Civil War, and advertised new lands for homesteading in the years that followed. But in 1917 it contracted with the leading illustrators of the day to recruit men, generate women volunteers, urge scrap drives, sell bonds, and underwrite relief programs. Rather than being timid, routine, and passive as the stereotypical bureaucrats' advertising program could be expected to be, it was so innovative and the quality of its

1927

The famous Sears catalogs began in 1888 and until 1893 carried only watches and jewelry. In 1894 they added sewing machines and saddles and musical instruments, and the firm went on from there. Note that the 1927 cover drawing is by Norman Rockwell. Sears and the Reader's Digest are famous for moving more information in fewer words than any other two institutions in America. For a century, Sears advertising copy has been a masterpiece of the What-it-is and What-it-does school of copywriting.

artwork was so high, that it came to be the image to be copied and had a major effect on "how advertising looked" into the 1920s.

Second, was the war's effect on advertising's attitude toward women. Ever since the introduction of national brands, the advertisers had recognized the importance of women in choosing what would be bought. At the turn of the century the advertising profession operated on the assumption that 80 percent of all purchasing decisions were made by women. The national magazines directed their ads to women and even such presumably masculine purchases as automobiles and insurance were written with copy designed (by men) in the way they assumed the feminine mind worked. But as a result of the shift of staffing patterns during the war, by 1920, 25 percent of all women worked outside the home, and as America became more office oriented, half of all people employed in the financial community were women, as were 90 percent of all typists and clericals across the economy. (David Potter says that man subdued the soil frontier with the plow, and woman the urban frontier with the typewriter.)

By the end of the war, then, the advertising world was assuming that most ads were read by women, most of the products were purchased by women, and that women should be the prime targets of their efforts. Style and fashion made this even easier than in the past. The rejection of so many of the prior constraints accompanied the disillusionment of the war experience, and the emancipation of women was reflected in the abandonment of the corset, hobble skirts, and eight-button shoes. These were replaced with the short skirts, bobbed hair, and bright make-up of the Twenties and the splash of color on everything. Manufacturers picked this up quickly and "the ensemble" swept the fashion industry. With this trend the advertisers could sell complete sets of hats, handbags, jewelry, gloves, shoes—different for every outfit—completely changed with every Fall report from Paris.

Advertising in the Roaring Twenties

If we accept that 80 percent of the readers of advertisements were women and 99 percent of the writers and designers of advertisements were men, what world were they picturing in their ads? This paradox intrigued Roland Marchand and he centered his attention on the advertising industry's advice to itself via the professional journals of the Twenties. He found the following:

Women were emotional and filled with "inarticulate longings," therefore advertisements should "portray idealized visions rather than prosaic realities." Keep the copy paragraphs short, personalized, and intimate. Since the recent induction tests for the Army had shown that the average American male had the mentality of a child of twelve, it was assumed that women did too.

To fit these requirements, the ads of the Twenties were filled with tiny little "slice-of-life" vignettes—miniature short stories where the woman was concerned about the

1914–1968

Trademarks and the march of time. A few of the classic symbols have not changed in a hundred years—the Uneeda Biscuit boy, the Bon Ami chick, Mr. Peanut—but others have been modified to keep up with current style and fashion. The Morton Salt "When It Rains It Pours" girl changed every ten or twelve years. Here are six versions from 1914 to 1968.

1902–1988

One aspect of the development of a corporation's image through the years is its logo. Here is a sampling of J.C. Penney's as it went from the founder's Golden Rule Store in 1902 through "Company," "Apostrophe S," "S without the apostrophe" and "Penney without the S"—where it stands as of this writing.

1928–1935

Fleischmann's Yeast turned to the great medical minds of Europe to protect America's health. Dr. Mayer (Belgium's Great Surgeon), Dr. Pritz (Berlin war hospital head), Drs. Delory and Hufnagel (of Paris), Bruusgaard (Oslo), Cherubini (Rome), and Brandweiner (Vienna) all contributed their expertise. Were they real? No one was sure even then.

impression she was making, her success in "holding her husband," the health or intelligence or success of her children. There were lots of offers for consolation; "write Betty Crocker" or "Dorothy Dix" and send the attached coupon. Astonishingly, Betty and Dorothy wrote back (tens of thousands of letters written by huge staffs at the companies' public relations offices). Marchand found such confidantes

for deodorants, Kotex, Lux, S.O.S. scouring pads, Camay, cast iron pots and pans, and literally dozens of other precursors to Ann Landers and Dear Abby.

The women shown in the ads were always bright and eager typists making a good impression in the office, or capable mothers running a neat and caring home. The men in the ads of the time were invariably businessmen. No laboring man seems to have bought anything. If the businessman was ever shown away from his desk, he was either playing golf or tennis and dressed accordingly. Any ills were shown threatening his chance for promotion; halitosis, constipation, pink toothbrush, foot odor, and drooping socks could all hold back his climb up the ladder of prosperity. All the males pictured were on salary; no one was paid by the hour. Everyone was either chauffeured to his office or drove a very long, four-door car; no one in any ad was seen on a streetcar or a bus.

Then who was writing these ads? National ads came overwhelmingly from New York or Chicago, regardless of where the product was manufactured. A late 1920s study of the major ad agencies showed that their mid-level salaries were five times the national average, that 66 percent of their copywriters had servants in their homes, well over half came to work directly from graduation at an Ivy League school, only one in five went to church, and 40 percent had not visited outside the major urban centers in the previous ten years. A case could be made that an image of America as seen in national advertisements might well be flawed.

What Were They Advertising?

Lots more cosmetics and goods to improve the appearance. There were just as many ads for distant real estate as in the days of the frontier and homesteading—although now they were selling towns. A typical *Saturday Evening Post* in the Twenties was filled with double-page spreads asking "Where are the ambitious young men of the crowded old states and cities to go?" (Answer: Jacksonville, Florida.) "The luckiest children in America with a larger chance in life!" (The Pacific Northwest courtesy of the Northern Pacific Railroad). "Low rates to the Opportunity States—Land is cheap . . . unusual opportunities to Men Who Want to Succeed" (the Great Northern Railway offering one-way tickets from Chicago to Seattle, Tacoma, or Portland for $25, two trains daily).

And an endless stream of new inventions to save time, eliminate the need for servants, permit the wife to leave the house, and improve the life of everyone. It is impossible to overstate the contribution advertising has made to the introduction of new technology. It has shown the new machines, demonstrated their role in the ordinary lives of the citizens, and even shown the customer how to use the gadget successfully. It is fashionable to claim that most of the innovations were unneeded, had been gotten along without very well, and cost more time and energy to acquire than they ever gave back.

This is nonsense. The early ads for the electric light bulb, the hand iron, the vacuum sweeper, the washing machine drive home how exhausting and time-consuming the simplest tasks of home hygiene used to be. The early ads explaining the use of an electric fan are sobering, not to mention the earnest assurance that you could safely preserve food with electricity instead of with melting ice (which had to be replaced daily after carrying the melted water to the sink).

The Twenties, of course, are also the time of general distribution of the telephone, electric phonographs, cameras for everyone, and radio in the home. All of these were indeed intrusions and users of time instead of savers, but it is hard to prove that they were more destructive than enriching. And for the advertiser, the radio opened a whole new continent. It is surprising to recall that for the early years of broadcast radio there were no ads at all, and many presumed it would always be what the Public Broadcasting Service has now become. However in 1923 the National Carbon Company sponsored the first regular entertainment program ("The Ever-ready Hour"), and by the end of the Twenties advertisers were filling the air time around the clock. Installment buying had been invented and made common, there was much to be bought, and good things to be enjoyed.

Depression

But the better life stumbled and prosperity collapsed into the worst Depression in American history. Twenty-five percent of the country was unemployed, there was little money to be spent and therefore few goods sold. Advertising revenue fell from a 1929 high of $3.4 billion to a 1933 low of $1.3 billion. Not only were many advertising agencies wiped out forever, but the advertisers, desperately short of money, began asking, "Just what was advertising good for? What part of my money was bringing in sales? Where? and Why?"

From this began the age of research. George Gallup began polling and selling his results; A.C. Nielson began selling indexes of food and drug sales determined by weekly visits to drugstores and by checking inventories; motivational psychology and eye-tracking and store interviews and test cities all had their advent.

At the same time, advertising went for the hard sell. The ads of the Thirties are jammed with text; the traditional slice-of-life stories became even more threatening; and contests, premiums, prizes, and two-for-one promotions were everywhere. This resulted in a surprising backlash. There had been consumer reactions in the Progressive period when the "muckrakers" had inspired the first government regulatory agencies of the Federal Trade Commission and the Pure Food and Drug Administration. But with the savage reaction to "the Depression that business had caused" advertising was painted with the same brush and the Roosevelt legislative program went directly after the advertising scene. The Pure Food, Drug, and Cosmetic Act of 1934, the Wheeler-Lea Amendment to the Federal Trade Commission Act, the advertising regulatory sections in the Securities

1931

From the turn of the century, the advertising agencies believed that 80 percent of all purchasing decisions were made by women. By the 1930s, many believed it to be even higher, and "the American wife and mother" were perceived as advertising's primary market. (Oddly, 90 percent of the ad writers were men.) Young & Rubicam used this same "Supreme Court" image (with all the members of the family dressed in black robes) ten years later. Their joint theme was that the ultimate test for any product was whether it appealed to the average family.

and Exchange Commission, the Post Office laws, and the Alcohol and Tobacco Tax Division of Internal Revenue all created heavy supervision and control over the way advertising was practiced. At precisely the same time, a consumer revolt coalesced and a series of popular, commercial books dramatized the harshest and most questionable advertising techniques. From this came the Consumers Research and Consumers Union organizations which began to test and monitor and publicize products and product claims.

The Thirties ended with a much chastened advertising community. Radio had proved to be a blessing. Soap operas (begun in 1932 and so named for the soap companies that sponsored them) completely dominated the day time, and comedies and variety shows the nights. Contrary to the present television format in which each commercial is sold independently, in 1930s radio the whole show advertised only one product: Fibber McGee and Johnson Wax; Bob Hope and Pepsodent; Bing Crosby and Kraft Cheese. Brand loyalty had never been so high.

1936   1955   1965   1968

FIFTY YEARS OF BETTY CROCKER

Betty Crocker was actually invented in 1921 ("Betty" was thought to have a warm and friendly sound; Crocker was the name of an emeritus director of the company), and a male correspondent answered her mail using this name until 1936 when she was finally given a face and torso modeled after a number of women in the Home Service Department. Her face has been repainted six times, and the 1986 version (she is supposed to look like a careerperson who comes home to use her kitchen after 6:00) seems to look younger than the original Ms. Crocker.

1972   1980   1986

1968

1969   Cybill Shepherd

THE BRECK GIRLS

There have been some two hundred Breck Girls, all done in pastel, and (considering the majority were high school age or younger) the art directors have had a remarkably high batting average at identifying potential celebrities. Among their teenage models were Brooke Shields, Kim Basinger, Cybill Shepherd, Jaclyn Smith, Cheryl Tiegs, and Rosemary Trible. Like the trademarks, they provide a cultural history of hair and makeup through the years.

During the early days of the women's movement, Breck was so fearful of being accused of exploiting beautiful young girls that the Breck Girl was banished, and when she finally returned in 1988, she was a 28-year-old Phi Beta Kappa from Atlanta with a career and one child.

The original concept was created by the pastel artist Charles Sheldon, who did 107 of the portraits from his Massachusetts studio, and then Ralph William Williams took over and continued the style for nearly a hundred more. Williams, samples of whose work are reproduced here, was an established artist before he joined Breck, being internationally known for his stained-glass windows in churches and cathedrals. The Breck series, presumably, continued his work with heavenly models in both locales.

1973   Jaclyn Smith

1974   Kim Basinger

1974   Brooke Shields

1939

This picture was a part of the famed Farm Security Administration photo record of Depression America, and the barn was located in Garrett County, Maryland. It could have been anywhere. Barn sides glorifying Clabber Girl, the Gold Dust Twins, and Bull Durham could be found in every state. The local advertising agent would offer to paint three sides of a barn any color the farmer wanted, free, if he would let the agent put his product's name on the side that faced the road. (The FSA photographer was John Vachon.)

National magazines were plentiful and had audiences of millions. When the U.S. entered World War II in 1941, both radio and the periodical press assumed they were the way of the future. They dwelt in Error's Wood.

Post-War . . . Deceptive Déjà-vu

The early post-World War II years were much like post-World War I, thus deceptively masking the confusion to come. Many more women had been brought into the pay economy, so they were even more a target for the advertisers' attention than before. The economy boomed for a decade buying and selling all the products that had been unavailable during the war itself (and unaffordable during the Depression years before it), and the advent of commercial television provided yet another window in which to display the wares. Two minor tremors rippled through the scene which presaged the convulsion to follow.

First, rather than there being a dramatic reaction to the

previous social conventions as the Roaring Twenties had followed the Armistice, World War II was followed by fifteen years of a thirst for just the way things had been before. Clothes, homes, furniture, cars were all made to look very much like they had at the end of the Thirties. The "reaction" this time did not occur until the Sixties, and when it arrived it would force advertising to sell to a very different audience from that which it had known before in ways very different from those that had worked for thirty years.

And second, two advertising directors broke the traditional attitudes on how an advertisement should look and work, and they suggested two rather different paths for the future. David Ogilvy believed in treating the customer as an intelligent peer who was reading his ad to learn something about the product under discussion. The ad was not to be a wildly shouted announcement of some dramatic event, but a dignified explanation of what was being sold. It spoke quietly in a dialogue between me-and-thee. Ogilvy devised unique hooks to capture the reader's attention, and then repeated these themes to link his ads together: the Hathaway man's eyepatch, the Schweppes salesman's Vandyke, the quietly ticking clock in that dignified Rolls-Royce. Ogilvy used handsome, colored pictures, and no humor. He believed there was nothing funny about advertising in general, and certainly nothing funny about an Ogilvy ad in particular. "People don't buy anything from clowns," he said.

Bill Bernbach went just the other way. His ads were hilarious, usually black and white, and limited to a single selling point. They frequently had only a sentence or two to a page. (Ogilvy often had more words in his ads than there were in the editorial columns beside them.) Bernbach's campaigns such as Volkswagen, Levy's Rye Bread, and Alka-Seltzer stopped the reader cold—his humor flattered the reader into thinking he was sophisticated enough to understand it, but it was used only to make a point about the product. Bernbach believed, "The purpose of an ad is to persuade people to buy. . . . The persuasion is in the idea and the words. And anything, however expert, that slickly detracts from that idea and those words is, for my money, bad design. . . . Your job is to simplify, to dramatize, to use all your talents to make crystal clear and memorable the message of the advertisement." Here were two men who took advertising seriously, had developed a philosophy of the profession. They had refined the techniques for capturing attention, displaying the product, and convincing the reader he should buy. They came just before everything came unstuck.

Chaos and Old Night

We have watched advertising progress in a fairly straight and logical line for its first 175 years. In the 1960s and 1970s, a series of developments began that appeared to run in exactly opposite directions. Logical sequences disappeared in a swirl of contradictions. Herewith an enumeration and checklist:

The Creative Revolution. It began with an apparently

benign innovation. For decades, the creative source of an ad had been the words of the copywriter. He had determined what the thrust of the ad was; he chose the words that would express this purpose; and after all these were determined, the completed concept was passed to the graphic artist to select type, picture, and format to bring visual order out of the various elements.

In the years before World War II, a number of highly skilled designers had fled Russia and the Continent, bringing with them the artistic philosophies of the Bauhaus, the Dutch design schools, and the poster and scenery design disciplines of the Russian schools of applied art. Dr. Mehemed Fehmy Agha became the art director of *Vogue* and *Vanity Fair;* Alexey Brodovitch (who had been a set designer for Diaghilev's Ballet Russe) became art director for *Harper's Bazaar;* and the Austrian Herbert Bayer began the startling corporate art campaigns of the Container Corporation of America. Brodovitch hired a young photographer named Richard Avedon; Paul Rand took over the art direction of *Esquire* and *Apparel Arts.* The result was that the designs of these strong figures began to overwhelm the words they created around, and by the Sixties the complete ad had become a visual statement, not just a literary one. This began a new tradition: copywriter/graphic artist teams were assigned as equals to each new advertising project.

The Boutique Agencies. The Design Revolution brought about a quantum advance in the appearance and style of Sixties and Seventies advertising, and it had two spillovers: First, since the idiosyncratic style of the designer was so closely identified with a single artist and a single copywriter, the creative skills of the new teams worked much better in small agencies rather than in huge advertising companies where the product was produced by assembly-line accretion. The result was that accounts rushed away from the old-line, traditional agencies and took their campaigns to the small, innovative, "boutique" advertising companies which were fast, flexible, and could reflect the accounts' products and purpose. By the end of the Seventies, the leading advertising journal could declare, "We will never again see agencies larger than thirty-five to fifty employees."

Overkill. The second result of the new advertising was tremendous success. The ad agencies began to make money faster than they knew what to do with it. Many of the most popular firms accumulated so much so quickly that the Internal Revenue Service threatened to change its traditional treatment of accepted business costs and deductions. Either the agencies had to "do something" with these "enormous reserves of capital or declare it profit." They decided to pour it into in-house research. The agencies hired specialized advisers on the most esoteric aspects of the marketplace; they built audition rooms for in-house television creation; they installed packaging laboratories, departments of behavioral psychologists, and they got larger and larger and more bureaucratized by the year. What had started as small, flexible, idea-houses became as large and sluggish as anything from the Thirties.

1953

In the early years after World War II a new phenomenon appeared in advertising: the corporate image. Up until then, an advertisement sold a product. As time progressed, fewer products were sold (and what were were so very similar—soap, cereals, cosmetics) that ads increasingly sold companies and services that were intangible and could not be pictured as objects.

Among the earliest of these corporate-image ads were those from Continental Can, Magnavox, and the most seminal, those of William Golden for the Columbia Broadcasting System. Golden invented the CBS eye in the early 1950s, intending it for a single-use ad in a situation where he wished to distinguish the company's television projects from its radio programs. Frank Stanton, President of CBS, was so taken with the image that he decreed it should be used indefinitely to symbolize all of the activities of the corporation. (Golden later reported that the thing he remembered most about the original was that he could not find a stock picture of clouds and had to send a photographer out to take one from an abandoned Coast Guard tower.)

Magazines. Right in the midst of this trend, paper pages that had carried print advertising to the world began to disappear. Ever since Dr. Kinsman had invented the Sunday School monthly to display his patent medicine ads, magazines had carried the major load of national advertising. The rich supply of ad money had supported the publication of enormously popular, entertaining, and even educational periodicals. But by the Sixties these, too, had grown so large they began to collapse of their own weight—like the legendary dinosaur, too large to live.

Collier's and *Women's Home Companion* were the first to go, expiring in 1957, and presaging things to come. The venerable *Saturday Evening Post* with a circulation in the millions, simply could not charge enough for its advertising space (without exceeding the possible profit on the item advertised) to print and distribute that many copies. It tried a variety of ways to limit its readership so it could promise its advertisers a more certain audience for their particular products, but nothing worked and the *Post* gave up in 1969. *Look,* also selling millions and still growing, reached a point in 1971 where it could no longer be produced profitably and it died. These were quickly followed by *Life* and *Holiday* and a dozen other long-time titles. Print advertising, which had built the edifice, had priced itself beyond reality, and

ARROW
COLLARS
& SHIRTS
FOR DRESS

1913

with it went thousands of empty pages on which to design and print the ads the industry had now become so skilled at creating.

Television. Television saved the day, but at major cost to print advertising. The money, the professional acclaim, the challenge to the next generation of both copywriters and graphic designers moved to the tube, and the thrust of advertising went from the perfect page to the perfect two-minute commercial. But what was sold had changed, too. The goods had become "parity products." In every category there were four or five major companies that produced essentially the same thing. A row of five detergents looked, and smelled, and cost, and washed essentially the same way. Cereals, soaps, cosmetics, coffee, margarine came in different packages but with substantially the same ingredients. Rosser Reeves said: "Our problem is—a client comes into my office and throws two newly minted half dollars onto my desk and says, 'Mine is the one on the left. You prove it's better.'"

Segmenting the Audience. From the challenge of the identical competitive product came the elaboration of "segmenting"—the conclusion that you can't sell or even advertise to everybody. The agencies examined what they were asked to promote and asked Who is really going to buy this product? and then examined where to place the ad so that that particular audience would see it. They designed ads that "looked like" the identified audience, talked like it, were shown doing the things that audience did. They frequently sold the identical product in four or five different packages at different prices and different sizes and different quantities to appeal to the different customer elites.

They exploited the intimacy of the television screen to retell slice-of-life stories just as they had in Barnum's day and in the Depression-era comic strip ads. Then, as television commercials became more and more expensive, they cut and shortened the message so the sales story was told in seconds rather than minutes. From this came the blizzard of snappy slogans. M&Ms began to melt in your mouth, not in your hands, and Wonder Bread built strong bodies 12 ways. Fairfax Cone convinced us that "When you care enough to send the very best" you sent Hallmark, and "Aren't you glad you use Dial?" A single ad writer by the name of James J. Jordan added "Ring around the collar," "Delta is ready when you are," "Us Tareyton smokers would rather fight than switch," "How do you handle a hungry man?," and "Zestfully-clean" to the American vocabulary. (As television time cost ever more, McDonald's "You deserve a break today" cost so much to say that they abandoned it and told their agency simply to flash the Golden Arches where the slogan had been.)

Research. The need to refine the message and focus its audience with precision drove research to metaphysical heights: focus-group interviews, motivational studies, brain waves, perspiration rates, pupil dilation measurement, and computer models producing printouts by the bale. Such costly support activities exceeded the resources of the bou-

As we saw Betty Crocker and the Breck Girls change through the years, here is the Arrow Shirt Man as conceived by J.C. Leyendecker in 1913 (opposite) and Le Roy Neiman in 1986 (below).

1986

This is another one of the All-Time Great American Ads, appearing in "Best" lists for thirty years. It was written by Henry Slesar of the Fuller & Smith & Ross agency in 1958, and it has been translated into all the major, printable languages including Chinese.

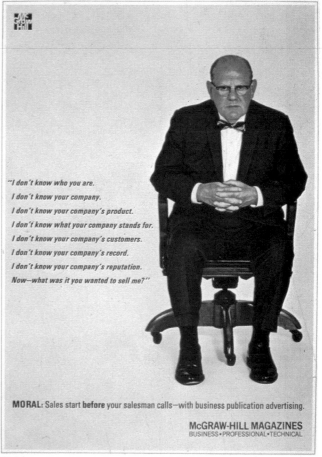

1958

How much longer can we hand you this line?

Forever, we hope.
Because we don't ever intend to change the Volkswagen's shape.
We play by our own set of rules.
The only reason we change the VW is to make it work even better.
The money we don't spend on outside changes we do spend inside the car.

This system gives us an immense advantage: Time.
We have time to improve parts and still keep most of them interchangeable.
(Which is why it's so easy to get VW parts, and why VW mechanics don't wake up screaming.)
We have time to put an immense amount

of hand work into each VW, and to finish each one like a $6,000 machine.
And this system has also kept the price almost the same over the years.
Some cars keep changing and stay the same.
Volkswagens stay the same and keep changing.

1969

You don't have to be Jewish

to love Levy's
real Jewish Rye

c. 1965

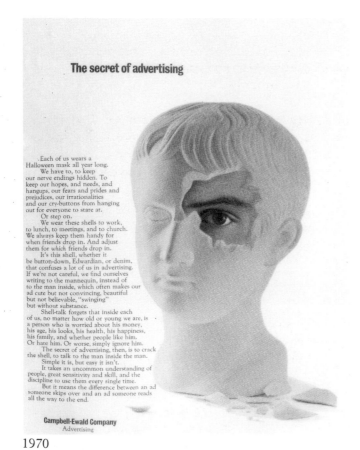

The secret of advertising

Each of us wears a Halloween mask all year long.
We have to, to keep our nerve endings hidden. To keep our hopes, and needs, and hangups, our fears and prides and prejudices, our irrationalities and our cry-buttons from hanging out for everyone to stare at.
Or step on.
We wear these shells to work, to lunch, to meetings, and to church. We always keep them handy for when friends drop in. And adjust them for which friends drop in.
It's this shell, whether it be button-down, Edwardian, or denim, that confuses a lot of us in advertising. If we're not careful, we find ourselves writing to the mannequin, instead of to the man inside, which often makes our ad cute but not convincing, beautiful but not believable, "swinging" but without substance.
Shell-talk forgets that inside each of us, no matter how old or young we are, is a person who is worried about his money, his age, his looks, his health, his happiness, his family, and whether people like him. Or hate him. Or worse, simply ignore him.
The secret of advertising, then, is to crack the shell, to talk to the man inside the man.
Simple it is, but easy it isn't.
It takes an uncommon understanding of people, great sensitivity and skill, and the discipline to use them every single time.
But it means the difference between an ad someone skips over and an ad someone reads all the way to the end.

Campbell-Ewald Company
Advertising

1970

There's one gap that's common to both generations and Talon keeps it closed.

1972

1987

OPPOSITE ABOVE LEFT AND RIGHT:

Advertising of the 1960s was dominated by the style and philosophy of two men: William Bernbach and David Ogilvy. Both minimized "research" and believed in the art of persuasion— what "felt right" as the proper way to sell each product. Individually or through their agencies of Doyle Dane Bernbach and Ogilvy and Mather, they produced dozens of memorable campaigns that are still considered classics in the field. These images are from DDB's series for Volkswagen and Levy's bread.

OPPOSITE BELOW LEFT:

A Seventies corporate ad, not selling a product but a company and its services. Here Campbell-Ewald seeks the answer to the eternal question: How do you get the customer to keep reading "all the way to the end?"

OPPOSITE BELOW RIGHT:

The agencies of the Sixties are remembered for being small, innovative, and aggressively independent. They relied heavily on humor and granted the reader the assumption of intelligence and being a peer of the advertiser. Following the tradition, the Talon ads approached their product with a light touch.

ABOVE:

The rules of what is permissible in advertising now allow much greater interaction by the models than before. Here we see examples of such recent phenomena as expensive designer jeans made from the traditional workman's denim, and the explosion of the youth market which now drives much of the gross national product.

tique agency, and the huge sums of money resulting from nationwide advertising contracts (that washed in and out in feast and famine waves) set the agencies up as targets for the Eighties' mania for mergers and takeovers.

The Mega-Agency. Thus in the final decade of advertising's two-hundred-year history, everyone rushed to the other side of the boat, and agency after agency combined, bought out its neighbor, amassed stock in its competitor and melded into a far smaller number of huge corporations until accounts from five fiercely competitive manufacturers could be served within one house in five offices, side by side, down a single hall. Once again, everything that had been tried and learned in the first hundred years was being tested all over again in the second.

And that is enough for this introduction. All we were trying to do here was draw a hasty timeline of the first two hundred years of American advertising. Now we are going back to fit specific stories and experiences on to this line, so we can get a better understanding of how advertising got to be what it is today. Just as we have noted that everything seems to "come 'round again," we will try to discover in some detail what actually was learned in those earlier experiments. Let's slow down the cadence, turn up the light, and get a magnifying glass.

THE "IVORY" is a Laundry Soap, with all the fine qualities of a choice Toilet Soap, and is **99 44-100 per cent. pure.**

Ladies will find this Soap especially adapted for washing laces, infants' clothing, silk hose, cleaning gloves and all articles of fine texture and delicate color, and for the varied uses about the house that daily arise, requiring the use of soap that is above the ordinary in quality.

For the Bath, Toilet, or Nursery it is preferred to most of the Soaps sold for toilet use, being purer and much more pleasant and effective and possessing all the desirable properties of the finest unadultered White Castile Soap. The Ivory Soap will **" float."**

The cakes are so shaped that they may be used entire for general purposes or divided with a stout thread (as illustrated) into two perfectly formed cakes, of convenient size for toilet use.

The price, compared to the quality and the size of the cakes, makes it the cheapest Soap for everybody for every want. TRY IT.

SOLD EVERYWHERE.

1882

The one that started it all: the first advertisement for Ivory Soap. This appeared in one of the few national magazines that existed at the time, a religious weekly called The Independent, *in its December 21, 1882, issue. Note all the elements that would reappear through a hundred years of Ivory advertising: the 99 and $^{44}/_{100}$ percent purity, the enumeration of suggested uses, the reminder that it was equally appropriate for skin and cloth, the convenient notches, and the phenomenon that it floats.*

Cereals, Soap, and Sex

WE ARE NOW GOING to get specific—depart from the flying generalizations of our timeline and get down to details. We are trying to find out how American advertising got to be what it is, and to do so, we need to go back to the years shortly after the Civil War. Here we will find the foundations of the four-color double-page spreads in this week's *Time* and the soul of tonight's TV commercials. About half of both of these will be dignified straightforward presentations of their products with clear-cut advertisements asking us to buy. The other half will be far-out, off-the-wall attempts to grab our attention, colossal productions to sell a miniscule product—frequently forgetting to mention what the product is in anything but the most oblique way until the very end. The ground rules and protocols for both of these approaches were set between 1875 and 1900. Cereals and soap. Sex came later. Soap came first.

SOAP

First, the product itself. In 1875, soap as we know it barely existed at all. There was no distinction made between hand soap and clothes soap (and, surprisingly, there would be no difference until the 1920s). Soap was soap. If you lived in town in 1875, you bought your soap from the grocer, who kept it in huge slabs that stood vertically at the end of the counter. He cut off the chunk you requested, charged you by the pound, and wrapped the piece in brown paper. The soap itself came in various shades of translucent yellow, had no particular odor, and had to be kept dry. If a piece sank to the bottom of a wash tub, it melted into sludge and disappeared within an hour.

If you lived on a farm or in a small town, you made your own soap, and it was an expected part of housekeeping. It was not particularly difficult, but the product was unpredictable. You kept the wood ashes from the kitchen range and the heating stove in an outside barrel, and at monthly intervals or so, you poured water through the ash barrel and caught the runoff at the bottom which by the time it had gone through the ashes had become lye.

You then put your used bacon and cooking grease in a pan, put in some fat cuttings from pork or beef, and heated it all until it melted, adding the lye and a spoonful of table salt a little at a time. What you got was "soft soap" which never hardened and was kept in a tub. If you wanted to buy soda in place of using your own wood ashes, you got "hard soap." Both worked very well.

The problem was that the process of conversion (the "saponification") was almost mystical. Neither granny in the kitchen, nor the soap makers out by the packing house, knew when it would work, or precisely what the final product would look like. One of the most popular recipe books of the time suggests the kind of concern: "The great Difficulty in making Soap come is the want of Judgement of the Strength of the Lye. If your Lye will bear up an Egg or a Potato so you can see a piece of the surface as big as a Ninepence it is just strong enough." When it did work, though, it was a clear, not unpleasant kind of jelly, which gave fairly good suds and did clean clothes. It took about two bushels of ashes and eight pounds of grease to make a bucket of soap. This was enough for the family wash that traditionally was done once a month. (The weekly "Monday

You need only one soap
IVORY SOAP

Pure__First quality,
Not expensive
Will wash anything
No chapping IT FLOATS

1898

1898–1965

The original wrapper did a good job of camouflaging the dust that collected on old-time grocery shelves. In 1936, the wrapper appeared in wax paper to insure freshness. 1943 brought the hint of waves and water, 1960 had a red ribbon, and 1965 had all the traditional elements but with a modern look. The package is still a major element in projecting the product.

"AUTUMN LEAVES"   FROM A PAINTING
                        BY W. GRANVILLE SMITH.

THE brilliancy of the autumnal foliage lasts but a short season at most; when the biting frost has completed its work, the trees shed their dead and lustreless leaves and wait for nature to clothe them anew.
So with our garments; unless protected they must be discarded at the end of the season, not worn out, but ruined by the biting alkalies of common soaps and soap powders.
You can protect your clothing and secure from it an extra season's wear by requiring your laundress to use only IVORY SOAP.
IVORY SOAP IS 99⁴⁴⁄₁₀₀ PER CENT. PURE.

1897

washday" did not become a tradition until after 1890.)

Thus the market for soap in the 1870s was still restrained at best. Baths were almost as rare as clothes washing. No "bathrooms" were built in houses until the end of the 1880s, and bathing was done in a portable tub usually placed in the warmest room in the house near the spot where the water would be heated. In the working man's home this would be the kitchen; in the rich man's home, it would be his bedroom, but the hot water had to be carried up the stairs a pail at a time and, even more daunting, had to be carried out in the same manner. Social historians believe that the colonial American bathed very frequently, but the Victorian American scarcely did it at all, mainly from reluctance to be seen in the nude. Children were not supposed to see adults unclothed ever, and servants were not to see either one after the age of six.

This, then, was the business scene into which the sons of William Procter and James Gamble set out to make their fortune in the soap and candle business.

The Saga of Procter & Gamble

The two fathers had come down the Ohio on rafts, independently, looking for work in the early 1800s. They were each headed for somewhere else, but rather accidentally got stopped in Cincinnati. Gamble was from Ireland, and Procter came from England in 1832. They fell in love with the daughters of Alexander Norris, who blessed their respective marriages and suggested they go into business together. They did, bought a candle and tallow works, and the two families got along remarkably well through three generations and seventy-five succeeding years. The Gambles ran the factory and the Procters ran the office or "store."

Up to the Civil War, the money came in from the candles; soap and lard were essentially by-products, with the oils that had to be floated off the top of the boiling mix as marginal products—marginal and the ones that had to be pushed, since they wouldn't sell themselves. Thus they had to be advertised and the first copy from a company that would lead the world in advertising a few decades down the line read:

Oils for lamps and machinery. A fine article of clarified Pig's Foot Oil, equal to sperm, at a low price and in quantities to suit buyers. Neat's Foot oil ditto. Also No. 1 & 2 soap. Palm and shaving ditto. For sale by Procter & Gamble Co., east side Main Street 2nd door off 6th Street.

Cincinnati Gazette, June 29, 1838

When the Civil War came, the company's location on the Ohio put them in exceptionally good position for war contracts. The production shifted toward boxes of yellow soap sent to the western armies. The big packet boats went to Pittsburgh weekly, the smaller packets to Memphis and Wheeling semi-weekly, and a daily boat to Louisville. Sons of the founders would push wheelbarrows around town each morning picking up cooking fats from households and meat scraps from restaurants and the steamships on the river. They paid for their haul with small bars of hard soap.

By 1875, the Procter & Gamble company was firmly established in Cincinnati and neighboring towns, with soap-making producing 25 percent of the company's sales, and kitchen lard and candles making up the rest. A Frenchman by the name of Michael Eugene Chevreul had finally isolated a formula for the fats and lye that gave a uniform, predictable product, and Procter & Gamble produced a variety of yellow soaps that went between harsh and gentle with names like Town Talk, Mottled German, Duchess, and Oleine. Advertising was still limited to less than the money they spent on lining paper and stationery, but they were on the threshold of the breakout.

The sons had gone away to college and come back with the knowledge of chemistry then available at Kenyon, Yale, and Princeton. The lost grail of soapmaking was the legendary bar of "castile," a pure white soap, mild, made of pure olive oil, shudderingly expensive, and imported only from Europe in the smallest of quantities. In 1875, James N. Gamble hired their first full-time chemist, an Englishman by the name of Gibson, and the two of them set out to see if they could duplicate the qualities of castile with the materials available in Cincinnati. In order to be "commercial" it also had to contain less water (to last longer) and not melt into mush after a couple of washes. In 1878, James came out of the one-room lab triumphant: he had invented white soap. The collective cousins clustered around, tested its manufacturing, shipping, and sales quality, and declared it good. They named it P&G White Soap, designed a special wrapper for each individual bar (cleverly checkerboarded to hide the inevitable dust that collected on grocers' shelves of the time), and put The Product on sale.

It went well in the local area, but did not shake the commercial foundations of anything.

A few months after it started, the company suddenly received letters from a number of down-river grocers for reorders of "that soap that floats." Neither the front office nor the factory could figure out what they were talking about. Pressure on the staff revealed that a minor mistake in production had been made the previous month. Like all soaps (even today) the fats and alkalis had been dumped into the vats, boiled, and after the glycerins were skimmed off the top, the soap was stirred until smooth by huge "crutchers," much like the paddles in a hand ice cream freezer.

The previous month, the man in charge of the stirring had gone to lunch without stopping the crutchers and they had churned around for an extra hour. When he returned he discovered his error, saw that the soap was considerably more whipped than usual, but concluded that since its contents had not changed it was still white soap, and thought that the bubbles would settle out once they were poured into the frames. He poured out the contents, assumed that nothing was wrong, and the contents were simply as before. What in fact had happened was that the whipped bars were now lighter than water and, when used in murky river water or even sudsy tubs, miraculously popped back up to the surface to be re-seized. Unintended result: It Floats.

One more step was needed to reach Perfection. The following year, on a Sunday morning in the Spring of 1879, Cousin Harley Procter of the front office was brooding on the potential of James Gamble's White Soap while sitting in the Church of Our Savior in Cincinnati. The Anglican lesson was being read from the 45th Psalm, and the words hung in the air with letters of fire: "All thy garments smell of myrrh and aloes and cassia out of ivory palaces whereby they

have made thee glad." Eureka. Not White Soap. Ivory Soap. The name was changed the following week, and the first official use of Ivory as a registered trademark was July 18, 1879.

Now, Deliberate Exploitation

Up until this point, most of the progress had come from a lucky mixture of intelligent search and serendipity. From here on, progress was based on wise choices and deliberate action.

Step One. In spite of the various names soap makers used, in the mind of the buyers you simply sent the youngster to the store to buy soap. Like lumber—you didn't ask for a particular brand of two-by-fours or studding—soap was soap. Harley Procter knew that with his floating white soap he had a specific, identifiable brand. It had purity, it could be used for multiple purposes (even "bathe babies in the nursery"), and it was identifiable by color and that ability to float. He was determined to tell people about it through advertising.

Step Two. In the grocery business, you used local advertising in your trade area to tell people what was in your store. If you were selling beyond your immediate delivery area, you sold to the jobbers and the wholesalers and you let them push the product beyond your personal control. Harley deliberately decided to ignore this approach, and set out to convince the individual buyer that what she wanted was Ivory Soap, specifically. His ads were going to talk directly to the person who would make the purchase, and the copy was going to describe why the product was better than any other and how it could be used to benefit the specific, individual buyer. This appears fairly obvious now, but it wasn't at the time. Up until Procter & Gamble, you glorified the product as an institution, a public entity, standing high on a hilltop, not something produced just for *your* very own benefit.

Step Three. Harley was convinced his soap was exceptional, but he wanted some way of saying it that didn't sound like somebody selling a horse at auction. He worked through a syllogism. What was the purest soap known to man? Imported, Mediterranean castile. How pure was that? He bought three bars that had originated in three different places and sent them to a chemists' in New York City, asking them to test them to establish a definition: if castile was pure soap, what was castile? The chemists declared that castile was the purest known because it consisted of *nothing* but fatty acids and alkali. Anything else that appeared would be "foreign and unnecessary substances."

Having established a benchmark for purity, Harley and James sent in random samples of production-line Ivory and asked how this simple white soap compared to top-of-the-line castile. To the cousins' delight (and apparent genuine surprise), when the report came back it showed the impurities in Ivory came to uncombined alkali—0.11 percent; carbonates—0.28 percent; and mineral matter—0.17 percent. "Total foreign and unnecessary substances" in Ivory

THE GIFT.

WHAT better gift to give a queen Now some may think 'tis not the kind
Than what will beautify and clean? Than will suit the royal mind;
Will make her robes and laces fine That rubies rare or diamonds bright
Like snow upon the mountain shine, Would prove more pleasing to her sight.
And give her cheeks that ruddy glow But well we know our loaded cart
Which only those who use it know. Of Ivory Soap will glad her heart.

If your grocer does not keep the Ivory Soap, send six two-
cent stamps, to pay the postage, to Procter & Gamble, Cincinnati, and they will send you *free* a large cake of Ivory Soap.

1883

NATURE washes the earth, and every field and
tree blossoms into life. She uses no other agent
than pure water, air and sun. Get as near to
Nature's way as you can. The nearest thing to water,
air and sun is Ivory Soap: light as the water, bright as
the air, white as the sun. No acids. No chemicals.
Just soap. IT FLOATS.

1902

WHEREVER there is stainless white cleanliness there
you may find Ivory Soap. You know how good
it is in the bath; it is just as superior for linens, flannels
or garments of other materials requiring special care
in the washing. Because Ivory Soap is pure the best
work is more certain to result from its use.
IT FLOATS.

1903

SOME have only themselves to keep clean, but the
housekeeper has many and varied tasks of cleanliness.
It is not, however, now necessary that she should have for
these, several kinds of soap each fitted to clean only one
thing. Ivory Soap is pure, and because of its purity it is at all
times the soap to select when soap is needed. It drives away
dirt with all its unpleasant consequences, and your confidence is increased every time you put it to a hard test.
IT FLOATS.

1903

The man in the bow: "Let's have a bath!"

The man in the stern: "All right! Here's
the Ivory Soap."

IT FLOATS—but that is not the only reason
why you should use Ivory Soap for the bath.
Other reasons are: It is the purest soap there
is. It lathers freely, rinses quickly, and leaves
the skin cool and clean and smooth.

There is no "free" (uncombined) alkali in Ivory Soap.
That is why it will not injure the finest fabric or the most
delicate skin.

Ivory Soap - 99 44/100 Per Cent. Pure.

1906

A Prominent Horticulturist Writes:

"I have found a home insecticide that costs
next to nothing and is vastly superior to the
expensive ones on the market: Melt a quarter
of a pound of Ivory Soap and add to it a pailful
of water, and it is ready to apply to your
bushes with a whisk, an ordinary garden
spray or a watering can."

"Plant Pests—How to Overcome Them," a 16 page book,
containing information of great value to every man and woman who grows flowers, either for pleasure or profit, will be
mailed on application to THE PROCTER & GAMBLE CO.,
Cincinnati, Ohio.

Ivory Soap - 99 44/100 Per Cent. Pure.

1906

An automobile is like everything else. To do its best and
look its prettiest, it must be clean—engine, body and brasswork.
To keep the engine clean, get hold of the best machinist
you can find.
To clean the painted parts, use Ivory Soap, tepid water and
a couple of soft cloths.
To clean the brasswork, use Ivory Soap paste. This is
the way to make it:

To one pint of boiling water add a quarter of a cake of Ivory Soap,
shaved fine. Boil ten minutes after the soap is thoroughly dissolved.
Let it cool. Keep in a glass jar with a tight-fitting top. Apply with a
soft cloth. Polish with another soft cloth.

It is better than polishing compounds, because, containing no
"gritty" substance, it will not injure the lacquer which covers brasswork, just as a thin coat of varnish covers furniture.

Ivory Soap
99 44/100 Per Cent. Pure.

1906

Make a good article. *Keep on making it good.*
Tell people how good it is. And they will buy it; *and keep on buying it.*
Ivory Soap is a case in point.
From the beginning, the idea has been to make it so good, so pure, so
satisfactory in every way that people who have used it once would continue to buy
it. They do.

And because it is pure, because it is good, because it is satisfactory in every
way, Ivory Soap is equally available for bath, toilet and fine laundry purposes.

Ivory Soap . . . . 99 44/100 Per Cent. Pure.

1908

Who wants pure soap?
Pretty nearly everybody.

Why do they want it?
Because it is pure.

Where can they get it?
At any grocery store.

How?
By asking for Ivory Soap.

Is Ivory Soap absolutely pure?
No.

How nearly pure is it?
99 44/100 per cent. pure.

Is there a purer soap than Ivory?
No. Not one.

For bath, toilet and fine laundry purposes;
for the nursery; for shampooing; for everything and anything that necessitates the use
of a better-than-ordinary soap, Ivory Soap is
unequaled.

Ivory Soap . . . . It Floats.

1909

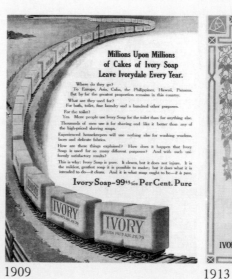

Millions Upon Millions
of Cakes of Ivory Soap
Leave Ivorydale Every Year.

Where do they go?
To Europe, Asia, Cuba, the Philippines, Hawaii, Panama.
But by far the greatest proportion remains in this country.

What are they used for?
For bath, toilet, fine laundry and a hundred other purposes.

For the toilet?
Yes. More people use Ivory Soap for the toilet than for anything else.
Thousands of men use it for shaving and like it better than any of
the high-priced shaving soaps.
Experienced housekeepers will use nothing else for washing woolens,
laces and delicate fabrics.

How are these things explained? How does it happen that Ivory
Soap is used for so many different purposes? And with such uni-
formly satisfactory results?

This is why: Ivory Soap is pure. It cleans, but it does not injure. It
is the mildest, greatest soap it is possible to make; but it does what it is
intended to do—it cleans. And it is what soap ought to be—*it is pure.*

Ivory Soap-99 44/100 Per Cent. Pure

1909

Wherever Ivory Soap goes, it carries with it
the Spirit of Cleanliness. The white floating
cake suggests cleanliness. Its bubbling, copious
lather feels clean. Its purity and quality have
come to mean cleanliness at its best.

IVORY SOAP . . . . 99 44/100% PURE

1913

A SAMPLING OF EARLY IVORY ADS

*From the beginning, Procter & Gamble believed that keeping the name in front of the consuming (or at least reading) public
would sell the product. "Keeping" meant continually, endlessly, remorselessly, but not repeatedly. For decades P&G never*

1904

1904

1904

1905

1907

1907

1907

1908

1916

1916

1917

1920

repeated a single ad after it was run; therefore the pressures on its agency for new ways to say the same thing were monumental.

Above a sampling of only a few of the themes pursued in just two decades up to 1920.

53

equalled 0.56 percent, lower than any of the three castiles.

Recognizing a slogan when he saw one, Harley subtracted the 0.56 percent from 100 percent and got "99 and $^{44}/_{100}$ per cent pure," one of the most famous tradelines in history, still as recognizable today as it was a hundred years ago.

Step Four. The great strength of the slogan was that it quietly stated an atmosphere of *quality*. That the product deserved the buyer's attention because it was pure, uniform; that you could always depend on getting exactly what you expected Ivory to be; and that this quality seemed to matter to the company that made it so much that this was what they chose to brag about. It was this general theme—"dignified class"—that Procter & Gamble managed to sustain through decades of public advertising.

The cousins immediately met the problem that we have discovered before. There really were very few places where you could place advertising for a *national* audience in their time, but they started with a six-inch ad in a religious weekly, *The Independent*, on December 21, 1882. From there, as more and more magazines came to life, Ivory appeared in country weeklies, farm journals, and ultimately in the new popular magazines like *Ladies Home Journal*, *Good Housekeeping*, and *Harper's Weekly*. The quiet theme of "quality" was deliberately followed in the makeup of the early ads. Ivory was the first of the advertisers to hire "big name," recognizable artists and copywriters to do its pieces. The ads went quickly to the back-of-the-front-cover spot, and P&G was one of the first advertisers to embrace four-color printing when it became available in 1896. (They actually sent staff members to France to see how it was done, and brought back specifications and techniques which the company gave to American magazine publishers to hasten their use of the European invention.)

The first Ivory baby ("safe enough to use on . . .") appeared in 1887, with a rather startling head of a 40-year-old man apparently pasted on a six-month-old body. The baby image improved steadily, however, and by 1900 such famous artists as Jessie Willcox Smith, Maud Humphrey, and Elizabeth Shippen Green were doing such a good job that the ads were popular as "suitable for framing" giveaways in return for a soap wrapper. Maud Humphrey's graceful images were especially popular as she illustrated one book after another and created over 300 covers for the major magazines of the time. (Ironically, she is now better remembered for being the mother of the movie actor Humphrey Bogart.) By the 1930s, the Ivory babies were being immortalized by such famous photographers as Edward Steichen and Anton Bruehl.

When You Get Successful, How Do You Keep the Competitors at Bay?

The Ivory ads were enormously successful right from the start. Ivory sales exploded, and Procter & Gamble quickly became one of the nation's leading manufacturers—and the target of competition from every side.

How did they defend themselves? Two ways. The first was to keep up endless, saturation advertising, essentially staking out a territoriality that seized the high ground in every market. They made no secret of it. In a May 15, 1911, *Saturday Evening Post* ad, they used up a full page of space to say:

> Advertising has been a factor—an important factor—in the success of Ivory Soap.
>
> But—would you buy Ivory Soap if you could get better soap for the price you pay for Ivory? No!
>
> Would you buy Ivory Soap if you could get another soap, as good as Ivory, for less than you pay for Ivory? Of course not.
>
> Advertising is merely an evidence of a manufacturer's faith in the merit of an article.
>
> Continuous advertising is proof of the public's confidence in it.
>
> Ivory Soap has been advertised, *continuously*, for more than thirty years.
>
> Ivory Soap . . . . .99 $^{44}/_{100}$ Per Cent Pure

But the second defense was even more interesting than the conviction that "continuous advertising is proof of the public's confidence" in a product.

The two families were acutely conscious that they had gotten their initial position through their laboratory, and since 1878 P&G has had an almost superstitious regard for constant, state-of-the-art research. For years, until the time of electronics and high tech, the proportion of Procter & Gamble's income devoted to research and development was among the highest in the nation.

It brings new products on line constantly, and then makes them compete against its own traditional brands. Every name must stand on its own, and if it cannot hold its own, it is dropped.

The company invented P&G White Naptha laundry soap in 1902 to defend itself against a growing competitor, Fels-Naptha. By 1920, the P&G version was the largest-selling brand of soap in the world.

P&G developed a hydrogenation process that resulted in Crisco in 1911. It came up with Ivory Flakes in 1919, Chipso in 1920, and the latter wiped out its own Naptha as the U.S. laundry soap of choice. It invented Oxydol in 1929 and wiped out Chipso. It came out with Tide detergent in a box in 1946, and did in all its granulated soaps. It invented Liquid Tide in 1984, which has displaced almost all dry detergents. Its Camay, Zest, and Safeguard fight each other against Ivory. Its own Cheer, Dash, Bold, and Era struggle with its Tide. Its flouride triumph of 1955, Crest, fights with its Gleem; Prell fights with its Head & Shoulders; Charmin competes with its White Cloud toilet tissues—

1901

The famous illustrator J.C. Leyendecker was only in his twenties and at the beginning of a long career when he painted this detailed ad, but he already understood the proper solemn and reverent attitude appropriate to THE PRODUCT.

Strong and serene, as mighty forest tree
That braves the blast and dares the storm, is he
Who wisely lives, and living, learns to know
The health and strength which Quaker Oats bestow.

AT ALL GROCERS IN 2-LB. PACKAGES ONLY.

When you write, please mention "The Cosmopolitan."

1897

THE
EASY FOOD
·
EASY
TO
BUY
·
EASY
TO
COOK
·
EASY
TO
DIGEST

QUAKER

WHITE OATS

Ceres, fair goddess of the harvest fields,
Now to the world her choicest treasure yields.

AT ALL GROCERS IN 2-LB. PACKAGES ONLY.

1897

while its laboratories grind out new products to displace what it already has on the market. An interesting way of doing business.

CEREALS

With Ivory Soap we had one product beginning in a clear field with a twenty-year running start before the competitors closed in. We also had a product that pretty much spoke for itself. It claimed to wash bodies and clothes, and from the customer's point of view, either it did and you bought it again, or it didn't and you went back to your old ways.

With breakfast foods, it was exactly the opposite. One day there were none, ten years later there were dozens, all savagely going for each other's throats. No one even considered saying, "This is something you eat for breakfast, you'll like the taste." Instead, each carton was filled with "The Road to Wellville," a raise in salary, better relations with your wife, fewer trips to your doctor, "Through the Alimentary Canal with Rod and Camera." Let's see how it developed.

Oats for People

Up to the Civil War, there was no particular food one ate just for breakfast. Our ancestors ate fried hominy grits and fried potatoes just as they did for lunch and supper, and they had fried bacon, fried pork, fried ham, two or three eggs, an apple, and coffee before they went out to work. In New England, they had fried pancakes.

The first innovation came from a German miller, Ferdinand Schumacher, who emigrated to Akron, Ohio, in 1856. He built a water wheel mill, ground the usual animal feed and flour, and, for his neighboring German friends, put some oats for porridge through a hand grinder in the back room. The non-German Ohioans professed to be shocked at this use of animal feed for human consumption, but the idea of boiled oatmeal became sufficiently popular in the area that Schumacher soon named his building the German Mills American Oatmeal Factory and within a few years was producing 20 barrels'-worth a day. By the end of the Civil War, he was selling one-pound glass jars of milled oats in

ABOVE LEFT:

Nearly a hundred years before Claymation, the admakers were using clay figures to sell products. Quaker Oats' artists sculpted scenes in bas-relief, lit them sharp vertical, and printed the photograph in the new halftone style.

LEFT:

At a time when men's Union Suit ads were being painted over to remove all sexually identifiable bumps, Quaker Oats was using explicit clay models of Ceres to catch the reader's eye. The "Easy to Cook" theme was the result of a technological breakthrough: up until the 1880s, oat cereals had to be soaked and boiled overnight. In the 1890s, the Quaker Company invented "rolling" the oats into flakes (rather than grinding them to grits), and thus cut the cooking time to an hour.

Cincinnati, New York, and Philadelphia. He was also sending 50-pound sacks back to Germany for sale in the old country.

Oatmeal became increasingly popular in New England. There it was used only as a breakfast food (to take the place of fried grits), but its preparation required considerably more forethought than grits did. The oatmeal was usually put in a pan when the housewife went to bed, and she let it simmer on the kitchen stove until the following morning, by which time it had softened sufficiently to be eaten. After 1890, oatmeal was usually prepared in a double-boiler, and put on a hot flame an hour and a half before it was to be served. Quaker Oats offered double boilers as a premium, in return for five pictures of the Quaker man and one dollar.

Quaker Oats

It was the Quaker, indeed, who started the idea of a marketed breakfast food. While Dr. Kellogg and C.W. Post to come were single-person entrepreneurs, Quaker Oats was a full-dress corporate entity from the start. Schumacher ground the meal; Henry Parson Crowell, a neighboring competitor who ran a mill at Ravenna, Ohio, quit work and gave himself over to full-time selling of Schumacher's product; and Robert Stuart, a miller from Cedar Rapids, Iowa, joined the team to concentrate on packaging, production, and shipping. (Schumacher would never have let the upstarts in—he was producing 2,000 180-pound barrels a day—but suddenly his American Oatmeal Factory burned to the ground and he needed help and capital to rebuild it.)

Until 1875, flour was sold by the barrel with little attention to cleanliness, and none for any brand distinction. Schumacher had accumulated orders throughout each year to be ground in September and shipped immediately, so any mildew that might appear would have had to have been generated in the buyer's store and could not be blamed on Schumacher's storage. Henry Parson Crowell revolutionized the whole procedure.

Schumacher's barrels had gone to jobbers and wholesalers to unload as best they could. Crowell headed directly to the consumer. He created a two-pound box of the meal, sealed it at the factory and guaranteed it to be clean and of honest weight. He printed the cooking instructions on one side of the box, and searched for an image to put on the other side. He finally saw a picture in an encyclopedia of a Quaker who, he believed, looked "earnest, hard-working, and virtuous." He had an image drawn that appeared the very personification of friendly rectitude with a scroll in the Friend's hand on which the single word PURE could be easily read. The whole thing was registered in 1877, and it became the first trademark for a breakfast cereal in history.

Schumacher had taken great pride in the fact that he had become the world's greatest producer of oats without ever having spent a penny on advertising. He had stated on many occasions that word of mouth and quality were all that were needed for success. Crowell believed just the opposite. He was convinced that the secret of success lay in reminding the

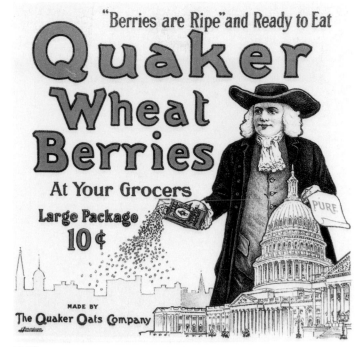

"Berries are Ripe" and Ready to Eat
Quaker Wheat Berries
At Your Grocers
Large Package 10¢
MADE BY
The Quaker Oats Company

1910

When Quaker Oats brought out its first cold cereals, it named them Puffed Rice and Wheat Berries. Shortly thereafter, it opened an account with the famous advertising agency, Lord & Thomas, under Albert D. Lasker. Lasker assigned the account to Claude C. Hopkins who promptly changed the names to Puffed Rice *and* Puffed Wheat *so he could write ads pressing "Puffed" for the two products. When the products were started, they sold for 10 cents each, but Lasker got the company to raise the price to 15 cents and invest all of the extra nickel in advertising.*

Hopkins also invented the slogan, "Shot From Guns," and kept the account for thirty years.

customer daily of the existence of Quaker Oats. Not just in print. Lots of people who ate oatmeal did not read every day, but every day someone ran out of oatmeal and Crowell wanted to be sure that these someones were reminded that they should buy more, quickly, and when they did buy, what they bought were Quaker Oats. He proceeded to thin the profits with every variety of advertising he could think of.

He took out space in local newspapers and weekly farm reports. He painted the Quaker on the sides of covered bridges, barns, and silos beside every road his agents could get a horse down. When a farmer would accept money for a single wall ad, it was considered preferable, but if he resisted, Crowell would pay for painting the whole barn. (The words and pictures were put on the roof and the wall facing the road; the farmer could choose any color for the other three sides.)

Crowell designed a filling machine that could handle half-ounce miniature boxes of Quaker Oats and he went from town to town hiring school boys to leave one box inside each screen door in the community. He got attractive students from home economics classes to cook oatmeal in front of grocery stores, and he set up long booths at county fairs,

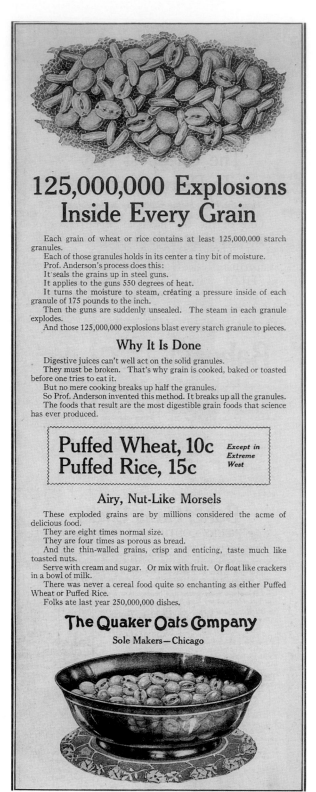

125,000,000 Explosions
Inside Every Grain

Each grain of wheat or rice contains at least 125,000,000 starch granules.

Each of those granules holds in its center a tiny bit of moisture.

Prof. Anderson's process does this:

It seals the grains up in steel guns.

It applies to the guns 550 degrees of heat.

It turns the moisture to steam, creating a pressure inside of each granule of 175 pounds to the inch.

Then the guns are suddenly unsealed. The steam in each granule explodes.

And those 125,000,000 explosions blast every starch granule to pieces.

Why It Is Done

Digestive juices can't well act on the solid granules.

They must be broken. That's why grain is cooked, baked or toasted before one tries to eat it.

But no mere cooking breaks up half the granules.

So Prof. Anderson invented this method. It breaks up all the granules. The foods that result are the most digestible grain foods that science has ever produced.

| Puffed Wheat, 10c | Except in Extreme West |
| Puffed Rice, 15c | |

Airy, Nut-Like Morsels

These exploded grains are by millions considered the acme of delicious food.

They are eight times normal size.

They are four times as porous as bread.

And the thin-walled grains, crisp and enticing, taste much like toasted nuts.

Serve with cream and sugar. Or mix with fruit. Or float like crackers in a bowl of milk.

There was never a cereal food quite so enchanting as either Puffed Wheat or Puffed Rice.

Folks ate last year 250,000,000 dishes.

The Quaker Oats Company

Sole Makers—Chicago

1913

On Labor Day at the 1904 St. Louis World's Fair, the first Puffed Rice was exploded from eight Spanish-American war cannons. The company loaded the barrels with dry rice grains, sealed the pieces, put flames around the metal for forty minutes, and when the guns were unplugged, out sprayed streams of Puffed Rice—which was then coated with caramel and sold as candy. Quaker licensed the idea to a candy maker, and it wasn't until 1909 that anyone thought to use the exploded grains as a breakfast cereal. The new application was an immediate success.

ladling hot oatmeal to anyone who wanted to step in out of the sun. Free.

He was the first advertiser to go all out for premiums *inside* the carton. He redesigned the filling machine to drop in silverware, china saucers, glass bowls, and drinking glasses, over which he poured the two pounds of dry oatmeal. He printed endless four-color chromo-lithographs of adorable children and nostalgic scenes "suitable for framing" on the front, with high praise for Quaker Oats on the back. He selected the precise colors of red, blue, and yellow that represented the Quaker label and saw that they were used on billboards sited opposite railroad platforms, on streetcar posters, and on metal signs hanging from farm fences. Calendars, cookbooks, blotters, and church fans described the glories of rolled white oats.

Crowell was one of the first to use scientists' endorsements, one of the first to run week-long cooking schools at Lyceums, and his finest effort was the 15-car railroad train he ran from Cedar Rapids to Portland, Oregon, in 1891. He dressed five portly men in Quaker costumes and put them on top of the engine and various cars. When the train would reach a station, everyone would jump down and, accompanied by the prettiest girls from the local high school, distribute boxes of Quaker Oats to everyone on the platform. When the train reached Portland many days later, a sample was given to every house in the city "to introduce the healthful attributes of hot oatmeal to the Pacific Northwest."

We're Selling Health Here

The first decade of Quaker advertising stressed the ease of digesting oatmeal, indeed pre-Civil War doctors had dispensed it in folded apothecaries' papers to be used as a gruel for colicky babies. Early in the game, miller Schumacher conceived of the idea of mashing the oats between stone rollers in place of grinding it with stone millwheels as flour was made. (The millwheels ground the oats into a coarse dust and, in later years, Dr. Kellogg would claim that the reason he invented dry cereal "was to displace the half-cooked, pasty, dyspepsia-producing breakfast mush" of boiled oatmeal.) Schumacher changed from flour to flakes because in the millwheel process you got 25 percent unsaleable waste. With rollers, everything turned into splintered flakes and you could sell it all. A delightful and unintended benefit proved to be that you could cook the rolled variety in an hour and a half instead of the overnight preparation previously required by the oat flour. Crowell, knowing a good thing when he saw it, then sold Quaker Oats through the 1890s as "The Easy Food—Easy to Buy—Easy to Cook—Easy to Digest: Quaker White Oats."

By the turn of the century, the case for cooked oats became much more serious. A typical *Saturday Evening Post* full-page ad would show two sets of children. The pair on the left, looking down and out of the picture frame, were gaunt, close-cropped, and slightly soiled. The pair on the right were well scrubbed, looked directly at the viewer with brushed hair, ribbons, and fluffy dresses. The headline read:

"How Much of This Difference is Due to Oatmeal?"

The copy then explained that the Quaker Oats Company had "canvassed hundreds of homes which breed children like these—the wan and anemic, red-cheeked and strong—the capable and the deficient." And this is what they found:

"IN THE TENEMENTS   Among the homes of the ignorant in our largest cities . . . not one home in twelve serves oats . . . The average child of the tenements is nervous, it matures undeveloped, and exhibits the lack of mental and physical power . . . The trouble is largely due to lack of proper nutrition.

"ON THE BOULEVARDS   In the homes of the educated, the prosperous, the competent, seven out of eight regularly serve oatmeal. Out of fifty professors interviewed in one university, only two did not serve it. Out of 12,000 physicians of whom we inquired, four-fifths serve oatmeal in their homes . . . Boston consumes 22 times as much oatmeal per capita as do two certain states where the average education is lowest . . .

"A canvass of 61 poorhouses shows that only one in each 13 of the inmates came from oatmeal homes . . . Hardly two percent of the prisoners in four great penitentiaries were fed on oatmeal in their youth . . .

[What were they missing?] "Oats contain more proteids [sic], more phosphorus, more lecithin than any other food. Oats . . . supply what brains and bodies require."

Dr. Kellogg in Battle Creek

By the time the oats and felons connection was being made, *Saturday Evening Post* readers were fully conditioned to this kind of reasoning thanks to even more vigorous advertising by Dr. John Harvey Kellogg of the Battle Creek Sanitarium. Dr. Kellogg gave us cold, dried, already-prepared breakfast food. It resulted from an unlikely sequence of events.

It began with a clergyman named Sylvester Graham, who had died in 1851. He had spent his adult life trying to convince Americans that white bread was weakening the nation. His solution was to eat coarse brown bread and whole-wheat crackers. The crackers came to be called Graham crackers and, of course, are still with us. (Many believe nothing better has ever been invented for dipping in cold milk between three-thirty and four o'clock in the afternoon.)

The whole-grain diet promulgated by Rev. Graham was picked up by the Shakers and the Seventh Day Adventists around 1850, and became a part of their church doctrine: whole-grain foods, no meat, limited fats; no alcohol, no tobacco, no coffee (all of the latter were artificial, not God-given, stimulants).

At mid-century the Adventists selected Battle Creek, Michigan, as their national headquarters, and shortly thereafter started a small hospital which, by 1866, had grown into a nationally known institution called the Battle Creek Sanitarium. A similar health institution called the Glen

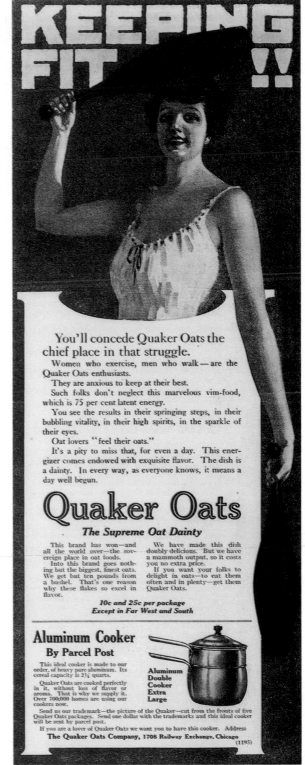

1916

"Women who exercise, men who walk—are the Quaker Oats enthusiasts." The Indian clubs are somewhat over-sized, but the healthy woman in the 1916 version of a leotard has all the elements of present-day fitness enthusiasts. Five trademarks and a dollar would get you a double boiler in which to prepare your hot, morning cereal.

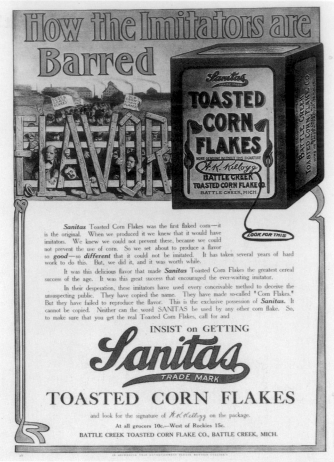

1907

1908

This is one of the last ads for Dr. John Harvey Kellogg's corn-flake invention issued under the trade name "Sanitas." Dr. Kellogg, director of the Battle Creek Sanitarium, invented foods which he sold as a hospital sideline under the name of the Sanitas Nut Food Company. Dr. Kellogg's accountant brother, Will, got him to kill the name "Sanitas" on the grounds that it reminded him of plumbing, washable oilcloth, and refrigerators.

"When Johnny comes Marching home again With a common Imitation—Send Johnny a Marching back again With a note of Explanation: Never send me anything but Kellogg's—the Genuine Toasted Corn Flakes." By 1911 there were 108 brands of corn flakes being made in Battle Creek alone.

The Kellogg brothers had been producing their corn flakes for eight years when C.W. Post introduced his version in 1906. Post was soon making nearly $2 million a year in profits on Post Toasties, and Kellogg's began fighting back with its "the only genuine" campaign. W.K.'s signature was to be the hallmark.

1907

Haven Water Cure was operating in Skaneateles Lake, New York, under the leadership of Dr. James Caleb Jackson. (Clara Barton and Elizabeth Cady Stanton took the cure there every summer for years.) The doctors at the two institutions exchanged information and diets, and in 1870, Dr. Jackson invented a recipe for mixing the whole-grain elements into a single cookie, which he dubbed "Granula." He made it out of graham flour and water baked into thin, hard sheets and then ground into peanut-sized kernels. These were again baked and ground into smaller pellets about the size of . . . Grape-Nuts (which would not be invented until 1898).

The result was believed to be extraordinarily healthful. It was pre-digested because of the repetitive baking, but was so hard to swallow that the accepted form of preparation was to fill a drinking glass one-third full of Granula when you went

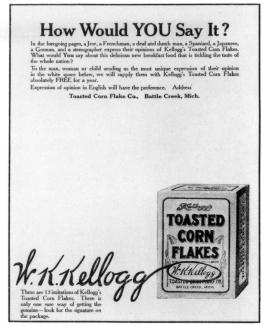

1908

to bed. You filled the remainder of the glass with whole milk, let it stand overnight, and in the morning the Granula would have swelled up to fill the glass. The milk would have separated into cream and skim, and you poured the whole glassful into a bowl and ate it for breakfast.

During the 1870s a series of doctors ran the Battle Creek Sanitarium and ultimately it was taken over by Dr. Kellogg who, in the next thirty years, made it one of the leading health spas in the nation. By 1900 it served 1,200 paying guests at a time, and its list of "repeaters" (came every summer for years) included John D. Rockefeller, J.C. Penney, both Kress and Kresge, Robert LaFollette, Percy Grainger, and long lists of internationally-known entertainers. Sojourner Truth lived her final years at the "San," as it was routinely called in the national press. The Sanitarium was sponsored by the Adventist Church so Dr. Kellogg had to conform to its vegetarian-no-stimulants dietary rules, and he was thus pressed to come up with new and tasteful food dishes that would appeal to his guests' palates yet contain no meat or caffeine. From this, civilization as we know it received cold breakfast food.

In 1878, Dr. Kellogg invented his first, pre-prepared health food, which he called "Granola." Its contents were remarkably like Granula, but he had added wheat to the traditional oatmeal and cornmeal mix, and baked the combination until it was more like zwieback and could be eaten soon after the milk was added. It was the first cold cereal boxed and sold by a brand name, but its sales were generally small and was considered mainly as just another of the Sanitarium's many spin-offs. (Dr. Kellogg wrote health books, sponsored Chautauqua-style lectures and string quartet concerts, and ran week-long back-to-health campaigns all over Europe and America.)

In 1880, Dr. Kellogg asked his younger brother, Will, to

One of W.K.'s favorite devices was to put obscure ads on a sequence of pages in a newspaper, with the ultimate explanation revealed on the final page. These are three samples from a series in Hebrew, French, sign language, Spanish, Japanese, German, and Gregg shorthand—all extolling Kellogg's in a single Saturday Evening Post.

come to the Sanitarium and keep an eye on its business affairs. John Harvey had always been the go-getter in the family; Will was quiet and reserved, and their parents worried about him. But "W.K." quickly saw that there was a great deal more money to be made in selling breakfast food than in running a hospital.

Following his creation of Granola, Dr. Kellogg turned to the potential of corn as a food, and he boiled it, mashed it out on rollers, chilled the blobs so they could be peeled off, dried them, baked them, and called them corn flakes. He marketed the result as Sanitas Toasted Corn Flakes produced by a bakery parallel to but separate from the hospital's kitchen. The Doctor called this spin-off the Sanitas Nut Food Company. His product was not a success.

It had a short shelf life (went rancid before it could be sold), got soggy in damp climates, and didn't taste too good either. Accountant W.K. Kellogg stepped into the production sequence and made changes. He wrapped the box in wax paper and began to advertise "freshness." (He later put the wax paper inside the box, thereby saving two inches of paper per wrapping and $250,000 per year.) He saw to it that the company never produced more product than it had orders on hand for so nothing was stored to get stale, and he added malt flavoring to improve the taste. He eliminated Dr. Kellogg's "Sanitas" name on everything because, he said, it

The cheaper brands pay him more profit on each package, but do not sell so fast.

Nor do they make *satisfied customers.*

When the dealer takes corn flakes home himself he takes home Kellogg's.

That's worth remembering.

"Don't merely say 'Corn Flakes'—say 'Kellogg's, Please.'"

ALWAYS READY

That's the great thing about Kellogg's. It saves the housewife countless steps. An open package, a few bowls and a pitcher of milk or cream, and breakfast is ready.

And it's a satisfying breakfast, too.

It can be served with fruit in many delicious combinations for variety.

Always heat for a moment in an open oven to restore crispness.

W. K. Kellogg

132 B.

The SWEET HEART *-- OF THE CORN --*

1907

had "the connotation of plumbing, washable oilcloth, wall covering and refrigerators." He got the Doctor to let him have the rights to the product and in 1906 he began to put the words "The Genuine Bears This Signature—W.K. Kellogg" on every carton. He was in business.

W.K. was wildly in favor of advertising. He wrote all his own copy, and prided himself that he always spent as much on promotion of his products as he returned to the stockholders as dividends. His campaigns were imaginative and changed constantly. One of his best known was a blizzard of appeals for people to stop eating Kellogg's Corn Flakes so their neighbors could have some. He put up the first blocklong, "80-foot-high," animated electric sign on Times Square. It had a winsome boy crying moveable electric tears until the words "I got Kellogg's Toasted Corn Flakes" appeared and the tears magically stopped and a grin flashed across his face. W.K.'s only major error was his success with the brand name. Corn Flakes became one of the first trademarks to go generic (as cellophane, linoleum, aspirin, and nylon would in the future). Following a law suit, a court ruling said that corn flakes had become so common as to be

descriptive and anyone could make them so long as the words were used lower case. In 1911 there were 108 brands of corn flakes being made in Battle Creek alone.

Then What Are Post Toasties?

Of the many firms going after a part of Dr. Kellogg's cold breakfast idea, none was as determined as Charlie Post's. C.W. Post had been a Texas real estate developer in Fort Worth, but he had severe digestive problems and had entered the Battle Creek Sanitarium in 1891 being transported from the train to his hospital bed in a wheelchair. He stayed at the San from February through November, when Dr. Kellogg told him that there was no more that he could do for him, and told his wife that he suspected her husband had little longer to live.

The Posts moved into the home of a Christian Science practitioner there in Battle Creek, and, to his astonished delight, within a day C.W. was able to eat his first full meal in two years and the next day was able to dress and walk about. He was convinced that the secret to good health was simply to think you are healthy and to eat in moderation. He

This "Sweetheart of the Corn" was a "typewriter" in W.K. Kellogg's office. Through the next seventy-five years, the symbol would be re-painted and re-issued with appropriate modifications to her hair, figure, and dress to conform to current fashion.

W.K.'s invention of a wax paper wrapper "to deliver the flakes . . . as fresh and crisp as they are when they come from our ovens" was his favorite innovation. He soon figured out a way of putting the wax paper on the inside, *thus saving two inches of paper per box and $250,000 in one year.*

1914

was eager to share his discovery, so he wrote a series of books which he in turn reduced to a single pamphlet called "The Road to Wellville." This secret to health was dropped into Post product boxes for the next thirty years.

Post bought a farm house at the edge of Battle Creek and took in boarders looking for the recovery of their own health. He named the home La Vita Inn and advertised it as a "place for cure through dietary and mental influence." He shared Dr. Kellogg's belief in pre-digested, non-stimulant food, so he had the Sanitarium's challenge of coming up with something edible for the two meals a day the Inn provided. His first invention was a substitute for the coffee that his visitors expected to drink to start their day—but which Post denied them.

After many experiments on his wife's kitchen range, Post settled on a mixture of 22½ percent wheat berries (the heart of the kernel without the husk), 67½ percent bran, and 10 percent New Orleans molasses. The mixture was browned in open pans on the stove, and then put in a roaster that steamed out the moisture but returned the oils from the wheat. He had invented Postum, which he said firmly "was not a substitute for anything. It is a pure food-drink, and stands on its own basis as a separate and distinct article."

Post served Postum at the Inn and then very quickly began to advertise it in ever-widening circles around Battle Creek. He wrote his own copy and deliberately used "plain words for plain people" instead of the Olympian medical phrases that Dr. Kellogg employed with the Sanitas products. One of Post's favorite devices was to use intentionally bad grammar in his headlines to imply he was talking ordinary language to ordinary folk.

The no-caffeine coffee substitute became enormously popular at a time before decaffeinated coffee existed. The same appeal the ads for the latter now use—coffee nerves, acidity, sleeplessness—had all been used by Post by 1900. Postum sold so well so quickly that its imitators swarmed in to try to seize the wholesale market by promising a larger mark-up than Post's but letting the grocers sell the product below Postum's standard price. When Post reached the point that he was selling Postum by the tens of thousands of dollars' worth a month, he decided to take the opposition seriously. His counter-attack was unusual and imaginative.

He himself created a new, competitive brand which he called Monk's Brew and he sold it for one-fifth the price of Postum. It was, in fact, 100-percent genuine Postum and was priced at a nickel a box. As Post explained to the National Association of Manufacturers ten years later in 1910, "This was sent out to the wholesale and retail grocers with the statement that as they seemed to want a cheap cereal coffee, we were ready to furnish it." Monk's Brew wiped out the competitors in less than a year, underselling what they could make on their brands by more than half. Post said, "We took back from the grocers literally carloads of Monk's Brew, which would not sell even at five cents. When those packages came into our factories, they were cut open, the contents carefully examined to see that they were in good condition, and poured from the five-cent packages directly into the twenty-five-cent packages . . . where they sold rapidly at five times the price offered under the unknown name of Monk's Brew." In the year of the great struggle, Post lost $46,000, but the next year his profit went to $385,000, and never slackened for the remainder of his life.

By 1900, Post's Battle Creek factory was using 1,500 bushels of wheat a day. Very shortly thereafter Post was using that much in an hour. The difference was Grape-Nuts. He invented it in 1897 and it went on the market in January 1898.

63

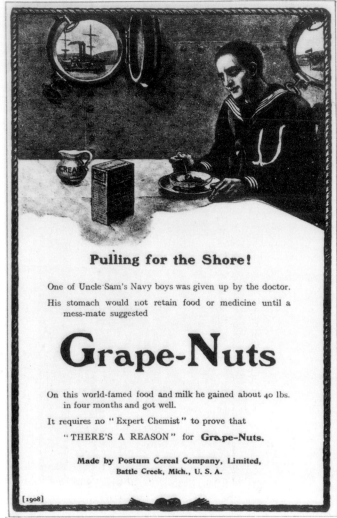

1908

The copy reads: "One of Uncle Sam's Navy boys was given up by the doctor. His stomach would not retain food or medicine until a mess-mate suggested Grape-Nuts. On this world-famed food and milk he gained about 40 lbs. in four months and got well." C.W. Post himself had been unable to retain food and, as both he and his wife always said, had "been given up on by the doctors." He was convinced that whole-grain food and positive thinking had restored his own health.

Why "Grape"?

With Postum going so successfully as a drink, and Dr. Kellogg doing so well with corn flakes, C.W. Post felt he needed a breakfast food, too. He always swore (frequently in court) that his resultant idea had no link to Granula or Granola, and Grape-Nuts came to be made as follows: He took whole wheat and malted barley flour and added yeast, mixed the combination together and baked it into loaves just like homemade bread. He then sliced this, re-baked it slowly for 24 hours, and ultimately ground up the very firm product he'd gotten so far. He maintained that the repetitive baking had reduced the starches to dextrose or grape-sugar, and the flavor had become nut-like. Ergo, Grape-Nuts.

It was not, Post maintained, a breakfast cereal. It was a scientific health food. As his ads declared, "it made red blood or it made red blood *redder*." It steadied nerves and benefited the circulation, and by 1909 Grape-Nuts was outselling Postum two to one. The two products complemented each other nicely. More Postum was drunk in the cold winter and more Grape-Nuts sold in the hot summer. The wheat husks that had to be stripped off to get the kernels for Grape-Nuts could be used as the bran for the Postum.

(One of the most bemusing things about the whole Battle Creek advertising approach was the way the various campaigns appeared to be made up wholly out of the vivid and dramatic vocabularies of the inventors—and then decades later science wrote reality under them. Post maintained, apparently intuitively, that his bread crumbs improved the blood. In 1911 Casimer Funk in the Lisner Institute in London discovered Vitamin B, the first vitamin known to science, and located it in the center of the wheat kernel. Dr. Kellogg and the Quaker people were convinced that "roughage and fiber" had an endless series of benefits for the human diet. Now, nearly a hundred years later, the nutritionists tell us that wheat fiber has proved to be exceptionally effective in preventing cancer and that oat fiber may be the best countermeasure short of insulin itself in helping diabetics—as well as normal metabolics—deal with excessive sugar.)

Post rarely suggested that his products tasted good. Always their benefits were for health: Postum fought "coffee neuralgia," heart disease, "lost eyesight through caffeine," the "poisonous alkaloids" in coffee, and "coffee heart" which would send the reader "to his or her long home." Grape-Nuts prevented appendicitis, and was recommended for tuberculosis, malaria, and loose teeth.

The Post ads were loaded with testimonial letters on how the various products had made life sweeter for the authors. Nowadays we tend to assume that this copy is the product of creative ad writers. Oddly enough in the early 1900s they really did come from the public, but C.W. stimulated them in a novel way. He would pick some minor magazine well out of the mainstream and run contests. For example, the *New York Magazine of Mysteries*, November 1904, offered cash prizes for the top off a Postum package, and . . .

325 boxes of gold and greenbacks will be sent to persons who write the most interesting and truthful letters on the following topics:
1) How have you been affected by coffee drinking, and by changing from coffee to Postum?   2) Give name and account of one or more coffee drinkers who have been hurt by it and who have been induced to quit and use Postum.

His conscience was clear; he had it in writing.

He also genuinely believed his "The Road to Wellville" pamphlet which was distributed free literally by the millions. It was an 11-page booklet, copyrighted in 1903,

The products that built the C.W. Post empire. Postum, a non-caffeine substitute for coffee, came first (1895). With the profits from this, Post built his plant and developed his first cereal, Grape-Nuts, in 1898. He then developed his own brand of corn flakes, which he called Elijah's Manna (1906). The Manna infuriated the nation's ministers as exploiting a respected religious story for commercial gain (the trademark was actually illegal in England), and it took Post until 1908 to get the flakes turned into Post Toasties. He designed the package himself, giving us Cinderella sitting by the hearth, closely watched by her cat. Instant Postum was the first "instant" (dehydrated) product on the market, and was an instant success. Oddly enough, no other manufacturer produced an "instant" form of anything—coffee, tea, puddings—for twenty years.

RIGHT:

C.W. Post himself wrote an 11-page pamphlet in 1903 which was dropped into Post cartons by the millions for many years. It was called "The Road to Wellville," and extolled walking, deep breathing, moderate diet, positive mental attitude, and adequate sleep.

For years Post ads provided images of vigorous health for everyone, just ahead down the road. The text of the ad on the right opens with: "You who follow habit's ruts with leaden feet, whose cheeks have lost their glow behind dim-lighted walls, step forth into the sunshine! Drink the rare wine of mountain air, and beneath the vault of blue walk down the open Road to Wellville!"

Regrettably, C.W. Post had killed himself with a .30-.30 hunting rifle during a fit of post-operative depression in 1914, and was not able to see these images of his own vision. His themes, however, were carried on the by the company for decades. (His arch-rivals, the Kellogg brothers, lived on to be 91 each, with W.K. carrying on until 1951.)

OVERLEAF:

Another of the Wellville series, this drawn by the celebrated artist Franklin Booth. One wonders if the designer of the Wizard of Oz's Emerald City might have been influenced by Post Company images in his youth.

1919

ABOVE:

An early Norman Rockwell ad which not only foreshadowed his mature painting style, but anticipated later ad layout conventions by several decades.

1925

The Road to Wellville

Behold, the Shining Spires of Wellville!

You who envy the rosy cheek and sparkling eye, who arise each morning weary and unrefreshed, who go to meet the daily task with fagged brain and unwilling tread—lift up your eyes and see the spires of Wellville shining in the sun! Right about face! Make up your mind now to live in Wellville, the town of health, success and happiness. Avoid the dangerous ruts of habit. Remember Nature's simple teachings. Eat more sparingly of the heavy foods of civilization. Drink more milk. *Eat more often of the golden grain.*

Post Health Products of Battle Creek are made from nutritious grain. They contain, in abundance, the vital elements that build bone and brain and brawn. Post Health Products cost so little, they are so appetizing and so convenient that they have turned thousands out from the dangerous ruts of habit into the "Road to Wellville."

Postum Cereal Company, Inc., Battle Creek, Michigan

Post's Bran Flakes • Postum Cereal   Post Toasties (Double-thick Corn Flakes)

Instant Postum   Grape-Nuts

1925

Grouchy Husbands

EVERYTHING a moment before had been peaceful—and even comparatively quiet. Perhaps the youngster did make a slight disturbance at play, but it was unintentional—not anything over which a normal father should hit the ceiling. Perhaps some remark was made, innocently enough but from the eruption which followed it might have been criminal!

What is the cause of outbursts like that? Unreasoning fits of temper on the part of men who ordinarily are kindly husbands and fathers!

It isn't often that overwork is the cause. Men are made for work. Work leaves the healthy brain and healthy body pleasantly relaxed—not taut and straining. Responsibility shouldn't fray the nerves. Men are miserable without it. They really love their homes and families.

But when this love is manifested by periodic explosions over nothing—when any little disturbance is a signal to fly off the handle—something is decidedly wrong!

The chances are that the man isn't well. Nerves! He would be the first to deny it, of course.

Why men fly off the handle

"Never felt better in my life!" he sputters. But it doesn't. His very vehemence is indication of the trouble which is secretly worrying millions of men in America. They are fagged. They are wearing out prematurely. Instead of the glowing health which should be theirs, "the prime of life" finds many of them a burden on their feet, tired at the beginning of the day as well as *at the end* of it, irritable, exacting, pessimistic. They are not "sick," no; but certainly they are not well.

And nine times out of ten the reasons are these: they neglect exercise, they don't get enough sleep; they shun fresh air; they eat too much, and eat the wrong things. And worst of all, they unthinkingly load their systems with artificial stimulants—with drug stimulants—which contribute *nothing of real value* to their well-being, but which slowly and surely rob the body of its reserve strength.

Perhaps the most widespread offender among these artificial stimulants is caffein. It has no food value. It *seems* to give new energy, but this is a delusion. Actually it whips and goads the tired nerves to action when what they really need is rest.

Various forms of abuse have resulted in an alarming health record in America. The United States Life Tables for 1920 show that Americans pass the period of full health and vigor at the age of 31. These are cold, hard figures. But they become warm, human, illuminating, every time a grouchy husband goes on the warpath over nothing!

In 2,000,000 homes, people are eliminating one form of abuse by making Postum their regular mealtime drink. It is all wheat, skillfully blended and roasted. Instead of caffein, an artificial stimulant, it gives only the healthful elements of whole wheat and bran. It is delicious!—rich, full bodied, with the appetizing flavor of roasted wheat.

Here is a drink which every member of the family can enjoy together, with no fear of sleeplessness, ragged nerves, headache, indigestion—with no sign of a grouch! Made with hot milk instead of the usual boiling water, it is the ideal drink for children, too.

You—the wife, the mother—are in a wonderful position to improve the health of your family. Your most important contribution, perhaps, will be the selection of food which builds up, instead of tearing down. Postum is not a cure-all—but it is one easy step in the right direction!

Get Postum at your grocer's—or accept the offer of Carrie Blanchard, famous food demonstrator.

Carrie Blanchard's Offer

"I want you to make a thirty-day test of Postum. I want to start you out on your test by giving you your first week's supply, and my own directions for making it. You will be glad to know, too, that Postum costs much less per cup.

"Will you send me your name and address? Tell me which kind you prefer—Instant Postum or Postum Cereal (the kind you boil). I'll see that you get the first week's supply and my personal directions right away."

FREE—MAIL THIS COUPON NOW!

© 1925, P. C. Co.

1925

Held back by Coffee ..
this boy never had a fair chance

"A DUNCE" they call him . . . "a sluggard" they say. But Science lifts a hand in his behalf and says "You're wrong!"

Pin the blame on the real culprit . . . pin the blame on coffee. Yes—*coffee!* For thousands of parents are giving their children coffee, and coffee harms children mentally—and physically!

Why coffee harms children

Coffee contains caffein—a drug stimulant. A single cup often contains as much as *three grains* of this drug—20% more than a physician would give an adult as a medicinal dose.

Coffee can make quiet children more listless and sluggish. It can make active children nervous and irritable. It can keep children from getting the sound and restful sleep they should have.

More serious still—by crowding milk out of the diet of children, coffee is a cause of *undernourishment*. It robs children of their rosy cheeks and sparkling eyes. It lowers their vitality, lessens their resistance to disease, and hampers proper development and growth.

Read this amazing proof!

Studies made by responsible institutions among America's school children not only disclosed the fact that an alarming number of these children of grade and high-school age drink coffee—*but that children who drink coffee get poorer marks than those who do not drink it.*

A survey conducted by a world famous Research Institution among 80,000 school children proved conclusively that those drinking coffee were harmed mentally as well as physically. *Less than 16%* of those who drank coffee attained good marks! Over 45% of those who did not drink coffee attained good marks.

Another survey, conducted among large groups of undernourished children, brought to light this fact—*over 85% of the undernourished children received coffee once or more daily!*

No wonder medical authorities condemn coffee for children. No wonder public health and educational authorities warn parents against giving children a drink which is so harmful!

A hot, nourishing drink is important

"But" many parents say, "my youngsters need a hot drink in the morning." Of course they do. But why one that tears down? Why not one that builds up? Give them Postum made with hot milk. It contains no drug—no artificial stimulant.

Postum made with hot milk is not only a delicious hot mealtime drink, but as nourishing a drink as you can find. It is rich in proteins, in fats, in carbohydrates, in minerals—rich in the body building elements that children should have. What a contrast to coffee! What a difference to the child!

No wonder teachers find that boys and girls, right through high-school ages, who drink Postum made with milk are healthier, happier and better students.

Postum is a drink children love. Made only from whole wheat and bran, roasted and slightly sweetened. Begin giving it to your children today. Your grocer can supply you, or mail the coupon for a week's supply absolutely free. Postum is a product of General Foods.

GENERAL FOODS, Battle Creek, Mich.

1933

The many Post ads presented C.W.'s theories: "Health is natural. Sickness is man-made." "We unthinkingly load our system with artificial stimulants . . . [Caffeine] seems to give new energy, but actually it whips and goads the tired nerves to action when they really need rest and nourishment." Solution: try Postum for 30 days. The accompanying coupon will bring the first week's supply free.

three-by-five inches and slipped into all the products. (A special miniature edition went into the enormous numbers of Post products that were sold overseas. Ready-prepared breakfast cereals were not produced in Europe for many years, and all of the big four, Post, Kellogg, Quakers, and Shredded Wheat had a paradise abroad until World War I.) "The Road to Wellville" urged gentle exercise, drinking lots of water, deep breathing, and balanced menus. The latter, which have held up very well in the light of our present understanding of nutrition, did include Grape-Nuts for breakfast, Grape-Nuts for lunch, and Grape-Nuts sprinkled on the salad for supper. The power of positive thinking was explained in detail, mental suggestion was demonstrated, and proper amounts of sleep finished off the regimen. The total program could come right off a modern-day video cassette.

C.W. Post was clearly jealous of the success of W.K. Kellogg's Corn Flakes but waited until 1906 to try his own version. He got a taste that he liked (he claimed his flakes had more bubbles to make them float better, were twice the thickness, and stayed crisper in cream longer), and then he christened them Elijah's Manna and came up with a picture of the prophet in the desert sharing his cereal with the ravens.

Chocolate bran flakes. Probably the first of the candied breakfast foods that now so distress the nutritionists.

1925

1904

The Triscuit introduced as The New Toast.

Shredded Wheat as drawn by Norman Rockwell.

1927

Instead of this appealing to the contemporary churchgoers, it generated a firestorm of reaction from organized religion. Sermons were preached against the "sacrilege" and the "exploitation of the Bible for commercial purposes." Letters to the editors poured in, and the revival tent congregations were particularly outraged.

It took Post until 1908 to get the name and the advertising stopped, but he redirected the effort toward "Post Toasties" with a picture of Cinderella sitting by the fireside, kettle on the spit over a burning fire, black cat, and cream pitcher by her dish of flakes on the floor. Between September 1908 and September 1909 C.W. reported with satisfaction that his *profit* on Post Toasties had totalled $2,185,820.98, with Postum bringing in $1,400,000, and Grape-Nuts making $1,700,000 in the same twelve months. All this back in the days when a million dollars really was a million dollars.

SEX

We've been looking for the antecedents of the accepteds—the givens—the basic conventions of American advertising. How did what we have come to expect to find in an ad get started? We've seen the innovations of Messrs. Procter and Gamble, of Kellogg and Post; what we haven't yet seen is how the ever-present use of sex began. The rules by which we play in this field can also be credited to a single individual; he came later, but the truths he found seem to have held up better than anyone else's insights in this very complex terrain.

First, we must remember that the omnipresence of sex in selling still hasn't reached the point where we're selling sex. Sex is used to get the reader's attention to sell some other product—usually one that is far distant from the implied attraction. As the roadside signs read: "Sex! Sex! Sex! Now that we've gotten your attention, can we sell you a car?" Calvin Klein explains his deliberately shocking graphics by saying, "I don't want women flipping through 600 pages of *Vogue* and not even noticing my ads."

If ever there was an area of advertising that has had to be re-learned every ninety days, it is how to use sex in advertising successfully. What was permitted last year is taboo this, and vice versa.

The use of images of the opposite sex to draw the eye goes back to the 1850s. Wood engravings of the heads of beautiful women were common in patent medicine ads, and frequently were the only pictures on the page—thus achieving their purpose of "read me first" in a way that modern advertisers would pay great sums for. The woodblocks also represent the first of many anomalies about sex and advertising: most patent medicines were bought by women but the advertisers used women's heads to attract the women's attention to their ads. (Even today most female nudes appear in ads for women's products, not men's, and they appear in women's magazines, not men's or general periodicals.)

After the Civil War, the heads got bodies as ads got bigger, and the use of the attraction of sex was more apparent. Any circus ad had a full-length woman in tights which,

JUST A LITTLE.

1889

Apparently in 1889 it took only four inches of leg to get the attention of the top-hatted man on the sidewalk, and presumably this titillating sight was equally arresting to viewers of this poster. Note the product name was on a line with the lady's hose as well as beside her beguiling eyes.

By 1915 silk hose had become accessible to ordinary people (instead of their previous availability only to the rich), and the advertiser could reveal a good eighteen inches of stocking without being accused of bad taste. The sight appeared to be as interesting to this top-hatted man as four inches had been to his predecessor in 1889. Black-and-white newspaper versions of this same ad carried the caption, "A sight draft with interest."

1915

1913

If stocking manufacturers could show their goods with wind gusts, men's underwear could appear in candid pictures taken in the home—but a certain amount of retouching was demanded before it could appear in this Saturday Evening Post ad for general distribution.

as the press run progressed and the engraving crushed and wore, made her look increasingly nude and revealed. Mark Twain said if it hadn't been for the trapeze ladies in circus posters, he'd never have known what was going on under all those crinolines, hoop skirts, and bustles.

Patent medicine ads expanded into full torsos and bodies, and from our point of view, emphasized exposed bosoms and deep cleavage (see illustrations on pages 20 and 26); but, oddly enough, considering that this was high Victoria, it was not considered "in questionable taste." Exposed bosoms had been so common since Napoleonic days that they were not objects of attraction. Church posters and tent meeting hand fans show the biblical women in off-the-shoulder, peasant-type costumes, nothing hidden, scarcely to be noticed.

But in the 1880s, the shirt-waist took cloth right up to the chin, and the floor-sweeping skirts covered everything but the tips of the shoes. At last the advertisers had a target of titillation: a peek at the forbidden. From the 1880s until World War I, the artists' wind gusts could lift the hemline as high as the ankle, and readers could be brought to a full stop.

The Oxford University Press's vastly dignified history of costume notes the potential in the phenomenon:

> Since the concealed is so exciting, the long skirts also provided an almost endless game of trying to peek. The outer clothes might reach to the ground, but if they could in some way be rumpled, or caught up, or disarrayed in the dance or in a riding spill or in the classic piece of hypocrisy by the girl allowing her lover to push her on a swing, what naked delights might not be glimpsed.

By the 1920s, silk stockings for ordinary people arrived to replace the cotton lisle (silk had been limited to the rich until the war), and hemlines shot up. The advertising historian Robert Atwan believes that the Flapper's short skirt was specifically raised to show off the newly available silk stockings; other sociologists believe that it was the iconoclasm of the Jazz Twenties that lifted the hems, and the silk stockings were needed to cover the unattractive bare skin of the legs. A traditional vaudeville joke of the time went: "Q. Whatever happened to the girl in the black stockings? A. Nothing."

In any event, the advertisers had to learn an entirely new set of rules. The first uncovered kneecaps in advertisements

1918

1925

COLES PHILLIPS

© H. H. Co.

Holeproof Hosiery

TRIM ankles, demurely alluring. How they fascinate, captivate. And well she knows glove-fitting Holeproof Hosiery makes them so.

In this short-skirted era, Holeproof is becoming as famous for its sheerness, shapeliness and lustrous beauty, as it is for wonderful wearing qualities.

Leading stores are now showing the newest ideas for Spring in staple and fancy styles in Pure Silk, in Silk Faced and in Lisles for men, women and children.

HOLEPROOF HOSIERY COMPANY, MILWAUKEE, WISCONSIN

Holeproof Hosiery Company of Canada, Limited, London, Ont.

1921

A stylish drawing by Coles Phillips who drew dozens of ads for hosiery (see illustration on page 166). Phillips, whose ads appeared in all of the major magazines, pushed the line of what was acceptable further and faster than any of his contemporaries.

For Your Easter Hosiery, Madame

See these new styles—#895-#3765-#3785

Allen A
Hosiery
For Men, Women and Children
Underwear
For Men and Boys Only

Fresh lustrous silks for Easter. How much they mean to one's costume. Here are three new hosiery styles from Allen-A. In all the authentic shades for Spring. Beautiful in weave, even in color, as you expect Allen-A hosiery to be. Yet moderately priced.

Here are special values to appeal to the careful shopper. Ask your dealer for them. If he hasn't these new Allen-A styles, just write us direct. We'll give you the name of a store in your city that can supply you. THE ALLEN A COMPANY, KENOSHA, WIS.

No. 895 ... No. 3765 ... No. 3785 ...

1925

Thought to be the first time the back of a woman's legs were revealed in an advertisement. Up to this point, this was considered to be as firm a taboo as the imaging of the most private portions of the human anatomy. This ad appeared in the very center of the Roaring Twenties and clearly respectable standards were falling fast.

The kind of beauty that thrills

WOMEN have found that there's a most unusual kind of beauty about these Iron Clads—a fascination that holds your glance, and makes it hard to look away. It's not the kind of beauty which calls attention to the loveliness of the silk. But rather a mysterious quality which glorifies the wearer's own shapeliness and grace.

That is the kind of beauty that thrills. Nature's beauty. Beauty of form that's clothed in such a charming way that all its natural loveliness is revealed.

It's in the texture and the silk. And in that silk there's something else besides. There's Iron Clad wear—and wear—and wear.

ASK for IRON CLAD 907—$1.50 a PAIR

COOPER, WELLS & COMPANY
212 Vine Street, St. Joseph, Michigan
Mills at St. Joseph, Michigan, and Albany, Alabama

Iron Clad Hosiery

1927

Sex in advertising spelled out so the reader understands exactly what the advertiser hopes to achieve.

This photograph, taken by Edward Steichen in 1936, is thought to be the first photograph of a nude woman in advertising.

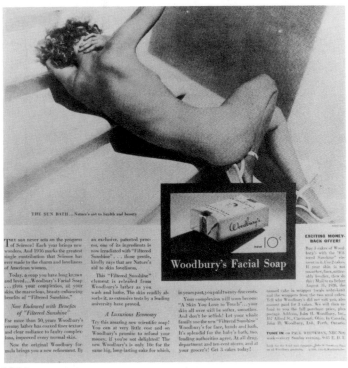

THE SUN BATH ... Nature's aid to health and beauty

Woodbury's Facial Soap

1936

---

appear in the early Twenties, but *backs of knees* were as forbidden as pubic hair is at this writing. The first ad showing the back of a knee appeared in 1925, and was considered far beyond the line of acceptability even in the Anything-Goes Twenties. But: It was the most remembered ad in the magazine by both sexes.

Male nudity was permitted—soap, underwear—but again it was used on products bought primarily by women. (Seventy percent of all male underwear is still bought by women.) Full female nudity was introduced with a photograph by Edward Steichen used to illustrate a Woodbury soap ad in 1936. Up to that time, the Woodbury and Palmolive campaigns of the late Twenties and Thirties had used sex in the copy but barely hinted at it in the artwork. The themes had been "you can keep your man if you keep your skin as attractive as it was when you captured him." "That schoolgirl complexion," "The skin you love to touch," "She's Engaged! She's Lovely! She Uses Pond's!"

The advertisers were using sex to attract male customers to sell "male products," but in a different way. Fully dressed women leaned on cars, beautiful women with blowing hair

73

drove speedboats, elegantly dressed women accompanied men in three-piece suits. The difference was that the woman was used less to arrest the reader's attention than to sketch a situation and imply a syllogism. That man's car attracted that beautiful woman. If I buy a car just like it, then . . . That man's suit has got him that woman. If I buy a three-piece suit with wide shoulders and a high collar, I too . . . This difference in treatment between male and female buyers apparently was arrived at intuitively, but now, 80 years later, the advertising researchers have validated it by vastly expensive studies: men remember sexual ads if there is an implied "situation," a plot to be thought up or a scene to be rationalized. Women remember sexual ads with the actual images of the specific people shown. Similarly, in ads with nude figures—either male or female—the women remember the name of the brand nearly 40 percent more frequently than men do. Men will remember the brand better if the picture has mountains or trees in it. (Literally. If the ad just had naked models in it, 37 percent of the men couldn't even remember seeing them, but if the models were involved in a suggestive situation, nearly 90 percent could describe it. Inexplicable datum: If nudes were present, males from cities of fewer than 25,000 recalled more brand names than males from cities of more than 250,000.)

Elliott White Springs

According to John Trytten, editor of *Sales Management*, advertisers use sex in advertising for one of two reasons. There are "those who think sex sells like mad" and "those who think advertising doesn't sell anyhow, so why not have a little fun for the money as it goes down the drain." Elliott White Springs put these together and gave us the approach to sex in advertising with which we have lived for the past fifty years.

Elliott Springs was the president of Springs Mills and seven other textile companies, three South Carolina banks, and a railroad. The railroad, the Lancaster & Chester Railway, was only 29 miles long connecting his mills to the main line of the Southern, but he papered the South with colorful maps of his tracks crisscrossing 15 states above the headline: "The Lancaster & Chester Railway System." Beneath, in microscopic type, were the words "and connecting lines." The L & C was the first railroad in the state to be fully dieselized (six locomotives), and consistently made a profit. President Springs' railroad interest was sometimes attributed to his University experience at Princeton, where the school was connected to the Pennsylvania Railroad by the four-car P J & B (Princeton Junction and Back).

Springs had graduated from Princeton in 1917 and rushed into the infant U.S. Air Force and World War I. He became a fighter pilot and ultimately the No. 3 U.S. air ace, having shot down eleven enemy planes. After the war he barnstormed around the country until his plane crashed in the first U.S. continental air race. With great reluctance, he joined his father in the family mills, where ultimately he became its president. By World War II, he had expanded the empire until it was the third largest textile producer in the country and had, among other things, the largest mill under one roof in the industry. By 1946 Springs Mills was driving 550,000 spindles. Springs had always written all the copy for the company's advertising, and at this point he decided he was bored with the traditional approach. Springmaid cloth was going to expand its reading public.

On December 12, 1946, he sent a memo to his New York office which read, "Why can't we combine the ridiculous with the sublime and get something worth while out of it? We'll take a typical sexy ad and revise it into a cartoon. Or take a cartoon and revise it into a sexy ad. This should please every one."

He continued to work the idea over in his mind, and on March 10, 1947, he wrote in reply to some rough drafts he'd received,

I want the ad to be subtle! I want it so designed that, when people first look at it, they will think it is serious. I want it to appear as if we were just imitating our competitors, and really trying to sell sheets with cheesecake.

A lot of dumb bunnies will then write in and bawl us out for being vulgar and stupid. Then some people will take a second look and catch the burlesque, and be very proud that they're so smart. They'll think they are the only one to get it, and write and tell us about it.

That is, they will if we do a good job . . .

His problem, he quickly learned, was his inability to get anyone to use the light touch. The artists kept giving him models that he thought should sell spark plugs and be displayed in non-franchised garages. The traditionally blown skirts were always too high. He kept pleading for "just a hint, just a hint." A February 1948 letter to his agent demonstrates his problem,

I am sending you under separate cover a furlined dunce cap. What I wanted was a subtle picture of a girl with her skirt agitated by the wind.
You send me a picture of a girl with her skirts blown over her head like she was standing over an air jet at Coney Island! It's about as subtle as the Can Can. Try again.

Yours very truly.

A subsequent letter shows the continuing problem:

The sketch of the girl and wind is fine. I'm glad to get it and, also, to have the skaters . . . But, in the future, make sure our model has on both a bra and a slip, if anything is showing. Keep the attention on one thing at a time. In this series we are selling material for pants, so don't make the model titillating.

The new sample sketch won't do. I said show the top of her stockings; not the top of her garter belt.

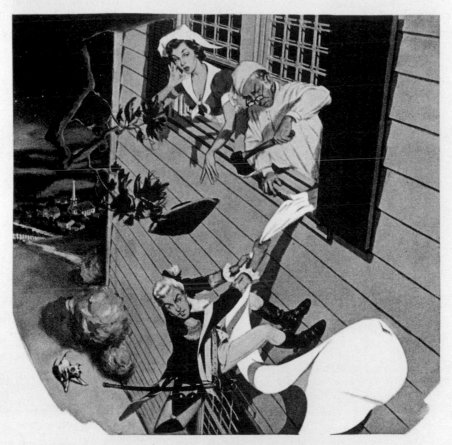

Bungled Bundling

In olden times throughout this land our maidens made their sheets by hand. They used a spinning wheel until it was replaced by cotton mill. Then, lovers found more than one use for strong sheets that could stand abuse. They used them to avoid grandsire and thereby to escape his ire. Our knight slid often down a sheet with eyes on girl and spurs on feet. But sometimes luck just wasn't there when grandpa's hatchet cut through air. Today we weave FORT SUMTER sheets in such a way that always meets with every family's bedroom need from restful sleep to militant deed.

Unlike old times when couples bundled and in the process often bungled, we make our SPRINGMAIDS much the best and proved it in a strenuous test. We took our own FORT SUMTER brand, woven and finished by skillful hand. Each sheet was washed 400 times—a test like that would slick new dimes. Two hundred times they were abraded, yet none were either worn or faded. That's equal to a generation of wear and tear and vellication. In speaking of FORT SUMTER covers, we really wish all fabric lovers, when homeward bound from some dull party, would test SPRINGMAIDS—they're all so hardy that you can get a running start and dive in—they won't come apart. The moral is to each of you: No matter what you say or do, remember that in cold or heat, you can't go wrong on a SPRINGMAID sheet.

© 1949, The Springs Cotton Mills

SPRINGS MILLS

200 Church Street • New York 13, New York

Atlanta   Chicago   Dallas   Los Angeles

For a set of 10 SPRINGMAID ads suitable for framing, send 25 cents to Springs Mills, New York.

ELLIOTT WHITE SPRINGS, *president of The Springs Cotton Mills, has written another book, "Clothes Make the Man," which was indignantly rejected by every editor and publisher who read it. So he had it printed privately and sent it to his friends for Christmas. After they read it, he ran out of friends, so there are some extra copies. It contains a veritable treasury of useless information, such as how to build cotton mills, how to give first aid on Park Avenue, and how to write advertisements.*

If not available at your local bookstore, send a dollar and postage to us.

He has also designed a sport shirt with 16 SPRINGMAID girls printed in 6 colors on SPRINGMAID combed broadcloth. It is made large, medium large, medium, and small. Send us $3, and we will mail you one postpaid in the United States. Or, if you want to make your own, send $2.50 for four yards of material 36 inches wide.

1948

Once he had gotten the images he wanted, he wrote the double entendre he visualized for the copy. Examples: "A buck well spent on a Springmaid sheet" [picture of a sleeping Indian brave]; a "deep-dyed villain with a handlebar mustache and diamond stickpin [Springs' description]. He has lured Nancy from the country to a hotel in the city. But Nancy is saying to him "Stop! You must take me home to mother." And the villain asks, "Why?" She points to the bed and says, "Because you can't go wrong on Springmaid Sheets." When he was unable to find euphemisms, he made them up: "In the museum in Naples there is a famous statue known as Venus Callipygus, which has a very tasty torso. We will henceforth refer to our end product as a Callipygian Camisole."

PROTECT YOURSELF

1948

Backs in Motion

1949

BE PROTECTED

Elliott Springs, president of The Springs Cotton Mills, says he is prepared to make everything shown in the picture.

1948

A buck well spent on a Springmaid Sheet

1949

These are two typical Springs layouts. He has used his leggy models to attract attention; he has put them in unlikely situations, which he hopes, in turn, will lead the viewer to read the text copy to see how the whole thing is justified. Note the company logo is always prominent and easily viewed.

Elliott Springs purported to be an expert on The Tease. He believed the best way of stopping readers who were scanning two hundred ads in a Saturday Evening Post was to show them something they didn't ordinarily see, but show so little of it it forced the readers to use their imaginations. He had the "Backs in Motion" ad redrawn repeatedly until the artist had the thin line of underpants "precisely right." Similarly the posture of the Indian brave in a "A buck well spent . . ."

Perfume and Parabolics

During the war, The Springs Cotton Mills was called upon to develop a special fabric for camouflage. It was used in the Pacific to conceal ammunition dumps and gun emplacements, but the Japanese learned to detect it because of its lack of jungle smells. To overcome this, when the fabric was dyed, it was also impregnated with a permanent odor of hibiscus, hydrangea, and old rubber boots. The deception was so successful that when Tokyo fell, the victorious invaders hung a piece of this fabric on a Japanese flagpole.

This process has been patented, and the fabric is now available to the false bottom and bust bucket business as SPRINGMAID PERKER, made of combed yarns, 37″ wide, 152 x 68 approximate count, weight about 3.30, the white with gardenia, the pink with camellia, the blush with jasmine, and the nude dusty.

If you want to achieve that careless look and avoid skater's steam, kill two birds with one stone by getting a camouflaged callipygian camisole with the SPRINGMAID label on the bottom of your trademark.

SPRINGS MILLS

200 CHURCH STREET · NEW YORK 13, NEW YORK
CHICAGO   DALLAS   LOS ANGELES

Coming soon ... SPRINGMAID sheets, pillowcases, diapers, broadcloth, poplins, and tubings.

1948

Springs wrote all his own copy and it was hard to decide which he preferred more—double entendre or puns. In either event, not only did the copy get written about in the local press and discussed in Letters to the Editor, but surveys showed greater copy recall and greater brand recall for his ads than for any other campaign in 1947–1951.

Springs believed it was fair to use any device to stop the reader, but he insisted that the ads actually sell some Springs Mills product—otherwise, he believed, the reader would feel manipulated and he would have lost whatever rapport had been established.

WE LOVE TO CATCH THEM ON A SPRINGMAID SHEET

We love to give the gals a treat and catch them on a SPRINGMAID sheet. We make them, Sir—and that's no jest. The sheets, we mean. They'll pass the test.

The cotton has a pedigree. We use the best machinery. Our whirring looms with warp and woof present the most conclusive proof that strength and texture we combine to make a sheet that's superfine. We have the best in workmen, too. They're capable, they're skilled, they're true. They turn out perfect sheets by dozens. We ought to know—they're all our cousins. And our new bleachery (we said) puts SPRINGMAID finish way ahead of all the rest—our joy and pride, but still we were not satisfied.

To make sure we were not mistaken, we had these sheets washed, mauled, and shaken four hundred times in laboratories that furnish facts and don't tell stories. Two hundred times they were abraded, yet popped up lovely and unfaded—(an ornament for any bed).

These tests were a simulation of a single generation of wear and tear and constant use, vellication, and abuse. To brides devoid of common itch for monogram or fancy stitch: Your children's children, with repeats, can count on these FORT SUMTER sheets. The moral is to each of you: No matter what you say or do, remember that in cold or heat, you can't go wrong on a SPRINGMAID sheet.

© 1949, The Springs Cotton Mills

SPRINGS MILLS

200 Church Street • New York 13, New York
Atlanta   Chicago   Dallas   Los Angeles   St. Louis   San Francisco
For a 1950 calendar showing all the SPRINGMAID ads, send
50 cents to Spring Mills, Dept. L-14, at the above address.

ELLIOTT WHITE SPRINGS, *president of The Springs Cotton Mills, has written another book, "Clothes Make the Man," which was indignantly rejected by every editor and publisher who read it. So he had it printed privately and sent it to his friends for Christmas. After they read it, he ran out of friends, so there are some extra copies. It contains a veritable treasury of useless information, such as how to build cotton mills, how to give first aid on Park Avenue, and how to write advertisements.*

If not available at your local bookstore, send a dollar and postage to us.

He has also designed a sport shirt with 16 SPRINGMAID girls printed in 6 colors on SPRINGMAID broadcloth. It is made small, medium, large, and extra large. Send us $3.00, and we will mail you one postpaid in the United States. Or, if you want to make your own, send $2.50 for four yards of material 36 inches wide.

1949

Finally getting both pictures and words on paper, Springs found himself with his second problem. No ad agency would take the account. He had expected resistance from the magazines, but not from the agencies. Instead, the owners insisted on changes in the words, wanted modifications of the pictures, or simply refused the business. (It took a brave man, incidentally, to say no to Elliott Springs. *Fortune* had

reported with obvious relish about his reply to his New York City manager who had been abused by a buyer and had threatened to kick him out of the salesroom. Springs told his employee: "According to the bylaws . . . the forcible ejection of mouthy customers is the privilege of the President only. . . . You could have sent him to my Lancaster office, which would have been much better, because the New York

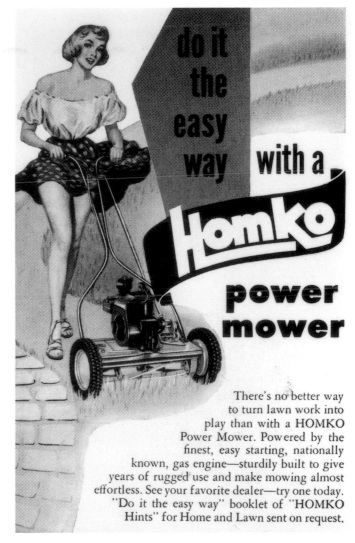

1952

Evidence that the Springs doctrine was far from universally accepted. The ad on the left was run in House Beautiful, *April 1952. It was re-run with modifications in* House Beautiful, *May 1952. Who ordered the repainting of the blouse and skirt hemlines? Advertising mythology always blames this sort of thing on 1) the account client's wife, 2) the magazine editor, 3) letters from readers. In fact, it is usually the advertising agency's anticipatory action taken in fear of negative backlash.*

office is on the ground floor, while the stairway at the Lancaster office has twenty-six steps with eleven-inch treads on a seven-inch rise. If the door at the bottom is open, the customer would then bounce all the way across Main Street, and his parabola would still clear traffic.")

Once the ads finally began to run—he was able to get the mustached villain printed only a single time in a single magazine—the industry journal, *Advertising Age,* condemned the ads as being in "bad taste" and felt they were degrading the image of all national advertising.

On the other hand, the second ad in the series (again Spring's words, April 4, 1949) "appeared in *Liberty* and *Look.* Since then we have received over 10,000 letters in response to it containing coins for reprints. *Liberty* increased the circulation of that issue 180,000 and raised the price on the next issue. Both magazines sold out on the newsstands." As one after another of the series was offered, *Time, Fortune, This Week* and the *Saturday Evening Post* began to accept

them. However *The New Yorker, Life,* and others not only refused to print them, but ran editorials and text copy protesting their public appearance.

In retrospect, it should come as no surprise that ultimately every major magazine accepted and printed some of the Springmaid series, and that they were enormously successful. Not only did they have one of the highest brand recall figures up to that time, but the sales of Springmaid Sheets sloped up without interruption until Springs' death in 1959.

Ultimately Elliott Springs rationalized his approach into a number of principles. Sex was phenomenally effective in getting the attention of a jaded reader. It worked, however, only if used with certain correlative devices: 1) You had to treat the reader as an intelligent peer; 2) Once you had the reader's attention, you had to offer some product benefit to justify stopping him, otherwise he would resent your impudence; 3) The actual sex image should be used not only with humor—a light touch—but with respect (Springs used both

1969

In an extensive research study of "Sex Appeal in Advertising," eight ads were shown to a large sample of readers; the majority of the ads contained nudity or visual evidence of recent love making. The above ad, having neither of these, had the highest over-all recall, and the highest brand name recall by both sexes.

male and female "sexy" models). The "object" must not be being taken advantage of. And 4) the most effective use of the sex should be what we now call The Tease. He described the kind of a sex symbol that stopped readers as revealing something that the reader was not supposed to see. He believed that a naked woman on a couch would be skipped right past, but an inch-and-a-half of stocking top revealed by a stooping model would bring both male and female readers to a literary stop.

The phenomenon of The Tease became the object of many studies, and one of the most graphic appeared in the Oxford history noted above. Prudence Glynn states:

> If you accept the Fundamentalist point of view or believe what you read in Freud it is possible to assume that all dress is erotic in that it conceals something, which by tradition is not acceptable to the public gaze. Inquisitive as he is, and prurient by nature, it follows that man has always been excited by what is concealed. It is always what is underneath which must be discovered, which goes a long way to explain why, in an age when clothing is largely unnecessary for survival, warmth, status, or decency, men and women still fill their leisure moments to such a degree in dressing and undressing themselves or one another. . . .

After noting the irony that the missionaries covered the naked savages, thus introducing the erotic unknown under a Mother Hubbard shift, Glynn notes her conviction that as long as there is an opposite sex, each will be in fact dressing for the other, and the hidden underthings not only interest the opposite sex, but give a hidden pleasure to the wearer him or herself.

Before Springs, sex in advertising was treated with an almost reverent dignity. "You don't kid around with the relations between the sexes." After Springs, it was much more frequently a throw-away, not to be taken too seriously, a chuckle between knowledgeable adults. Its critics feared that this casual humor would splash into the advertising, implying that it too was not too serious and that advertising and sales themselves were a part of a game. Its supporters saw it as candy coating that made the serious matters go down more easily.

Springs' rules and attitudes held for many decades, but began to take a series of contradictory modifications under the pressures of the woman's liberation movement, the *Eros* Supreme Court Decision, Calvin Klein, and the Joint American Association of Advertising Agencies—Association of National Advertisers Interchange Committee on Poor Taste in Advertising. We'll see the impact of these in our chapter "Lingerie, Hosiery, and Underwear." However the use of humor, the wink understood only by me-and-thee, and The High-Class Tease have been built and embellished on foundations set and aligned by Elliott White Springs. His innovations can still be seen in tonight's television commercials and in the four-color spreads of this week's magazines.

LEGS CAN NEVER BE TOO LONG OR TOO SEXY.

THE VERY LEGGY PANTY COLLECTION by **MAIDENFORM**®
Hi-leg panties for the look you love.

Available in choice of fabrics, trim, and colors.

M 185

Printed in U.S.A.

1987

Col. Springs would be hard-pressed to recognize his "Tease" today. Either his rules have changed or the wind is stronger. See the illustration on page 69; the two ads were run almost exactly one century apart.

MICHELIN TIRES

"Your Change, Sir!"

IF you buy a Michelin Universal and hand your dealer the same sum that you've been paying for other good tires, you'll get back a substantial sum in change.

Michelin Tires are the most durable that money, brains and experience can produce, yet they are almost as low in price as the cheapest makes.

Free on Request: Tire Users' Handbook, *fully illustrated and printed in colors. Fifty-six pages on tire economy, written in an easy, non-technical style.*

Michelin Tire Co., Milltown, N. J.
Canada: Michelin Tire Co. of Canada, Ltd.
782 St. Catherine St., W., Montreal

Michelin Universal Treads and Red Inner Tubes

Inch Sizes	Straight Side	Q. D. Clincher	Red Tubes
30 x 3½	. . .	$20.70*	$3.95
32	$23.10	. . .	4.10
34	24.60	. . .	4.50
31 x 4	. . .	29.15*	4.80
32	31.35	31.35	5.40
33	32.20	32.20	4.95
34	32.75	32.75	5.80
35	. . .	33.55	5.30
36	35.50	35.50	6.15
34 x 4½	43.30	43.30	7.60
35	45.55	45.55	6.80
36	46.50	46.50	8.00
37	. . .	48.10	7.25
35 x 5	53.10	53.10	9.35
36	. . .	54.35	9.45
37	55.00	55.00	9.60

*Soft Bead Clincher
Prices subject to change without notice

1917

The Great Names Go Back So Far

OUR COMMERCIAL MEMORY is clearly generational. Our children ask us, "Mom, were there cars when you were a kid?" and we are insulted. "Dad, what was television like in olden time?" and we don't quite know where to start our reply. For each of us, all the world's products—and their advertising—seem to have begun just a few years before our own memory begins. We adults are just as out of phase on our commercial recall as are our children. We simply start a bit farther back.

This situation came home to the authors the first time we saw the pneumatic Michelin Man (we have since learned that "everybody" knew him as Bibidendum "back then") in a *Saturday Evening Post* for *1917!* We'd assumed he was invented about 1960. Since then we find our editors, the art directors, the museum curators and the advertising agency staffs we've been working with have just as many blind spots as we. "You mean Chiclets go back to 1899?" We do, and here's an album of some of the ways our household names looked when they started. We think you'll share our surprise with how far back those great names do go.

This is Bibendum, the Michelin Tire trademark since 1896, when he first appeared on an advertising poster drawn by a cartoonist named Maurice Rossillon (who signed himself O'Galop). The first poster set the trademark image for now nearly a hundred years. It showed Mr. Bib with a champagne glass raised high, and the pneumatic character shouting, "Nunc est bibendum . . . A Votre Santé" (Now we can drink . . . To Your Health). The champagne glass was filled with broken glass, broken bottles, and long, sharp nails. The copy across the bottom of the poster read: "The Michelin tire drinks all obstacles." Mr. Bib (as the company now calls him), was about to absorb the dangers of the road without the slightest hesitation.

ARROW COLLARS AND SHIRTS

ARROW Collars are made in the greatest variety of styles and heights, in such a careful way, of such excellent fabrics, that even the most fastidious, to whom cost means nothing, give them preference.

2 for 25 cents

ARROW Shirts fit most men comfortably. They quickly reflect the tendencies of fashion. They do not lose their original freshness of color, and render such sterling service that the label will serve as your guide to shirt satisfaction.

$1.50 and up.

CLUETT, PEABODY & COMPANY, INC., TROY, N.Y. Send for Booklets.

1913

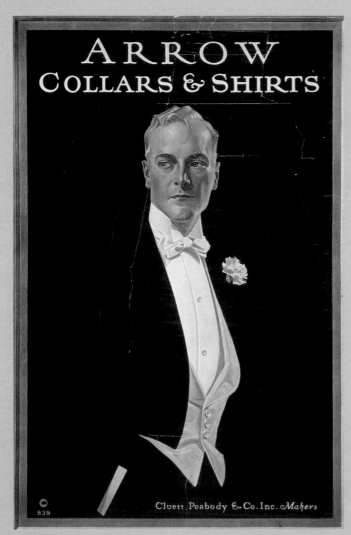

1927

Arrow Shirts started as collars. Period. The company was founded in 1851, and it made starched collars and only collars for seventy years. In 1885, a man by the name of George B. Cluett bought the company and changed its name to his. Four years later, he was joined by Frederick F. Peabody, another collar maker, who brought with him his trademark "Arrow" and an inspired feel for advertising.

He conceived of a masculine image, straight, tall, clear-eyed, square-jawed—the "Arrow Collar Man," who became as much a symbol of the turn-of-the-century male as Charles Dana Gibson's Gibson Girl was the model female. A series of leading artists created the image, but J.C. Leyendecker's expression led all the rest.

By the outbreak of World War I, Cluett-Peabody was stocking 400 different models of detached collars, and employing 6,000 workers to make them. While abroad, the doughboys had discovered a foreign shirt with a soft, attached collar that had had great appeal. Arrow, ever-responsive to its customer's needs, began selling its collar with a shirt attached in 1921. Unfortunately, the shirts shrank.

Technology soon came to the rescue, however, with an invention of Sanford Cluett (one of the founder's nephews), who personally devised the "Sanforizing Process." This is still controlling shrinkage both in Cluett-Peabody's products and in its competitors' (to which the inventors license the process for over $10 million a year).

The Arrow collar still thrives, but against odds. Seventy percent of all shirts currently sold are sports models.

Irreproachable 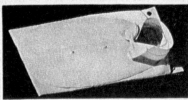 *Immaculate*

ARROW SHIRTS

Don is just as comfortable as it is smart. It opens in the back and has a bosom so contrived that it will not bulge. The fabric is exquisite white piqué, of patterns fine as snow crystal. Don is an aristocrat in style.

CLUETT, PEABODY & CO., INC., TROY, NEW YORK

1909

1980

"Hasn't scratched yet!!!" Bon Ami cleanser soap was invented in 1890 by the Manchester, Connecticut, firm of J.T. Robertson Soap Co. The chick which still hasn't scratched was thought of by one Louis H. Soule, the firm's promotion man in 1901. He intended it for a single advertisement, but it went over so well the company registered it as its trademark.

1925

"Black and Decker with the Pistol Grip and Trigger Switch." Apparently this 1925 ad man was playing to the male's preoccupation with weapons which had done so well twenty years before. He seems to be saying, buy a Black and Decker drill, the next best thing to an automatic on your workbench. Before they got into the hand tool business, Duncan Black and Alonzo G. Decker were manufacturing in Baltimore, making such unlikely gadgets as milk bottle cap machines and currency-cutters for the U.S. Mint. In 1916, they invented the first portable electric hand drill, and the company has been at it ever since producing them in awesome quantities. Among other famous firsts, a Black and Decker drill dug out the first moon samples during the Apollo 15 mission.

"The Voice with a Smile"

"Hail ye small, sweet courtesies of life, for smooth do ye make the road of it."

Often we hear comments on the courtesy of telephone people and we are mighty glad to have them.

For our part, we would like to say a word about the courtesy of those who use the telephone.

Your co-operation is always a big help in maintaining good telephone service and we want you to know how much we appreciate it.

BELL TELEPHONE SYSTEM

c. 1950

Alexander Graham Bell invented the telephone in 1876, and handed it over to the Boston bankers in 1877, washing his hands of it. The financiers created a monumental holding company of nearly two dozen regional phone companies, and called it the Bell System.

In its glory days, the Bell System owned 80 percent of all the telephones in the United States, and for nearly a century ran endless ads like "We may be the only phone company in town, but we try not to act like it." For decades its ads suggested with great success that the company was really not in business to make money, but mostly to be a friendly neighbor simply trying to make life easier and happier for the local community.

Ultimately, however, this soothing ad campaign failed to protect the company against an anti-trust break-up, and now, in the face of aggressive competition, AT&T's ads are as savagely combative as anyone else's. (A current series suggests failure to use the proper phone company can result in family discord, lost jobs, professional embarrassment, summary firing, and worse.) "The Voice with a Smile" ad here was from the "caring, friendly" days, and it reminds us that a benevolent monopoly may have been possible after all.

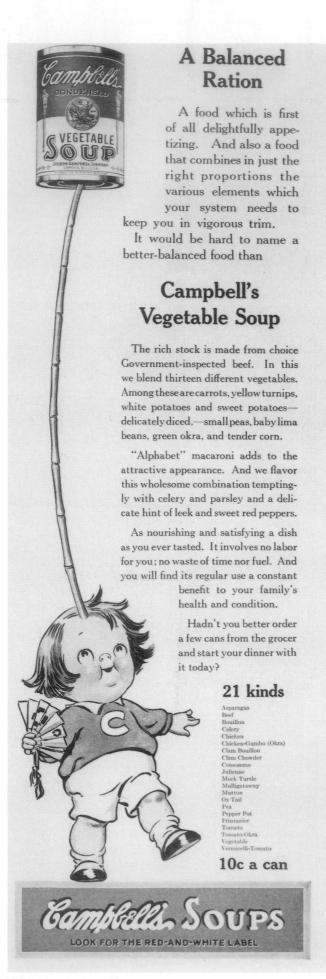

A Balanced Ration

A food which is first of all delightfully appetizing. And also a food that combines in just the right proportions the various elements which your system needs to keep you in vigorous trim.

It would be hard to name a better-balanced food than

Campbell's Vegetable Soup

The rich stock is made from choice Government-inspected beef. In this we blend thirteen different vegetables. Among these are carrots, yellow turnips, white potatoes and sweet potatoes—delicately diced,—small peas, baby lima beans, green okra, and tender corn.

"Alphabet" macaroni adds to the attractive appearance. And we flavor this wholesome combination temptingly with celery and parsley and a delicate hint of leek and sweet red peppers.

As nourishing and satisfying a dish as you ever tasted. It involves no labor for you; no waste of time nor fuel. And you will find its regular use a constant benefit to your family's health and condition.

Hadn't you better order a few cans from the grocer and start your dinner with it today?

21 kinds

Asparagus
Beef
Bouillon
Celery
Chicken
Chicken-Gumbo (Okra)
Clam Bouillon
Clam Chowder
Consomme
Julienne
Mock Turtle
Mulligatawny
Mutton
Ox Tail
Pea
Pepper Pot
Printanier
Tomato
Tomato-Okra
Vegetable
Vermicelli-Tomato

10c a can

Campbell's SOUPS
LOOK FOR THE RED-AND-WHITE LABEL

1916

Campbell's Soups has been canning soup in Camden, New Jersey, since 1869. It invented the idea of taking the water out ("condensing" the soup) in 1898, and began advertising in 1899. Campbell's started by putting its signs in streetcars (the famous red and white can that Warhol copied was based on Cornell University football colors), but soon began buying the first-page-after-the-editorial-content in national magazines and embraced color printing as quickly as it was available. This printing location was so firm that "after the Campbell ad" became a part of advertising cant.

The Campbell's Kids first appeared in 1904, having been invented and drawn by Grace Wiederseim of Philadelphia. She claimed the original purpose was to appeal to women, but the company soon added jingles, and the Kids engaged in endless adventures for well over fifty years. In the days before Saturday morning television, cutting out Campbell's Kids and making scrapbooks was at the top of youngsters' free- (and sick-) time amusements.

1906

To the aficionado of bubble gum, "Fleer's" means Dubble Bubble. In fact, Frank H. Fleer started with a flavoring company which, in 1883, got interested in chewing gum, and after a number of increasingly successful names and flavors, invented Chiclets in 1899.

The name Chiclets came from "chicle," the sap of the sapodilla tree from which chewing gum is made. It was introduced in this country by General Santa Ana of Alamo fame. In spite of the Texans' feeling about him, the General spent several years of exile from Mexico living in New York City. Santa Ana loved to chew unflavored chicle (which is sweet, like sugar cane), and brought it with him when he fled north.

Fleer & Company did well with Chiclets, but apparently preferred money to the product, and sold it in 1909. Dubble Bubble was not perfected until 1928, and Chiclets, still thriving, is now made by the Warner-Lambert Company.

1894–1975

A CENTURY OF COCA-COLA ADVERTISING

On May 8, 1886, Dr. John Styth Pemberton, an Atlanta pharmacist, mixed up a syrup which, when cut with carbonated water and tested at Jacobs' Pharmacy, was declared to be Delicious and Refreshing by all who sampled it. The drink went on sale at once, and the first year Dr. Pemberton sold an average of nine drinks a day. He died two years later, and an Atlanta businessman by the name of Asa Candler bought up the rights and the secret formula. The latter—"7X"—is still made from "all-natural ingredients" and is believed by commercial historians to be the "most jealously guarded trade secret in the world."

For the first decade, Candler sold the syrup to soda fountains around the South, and it was a druggist in Vicksburg who thought of bottling the drink in his back room and selling it to plantations and lumber camps along the Mississippi. The folks at the Atlanta headquarters loved the idea of local bottling, and by the end of World War I there were nearly a thousand locally owned and operated bottling companies—all mixing carbonated water with the caramel syrup they bought from Atlanta. Pemberton began the Coca-Cola advertising tradition by painting squares of oilcloth to hang from drugstore awnings. Candler picked up the torch, and the phrase "Drink Coca-Cola Delicious and Refreshing" was then repeated endlessly on walls, fences, trays, blotters, calendars, store signs, clock faces, pocket knives, playing cards, etc., etc. Through the following century, the company has made "refreshment" the central theme, and tried to link the product with "the pleasant things of life, distinctive and acceptable anywhere."

1892

Having been invented by a pharmacist, it is not surprising that the earliest Coca-Cola ads stressed the tonic effect of the drink.

1904

The first Coca-Cola model was the Metropolitan Opera star Lillian Nordica (see illustration on page 29) in keeping with the celebrity fashion at the turn of the century. She was soon followed by Hilda Clark (above) who was the first of Coca-Cola's just ordinary (but always beautiful) women from middle America. Clark was, in fact, an actress, but unknown and unrecognized on the stage, and she stayed that way, being known to history only as the Coca-Cola Girl.

1905

From the beginning Coca-Cola's success drew imitators like flies. Here is an imaginative brand which was given a copyright in 1905. The company deliberately designed the "hobble-skirt bottle" in 1915 to make it easier to tell the genuine product, and since then has vigorously defended its patent on "Coca-Cola," "Coke," "Coke Classic," and all the rest to and including the "Dynamic Ribbon" device.

While Coke women have usually displayed their healthy vigor by or on the water, they have been equally robust on the golf course.

1906

c. 1916

A drink for all seasons, and the first of dozens of Coke models to be seen by the sea.

The company was much enamored of cut-outs that stood in store windows, and festoons that were hung around soda fountain mirrors. All of these were changed regularly throughout the year so the word Coca-Cola was continually in sight featured in ever-new images for the shopper and the traveler.

1917

1923

This model is on the water by means of
an unusually sturdy surfboard. The rolled
hose are classic Twenties' fashion.

1924

In 1923, the company introduced the six-bottle carton,
and by 1929 Coke in bottles finally exceeded Coke in
glasses served from soda fountains.

1925

Coca-Cola not only supplied the product but by its advertising images made the corner drugstore the place to meet
after the game or movie, and created the image of a wholesome, pleasant spot for teenagers and families to gather.

Don't Wear
A TIRED THIRSTY FACE

You look the way you feel. • Refresh yourself with an ice-cold Coca-Cola, and bounce to a happy normal. • An ice-cold Coca-Cola is more than just a drink. It's a very particular kind of drink—combining those pleasant, wholesome substances which foremost scientists say do most in restoring you to your normal self. Really delicious, it invites a pause, a pause that *will* refresh you.

Refresh yourself
Bounce back to normal

1933

Here Coca-Cola's ever-cheerful advertising recognizes the problems of daily stress at the depth of the Depression.

1934

Johnny Weissmuller and Maureen O'Sullivan, the Thirties' Tarzan and Jane, here appear on a tin tray. Drugstore Cokes were served in the classic, bell-shaped Coca-Cola glasses etched with the logo. The glasses, of course, required an appropriate tray for delivery to the customers' table.

Drink Coca-Cola
Delicious and Refreshing

Thru 50 years... 1886 to 1936
The pause that refreshes

Fashions in clothes change. But human thirst is always the same. Since the first ice-cold Coca-Cola made a pause refreshing in 1886, its fame has spread...from city to city...country to country...around the world...welcome everywhere, because ice-cold Coca-Cola is what refreshment ought to be...pure...wholesome...delicious.

ICE-COLD EVERY DAY IN THE YEAR 5¢

1936

"The Pause That Refreshes" was the all-time greatest slogan, first appearing in 1929 and leading all the other tries for recall and acceptance. In this Saturday Evening Post layout, the sandy lady on page 90 has joined her 1930s successor.

The pause that refreshes

Drink Coca-Cola
Delicious and Refreshing

1939

The Coca-Cola Girl not only attempted to capture the look of middle America, but was specifically designed to "have sex appeal, but a man can take her home to Mother," according to Company prose. As the years went by, the Coca-Cola Boy was usually a sportsman and an "all-around good guy."

1943

1949

1951

The figure with the bottle cap is known as The Sprite by the firm, and here the ad department tried to catch up and re-embrace the word "Coke" that the customers had been using for years. The need to clarify the name became particularly acute when the product began to appear with American troops around the world.

The company followed the troops in World War II at the military's specific request. It set up bottling machinery as close to the fighting fronts as possible, the first unit appearing in Algiers within days of the initial landings. Sixty-four plants were operating by V-J Day so the American soldier rarely lacked the familiar product from home.

ABOVE:

Homage to the bright red American icon: the Coke machine (here still dispensing bottles; not yet cans).

The company started its tradition of holiday ads in 1931, and the endless series of Coke and Santa Claus has been based on an image of the figure as envisioned by the artist Haddon Sundblom. Some social historians attribute the difference between the somewhat threatening European Father Winter symbol, and the plump, cheerful American Santa to the years in which Sundblom showed us how Santa really looked via Coca-Cola calendars, billboards, and ads.

1951

Always that uniquely shaped Coke bottle. The industrial designer Raymond Loewy declared the two most perfectly designed containers ever made were the Coke bottle and the egg.

1960

ABOVE AND RIGHT:
"It's the real thing" first appeared in 1942 and was re-introduced in 1969.

Throughout the hundred years of Coke advertisements, people drinking Coca-Cola were always popular, in the best of fashion, and, of course, showing good taste.

"Things Go Better With Coke" first appeared in 1963. By 1969 the slogan had been expanded to "Things Would Have Gone Better With Coke" and the successive spokespersons for the theme were shown in photographs of such witnesses as Marie Antoinette, Julius Caesar, Captain Bligh in a boat, and Napoleon on Elba.

People go better refreshed. The never-too-sweet taste of Coca-Cola gives that special zing...refreshes best.

1964

"Things would have gone better with Coke."

1969

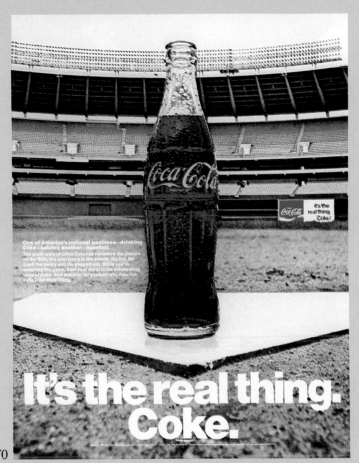

1970

In case you wondered what the company thought this slogan meant, company prose described it as reflecting "the resurging, positive spirit of the 1980s" and "reaffirming the leadership of Coca-Cola." The slogan is presented here by Bill Cosby, the 1980s equivalent of Madame Nordica, the company's first celebrity endorser.

1980

"Have a Coke and a Smile" was launched in 1979, and proved to be the most successful slogan since "The Pause That Refreshes." In the 1980s the traditional white, middle-class, middle American Coca-Cola look began to widen across broader age, class, and ethnic lines.

1983

1986   The theme expressed in youth's vernacular.

Matthew 22: Verse 14. Almost.

1988

1881

The Coats family began manufacturing thread in their native Scotland around 1820. A second generation split off to find their fortune in America, and acted as American salesmen for the family firm. A third generation decided to make the thread here instead of importing it, and opened a factory in Pawtucket, Rhode Island, in 1869. Both they and their chief competitors, the Clark family, had begun their trade by making copies of Kashmir shawls in their hometown of Paisley. (Paisley shawls are thus named after the Scotch town, not the Indian source of the design.)

In 1896, the Coatses and the Clarks decided to merge into the present Coats and Clark company. The accompanying 1881 trade card is thus pre-merger. Footnote for those loyal customers who have been buying the famous "O.N.T. Clark Super Cotton" thread for years: "O.N.T." stands for "Our New Thread" and was so declared in 1866 when the company expanded its product line from the thick, stiff product used in power looms, and added its new invention, a thin, stronger, smoother thread for use in the new sewing machines of the day.

Cracker Jack
The more you eat, the more you want

5c

Sing a song of Five Cents,
A pocket in the back.
What are pockets made for?
To fill with Cracker Jack.

It's not hard to tell why when you taste the delicious combination of popcorn, peanuts and molasses candy with the natural color and flavor. **Everyone can eat it freely—everyone should. It's more nourishing than corn, potatoes, milk, eggs, raisins, etc. Just realize that.**

The best of ingredients are used in making Cracker Jack. It is untouched by hands in making and packing and reaches you as-good-as-made, every time.

The ideal confection, with a premium in each package that gladdens the youngsters' hearts.

Write for the Cracker Jack Riddle Book. Sent free on request. Address Dept. I.

RUECKHEIM BROS. & ECKSTEIN, Inc.
Brooklyn, New York
Bush Terminal Building No. 20

Also makers of Angelus Marshmallows. Three kinds—mint, white, strawberry. Try a package, 10 cents.

In the Triple Proof Package that keeps out moisture, germs and dust.

1916

F.W. Rueckheim and his brother, Louis, sold popcorn from a stand in Chicago, and then broadened into the candy-making trade. By 1893 and the Columbia Exposition, they had perfected a mixture of popcorn, peanuts, and candy coating which sold well on the fairgrounds. "Crackerjack"—meaning "just great, excellent"—was a common slang term of the time and the Rueckheims seized it for their confection. They also embraced the wisdom of the N.W. Ayer advertising company and went national.

They improved their ability to keep the candy from sticking together in a solid block while being shipped (1896), they designed a wax paper liner to keep the product dry and fresh (1899), had the good luck for the tradename to be included in "Take Me Out to the Ball Game" lyrics (1908), and they started including a "toy surprise inside" in 1912.

The figure of sailor Jack and his dog were put on the box in 1919. They had been drawn with F.W.'s grandson, Robert, and Robert's dog, Bingo, as models. Cracker Jacks still sell in great quantities (now owned by Borden's, they ship over 500 million boxes a year), and the classic slogan, "The more you eat, the more you want," is holding up well.

1907

Dr. Pepper was created in 1885, and for nearly forty years was a specialty known and loved only by Texans. It started in Waco (tradition has it a counterman in a local drugstore conceived the taste and named it after his pharmacist boss), and the ultimate formula was perfected by a local ginger ale bottler.

Not until the 1920s was it sold outside the state, but once the owners decided to go national they invested thousands of dollars in advertising, and nailed the slogan, "Drink a bite to eat at 10–2 & 4 o'clock. Dr. Pepper—Good for life!" to their mast. Up until the proliferation of diet/sugarless/caffeine-free drinks, Dr. Pepper was consistently Number Three, immediately below Coca-Cola and Pepsi-Cola. During its first forty years its symbol was the lion; after 1978 Young & Rubicam urged us to declare ourselves: "I'm a Pepper, too!"

1925

How can you invent an ice cream bar? Surely there have been blocks of ice cream dipped in chocolate since Roman times? No. Not until 1920 could anyone figure out a way to weld hot chocolate to frozen ice cream, cool the chocolate down fast enough so that the ice cream wouldn't melt from the hot candy, and end up with everything still holding together.

One Christian Nelson, a schoolteacher in Onawa, Iowa, achieved the great breakthrough by endless experimentation, first finding the precise temperature needed to keep the chocolate dippable but the ice cream hard. He then concentrated on keeping the hardened chocolate from flaking off, and after many tries came up with a mixture of yellow cocoa butter, dark chocolate, sugar, milk, and water, with the secret lying in the cocoa butter. It worked every time he tried it.

With the product in hand, he headed for a major creamery company to produce it, but, almost by accident, met a young man by the name of Russell Stover who offered to work as his business manager and urged him to produce the bars himself. With the help of Stover's wife (later to found the Mrs. Stover's candy chain), they came up with the name Eskimo Pie, and Stover suggested they be wrapped in the new aluminum foil. At this point they began to advertise, with the accompanying ad as a result.

There is a major footnote. In order to ship the product beyond the limit of railroad refrigerator cars, Nelson pursued the cooling question and ultimately created the dry ice industry, which for years was primarily owned and operated by Eskimo Pie.

1884

This is a ringer. When the authors sent a facsimile of this trade card (found in the Library of Congress's copyright archives) to the Goodyear Company for background information, Goodyear replied with charming candor: "To be honest we have been endeavoring to determine which Goodyear Rubber Company produced [the 1884 card]. We can tell you it was not this Goodyear. Our company was founded in 1898 and our first rubber plantation began operating in Indonesia in 1916. We took our name in honor of Charles Goodyear who discovered vulcanization—making possible the wide use of rubber. He died in 1860, some 38 years before our company began and there was no Goodyear family in our organization. Apparently, several other companies were named after Charles Goodyear and we have to assume your trade card belongs to one of those. . . . " They wished us all the best.

c. 1892

1902

1933

"Spikenard and Dog Grass"—ingredients to make the mouth water. Charles Elmer Hires was a Philadelphia pharmacist who had made a youthful fortune making fuller's earth. In 1870, when he was twenty, he married his neighbor's daughter and took her on a short trip to the beach. Their landlady served them some root tea that Charles found so tasty he went home and began to experiment with various combinations himself, ultimately ending with a mixture of "hops, ginger, sarsaparilla, juniper berries, spikenard, birch bark, and dog grass." The Hireses tried the concoction on friends and neighbors who declared it good.

His friend the Rev. Dr. Russell H. Conwell (who later founded Temple University) urged him to go public with the drink in the interest of temperance, and, to appeal to the Pennsylvania miners who were unusually in need of such a substitute, call it "Root Beer." Hires did, sold it in great quantities at the Philadelphia Centennial Exposition of 1876, distributed it to pharmacies in packets of dried flavorings (1877), made it into a liquid concentrate in the 1880s, sold it in bottles in 1893 and as a syrup for soda fountains in 1905. As can be seen in the 1933 Saturday Evening Post ad, the customer still had these options as late as the Depression years.

The small print in the 1891 ad assures the buyer that: "Hires Rootbeer gives the children strength to resist the enervating effects of the heat, bridges the convalescent over the trying part of a hot day, helps even a cynic to see the brighter side of life."

The United States Rubber Company had been making canvas and rubber shoes since the 1880s, but in 1916 the managers decided that their most popular variety should be given its own brand name. They intended to call them Peds from the Latin word for foot, but this was too generic to be copyrighted, so they moved to Keds and got a winner. The style has fit into the fashion of the day through seven decades, and if you take the hats off the women, the artwork could probably be run in tomorrow's newspaper with barely a second glance.

1886

Keds

the finest, best looking, best made *canvas rubber-soled shoes*. Made by United States Rubber Company, the largest rubber manufacturer in the world.

Wear Keds and you get style, fit, comfort of the highest order. A rare combination in shoes, you say. Yes, but prove it in Keds. The tops are of a specially woven, fine grade of canvas. The soles are of tough, springy rubber. Keds will stand the most critical examination.

The best-shod folks on the face of the earth are the Americans. And the women are ahead of the men! Milady of the United States looks her best when she feels at the best. That's why she should wear Keds.

Your dealer is the one to supply you with Keds. He's the one to make you happy with proper fit, style, size.

Think of being able to get three pairs of beautiful, trim, dainty white Keds for the price of a single pair of the leather-sole kinds! You can have a pair of Keds for every occasion and not strain your pocketbook, either. That's one of the advantages of Keds. Certainly fine for daily business use.

HOW TO GET THEM—Figure out what you want to spend, then ask the dealer for the brand according to the price. You'll know you're right when you see these trade-marks.

| NATIONAL Keds | $1.50 up | CAMPFIRE Keds | $1.25 to $2.00 | CHAMPION Keds | $1.00 to $1.50 |

MEN! BOYS! GIRLS! There are plenty of styles of Keds for you, too. Everything we have said about Keds for women applies to Keds for you. All the good looks, style and comfort women folks enjoy in Keds is right there for you. Ask for them by the same names.

United States Rubber Company
New York

1917

Chase & Sanborn coffee is a parable of American advertising in miniature. The firm was founded in 1861, when Caleb Chase and James Sanborn, two Boston tea and coffee merchants, joined together. A generation later they were the first coffee dealers to sell their goods in sealed tin cans (1879).

They advertised heavily, moving with the fashion from sales cards to magazines and were one of the earliest firms to exploit the advertising potential of radio. The Chase & Sanborn Hour with Edgar Bergen and Charlie McCarthy created one of the classic formats of the medium—and kept the company as Number One in coffee sales and one of the leading food manufacturers in the country right up to World War II.

After the war, General Foods challenged its standing in the coffee competition with major advertising of its Maxwell House brand. Chase & Sanborn decided it wasn't worth the costs required, quit advertising the product nationally, and shifted its sales to the restaurant and fast food field. While Chase & Sanborn coffee is still a profitable part of its new owner's (Standard Brands) product list, it sells only 1.3 percent of the supermarket and corner grocery coffee.

c. 1880

Blue jeans, the great American contribution to clothing the human form, can be traced to 1850, when Levi Strauss arrived in San Francisco with a load of dry goods to sell to the Forty-niner Gold Rush prospectors. Strauss soon ran out of the pants he'd brought from the effete East, and, rather than sending back for more, decided to make some work trousers out of the canvas he'd planned to sell for tents and wagon covers. This, he believed, should really hold up to the wear and tear of the California mountains.

His first models were cut from sailcloth, and they wore beautifully but tended to abrade the customers, so he shifted to denim which was softer and almost as tough, and he nailed copper rivets at the seam junctions to guarantee that nothing would separate under stress. (Denim itself has a long and honorable tradition. It was created in France, and was originally called serge de Nîmes, the "de Nimes" being corrupted to "denim" when it got to California. Legend has it that Columbus's sails on the Santa Maria were made of denim, which from the beginning was woven of a tough blue yarn in the long warp threads, and a white, flaxen color cross-wise in the woof.)

The blue jean "Levi's" (one of our earliest trademarks) spread from the West to the East and then to Europe and soon became the worldwide uniform of the working man. By the turn of the century Levi Strauss was the world's largest producer of brand clothing, and now has distribution centers in over 70 countries.

In the 1930s, easterners returning from western dude ranches began to popularize the cowboy pants as upscale sports clothing and leisure wear. The first zippers were put in the models in the 1950s; the counter-culture embraced them in the 1960s; and President Carter brought them into the White House in the 1970s.

Sassoon designer jeans appeared in 1976; Gloria Vanderbilt signed the back hip pocket in 1977 and ran the price up to $34. Her gambit was such a success that Calvin Klein and Jordache joined the movement in 1978. In a triumph of modern-day advertising, the young model Brooke Shields assured the world that nothing came between her and her Calvins in 1980, and the proletariat's blue denims had apotheosized.

But Levi Strauss still sells more blue denim pants than any other manufacturer in the world.

c. 1969

FIVE CENTS THE CAKE

FOR SAVING LIFE

LIFEBUOY SOAP

BUOY SOAP

"A LIFE-SAVER"

FOR PRESERVATION OF HEALTH

The use of this wonderful cleanser throughout the entire house= hold not only ensures perfect cleanli- ness but also ensures freedom from the danger of infectious diseases. Lifebuoy is a sanitary disinfectant soap which can be used everywhere the same as ordinary soap.

Five cents at dealers, or by mail, two cakes ten cents
ILLUSTRATED BOOKLET, "THE GREATEST LIFE-SAVER," FREE
LEVER BROTHERS LIMITED, 111 FIFTH AVE., NEW YORK

1902

LIFEBUOY

5 cts.   5 cts.

CLEANSES   DISINFECTS

AT YOUR DEALER'S   AT YOUR DEALER'S

BEST ANTISEPTIC ON THE MARKET
"I am using Lifebuoy Soap in the Nurses' Home, and have used it in my family for years. I consider it the best antiseptic soap on the market."
ELIZABETH C. HOWLAND (Matron Nurses' Home), 18 Park Avenue, Springfield, Mass.
SANITARY—ANTISEPTIC—CLEANSER—DISINFECTANT

Trial carton of two cakes of Lifebuoy Soap by mail 10 cents, if your dealer cannot supply you. Mention *Collier's*. Costs us 13 cents alone for postage, hence soap free. Money refunded to anyone finding cause for complaint. Valuable booklet free.
LEVER BROTHERS LIMITED   NEW YORK OFFICES: 111 FIFTH AVENUE

1902

Lifebuoy was introduced by the British firm Lever Brothers in 1894. From the first it had a healthy dose of carbolic acid in each bar, which gave it various disinfectant properties and a clinical fragrance. Anyone who went to a hospital in the first half of this century was overwhelmed with the smell of pine tar, Lysol, and carbolic acid, so it was easy to convince the customer he was washing himself clean. In the early days Lever was marvelously responsive to epidemics. The moment one would break out anywhere in the English-speaking world, the local papers would be saturated with Lifebuoy ads.

By the 1920s, the company had softened the appeal and spread the advantages of Lifebuoy as a beauty soap and a preparation for dates in evening gowns. Came the Depression, and the focus shifted from skin care to social disgrace (an even greater threat to well-being than the epidemics had been): Lever discovered "B.O."—Body Odor. This was explained in the then popular comic strip story format in print ads, and on the new radio shows as a rolling fog horn booming "B.O." from the shoals of danger and social disaster. Lifebuoy, essentially the deodorant soap that began it all, would "protect" its customers.

Maxwell House Coffee is named for the Maxwell House Hotel in Nashville, which introduced this particular mixture of coffees to its guests in 1892. Maxwell House started its long-running slogan "Good To The Last Drop" in 1907. Company tradition says it came from a remark made by Theodore Roosevelt while dining in the hotel. So many people have asked, "What's the matter with the last drop?", that at intervals the ads have said, "And that's good too!"

One of the ironies of the brand is that its present owner (General Foods) produces over one-third of all coffee sold in the United States, and 40 percent of its business is coffee. General Foods started as the maturation of C.W. Post's cereal empire, which in turn was based on Postum, a non-caffeine breakfast drink specifically invented to get around Post's greatest hatred: coffee.

Over this coffee the North and South pledged the new brotherhood years ago

MAXWELL HOUSE COFFEE TODAY—*America's largest selling high grade coffee*

1926

OVER 1892

At the time of this writing, Singer no longer makes sewing machines (it now produces defense equipment for the Pentagon and space machines for NASA), but no history of American advertising would be complete without noting the contributions of The Singer Sewing Machine to Western civilization.

The sewing machine had actually been invented and patented by the British in 1790. The American Elias Howe invented the sewing needle with a hole in it in 1846, and Isaac Merritt Singer of Oswego, New York, was busy being an actor, a sawmiller, and an occasional inventor without any interest in sewing machines at all. But by 1850 he had devised a large drill for cutting rocks, and a small one for shaping wooden display type. While on the road selling the latter, he heard how all sewing machines spent more time in the shop than in the home, and he set out to make a working, reliable one. Using nothing but already developed technology (which got him into monumental lawsuits) he came up with an efficient combination and created the Singer sewing machine—one of the world's most useful pieces of machinery.

In the course of his lifetime, he made the following contributions to the world scene: He created installment buying, selling the machine for $5 down and $3 a month (for a $100 machine). To mollify his many legal claimants, he created the Sewing Machine Combination and the nation's first patent pool. He licensed his technology to anyone who would pay $15 a machine, and divided the $15 among Howe and the others, proving that you could make money from your competitors' products. From the very beginning he sold and then manufactured the sewing machines abroad, and, as late as a century after the invention, the Third World was buying almost half of each year's production. The trade card here is one of an 1890s set which showed the Singer being used in a dozen different Asian countries, recalling Mahatma Gandhi's claim that the machine was a godsend to the common man. Gandhi used a series of Singers during his frequent stays in British jails.

Isaac Singer became very rich during his lifetime, produced 24 children from four women, only one of whom was his wife, and when finally driven from America by the shocked outrage of the press and his business partners, in the words of Moskowitz, Katz, and Levering, "took the sister of one of his mistresses and fled to Europe."

The Uneeda Biscuit boy is the story of early American advertising boiled down to a single parable that just happens to be real history. In the early 1890s there were hundreds of hometown bakers putting out generic crackers in barrels and plain cookies in square shipping boxes. Mothers would say, "George, here's a paper bag. Go down to the store and fill this with crackers."

1901

There were soon far too many bakers for anyone to make a decent living, so they began to combine. For eight years, savage merger fights reduced the market to three very large companies: New York Biscuit, American Biscuit, and United States Baking. In 1898, a Chicago lawyer by the name of Adolphus Green convinced the big three that they would all do better as a single unit; they worked out a deal and the National Biscuit Company was born with 114 bakeries firing 400 ovens. In its first year, NBC owned 70 percent of all the bakeries in America.

Green was convinced that to make it all work, he had to kill the idea of "a cracker is a cracker." A National Biscuit Company cracker—or cookie—was going to be one of a kind. He set out to make a unique product of a piece of food that had been around for at least a thousand years. Logical steps: First he wanted a name, a handle, a single thing to call it. He made a list and got it down to Bekos, Trim, Dandelo, Verenice, Nabisco, and Fireside. He took these to the N.W. Ayer & Son advertising agency, where the account was assigned to Henry N. McKinney. McKinney didn't like anything on the list.

He made his own list: Biscona, Hava Cracker, Taka Cracker, Usa Cracker, Takanoo, Racka, Pauco, Tanco, Onal, Nati, Wanta Cracker, and Uneeda Cracker. Green liked the last one, but he said it lacked class. The British called a cracker a biscuit, and so would he.

With the name chosen, they needed a package that, more than anything else, looked different from anything else but that would also ship well. (Crackers in barrels had had to be so tough they would not crumble, thus resulting in a piece of hardtack so hard it could not be nibbled.) Green wanted his biscuit protected against damp and mold so that the customer would be willing to pay a premium price to get a better product than the local, non-NBC baker could produce. The ultimate, innovative box and its water-tight liner were invented by a lawyer in the firm who cut up his wife's kitchen table, put a treadle underneath, and showed how the carton could be created by someone, sitting down, producing a uniform container with a minimum of effort and fatigue.

They now had a product and a package; they next needed an image and exposure. They gave N.W. Ayer an unprecedented amount of money for advertising, and Ayer came up with the Uneeda slicker boy carrying the watertight package in the rain. The boy was Gordon Stille, a five-year-old nephew of one of Ayer's copywriters. In 1900, Gordon sold 100 million boxes, which amounted to an average of six boxes for every family in America.

The idea of a unique name and image for what was essentially a generic product was methodically pressed through the whole National Biscuit Company line, and it is still so successful (nearly a hundred years later) that the words elicit an immediate, clear-cut image in the mind: Oreos, Fig Newtons (named after Newton, Massachusetts, where all the rich folks lived), Animal Crackers, Oysterette Crackers, and Premium Saltines. Green even applied his trademark identity theory to the company itself, selecting the incunabulist Nicolas Jenson's printer's mark—the Byzantine cross over the circle, in white lines on a red field—for the corporate image. The word In-er-Seal filled the circle in 1900; it was changed to NBC in 1918; and Nabisco in 1941. The design now appears in the upper left corner of products from Planters Peanuts to Milk Bone dog biscuits.

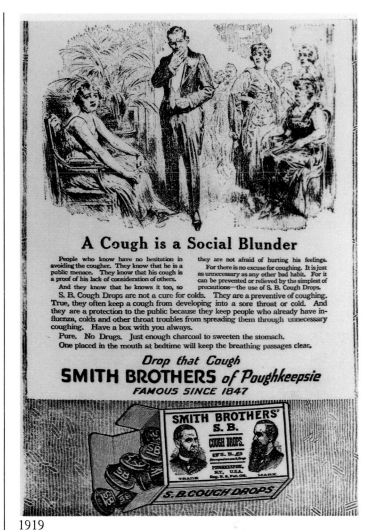

A Cough is a Social Blunder

People who know have no hesitation in avoiding the cougher. They know that he is a public menace. They know that his cough is a proof of his lack of consideration of others.

And they know that he knows it too, so S. B. Cough Drops are not a cure for colds. They are a preventive of coughing. True, they often keep a cough from developing into a sore throat or cold. And they are a protection to the public because they keep people who already have influenza, colds and other throat troubles from spreading them through unnecessary coughing. Have a box with you always.

they are not afraid of hurting his feelings.

For there is no excuse for coughing. It is just as unnecessary as any other bad habit. For it can be prevented or relieved by the simplest of precautions—the use of S. B. Cough Drops.

Pure. No Drugs. Just enough charcoal to sweeten the stomach.

One placed in the mouth at bedtime will keep the breathing passages clear.

Drop that Cough

SMITH BROTHERS *of Poughkeepsie*

FAMOUS SINCE 1847

1919

The ad says "Famous since 1847." The scholars have found Smith Brothers Cough Drop newspaper ads as far back as 1852, making this one of the longest running, continuously placed advertising campaigns in America. The fact that the one on the left is Brother Trade, and the one on the right, Brother Mark, may be the longest running advertising joke, as well.

The famous product was originally sold out of glass jars on pharmacy countertops and was called James Smith and Son's Compound of Wild Cherry Cough Candy. The company supplied small, paper envelopes for the shopkeeper to give the customer to carry the drops home. When the company went to the box, the bearded brothers appeared, and the product proceeded to sell through five generations of this family-owned business.

The advertising historian Julian Watkins called the campaign a classic of "continuous advertising, small space, plenty of insertions, simple copy." He could also have pointed out the integrity of the copy for this early patent medicine. The brothers stated firmly that the cough drops did not cure colds; they prevented coughing. (He might also have noted that the inclusion of charcoal to sweeten the stomach seems to anticipate our present-day copywriters' preoccupation with acid indigestion.)

1926

Anyone who has ever been to Vermont and tried to buy a jug of pure maple syrup will remember his sticker shock at the sight of the price. Maple syrup has always been expensive. In 1887 Patrick J. Towle, of Minneapolis, set out to see how much he could cut pure maple sugar with cane sugar and still have it taste like pure maple. He came up with a pleasant mix which he could sell at a price that ordinary people could afford for ordinary breakfasts.

He packaged it in a log cabin-shaped tin can which was instantly recognizable and which, when emptied, filled children's toy boxes for fifty years. World War II metal shortages drove General Foods (who had purchased the brand in 1927) to abandon the familiar can and go to glass bottles, and Log Cabin Syrup has never been the same.

OPPOSITE:

The Scott Brothers, E. Irvin and Clarence, had sold paper products from a pushcart in Philadelphia from 1879. When indoor toilets began to appear, the brothers bought tissue wrapping paper and repackaged it in convenient sizes to support the new invention. (The previous product had traditionally been yellow pads like small versions of our present legal tablets.) The tissue paper sold well until 1907, when the Scotts received a shipment of paper too coarse for the usual use but even more absorbent than expected. They promptly re-sold it as a paper hand towel.

During World War I, they invented the C-fold, wall-stored, one-at-a-time delivered paper towel and began to advertise nationally. The adjoining ad is from the March 25, 1916, Saturday Evening Post, and the spelling is right. Scott Paper still makes Scot Tissue Toilet Paper with only one T.

1918

Even as most people are astonished to learn that there really was a Clarence Birdseye who invented frozen foods, they are equally surprised that three generations of Maytags (starting with Frederick Louis in 1857) made washing machines in Newton, Iowa.

In 1894, the founder was producing washers that were essentially wooden tubs with an agitator sticking down through a hole in the wooden lid like a butter churn. An electric motor was added in 1911, and, as described in the accompanying ad, a gasoline engine was introduced during World War I.

Do-it-yourself laundry was available throughout the training camps, and by the end of the war, hundreds of thousands of men had seen a mechanical washing machine in action. They promptly bought one for their own household. In 1922, the traditional peg-studded, central agitator was replaced by a finned pillar that turned from side to side and the company was on the way to becoming the world's largest producer of mechanical washing machines.

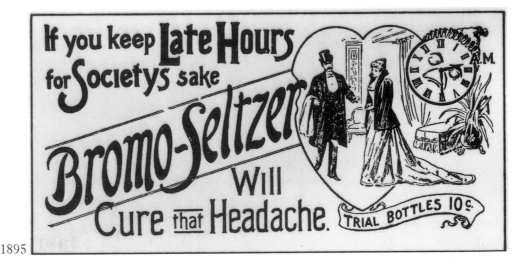

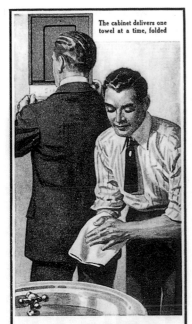

The cabinet delivers one towel at a time, folded

The Towel That Meets Your Demands

When you go into a public lavatory you expect a soft, absorbent, sanitary and individual towel. It must dry your hands and face quickly and thoroughly. It must leave a refreshed feeling of cleanliness. And it must be economical to buy. The towels that fill *all* of these demands are

ScotTissue Towels

The Soft, Absorbent, Original Paper Towel

To entirely satisfy those demands of yours has ever been our aim and we have stuck to it despite the inroads sometimes made by towels designed primarily to sell instead of to satisfy.

Our aim is realized — we now offer you a towel that will overcome any prejudice against paper or fabric towels.

We have minimized waste in towel delivery with the new ScotTissue Fixture, which delivers one towel at a time, folded, which is the way to use a ScotTissue Towel.

ScotTissue Towels should be recommended to you by jobbers and dealers. If you buy supplies for any public or semi-public lavatories, write us. We can show you the most efficient and economical towel service you can install. Write for samples and booklet: "Why You Should Install ScotTissue Towels."

SCOTT PAPER COMPANY
Manufacturers of ScotTissue Towels and Toilet Paper
723 Glenwood Ave., Philadelphia

In order to insure cleanliness ScotTissue Towels are always packed in a dust-proof carton	CHICAGO 113 E. Austin Ave.
	NEW YORK 30 Church St.
ScotTissue Towels in folded form for cabinet	SAN FRANCISCO 356 Market St.
	Address nearest office

ScotTissue Towels are packed in rolls for home use. There are many uses for ScotTissue Towels that every housewife should know about. Ask for the booklet: "Why You Should Use ScotTissue Towels in Your Home."

1916

Bromo-Seltzer goes back to 1887, when it was invented by the Emerson Drug Co. of Baltimore (the Bromo-Seltzer clock tower on the plant is now a National Landmark). From its earliest days it was advertised as speeding recovery from "overindulgence," and during the Roaring Twenties its ads showed young men in tuxedos staggering up hills, cheerfully supporting each other. Anticipating Coca-Cola's misjudgment over the modernization of the Coke formula, in the early 1970s Bromo-Seltzer was repackaged in a modern, sloping, blue plastic bottle with a white dosage cup for a top. Sales went into decline, and the company hastily returned to its traditional "high-shoulder" bottle which had held the tablets since McKinley's time.

With a name like Planters and a central packaging plant covering almost 100 acres in Suffolk, Virginia, it might be expected that Mr. Peanut comes from a deep southern heritage. Not so. Amedeo Obici and Mario Peruzzi, both Italian immigrants with fruit stands in Wilkes-Barre and New York City, joined together in 1906 to form the Planters Nut and Chocolate Company. "Planters" was chosen "because it sounded important and dignified."

Antonio Gentile, a schoolboy of Suffolk, Virginia, invented the Mr. Peanut symbol. Antonio had won a local contest for same, for which he was given $5 in 1916.

1918

Sweets after Sports

Concentrated energy in chocolates exactly answers the call of that "empty feeling" that follows a round of golf, a morning in the surf, or a battle royal at tennis.

People eat far more of Whitman's Chocolates in summer than they did formerly, and for three reasons:—

They have discovered that chocolates give "pep." Whitman's Chocolates are carefully packed and protected against summer's heat.

The exclusive plan of Whitman distribution, direct to exclusive sales agencies, even in the most remote summer resorts, assures fresh chocolates in good condition, and guaranteed.

Whenever you see the sign you know that the dealer's stock comes, not from a jobber, but direct from Whitman's. For your guests out-of-doors, supply

SALMAGUNDI
Ideal companion for "roughing it" out-of-doors. The handsome metal box gives protection to this popular assortment of Whitman's.

Whitman's
Chocolates

1925

Whitman's Chocolates go all the way back to 1842 with Stephen F. Whitman's candy store in Philadelphia, but the "firsts" for which we know them came after the turn of the century. The firm got the idea of putting a miscellaneous collection of its various kinds of chocolates in one box, putting a location index inside the cover, and calling it a "sampler" in 1912. The cover design was in cross-stitching like a traditional embroidery sampler.

Whitman was the first advertiser to use a four-color ad in the Saturday Evening Post, and from there on used highly sophisticated color graphics in regular displays. For years, people cut out Whitman candy ads for home framing because of the beauty of their artistic images.

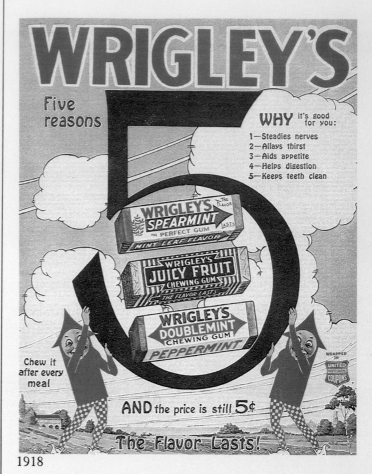

1918

There was a wise lady who lived in a shoe,
For her many small children she knew what to do;
She made them most happy with Wrigley's for all—
It kept them in trim at a cost VERY small!
MOTHER GOOSE UP-TO-DATE.

REAL Peppermint Flavor

Get the new Wrigley's Double Mint and have a delicious, lasting treat— REAL Peppermint—full strength.

Easy to remember: Double Mint. And hard to forget— once you've tried it.

The *satisfying* confection.

···*After every meal*···

1927

Enjoy Healthful Delicious
DOUBLEMINT GUM

WRIGLEY'S DOUBLEMINT CHEWING GUM

SHEPARD

1942

Here are the three famous flavors, all in place by 1914, and the only three kinds of gum that Wrigley's made for fifty-nine years. (Competitors' Dentyne and Dubble Bubble finally drove it to defensive innovation.)

Wrigley's started as a soap company, and as late as 1891 it was solely selling soap, throwing in small boxes of baking soda and chewing gum as advertising premiums. William Wrigley, Jr., moved from Philadelphia to Chicago in 1891, and in the process of opening up soap outlets noted how popular the gum giveaways were. He promptly abandoned soap for gum and made millions of dollars on a five-cent product.

Wrigley was a great believer in advertising; his perpetually repeated theme was: Tell 'em quick and tell 'em often. He felt that it was a mistake to cling too closely to printed vehicles, and thus put as much money into streetcar and subway ads, billboards, and later, radio and television, as he did into magazines and newspapers.

He invented the foil wrapper to keep individual sticks moist, and then was the first to put cellophane around the whole package to keep it even moister.

Wrigley's first gums were called Vassar and Lotta, but he abandoned these for Spearmint (named for a kind of mint whose flower is pointed like a spear), followed by Juicy Fruit, and Double Mint, introduced in 1914. With that, the company sat down to concentrate and soon had 70 percent of the world's gum business, selling it (with appropriate language wrappers) in twenty countries. As Wrigley got richer, he built office buildings and hotels, bought Catalina Island and the Chicago Cubs, but refused to broaden the product line or produce any good but gum. The spear of spearmint was the basis for the company's trademark cartoon figures for the Twenties and Thirties, and the double mint (so much flavor it must have twice as much mint in it), produced the image of beautiful women twins that proved so successful from the Forties through the Eighties.

Above are two of the famous Wrigley twins pictured in the airbrush style of Otis Shepard. Shepard joined the Wrigley company in 1932 and produced a stream of variations on the theme until his 1962 retirement. For years Shepard argued with Wrigley that the images were enough—no words were needed. Wrigley insisted that there be at least a little copy, even on the many streetcar, subway, and billboard signs where he who ran could only read a bit as he passed by. The doubled models are still a part of Wrigley ads, although under today's rules, male twins must appear occasionally.

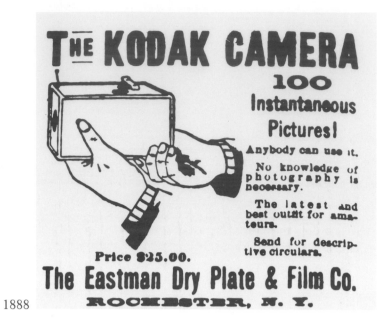

1888

The first "Kodak" went on the market in June 1888. This ad was run in September of the same year, and began the campaign that has extended for a century. The first ads sold the idea: "Anybody can use it." The camera produced crisp, clear pictures (if taken in bright sunlight), but the negative and therefore the prints were circular, taking full advantage of everything seen through the fixed lens. There was no viewfinder, but there was a line embossed on the top of the box that showed which way to point the new contraption.

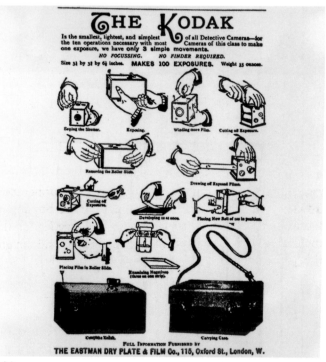

1888

This detailed "how to" ad was also run within the first six months of the invention, in this case in England. Eastman was "international" from the outset. Most owners sent the entire camera back to the factory after they had taken 100 pictures, but this ad (and the booklet that came with the camera) told the amateur photographer how he could develop the film himself, if he wanted to. The shutter described above snapped at 1/20 of a second, and was cocked by pulling up on a little dangling string that hung out of the box. There was no film counter, but the winding knob told him how far to advance each shot, and a memorandum book was provided with each boxed roll.

1889

This is the first appearance of the famous phrase " 'Press the button'—we do the rest." In the early days, George Eastman wrote all his own copy, and he carved the line out of a long ad he had composed. He said he read the copy again, and everything he'd written was simply a more complicated way of saying: Press the button—we do the rest. So he dropped the waste in the wastebasket. Many years later, when he was very rich, he said, "I can only add that no man was more astonished to find the phrase so universally popular. It has been highly gratifying to me."

The Hard Ones—
How Do You Sell A . . . ?

UP TO NOW we have seen the pioneers set the models for advertising products that were reasonably familiar. The customer at least knew what the product was; the challenge was to get him to buy one particular version. Let us now look at how the innovators solved the problem of selling something no one had ever seen before: a camera, a safety razor, and flying in an airplane.

On one level, the exercise is interesting simply to watch how the innovators led the customers from what the gadget is, to how to use it, to making it an essential part of the buyers' lives. On a more philosophical level comes the educational aspect: the maker simply wanted to make some money, but in the process of demonstrating his invention, he educated a whole society to a richer or more comfortable experience. And once again we are discovering how far back the givens of how we advertise today do go. How do you convince the customer that he shouldn't—can't—live without a home computer, an electric icebox, a gasoline automobile—a camera, a safety razor, or an airplane ride?

The Eastman Kodak

The Eastman Kodak was invented in 1888. People had been going to the photographer to "get their likeness taken" since before the Civil War. They knew what a camera was. It was a huge thing, weighed fifty to a hundred pounds and sat on a heavy tripod or on a table. The picture was made on a plate in the back. Fifteen years before 1888 the plate was a sheet of glass covered with a freshly made, dripping wet skin of collodion holding a solution of light-sensitive grains of silver bromide. Ten years before 1888 the camera was just as big, but the plates rushed from the darkroom were covered with dry gelatin holding the silver bromide. And ten years before 1888, George Eastman got into the act, buying his first photographic equipment for nearly a month's pay and taking lessons from a local, professional photographer, although Eastman's interest was simply as a hobby for weekends.

Eastman was then 23. His father had died when he was eight and his mother had started taking in boarders; George worked nights sawing filigree on picture frames. When he was 14, he dropped out of school to work as a runner for a real estate company. He then became an office boy for an insurance firm, and at 20 became a bookkeeper for the Rochester (N.Y.) Savings Bank. The camera he had bought with his first savings was "about the size of a soap box" (as he later described it) and it came with a tripod, "which was strong and heavy enough to support a bungalow," and a dark-tent with all the chemicals.

The chemicals were where the whole process broke down. They were volatile, toxic, and had to be carried to the site of the picture in huge bottles and clay crocks. The plates had to be dipped into the collodion and silver nitrate and rushed out of the darkroom to be snapped behind the lens and bellows of the camera.

Like everyone else, Eastman recognized that the weak spot was in the film, not the camera, so he proceeded to invent solutions in that order. He first took an idea he found in a photographic magazine, and developed a way to support the silver salts in dry gelatin instead of the wet collodion. With this he started a small Eastman Dry Plate Company (1881) to market same. He then worked out a way of getting rid of the glass plates by dipping tough, thin paper in hot

KODAK SIMPLICITY

has removed most of the opportunities for making
mistakes. No dark-room, few chemicals, little bother.

Kodaks, $5.00 to $108.00.

EASTMAN KODAK CO.
Rochester, N.Y.

1905

If it isn't an Eastman, it isn't a Kodak.

Bring your Vacation Home in a

KODAK

Add to the after-delights of your holiday with pictures of the
people, the places and the sports you are interested in. Every
step easy by the Kodak System.

Kodaks, $5.00 to $108.00.   Brownies, $1.00 to $9.00.

EASTMAN KODAK CO.
Rochester, N.Y.

1905

Kodak knows no dark days

With its allies, the Kodak flash sheets and a Kodak
flash sheet holder, your Kodak camera is ready for every
picture opportunity.

Ask your dealer or write us for our little booklet "By Flashlight." There's no charge.

EASTMAN KODAK COMPANY, ROCHESTER, N.Y., *The Kodak City.*

1917

Not only did Eastman open processing plants
in many foreign countries, but he early
advertised abroad and made "carry a Kodak
with you when you travel" a major theme of
his advertising. One of the first four electric
signs that went up surrounding Charing Cross
in London spelled out Kodak, and Eastman
was the first advertiser to use the sides of
Parisian omnibuses for his posters. He had a
monopoly on the space for three years.

Eastman had invented the word "Kodak" out
of the whole cloth. He claimed that his
mother's name started with a K and two Ks
were better than one. He wanted a word that
had no other meaning in any foreign
language, could not be mispronounced, and
took up little space. He marketed it so
successfully that by 1905 any camera, no
matter who manufactured it, nor how large or
how small it was was called a "kodak" and
Eastman discovered he was about to lose his
trademark. He hastily created "If it isn't an
Eastman, it isn't a Kodak" and hired such
famous artists as Edward Penfield (here) to
capture the reader's attention. Penfield was
the art director for Harper's and a famous
poster designer at the turn of the century.

Kodak kept explaining innovations to the
amateur as they were developed. Here is the
first flashbulb for the non-professional—a
cardboard holder on which the photographer
ignited sheets of flash powder. His partner is
not pinned in terror, but is only following
instructions to stand a precise distance from
the flash sheet and against a reflecting surface
to fill the shadows.

Movies you make yourself

There's something new in photography—a new pleasure and a fascinating
one—motion pictures the Kodak way. With the same ease that you make
ordinary snap-shots you can now film "movies" of your family, your friends,
your sports and pleasures, and show them on the screen in your own home.

The camera is the Ciné-Kodak, and to operate it all you do is train the lens and press the
button. A motor cranks the camera and gets
the scene in *action*.

The projector is the Kodascope—also Eastman-
made—and it not only allows you to show your own
movies but professional releases as well. Through
Kodascope Libraries, Inc., you can rent for

Kodascope projection famous feature films, Charlie Chaplin comedies, animated cartoons and
travel scenes, and show them in your own home.

Motion pictures the Kodak way mean a saving of 80 per cent. over cameras using standard
width film, and when you buy Ciné-Kodak film
you've paid for the finishing by Eastman experts.
You press the button; we do the rest.

Ciné-Kodak booklet and full information by mail, on request.

Eastman Kodak Company, Rochester, N.Y., *The Kodak City*

1924

LEFT:

*Home movies for the amateur explained, and
the assurance that there's nothing to it
reaffirmed. George Eastman's original slogan
also applies again: "You press the button; we
do the rest." (With the 16mm film, you had
to send the pictures back to the factory for
processing. The company would soon
introduce color slides under the same
arrangement.)*

RIGHT:

*This campaign aimed for the Christmas sales,
and the multiple colors exploited the current
style: bathrooms were in color, women's
ensembles and accessories had to match in the
smallest detail, you wouldn't want to carry a
black camera with a green dress, would you?
Unfortunately, in the growing Depression,
even $7.50 was over half-a-week's pay for the
average worker.*

A special **Christmas showing**
of the new 1931 Kodaks

For Christmas shoppers, new model Kodaks, Brownies,
Ciné-Kodaks . . . Ready now at Kodak dealers'

Give a KODAK

1930

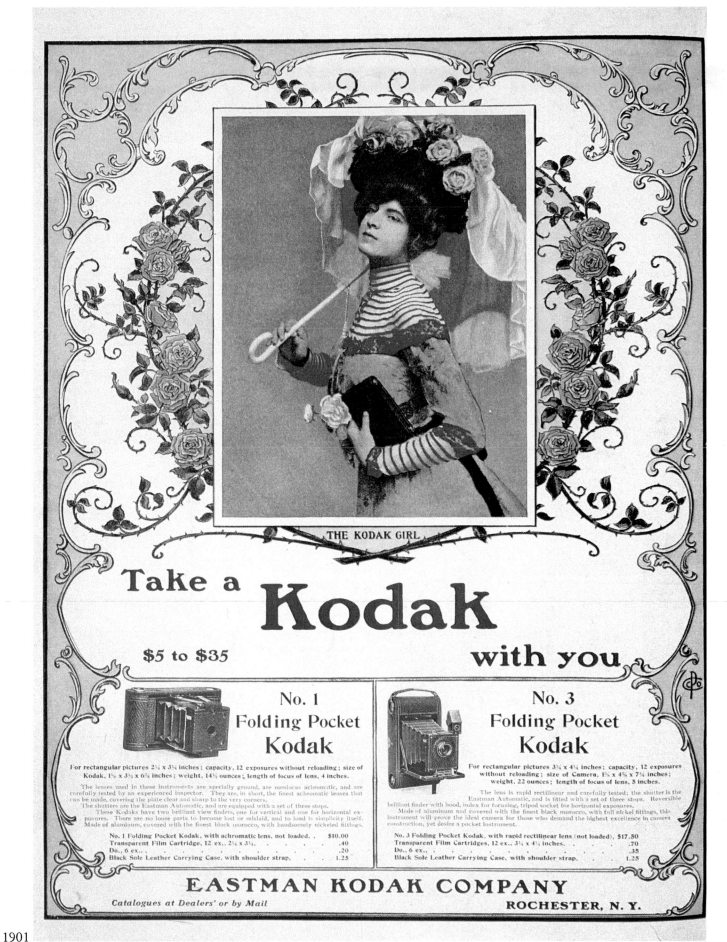

THE KODAK GIRL

Take a Kodak with you

$5 to $35

No. 1 Folding Pocket Kodak

For rectangular pictures 2¼ x 3¼ inches; capacity, 12 exposures without reloading; size of Kodak, 1⅝ x 3½ x 6¼ inches; weight, 14½ ounces; length of focus of lens, 4 inches.

The lenses used in these instruments are specially ground, are meniscus achromatic, and are carefully tested by an experienced inspector. They are, in short, the finest achromatic lenses that can be made, covering the plate clear and sharp to the very corners.

The shutters are the Eastman Automatic, and are equipped with a set of three stops. These Kodaks have two brilliant view finders, one for vertical and one for horizontal exposures. There are no loose parts to become lost or mislaid, and to load is simplicity itself. Made of aluminum, covered with the finest black morocco, with handsomely nickeled fittings.

No. 1 Folding Pocket Kodak, with achromatic lens, not loaded,	$10.00
Transparent Film Cartridge, 12 ex., 2¼ x 3¼,	.40
Do., 6 ex.,	.20
Black Sole Leather Carrying Case, with shoulder strap,	1.25

No. 3 Folding Pocket Kodak

For rectangular pictures 3¼ x 4¼ inches; capacity, 12 exposures without reloading; size of Camera, 1⅝ x 4⅜ x 7¼ inches; weight, 22 ounces; length of focus of lens, 5 inches.

The lens is rapid rectilinear and carefully tested; the shutter is the Eastman Automatic, and is fitted with a set of three stops. Reversible brilliant finder with hood, index for focusing, tripod socket for horizontal exposures. Made of aluminum and covered with the finest black morocco, with full nickel fittings, this instrument will prove the ideal camera for those who demand the highest excellence in camera construction, yet desire a pocket instrument.

No. 3 Folding Pocket Kodak, with rapid rectilinear lens (not loaded),	$17.50
Transparent Film Cartridges, 12 ex., 3¼ x 4¼ inches,	.70
Do., 6 ex.,	.35
Black Sole Leather Carrying Case, with shoulder strap,	1.25

EASTMAN KODAK COMPANY

Catalogues at Dealers' or by Mail

ROCHESTER, N. Y.

1901

Eastman invented the first folding camera in 1895, and by 1896 he had made 100,000 Kodaks and was selling between three and four hundred miles of film and paper a month. The Chicago Tribune said "The craze [of amateur photography] is spreading fearfully." Prints were now squared, and the viewfinder worked either vertically or horizontally. Eastman was among the first to use two colors of ink in his ads like this one which appeared on the back cover of a May Saturday Evening Post.

It is now almost fifty years after Eastman began selling his camera for the average man. The slogan is still there: "Only Eastman makes the Kodak"; the innovations are still coming: fast films, Photoflood lights, and Photoflash bulbs; do-it-yourself how-to instructions. But the advertising format reflects the cluttered look of the 1930s. Type in multiple sizes scattered all about; pictures in every shape, and the clean, single-point copy that George Eastman himself wrote has fallen to looking like the competitors'.

1935

castor oil (which made it translucent), and then coating the paper with his light-sensitive gelatin mixture held between a sandwich of collodion layers.

At about this time someone else invented flexible celluloid, and Eastman substituted it for his paper. This permitted him to roll the film up, cut it into sheets, and take it out of the darkroom. He quit work at the insurance company, and changed the firm's name to Eastman Dry Plate & Film Co.

Until 1888 photographic film was sold to professionals and only a tiny scattering of hobbyists. Eastman wanted every man in the street to experience the joy of photography (and buy his film). He was convinced that if he was to make photography popular, he had to make it simple—take out all the mixing and the chemicals—and he had to make it portable. He was convinced that the future of photography was just as much places as it was faces, and he was convinced that while it would be useful to take endless pictures of the kids growing up, if he could get the customers to capture vacations and distant scenery, he would sell many times more film than if he relied on portraits at home alone.

Given these specifications, he worked his way through his R and D with immaculate precision. He designed a foolproof, extraordinarily simple camera to hold the rolls of his new flexible film. The camera would be loaded in the factory and sealed. The owner had only to do four things: pull up on a little dangling string to cock the shutter; aim the box in the direction of the arrow embossed on the top; press

the button; and wind the film to the next number on the circle around the knob.

The picture that had been taken was two and a half inches in diameter—a perfect circle—and was printed as such. There was no viewfinder, you just aimed the box, and, when all 100 exposures had been taken you returned it to the factory. The Eastman Company unloaded the camera, made the 100 prints, reloaded the box, and returned it. All for $10. The camera cost $25. If anything went wrong, you just sent the box back and the company would give you a new one.

Having invented the product, Eastman wanted a name for it, and the magic word "Kodak" did not come casually. (When he tried to get it registered as a trademark in England in 1888 the Comptroller of the British Patent Office demanded an explanation of the derivation of the label. Eastman wrote back: "This is not a foreign name or word; it was constructed by me to serve a definite purpose." He told them, it was short; it was not capable of mispronunciation; it did not resemble anything in the art and could not be associated with anything in the art except a Kodak.) Eastman's mother's name began with a K, and he said that he had always liked K since there was only one way you could say it. Two K's were better than one, and he endeavored to keep what was between them as short as possible, because as frequently as he hoped Kodak would be written over the years, a short word would save a great deal of space. Thus: Kodak.

He immediately began to advertise in every magazine he

could think of that seemed to have readers who could afford $25 for an adult toy. At this time, shopkeepers and office clerks averaged $12 a week for 48 hours of work. Even managers got only three dollars a day, yet the product immediately sold beyond Eastman's wildest hopes. Within six months he brought out the Kodak 2, which contained only 60 pictures, but made a circular print three and a half inches across. He began at once with his belief that you should always sell at the lowest possible price to make a consistent, small profit. He cut the price of the film again and again, made the camera increasingly convenient, and lowered the cost with each model. Kodak 2 was more popular than the Kodak 1, and he found himself developing tens of thousands of rolls of film—which he processed and returned in five days. Even during the Christmas rush he took pride in the fact that the turnaround never exceeded ten.

Eastman wrote his own ad copy, and wrote the instruction manuals that came with the cameras. His technique seems to have been the one of writing down everything he wanted the reader to know, and then methodically blue-pencilling out all repetition and qualifications until he had the bare bones of the ad. He said that "I finally cut out everything else but: Kodak cameras. You press the button— We do the Rest." It became one of the best known slogans in English.

He believed in very simple messages, essentially no more than one thought to an ad. His use of white space would have satisfied an art director of today, but he did not believe in repetition of anything but the company slogans. The ads themselves might make the same point again and again, but they always illustrated it in a clearly different way. Furthermore, as the years went on, he brought out an endless series of innovations for his customers.

In 1891 he brought out the first truly tourist camera that could be loaded in strong sunlight, anywhere. In 1895, he brought out the first folding pocket camera that took oblong and larger pictures than the box cameras, but collapsed into a thickness of less than an inch. In 1896, he made his one hundred thousandth Kodak and was selling film in excess of three to four hundred miles' worth a month. He had cut the price of the cameras to $5 for the introductory, stripped model.

During World War I he bought full-page, colored ads urging the home front to send pictures of home and family to the boys in camp. Then he ran ads suggesting that you send camera and film to the boys in camp so they could take pictures and send them back to you. He quickly found that his advertising was almost too effective. Even after the invention of roll film and simple home developing, his customers kept sending the whole camera back, so the "we do the rest" was phased out.

The endless repetition of "Kodak" (he put it on top of buildings on Times Square and Charing Cross, he had a monopoly on the side of Parisian omnibuses for three years) likewise overshot. The buying public had come to think of Kodak and camera as synonymous and all his competitors' products were being called Kodaks, so the company slogan became "If It Isn't an Eastman, It Isn't a Kodak." (This seemed to reassure the company, but made very little impact on the amateur photographers of the world.) The cameras and the film, incidentally, were marketed worldwide almost from the start and Kodak film in foreign-language wrappers—and even non-arabic numbers showing through the little red hole in the back—were on every continent.

Eastman Kodak's endless innovation kept the name and the product constantly renewing itself: flash powder, photofloods, flashbulbs. Home movies in black and white and then in color even before the movie houses had them; color slides, color prints, projectors, sound-on-film, 35mm "candid cameras." The company's reputation for reliability and identification with its customers has awed its competitors for a hundred years. And its advertising has continually announced, explained, demonstrated, and steadily cut the costs—only to start over again on the next new product.

The Gillette Safety Razor

King C. Gillette was born in Chicago in January 1855, just six months after George Eastman had appeared in Waterville, New York. His newspaper editor father named him after a personal friend, one Judge King. The C came from his mother's family name, Camp. In his twenties Gillette sold hardware products on the road—a traveling salesman— and in 1889 (when he was 34) he went to England for a year and sold soap products for Sapolio. During this stint he learned the importance of constant, repetitive advertising.

In 1891 he became a sales representative for the Baltimore Seal Company, and he worked his routes from New York State throughout New England. He got to be great friends with the president of the firm, one William Painter. About this time Painter invented a little cork-lined cap that was crimped over the top of glass bottles (Eureka! the bottle cap), and this caught on so well that in its first full year it brought in $350,000 in royalties—and the president changed the company name to the Crown Cork & Seal Company.

According to Gillette, one night he and Painter were talking about the success of the product, and the president said to him, "King, you are always thinking and inventing something. Why don't you try to think of something like the Crown Cork which, when once used, is thrown away, and the customer keeps coming back for more—and with every additional customer you get, you are building a foundation of profit." Gillette replied that this sounded good, but it wasn't so easy to do. "How many things are there like corks, pins and needles?" Painter agreed, and said but "you don't know . . . it won't do any harm to think about it."

As Gillette later told the story, the challenge became an obsession to him and during his travels he spent hundreds of miles in coach cars and Pullmans brooding on the possibilities. For several years Gillette had used a patented "Star" razor to reduce the chance of cutting his throat with

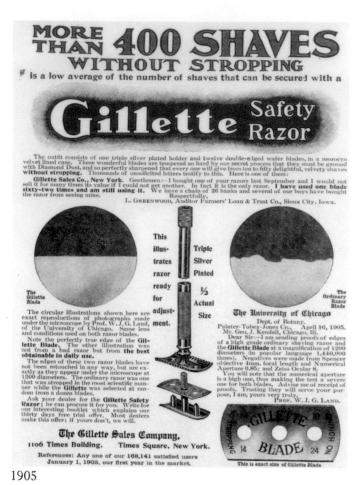

1905

1905

1906

ABOVE:

When the Gillette safety razor appeared, it sold at five dollars for the "handle" (two days' pay for the average worker of the time) and a dollar for 20 blades. A straight razor went for $2.50 and lasted a lifetime. Gillette perceived the instrument as a luxury item and sold it in jewelry shops, cutlery stores, and places like Wanamaker's and Lord and Taylor's. In fact it immediately sold briskly to buyers of all economic levels.

George Eastman would have approved of the copy in this ad. Short and to the point.

LEFT:

The February 24th back cover of the Saturday Evening Post. *The Gillette razor was not yet three years old at this point, but very well advertised. Note the statistical justification: "IF THE TIME, MONEY, ENERGY AND BRAIN-POWER which we have wasted in the barber shops of America were applied in direct effort, the Panama canal could be dug in four hours."*

Gillette believed in selling his razors with a me-and-thee dialogue between himself and the buyer. These were not a company product; they were King C.'s razors, and he put his face on every packet; his signature on every blade; and talked his selling case directly to the reader. Like David Ogilvy a half century later, he did not believe you could have too much copy so long as it was honest and to the point. And like Victor Kiam's "I liked it so much I bought the company" selling Remington electric shavers eighty years later, there was the right-in-the-eye look. Would I lie to you?

You adapted the razor to your facial contours by bending your wrist. Eighty years later technology took over, and Gillette introduced the Sensor model, the result of ten years' and $200 million worth of research. The Sensor follows the contours of your face via 13 moving parts, multiple laser welds, platinum-hardened chromium blades, and 22 new patents.

The product is a quarter-century old here, and is as common as a pen or a pencil, but the company still likes to think of it as a luxury item. This gold-plated handle is identical to the ordinary version, but the gold carton of special blades is doubly different. For twenty-seven years the carton has been the green of a dollar bill because King C. wanted his face "to be as recognizable around the world as Washington's is on the money."

---

the long, traditional, straight razor of the time, while shaving on swaying railroad trains. The Star was a little hoe-like razor, wedge-shaped and similar to what you would get if you cut an inch-wide section out of a barber's razor, anchored it to a handle at right angles, and then after each shave removed it from the handle, put it in a special holder and stropped it back and forth across a piece of leather. The Star was then returned and stored in a specially designed box. At this time, all razors had to be stropped on leather just before they were used, and then had to be taken to a barber or cutler several times a year to be re-ground for home use. Straight razors would last indefinitely, and indeed, it was traditional for the eldest son to inherit his father's razor at the time of the latter's death. Straight razors cost $2.50 apiece, a day's pay at the time.

By slow, logical steps (not in the blinding flash he always described at trade conventions) Gillette concluded that it wasn't the long, gleaming silver razor that did the work, but a tiny edge, possibly only a millimeter wide. If he could just duplicate that little edge and sell it polished and ground, the customer could use it until it grew dull and then simply throw it away. He soon found The Great Idea had two major flaws: one, "everyone," even the metallurgists at M.I.T., said you could not put a cutting edge on thin, flat sheet steel; and two, no one could see any advantage in throwing razors away and starting all over again. Why not simply buy a razor once, and use it the rest of your life?

1908

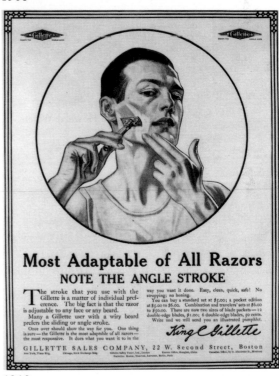

1910

1930

Gillette talked to hardware men and metal workers while he continued to sell Crown crimped bottle caps on the road, and he kept making models of razor blade holders in his basement. Not until 1899 did he finally come up with a combination that would actually shave his face. He then needed money to get the idea off the ground, but found that the people with the cash were unimpressed with his paper patent until the production of the actual goods had been worked out. A number of the backers finally talked one of New England's leading engineers—William Emery Nickerson—into taking on the task of designing the production machinery. Nickerson accepted the challenge and in six months had solved the problem of how to harden ribbon steel so it would hold an edge, and how to form a blade that had enough stability to function as a razor. There was some difficulty over what to call the company. Gillette, as the idea man, wanted their names immortalized, but Nickerson felt his name had an unfortunate connotation for a safety razor so they agreed on the American Safety Razor Company, and this came to life in September 1901. It took almost a year for King C. Gillette to get it changed to the Gillette Safety Razor Company.

By July 1903, Gillette, Nickerson, and their backers had decided to charge five dollars for the "handle," and one dollar for twenty blades. They began to sell contracts to department stores for distribution. The razor sold so well so promptly that the company reduced the number of blades in the carton to twelve for a dollar, thus increasing the profit margin by forty percent.

Most of this profit went into advertising. From the very beginning the company allocated twenty-five cents of every razor to promotion, and in April 1905 they raised it to fifty cents of every sale. The key to the safety razor campaign, oddly enough, was not that it kept you from slicing half your face away as was potentially so easy with a straight razor, but "No Stropping, No Honing." The elimination of the perpetual "getting ready to shave" was what proved to have the greatest appeal. The usual, "if you cannot buy a Gillette from your own supplier send five dollars to . . ." worked wonders, bringing in as many dealers' inquiries as it did individual customers.

The No Stropping, No Honing led the way to Gillette's basic advertising theme: the razor with the interchangeable blades saved time, increased comfort, and gave "more freedom for other activities."

From the outset, Gillette identified the blades with himself as an individual—not with a company or corporation. The razor was his idea. He used it. He found it comfortable. It was King C. Gillette's razor. His face covered one whole side of the blade package "heavy mustache, wing collar, stickpin, and wavy black hair" parted in the middle. Trivia lovers relish the thought that his picture was printed more often than any other modern man's—over 100 billion times.

The traditional story of how he came to pick his own face as a trademark runs: in the course of telling his ad people what he was looking for, he said he wanted a symbol as recognizable—internationally—as George Washington on the dollar bill. The ad makers, taking him at his word, put his own picture on the product, and for the first fifty years the razor blade package was printed in green ink in the same color as a dollar bill. The slogan, "Known the World Over" accompanied the visual identity for many decades.

The razor exceeded everyone's most optimistic hopes. In 1903 he sold 51 of the "handles" and 168 blades. In 1904 he sold 90,844 razors and 123,648 blades. In 1905 the razor figure tripled and the blades went up times ten. By 1917 blade sales exceeded 120,000,000 annually.

The early Gillette ads were marvelously detailed conversations between King C. and the customer. He explained what his razor would do, how you used it, why it was superior. He offered it in an endless series of boxes, metals, holiday wrappings—with the razor handle and the blue blade identical in all.

It was in 1917 that Gillette got his second greatest idea, (second only to the invention itself). He decided that he would give a free razor and pack of blades to every serviceman joining the Army, Navy, and Marine Corps to fight the Kaiser. His production people adjusted the concept slightly by suggesting that they sell the product at cost to the U.S. Government and let the government do the distribution. This was done, and the razor (which still sold for five dollars) was included in the Quartermaster's issue kit of shirt, pants, and shoes, thus introducing the product to a whole generation of young men.

Terror time came when Gillette realized that his original patent was going to run out on November 15, 1921. Commercial intelligence reported that Japanese manufacturers already had tens of thousands of razors in a bonded warehouse in Chicago waiting for the arrival of November 16. Six months before the deadline Gillette brought out a new model in a stripped version selling for a single dollar, and the crisis was averted. But the idea of cutting the cost of the razor and living off the blades opened a whole new campaign for the company.

The World War I period had been dedicated to getting the American male to shave himself instead of going to the barber. In the Twenties, the concentration was on getting a razor into every man's hands. The holder was sold essentially at cost, and the company sold millions to other manufacturers to be used as premiums with their products. They were put into coffee and tea containers, given free with shaving cream and soap, Wrigley used over a million as chewing gum premiums, and an overalls manufacturer put a Gillette in the pocket of all their pants. The razor became a break-even product; the profit was to be made on the blade.

The Depression Thirties were dedicated to keeping the price down by new forms of manufacturing. As hard as it is to believe, up until the mid-Thirties each blade was printed, etched, the holes punched out, and cut into the proper shape mechanically, but at that point every single blade was sharpened BY HAND, TWO SIDES, TOP AND BOTTOM. Not until the Depression was the technique of strip steel, mechanically honed and cut apart, embraced, thus producing 450 finished blades a minute per machine.

Finally, in the Forties (World War II), the company concentrated on getting every man into the *daily* shave habit. Not only is this far less common than most people realize, but to the makers' horror, after World War II, the beard came back. (Note how hair on the face has gone in and out with fashion for the whole life of the Republic: every one of the signers of the Declaration of Independence was clean shaven; the overwhelming majority of the Civil War leaders had a mustache or a beard.) The leadership of World War II was clean shaven, but Style came 'round again in the second half of the century, and the search for a symbol of macho manliness has again undone many millions of Gillette advertising dollars carefully spent throughout the past 80 years. A three-day beard on construction workers and television detectives is almost as costly as a full beard on a folk singer.

The invention of the electric razor looked like a major threat to King C.'s invention, but strangely, this never developed. While the electric razor was sometimes useful while traveling, the average customer liked the cleanliness of the cutting razor in the home. But Gillette's competition assaulted its premier position with the plastic-handled, throwaway version of the double-tracked, single-sided model, and at the time of this writing, the expendable razor (with a much-reduced profit margin) seems to be winning. The glory days of King C. Gillette's blue blades, and the annual World Series' "Look Sharp, Feel Sharp, Be Sharp" slogan seems to be a completed chapter in a corporate history that has gone on to diversification of products, leaving its razor—the original cutting edge—as only one among many.

Voluntarily Flying Through the Air

Even as the personal camera and the safety razor started from next to nothing and had to be introduced and sold to each individual citizen, the idea of flying from one place to another started from next to nothing and with the help of an innovative advertising campaign was built into a major industry in less than five years. Knowing how the Wrights' airplane grew steadily larger and more efficient, it could be assumed that the people flying in them (other than the pilots themselves) must have grown from a few to a steadily increasing number until there were many ordinary citizens flying from one place to another. Not so. At the beginning of 1926 there were *no* airlines carrying people inside the airplane, and by the end of 1930 there were dozens carrying thousands. And like the Kodak and the Gillette, there was a single invention that achieved the triumph: in this case, the corrugated metal Ford Tri-motor, soon to go down in history as The Tin Goose.

The Wrights' airplane did indeed develop with mind-shattering speed. The first man-carrying powered flight (of what was scarcely more than an oversized kite) came at Kitty Hawk in 1903. By the end of World War I in 1919—only 16 years later—every major nation of the world had hundreds of planes and many hundreds of trained pilots.

When peacetime arrived, it was assumed that the quickening development of the new transportation form would accelerate, but instead it dropped back to almost nothing. Ordinary people could think of nothing to use the airplane for.

At that time, even the newest, most powerful planes were made of wood, covered with stretched canvas. The engines were noisy, the twin wings (thought to be needed for maximum lift) were supported by wires and struts that gave off penetrating hums and (we now know) held back the plane. Anyone who hired a plane to take them anywhere had to sit in an open, unheated cockpit, sharing the great out-of-doors with the pilots.

Commercial aviation of any consequence began in the closing weeks of 1919 when the Post Office contracted with some ex-fighter pilots to fly the mail from New York to Washington. Three pilots were killed in separate crashes within days and, as mail runs were added to the West, the task became increasingly dangerous. Nine pilots were killed in 1920, even though all flying was in daylight.

The Postal Service worked frantically to catch up on safety, and by 1923, emergency fields were spotted every 25 to 30 miles along the routes, and emergency lights were placed at airports from Chicago to Cheyenne, Wyoming. By the middle of 1924, revolving night beacons flashed all the way from New York to San Francisco, and night mail service was inaugurated coast to coast. Although private citizens were taken up for sight-seeing and even flown under contract, there was still no attempt at regular inter-city passenger flights.

At about this time an inventor by the name of William B. Stout began looking at the bi-winged mail planes and was convinced that there was a way to put a small room for passengers inside the fuselage. Working from a variety of ideas the Germans had had, he first did away with the lower wing, which he believed caused more drag than lift. He then put the top wing within the fuselage, but spread it over a much larger surface into what he called a "bat wing." He thickened it and supported it inside as a cantilever, and then applied one of the Junker experiments: a metal skin. The Aluminum Company of America had just produced an alloy of aluminum and copper which was exceptionally strong yet light which they'd labeled Duralumin. They made a sandwich of it between pure aluminum sheets to resist corrosion. Stout corrugated it like a barn roof, and put it over metal rods (the Germans had been afraid to abandon the flexibility of a wooden frame).

With the metal skin bolted to the metal frame, to his delight, it flew beautifully. Edsel Ford, who had been watching Stout's development from the sidelines, convinced his father that Stout was on to something big, and Henry bought Stout's factory and models outright and made them a new division of the Ford Motor Company.

With the Ford engineering department available and plenty of money, Stout and then others from the firm threw themselves on the plans and designed the prototype "by committee." They moved the pilot's cockpit in front of the wing, put him indoors, and put celluloid windows around him. (Celluloid was the only plastic yet invented.) No pilot had ever flown "indoors," and when the model was sold in Europe, the European companies insisted the windows be removed so the pilot could keep the "feel" of the flight. The windshield in the first test model almost wrecked it. It blew back into the cabin into the flight wheel and locked the controls for several frightening minutes. Ford put new and heavier engines on either side, and ultimately put a third in the nose, thus, finally, creating the legendary Ford Tri-motor.

They flew thousands of trial flights between the July 1925 purchase of Stout's company and the June 1926 inauguration of the new plane, and Ford was sure he had a winner. He was a reluctant convert, however. He maintained throughout that flying was still 90 percent luck and instinct, and 10 percent science. He wanted to "reverse the percentages." (Stout was also good at epigrams; he once lectured his staff about eliminating all possible weight and one of the foreman translated the instruction into: "simplicate everything and add more lightness" which Stout painted on signs all over the plant.)

The Tri-motor was a total success from the start. It was fast for the time, stable, and reliable; it could take off in only three plane lengths and climb 900 feet a minute to 15,000 feet. It could both take off and land on only one engine if two should fail. It carried eleven passengers in wicker chairs, and was far more comfortable than any plane yet designed. (It was not a complete airliner as we know it today, however: for the first three years it had no heater in the cabin, and the noise was deafening. As the new "flight escorts" passed out coffee, they distributed cotton wads for the ears.) But with the availability of the new, safe, "indoor airplane," new airlines began springing up everywhere, and virtually every one operated one or more Ford Tri-motors.

Most of the new airlines started as scheduled flights between two specific towns. One line would fly between Los Angeles and San Francisco, another between San Francisco and Portland, another from Portland to Spokane, et cetera. Thus in 1926 you found Varney, National Air Transport, Stout, Pacific, and Boeing Air Transport coming to life. In 1931 all of these would merge into United Air Lines.

Colonial, Southern, Embry Riddle, Texas Air, Thompson Aeronautical Corporation, Interstate, Delta Air Service, Frank Martz Airlines, Southern Air Fast Express (SAFE), and Century Air Lines started in 1926 and became American Airlines in 1934.

The Fords quickly recognized that they would have no trouble convincing the new airlines to buy their Tri-motors. The problem was getting enough ordinary citizens to want to fly that the airlines would have enough customers and therefore enough money to buy more Tri-motors. Henry Ford set out to explain flight to the common man.

He went to the N.W. Ayer Company to design the campaign. Ayer assigned William Ashley Anderson to write the copy, and Ford sent Stout to explain what flying would some day be like. Between them, they created a series of seventeen ads trying to express in words the advantages, the exhilaration—and the need for—commercial flight. Recall, Stout had little more idea of the answer than Anderson. When the ads started, there was very little commercial aviation anywhere in the country. Most of the nation's airfields were nothing but open pastures with most of the tree stumps removed; and over half of all the scheduled flights were still in open cockpit World War I planes. But the seventeen ads were written. The Ford Company took space they had already contracted for (they had intended to announce the forthcoming V-8 to replace the Model-T in these pages) and for a year and a half the series appeared in the *Saturday Evening Post, Literary Digest, National Geographic, American Boy, Town and Country, World's Work, Review of Reviews, Spur, Vanity Fair,* and *Sportsman.* The journals added up to a combined circulation of 6,150,912 or twenty million readers.

About half way through the series, Charles Lindbergh flew solo from New York to Paris and reinforced dozens of Ford's assertions. He flew in a single-wing, metal-covered aircraft, and several thousand people immediately decided that if Lucky Lindy could do it behind one engine, surely they could do it behind three. The papers and the radio gave the Lindbergh flight saturation coverage, and then continued to fill the columns with articles about every aspect of aviation. The aviation historian David Weiss noted that as late as August 27, 1927 (three months after the flight of the *Spirit of St. Louis*), the *New York Times* was carrying seventy-four articles and features on flying in that single day's issue. In 1928, 60,000 tickets were sold in the U.S. for airplane flights; in 1929, 160,000 people flew.

Ford's "Lift Up Your Eyes" series continued and the sales of Tri-motors continued to rise. In 1927 Ford had sold twelve planes; in 1928 they sold thirty-nine. For the 1929 model they installed heaters, sound-proofing, leather seats, larger windows and more streamlining. They sold and delivered eighty-nine of this model which carried fifteen passengers and was both faster and more economical to fly. Admiral Byrd flew one of these over the South Pole on November 29, 1929. The safety record continued to make the Tri-motor one of the safest airplanes ever built in America.

At the same time as Ford was explaining flight to his prospective passengers, he was explaining commercial aviation to the owners. He built the largest concrete runway in the world (at Dearborn, Michigan), and then distributed its cost figures and blueprints to municipal governments. He used Ford Tri-motors to ferry Ford parts and products between plants and dealers, and then sent monthly reports on the amounts of gasoline and oil used, the cost of maintenance, and complete repair records to all the airlines so they could estimate comparable costs for their own corporations.

But Ford's production statistics for 1930 reveal a strange

AIR MAIL
is Socially Correct

5¢ for the First Ounce 10¢ for each additional Ounce

1925

In 1925, six years after the close of World War I, the government was in the airmail business and trying to sell the service. Commercial airplanes looked like the one behind the lady's head. They were exclusively mail planes, made of wood covered with fabric, bi-winged with the pilot sitting in an open cockpit toward the rear of his plane so he could watch the ailerons and tail flaps which controlled his flight. An inventor named William B. Stout was convinced that the plane should be made with metal rods inside and covered with a metal skin. He believed the mail plane could be enlarged so passengers could sit inside protected from the weather. He eliminated the lower wing, enlarged the upper, and put the pilot at the front of the plane. Henry Ford liked the result so well he bought Stout's company and went into the aviation business in July of 1925.

ACROSS THE FENCELESS SKY

When forest fires or tornadoes strew the paths of civilization with wreckage and suffering . . . when levees melt away before uncontrollable floods, and entire countrysides are inundated . . . when blizzards smother city and country under paralyzing burdens of snow and sleet, where does man look first for help from his fellow man?

Upward! For across the fenceless sky first aid will come!

Florida, storm-swept . . . Yokohama and Tokyo, shattered by earthquake and blasted with flame . . . the Mississippi Valley, sunk in its floods . . . and New England, ravaged with sleet storms and turbulent waters . . . all turned to the sky to re-establish communication with the outer world.

Everywhere above the earth, it seems, planes are flying on errands of mercy, drawing mankind closer together in bonds of sympathy and understanding. Not only in the service of stricken communities, but in the service of individuals who otherwise would be beyond the help of man.

For among the small items of the daily news we read of a child born three thousand feet above the dim coast of the Carolinas, as its mother is being carried to a mainland hospital . . . of a surgeon dropping from the sky through the rack and darkness of a north Pacific gale to save a wounded woman in Alaska . . . of a plane lifting a baby from a jungle village to the safety of Ancon Hospital in Panama, 250 miles away . . . of first-aid experts flying with their equipment from Washington to rescue entombed miners in Alabama . . .

So soon has this astounding miracle of man's conquest of the sky become an accepted fact of every-day life!

What may we expect next? Isn't it reasonable to expect that just as this federation of political states has been bound together by steel rails and surfaced highways, so the nations of the world will be brought into closer harmony when the skyways make possible smooth, safe transport from capital to capital . . . from the universities of one nation to . . . from the universities of another . . . from the industrial centers of one country to the markets of a neighbor? . . .

There is nothing visionary in this when considered against a background of achievement. Lindbergh's flight from Washington to the City of Mexico awoke all Central America to a new sense of nearness . . . to a friendlier understanding of neighbors . . . and to an immediate popular demand for regular air-lines connecting country with country.

The Ford Motor Company has sound industrial and commercial reasons for believing in a great epoch of air transport now being born. We measure our own achievement in terms of well over a million miles of useful commercial flying, and the safe transport of more than five million pounds of freight. And we are planning, building and operating our planes on the most advanced principles of safety, speed and economy of operation.

The great Ford Airport at Dearborn is the scene of continual and increasing activity. Passenger station . . . shops . . . research laboratories are pulsating gages of the progress being made. It is the Ford policy to plan in advance for great expansion.

Who has not thrilled with thoughts of the golden pathways that lead across the fenceless sky?

1928

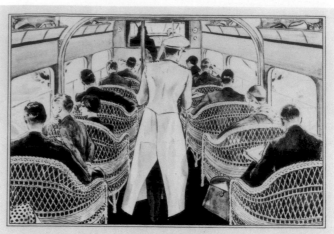

FIRST TIME UP!

You settle back in your wicker chair a little nervously as the engines roar. Then a burst of speed across the flying-field! Forty miles an hour . . . fifty-five! Someone shouts:

"Watch the wheels!"

Unless your eyes are fixed on the great balloon tires no perception tells when you have left the earth. There is only an astonishing feeling of stability; then comfortable relaxation as the motors are throttled down. The giant, tri-motored car moves upward on a cushioning ramp of air. . . .

Gradually you experience a sensation that is certainly one of the most extraordinary man has ever felt. You are transcending human nature. You feel immeasurably superior to the crawling beings in the miniature world immersed in silence two thousand feet below. Though ordinarily you may suffer from fear of heights, this fear does not touch you now, for there are no lines of perspective drawing you earthward!

Streets, monuments, buildings, vehicles and living creatures, are fractions of inches in size. Hedgerows, fences, and symmetrically plowed fields of red and brown earth form rug-like patterns, while distance gives the raw surfaces a velvety texture.

Boats, moving along a river the color of green onyx, push threads of cotton from their bows. Trains wind through the hills with lazy deliberation. Automobiles creep along ribboned roads. Sheep, cattle, horses graze heads downward in the fields, unaware that you are watching from the sky.

The air of other-worldliness that hangs over the earth below is emphasized by the fact that you are hardly aware of forward motion, though moving twice as fast as the fastest express trains, and it is as easy to stand poised on one foot in the cabin as on the floor of your own bedroom. Your fellow passengers move freely about, shifting the ten wicker chairs companionably, to play cards, to typewrite, to make sketches, or, gathering in groups, first on one side of the plane, then on the other, to study the panorama below.

You soon accept the truth of the reported safety of these giant commercial planes. What if a motor fails? With two, the plane can continue to its destination! If two fail—the remaining motor can extend the angle of descent to cover an area almost half the size of Delaware. And if all three fail the plane has a gliding range of miles.

Ford tri-motored, all-metal planes have demonstrated railroad efficiency for over a million miles of flight, carrying mail, freight and passengers . . . in tropical regions, in arctic regions, at sea level and over the highest mountain ranges on this continent.

Events of the last twelve months have put commercial flying in America on the level of stable industries. Great businesses have accepted it as a dependable means of swift transport, cutting two-thirds off railroad time. Business men no longer think of the mere thrill of "going up"; they think rather in terms of profitable service.

In the modern business world, the dawn of each new day presents a different scene . . . new products, new competition, new markets. To meet its challenge, you must be prepared. When the occasion comes for your first time up, it will not be to "joy-ride" in an antiquated and hazardous machine; but far more probably it will be to reach some distant meeting-place in advance of business competition!

1928

Ford experimented with Stout's design, starting with two engines and then adding a third, in pursuit of his traditional fetish for reliability. The ultimate result was the famous Ford Tri-motor which could take off with two engines and fly with one, and which was to become one of the safest airplanes ever designed. Ford got it into production in 1927, and almost every American airline started its business with the shining, corrugated aluminum Ford Tri-motor. Ford knew that he did not need to sell the aviation companies on the advantages of his machines, but he needed to sell the American public on the advantages of aviation. He therefore began a series of seventeen classic ads explaining "what flying would be like" for the common man. Neither Ford nor his ad writers really knew. When the ads began, the scheduled airlines of America owned a total of twelve planes, none older than six months.

Surprisingly, this drawing is completely accurate. Henry Ford himself suggested putting the pilots and "flight escorts" in uniforms. The moveable wicker chairs were used for the first three years, when they were replaced with aluminum-framed, leather chairs. Note width of individual units in comparison to present-day seating specifications. The windows were glass with sliding elements for opening by the passenger. Cruising speed: 105 miles an hour.

ending to the story—an odd outcome for an advertising campaign that had been so successful it was recognized by almost all literate Americans, and was quoted and discussed in editorials, books, and boardrooms in every community. The campaign's assumptions resulted in legislation, huge capital investments by local governments, and a sense of general familiarity by the man in the street. Yet in 1930 the Ford Motor Company built and sold only nine airplanes. In 1931 they unloaded fifteen, but in 1933 they sold their final two and went out of the aviation business forever.

No one has fully explained what went wrong. Depending on which aviation historian you believe, Ford's early involvement and his ultimate abandonment came from a mixture of: the Depression which hit the young airlines hard (on many major routes scheduled flights flew without a single passenger aboard); the fact that Douglas and Boeing were developing much more efficient two-engine planes which the Fords suspected would be the shape of the future; the fact that Harry Brooks, the son of Henry Ford's closest friend, was killed while demonstrating a new "Flying Flivver" at Henry's personal request; or that for the first time Ford's labor problems—coupled with the need to introduce a new automobile to fend off growing attacks from General Motors—were demanding Henry's full attention. Whatever the reasons, in July 1932, the Fords let anyone who had had automotive manufacturing experience go back to the production lines, and fired the rest of the 1,600 employees who had designed and built the 200 Tri-motors. Thus, having

LIFT UP YOUR EYES !

How long ago did Orville Wright circle the drill field at Fort Myer while a few score of astonished witnesses stared open-mouthed at the sight of this first man to fly with wings for more than an hour? . . .

How long ago did the intrepid Bleriot hop in his flimsy, scorched monoplane from France to land precariously on the cliffs of Dover? . . .

How long ago did Graham-White circle the Statue of Liberty, struggling dexterously with his hands to maintain equilibrium? . . .

It seems only yesterday!

Yet in the few brief years since then man has learned a new technic in existence. He has explored the earth's atmosphere, his noble machine climbing on after human faculties had failed. . . . He has skimmed lightly over the impenetrable ice barriers of the polar regions. . . . He has taken in his flight not only the gray, fog-blanketed waters of the North Atlantic, but the empty blue seas of the South Atlantic—the Mediterranean—the Pacific—the Indian Ocean—the

Gulf of Mexico. . . . He has soared confidently over the sands of Sahara and the Great Arabian Desert, where only the camel had dared venture before. . . . He has skimmed the terrible dark jungles of the Amazon, and scaled high above the silent places of Alaska. . . . He has flown in squadrons from the Cape of Good Hope to London. . . . In squadrons he has circled South America. . . . *In squadrons he has circumnavigated the globe!*

And in the ordinary routine of transportation service he travels on fixed schedules over airways that streak the skies of Europe and North America. Mail. Passengers. Express. The world is rapidly assigning special duties to this safe vehicle that cuts time in two.

Is there any epoch in all history that has been so sudden in growth from birth to universal achievement? . . . so dramatic in its nature and accomplishments? . . . so rich in promises for the future?

Perhaps the most significant thing in

the great accomplishment of young Colonel Lindbergh is that in him the world sees *the first outstanding example of a generation that is born air-conscious!* Just as the past generation was born to steam, accepting railway transportation as an accomplished fact—and just as the present generation has accepted the automobile as a customary vehicle—so does the rising generation lift up its eyes to the skies! It may be hard still for many of us to accept the fact, but it is certain that the aeroplane will give as great an impetus to advancing civilization as did the automobile.

In this firm belief the Ford Motor Company is devoting its activities and resources to solving the problems that still face commercial aviation. In factory equipment, in laboratory experiment, in actual flights, the Ford Motor Company is establishing a foundation for one of the greatest industries in the world has yet known. Within the last two years pilots have flown over the established Ford air routes, carrying freight, on regular daily schedules, a distance of more than 700,000 miles.

1928

Each of the ads in the series focused on a single aspect of what flying would be like. The copy was written by William Ashley Anderson of N.W. Ayer and Son, with "technical assistance" from the airplane's designer, William B. Stout, himself. With very little hard data, the copy was filled with dots and exclamation marks, but their readership and recall record put the series in everyone's list of The Hundred Greatest Advertisements. In this one, the theme read: "Just as the past generation was born to steam, accepting railway transportation as an accomplished fact—and just as the present generation has accepted the automobile as a customary vehicle—so does the rising generation lift up its eyes to the skies!" Charles Lindbergh's trans-Atlantic flight in May 1927, had a great impact on the nation's thinking. "If Lindy can do it on one engine, I ought to be safe behind three."

HARBORS AND PHANTOM PORTS

WHILE Chambers of Commerce labor earnestly for deeper river channels to bring them closer to the seaboard, and political wars are waged bitterly over preferential railroad rates that may jeopardize the markets of inland and isolated towns, *a thousand dry-land ports have suddenly appeared with wharves open to business from all the world!*

A thousand communities have at least sensed the opportunity for a place of importance upon the new map being drawn of channels and harbors that open to the sky. It is significant that upon these charts many great coastal harbors are conspicuously absent. For the ships of the air, following laws that have always governed the development of permanent transportation systems, *are being drawn only to the most efficient terminals.*

At whatever hour of the day or night this message reaches your eyes, somewhere above the United States planes are carrying commercial cargo at a hundred miles an hour to scheduled destinations. *These planes must have suitable landing fields.*

In the early days of automobiles, the stigma "bad roads" stuck to communities that failed

to grasp the need for better roads to smooth the way for the new machine. "Bad harbor facilities" have ruined many a promising seaport town. "Inefficient railway service" has hampered the development of cities that might have become important commercial centers. And now that a new and revolutionary leap forward is being taken in transportation, the towns and cities of today are going to be powerfully influenced by the degree of attention they pay to air-ports.

There are still less than 250 municipal airports worthy of the name. There are almost as many commercial and private ports. There are somewhat less than a hundred maintained by the Army and Navy. More than 3000 "phantom ports," improperly equipped, are of use only as emergency landing fields.

Few American air-ports can yet compare to the European "world-ports" of Croydon, LeBourget, Tempelhof. Great cities like New York are awakening to the full significance of this; though it still takes as long to get from a New York flying-field to the heart of the city as it does to fly from New York to Philadelphia. The really notable American

air-ports are being built in inland cities such as Detroit, Cleveland, Chicago, St. Paul, Salt Lake City, Wichita and Cheyenne.

What does all this mean to you? If you are a man of broad industrial and commercial interests, your traffic managers, forwarding departments and general sales managers can answer you best. *It is of vital importance to American business to promote and maintain efficient municipal air-ports!*

When the New York-Atlanta Air Mail was inaugurated in May, instead of one, two ships were required to take 32,000 pieces of mail from New York and Philadelphia. Business men had realized at once the value of a night mail service that would insure delivery in Atlanta at the same time as in New York.

Those who hesitate to employ the airplane will do well to recall that there are still many old-timers who refuse to ride in automobiles!

The great Ford all-metal, tri-motored planes, carrying millions of pounds of freight, transporting scores of thousands of passengers, flying on extended missions from the tropics to Arctic seas, have known no accidents to passengers!

1928

Here the theme is: ". . . a thousand dry-land ports have suddenly appeared with wharves open to business from all the world! . . .

"What does all this mean to you? If you are a man of broad industrial and commercial interests, your traffic managers, forwarding departments and general sales managers can answer you best. It is of vital importance to American business to promote and maintain efficient municipal air-ports!"

---

introduced America to "what flying will mean to you," the Fords stepped off the stage and watched the continuing development of American aviation as detached spectators.

There is an unusual footnote to the story, however: what finally happened to those 200 airplanes. They flew on and on. After their role was taken over by the Douglas DC-2 and the Boeing 247, like Washington streetcars and New York buses, they went south to Mexico and Central America, and then twenty years later they flowed to Asia and South America—and kept on flying right into the 1970s. They were almost indestructible.

One of the aviation historians, William L. Larkins, set out to trace every one of the original 200 (each had its registration number, which was carried with it from country

to country). While most of them went on from year to year and continent to continent, even the ones that came to abrupt ends, did it with a peculiar flourish. Many of Larkin's brief biographies read like the diary of Indiana Jones. Sample:

No. NC-8418
Ended April 1, 1931
Ovalle, Chile
A Pan American Airways inspection party walked away from a crash-landing at a one-way Chilean government airport, bounded by high cliffs of the Andes and strong cross winds. The pilot elected to dig a wing into the ground and cartwheel the plane rather than crash into the base of the cliff. [The *New York Times*

This ad wanted to invite women to fly, but the pre-Women's Liberation text was clearly written by a man. A portion:

"While man concerns himself with problems of engineering, and takes an artisan's pleasure in the mechanics of aviation and the organization of transport services, woman is swept aloft by the poetry of flight!

"The spirit of modern woman is a free spirit that looks to the adventure of the skies with unreasoning exaltation. The spectacular drama and glamorous thrill of flight has caught her imagination [. . .] a dazzling Peri leaping into the empyrean while the world of fact sinks below in its clouds of dust and smog. . . . For man no longer flies alone!"

1929

reported:] "All three engines were torn off and the fuselage crumpled like paper, but Clifford Travis, the pilot, saved the lives of the six persons in the cabin, all of whom were out of the plane within 30 seconds of final impact, climbing through the windows. . . ."

No. CV-FAI
Ended April 17, 1931
Mihinia, India
The plane hit a vulture in flight, damaging the engine cowl, and landed at Bamrauli Airport. The decision was made to refuel and continue on to Calcutta. The plane took off . . . and about an hour later hit another vulture, with the left wing, damaging the plane so badly that an immediate landing was considered necessary. This was done in a plowed field near the village of Mihinia about 45 miles east of Benares, India. In landing the plane turned over, ruptured an overhead gas tank, and the plane caught fire. [The *New York Times* reported:] "All four, including Prince Bibesco, escaped with various injuries."

No. NC-400H
June 11, 1934
Near Junin, Argentina
This Pan American-Grace Ford was flying in heavy rain when it made a forced landing in Mar Chiquita, a

lake near Junin, Buenos Aires Province, Argentina. Five were killed and five injured. The survivors sat on the wings for four hours until rescued. [The aircraft finally sank, but it was eventually brought to the surface, salvaged, and put back into operation four years later. The registration numbers were changed, however, and Larkins lost track of the unit.]

So what have we seen here? Three products designed to make money for their inventors. The camera could have been introduced and explained over counters by dedicated camera clerks, but clean, clear, honest, and straightforward advertising immensely telescoped the process and accelerated the satisfaction experienced by the amateur photographer. The trivial safety razor, honestly introduced and sold by Gillette's ads, mitigated the psychic irritations if not the dermal of the common man, and surely contributed to his comfort and well-being. The Ford advertising in some ways is the most unusual of the three, since it was describing something that had never been, and promising something that could only be guessed at at the time it was written and run. Yet it too was essentially honest and straightforward, trying to sell something the inventors genuinely believed would be a benefit to society (albeit a source of profit for themselves). The fact that their guesses proved remarkably accurate while they themselves abandoned the challenge makes it all the more intriguing.

WHEN FLEDGLINGS FLY

You've seen, perhaps, the robins pushing fledglings from their nest in spring . . the flurry of feathers, the frenzied teeterings, the terrified chatter, and then erratic swoops to fearful landings on some leafy shrub. . . . You've seen them later in the summer when you've become aware suddenly of a new beauty in the plump young robins singing lustily upon the lawn. . . .

If the Spirit of Conquest that launched the fledglings out into the world had ever faltered in courage or instinctive resourcefulness, you'd never hear the flute-like song of robins against the locusts' rasping violins.

Fledgling man is today launching himself into a new world of space. We can as yet see only the daring flights of those who lead the way across the skies. But who can say what argosies will sail along the paths where they first winged their way? *Were it not for the ambitious urge in the hearts of brave men,*

we would never see the conquest of the sky . . . we would never lift our faces from the brown still earth!

Were it not for bold hearts and quick, shrewd resourcefulness, we would have no skyscrapers reaching to the stars, no lacy bridges high over hungry floods, no tunnels through the darkness of the earth and rock below us, no roads of stone and steel, no webs of wire to guide the fluent lightning to our needs. . . .

In the life and growth of civilization, courage and quick, shrewd resourcefulness are the weapons of men, of businesses, and of communities, that achieve success. Even dollars and opportunities are but fledglings that must be launched with confidence and courage into a hostile world, sustained by everlasting energy and resourcefulness.

Who then are the courageous pioneers of today in our population of 120,000,000? Are

not the greatest of them the men who dare to launch and fly our winged ships of the air? Are they not the men who build the flying-fields, nests for these giant birds, upon the ragged fringes of blind and torpid cities? Are they not the captains of industry, of commerce, of transportation who are showing civilization safe ways across the free sky?

The services of airplanes are multiplying astonishingly. Progress, measured by months, has been breathlessly rapid. Already it is becoming impracticable to make forecasts, for stupendous accomplishments outdistance them. Our own tri-motored planes, in our own service have already carried well over six million pounds of freight; and the same kind of planes, operated by The Stout Air Services from the Ford Field at Detroit, have carried over sixty thousand passengers!

Those of us rising with the Dawn have already seen Winged Victory in the skies!

1929

In mid-century America, purchasable cosmetics were essentially limited to scents and hair dressings. Respectable persons would wear nothing that changed their God-given appearance. Here the firm of Apollos W. Harrison could claim genuine musk cologne because he owned the only two musk deer "ever imported alive into this country."

1857

A beautifully engraved, high Victorian Gothic ad, which gives the effect of three dimensions. Changing the color of hair was permitted at this time, and this Baltimore barber is offering his dye to men and women. The dye was named after Circassian women (from the Black Sea area) who were reputed to be so beautiful that they were the favorites of the Turkish Sultan's harem.

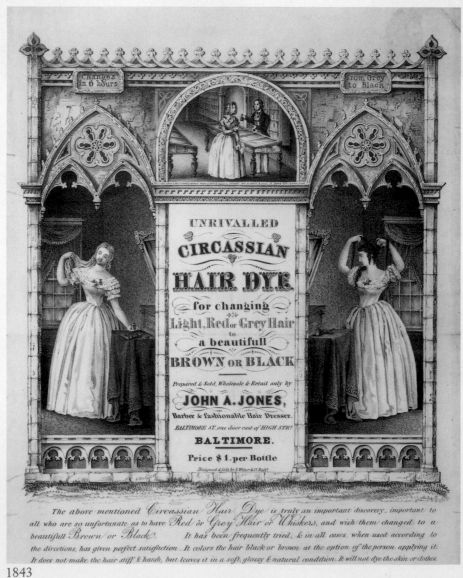

1843

Cosmetics—
How to Attract the Opposite Sex

IN OUR BOOK we have focused on the first two hundred years of advertising in the Republic, and thus we begin with 1789. This causes us to miss the brisk trade in cosmetic ads of the late colonial days. They filled the newspaper columns, right up there with land, stage schedules, and patent medicines. From 1750 to the Revolution, the Williamsburg and New York and Boston papers were full of products that guaranteed the reader to look like the highest fashion of aristocratic London and Paris.

White powder was sold by the pound in major quantities for the face and hair. Face powder was made of white lead (from lead plates immersed in vinegar and then scraped into dust); hair powder was made from ground rice (which gradually turned brown in firelight and candle fumes). Ads for beauty patches were common, and shipments of rouge and lipstick were received and announced regularly. The patches (which were primarily used to cover pock marks), were described as coming in fascinating shapes, and the rouge and lipstick could be had either in ground lead or plaster of Paris, each tinted with a variety of vegetable dyes.

Perfumes and toilet water were advertised for men and women, and with the difficulty of cleaning the brocaded and embroidered clothes (plus the erratic bathing of either sex), apparently the scents were sold as a necessity not a luxury. Yardley's lavender water appears in ads throughout the later colonial years, and seems to have moved like a staple. Then came the Revolution.

It started with the boycotts of English goods, quickly followed by plain, republican, homespun cloth, plain hair, and no cosmetics of any kind as a matter of principle. Paris too went republican, with any form of body paint smacking of the aristocrats, and its use not only being out of fashion but actually life-threatening. During the first thirty years of the American Republic, the only form of cosmetic advertising was for pomades (North African waxes and American bear grease) to control the hair.

Once the reaction to aristocratic artifice passed, fashion again looked toward London and Paris, but by then Wordsworthian Romanticism had arrived with its demure and natural look, followed by the well-scrubbed face and ringlet hair of Bronte time. Queen Victoria appeared and for her long reign no artificial cosmetics were tolerated for respectable women; anything applied to the skin could come only from home concoctions put on and taken off in the privacy of the bedroom. The favorites were lemon in water to "freshen" the skin of face, neck, and arms, and lard and water to soften hands. Again with the exception of hair dressings, up to mid-century there was nothing to sell, and therefore nothing to advertise.

In 1846 Theron T. Pond, a Utica, N.Y., chemist extracted some sap of the witch hazel tree, whipped in some water and called it "Pond's Extract." With the money that this balm made, the firm expanded and so did its product line with the manufacture of a plain, white, traditional cold cream. (In the second century A.D., the Greek physician Galen had whipped water into molten beeswax and olive oil for use as a softening cream for the hands. We now use mineral oil instead of olive oil with some borax to whiten the mix, but otherwise it is essentially still the original recipe.) The company's new product became Pond's Cleansing Cold

For Preserving & Dressing The
HAIR.

1860

Glycerine was a by-product of soap-making at the time and was an effective hair oil. It was shiny, moistening, and, since it absorbed water from the air, would keep its look of freshness through what is apparently here anticipated as an evening at the theater. Note opera glasses in the pouch.

1898

By 1898, face rouge and hair tint were permitted for elderly women, but only actresses wore lip rouge and eyebrow liner. Nice women could powder their shoulders, and a little scent on the handkerchief had always been both permitted and expected. This stunning model is selling "Parisian Rose" Perfume.

BEAUTIFUL
WOMEN CHEW
Primley's
CALIFORNIA FRUIT
Chewing Gum

And why shouldn't they? Gum is no longer considered fit for children only; people of the greatest refinement now enjoy it. Since PRIMLEY'S CALIFORNIA FRUIT GUM has become known, its delicious fruit flavor surpassing all others, people cannot say too much for it.

1893

The question of cause and effect has long been blurred in such campaigns as the modern Cover Girl cosmetics. Does the beautiful model use Cover Girl because she is beautiful or is she beautiful because she uses Cover Girl? J.P. Primley suggested the dilemma here on the back page of Collier's in 1893.

It Puts Off Old Age
by nourishing the entire system.
Quaker Oats makes your blood tingle; nerves strong and steady; brain clear and active; muscles powerful. It makes flesh rather than fat, but enough fat for reserve force.
It builds children up symmetrically into brainy and robust men and women.
You can work on Quaker Oats It stays by you.
At all grocers in 2 lb. Packages only.

1902

It was originally permissible to use barely detectable cosmetics to cover the hints of aging. In 1902, Quaker Oats got to the heart of the problem and pushed aging itself back. It is here declared to make your blood tingle, and to make flesh rather than fat—but enough fat for reserve force. Most surprisingly it promised to build "children up symmetrically. . . ."

The dye job here is clearly a triumph in the eyes of the satisfied customer. Note the unusual type treatment on J.J. Kromer. This distortion of perspective and "arcing" is now done with a Fotomaster camera. In 1864 it was done by hand.

1864

Beyond the early use of color to demonstrate the effects of the cosmetic, the surprisingly detailed explanation of how to shampoo your hair is noteworthy here. Cause? Up to this point, middle America was still washing its hair with bar soap. Bottled liquid was considered unnecessarily expensive and self-indulgent.

Your Hair Appears Twice as Beautiful—*when Shampooed this way*

Try this quick and simple method which thousands now use. See the difference it makes in the appearance of your hair.

Note how it gives new life and lustre, how it brings out all the wave and color. See how soft and silky, bright and glossy your hair will look.

1925

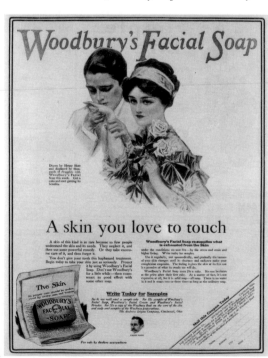

1911

This ad, which appeared in the May 6, 1911, Saturday Evening Post, is thought to be the earliest form of the famous slogan, "A skin you love to touch." John H. Woodbury's head had been a registered trademark since 1891, and was already well enough known to appear in burlesque routines and humor columns as The Neckless Head. Woodbury's was one of the first to market a skin soap as distinct from just soap.

1916

The nineteenth-century tradition of making cosmetics in the home was still active as shown in this 1916 Sunkist ad. Sunkist was the trademark of the Southern California Fruit Exchange, which had been organized in 1893. The brand name was adopted in 1908, and was remarkably candid about its "Practically Seedless" Lemons.

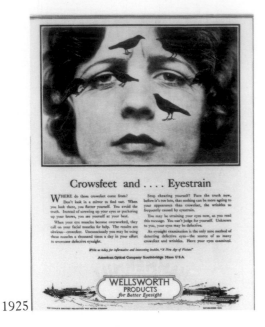

A longtime problem graphically presented by the American Optical Company.

Comedones—at least one of the world's ills which no longer seem to be among advertising's major concerns. In the 1920s and 1930s, many such threats to our well-being (and explanations for failure to get a raise, an invitation, a mate) appeared. Comedones joined such copywriters' problems as halitosis (bad breath), pityrosporum ovale (dandruff), and tinea trichophyton (athlete's foot).

Cream, which in turn became one of the longest-lived and most useful cosmetics ever invented.

In 1859, a kerosene dealer in Brooklyn heard about the Titusville oil strike, and went out to get some cheap kerosene. Instead of the coal oil, he found the oil field workers claiming wonder cures from some fatty grease that accumulated on the drill rods. The grease was described as unusually effective as a salve for curing cuts and burns. Robert Chesebrough returned to Brooklyn with the paraffin-like stuff, and once he figured out how to produce it from raw crude oil, Vaseline Petroleum Jelly was born. Vasel comes from the German *wasser*, for water, and ine from *elaion*, Greek for olive oil. Between Pond's Cold Cream and Chesebrough's Vaseline, the first truly American products were created which would meet the definition of The Food, Drug, and Cosmetic Act of 1938. According to the law, cosmetics were

articles intended to be rubbed, poured, sprinkled, or sprayed on, introduced into, or otherwise applied to the human body or any part thereof for cleansing, beautifying, promoting attractiveness, or altering the appearance . . . except that such term shall not include soap.

"Gone with the Wind" Cosmetics

By the Civil War, most purchased cosmetics were bought by men in barber shops. The beauty aids demonstrated by Scarlett O'Hara were historically accurate. Women were expected to keep their skin as white as possible with hats and veils, and redden their lips and cheeks by biting the former and pinching the latter. Sarah Josepha Hale, the editor of *Godey's Lady's Book*, like most upper-class women of the time, made her own cosmetics. She included the recipe for her hand lotion (lard, rose water, and coconut milk) in the magazine, and recommended her own bedtime beauty treatment: she soaked brown butcher's paper in apple vinegar and laid strips on her temples and across her eyes to "ward off crow's feet."

The major advertising of the products was directed to the males. They were permitted to grease, dye, and condition their hair, mustaches, and sideburns, and newspaper ads were frequently targeted as much at the barber as the customer. The following is an ad from 1851. Henshaw, Edmands & Co. of No. 36 Indian Street, Boston, Mass., were offering:

Bear's Oil	gal.	2.00
Buffalo Oil, for the hair	doz.	1.75
Cologne water, real Farina's	doz.	2.62
Freckle Wash	doz.	3.00
Gilman's Liquid Instantaneous Hair Dye	doz.	8.00
Hair Powder, perfumed, French ½ lb. papers	lb.	12.00
Indian Hair Dye	doz.	4.00
Lavendar Water, fancy	doz.	1.25

Macassar Oil, genuine	doz.	8.00
Macassar Oil, imitation	doz.	.62
Toilet Powder, perfumed	doz.	1.00

With the close of the Civil War, American inventiveness began to focus on the cosmetic tradition, and a series of American discoveries affected cosmetics everywhere. In 1866, one Henry Tetlow discovered that oxide of zinc, intended for artists' paints, when dried and ground made an excellent face powder base. It was harmless and cheap and is still the basis for makeup powder. Soon after, talcum powder was invented. This is simply magnesium silicate ground up, and it has since been dusted on hundreds of millions of babies and recently-bathed adults.

As the nineteenth century closed, cosmetics began to proliferate. Elderly women were permitted to tint their hair (hair was worn in great swirls in those days of the Gibson Girl and Lillian Russell), and women were permitted to powder their arms and décolletage without their morals being questioned. Theatrical stars and opera singers left their stage make-up on when they appeared in the streets, so when the convulsion of style change appeared at the outbreak of World War I, the average woman knew what lipstick, rouge, and eyeliner were supposed to look like. (Mascara had been introduced to the States by Empress Eugenie when she visited Newport and Saratoga toward the end of the century; and Florence Nightingale Graham opened her first New York Salon for beauty skin care. After it became very popular, she changed her name to Elizabeth Arden.)

World War I really began the cosmetics industry. Hair was cut short when the maid who helped comb it each day went into the munitions factory, and the independents of the women's emancipation movement bobbed it to assert their new freedom. When the war was over, the liberation of style continued by abandoning the hour-glass figure of 1915 for the flat-chested, short-skirted silhouette of 1920. Heavy, bright, glossy lipstick painted in a Cupid's bow dramatized the mouth, eyebrows were plucked, and mascara was brushed along the Flapper's lashes.

Before the war, a Parisian hairdresser by the name of Marcel had started to arrange hair in symmetrical waves (set with hot curling irons), and by the war's end, Charles Nestlé had invented the electric heat and chemical permanent wave and made it cheap enough that "shopgirls can afford it." Lip rouge had been sold in pots and spread by the fingertips at the opening of the war; the first lip*sticks* were produced by the Scovil Manufacturing Company of Waterbury, Connecticut, during the war, and were available as solid, extendable bullets by the early Twenties.

Advertising fell all over itself trying to keep up with the new products, the new colors, the new beauty shops, the new styles of hair, makeup, and textures. Very quickly, the advertisers found that it was easier to follow the images of the most successful movie stars than to try to show the customers how they should look and which cosmetics would

1928

A classic case of advertising going for the throat. The image of "tiny criss-cross lines" giving "your throat a crepe-like texture" is imaginatively graphic, with the reinforcing "crepy throats" to set the neologism.

achieve the end they sought. Thus the ads showed the Clara Bow look, then the Jean Harlow and Claudette Colbert image, and finally the Norma Shearer and Madeleine Carroll open-faced, white teeth and large-mouth style—with pale lips but flaming fingernails. World War II used Rita Hayworth as the model, and the Fifties showed the customer Audrey Hepburn with pale lipstick but large, dramatized eyes. Obviously, the advertisers shifted styles and colors as quickly as required.

By the Sixties, color was out and suntan was in, and the cosmetics of appearance began to meet the working chemicals. Tanning lotions ultimately gave way to sunscreens. Deodorants (which are antiseptics controlling odor-producing bacteria) yielded to anti-perspirants which prevent the perspiration from appearing in the first place.

By our own time, the advertising researchers have determined that the average customer is using between eleven and twelve cosmetics at any one time. The classic cold cream of a hundred years ago is the base for (with minor modifications)

He remembered—

That Schoolgirl Complexion

1928

"That Schoolgirl Complexion" was another of the classic cosmetic slogans of the interwar period. Palmolive was the other personal soap (along with Woodbury's) which broke away from the generic soap stream. Palmolive was actually invented in 1898 and named after its constituent oils.

foundation cream, astringent cream, cleansing cream, hormone cream, vanishing cream, lanolin cream, nourishing cream, and marrow cream. Color variations for powder, eye makeup, lipsticks, and nail polish have reached such a point that a single company may be producing over 300 shades of identified, named, and formulated reds at any single time. (Automation has vastly assisted the industry. Mabelline, for example, mixes its Great Lash in 500-gallon vats which yield 120,000 packages of .43 fluid ounces with each production batch.)

Thus we meet the cosmetic advertiser's greatest challenge. How does he differentiate his product from his competitors' when both are so very much alike? Early in the game (in the Teens and Twenties), the copy pressed hard on convenience and how well the cosmetic held up. "No messy . . . ," "Never hardens," "The delicate fragrance lasts. . . ."

This approach was followed by emphasis on health and aging in the Thirties and Forties. "Never irritates," "Good

for your skin," "Keeps that schoolgirl complexion." By the Fifties and Sixties, the emphasis was on the beauty of the models shown using the product, and total integration of hair style, bone structure, the color of eyelids, lipstick, and fingernails.

By the Seventies and Eighties, the advertisers had essentially given up describing how or why their products worked, and instead hinted at the "experience." Perfume makers showed fantasy scenes that permitted the user to imagine her own dream sequence which might result from the use of the product. Since it was impossible to describe the difference between the actual scents, a great deal of time and money was spent on the packaging, so when the customer thought of the trade name, she immediately thought of a particular bottle or the color of the carton. Instead of selling the innovative new contents or the purity of the ingredients as is typically done for new product lines (we rarely hear of a breakthrough in eosin, for example, the red crystalline flourescent dye in lipstick wax, or a quicker acting titanium dioxide in the fatty acid, glossy brands), the cosmetic advertiser instead employed the "Modess Method," showing the product name in large, uniquely drawn letters, with the copy limited to variations on the word, "because . . ." followed by real or implied suspension marks. The customer was permitted to fill in the reasons for purchase, based on her confidence in the product line and the beauty of the models shown using it. Men were shown simply patting lotion on their face and shouting, "I needed that."

The nearest approach to announcing the latest chemical content is the surprisingly straightforward device of putting a sample of a perfume on a sealed piece of paper and inserting it in the customer's catalog or magazine. The first of these "fragrance strips" appeared in 1984, and quickly became increasingly common to the point where as many as three brands have been inserted in a single magazine, thus producing an unusual blend once all three have been ripped and sampled. With the success of the perfume, strips containing a variety of lipsticks, blushes, mascara, and nail polish soon followed. While the device is arresting, the impact is not cheap. A perfume strip was costing five cents each in 1988, and mascara strips ran ten cents apiece—times, of course, the hundreds of thousands of copies in the press run.

The Law

If the cosmetic advertiser's major problem is coming up with ways of differentiating his product from his competitor's, his second largest is staying within the law—in this case the boundaries of the regulatory agencies' guidelines.

Cosmetics were supposed to be included in the original Pure Food and Drug Act of 1906, but during the early markup they were dropped for fear that their presence might trivialize the serious intent of the rest of the bill. Various health and consumer groups began to press for changes in this situation in the early Thirties, and ultimately the Food,

"Particularly when a 'close-up' is being made do I appreciate the California lemon rinse. Under the strong studio lights the slightest imperfections seem magnified many, many times. That's when everything has to be just right."

Betty Compson

"I always feel that I can do myself justice only when I have full confidence in my appearance. When my hairdresser uses a lemon rinse after my shampoo, I know that my hair is at its very best."

Marian Nixon

"I am very particular about the treatment my hair receives. Everyone who appears before the camera has to be. That is why I never consider my shampoo really complete without a lemon rinse after it."

Mary Nolan

"If I were making a list of beauty suggestions, I would place the lemon rinse right up close to the top. I know my own hair is much more 'satisfying' when I use it."

Constance Bennett

Lemon rinse *Reflects the Charm* in your hair

"THE *REAL* SECRET of beautiful hair is simplicity itself!"

Hollywood's glorious stars, who know beauty as others know their A-B-C's, say this.

"Hair and scalp must first be really and truly *clean!*"

Shampoos alone, they find, are not enough. Soap removes the dirt and grease *but forms curds on the hair.* It leaves behind a sticky, luster-dimming film. As long as it remains,

the natural beauty of your hair is hidden.

Ordinary water rinsings will not remove soap curds. Yet they yield readily to the fresh lemon rinse.

So use this simple method. After a first rinsing in clear, warm water, use the fresh juice of two California Sunkist Lemons in a quart of water. Rub thoroughly into scalp. Then rinse again with clear, cold water.

Hair and scalp thus rinsed are really clean. All hair is soft and silky—*alive* with natural charm. Whether it is bobbed, or long—straight or wavy—blonde, brunette or auburn—it is better for this treatment. For lemon cannot *change* the hair itself in any way. It merely *finds* the brilliance you have allowed soap curds to hide.

Sunkist
California
Lemons

Buy them by the dozen for their many uses

FREE—
Book of Natural Beauty Methods

Send coupon now for new, *free* booklet, "Lemon, the Natural Cosmetic". Read interesting facts beauty experts have spent years to learn. Discover how you can have prettier hair, skin and hands by simple, natural methods—at home or at your beauty shop.

Since lemons are useful in so many ways it pays always to have a dozen on hand. To be sure of dependable quality, ask for California Sunkist Lemons. They are fresh in your market every day in the year—wrapped in tissue bearing "Sunkist" trademark.

MADAM: *A copy of Rolf Armstrong's painting "The Reflection of Charm", suitable for framing—for 10¢, shipping cost.*

These beautiful, full-color reproductions disclose all the soft shadings of the original pastel. They are 12 by 19 inches in size, on heavy art paper, ready for framing. No advertising of any kind. Merely send coupon with 10 cents in stamps to cover part of packing and mailing costs. If you wish the beauty booklet *only,* send no stamps.

CALIFORNIA FRUIT GROWERS EXCHANGE, Dep. 1266-A.
Box 530, Station "C".
Los Angeles, California

☐ Please send FREE booklet, *Lemon, the Natural Cosmetic,* telling how to use Lemons for the skin, manicuring and for beautifying the hair.

☐ Enclosed 10 cents in stamps to cover mailing costs. Please send me the full-color reproduction of Rolf Armstrong's painting "The Reflection of Charm," suitable for framing. (No advertising.)

Name
Street
City   State

1930

A stunning fashion ad from Foote, Cone & Belding, still urging the use of Sunkist California Lemons —with the inevitable coupon to be sent in at the end. While the coupons of the 1920s and 1930s were somewhat intended to introduce samples of products to new customers, their primary purpose was to determine readership—what was the pulling power of this particular ad, and which of the magazines where it was placed drew the most send-backs for the dollars invested?

1966

Incredible how far man has evolved.

ROYAL PUB
by REVLON
Today's most virile cologne and after shave

1973

These two ads were created seven years apart. Question: Were they by two designers who accidentally hit on the same layout, or did the 1973 designer find the 1966 image in the files?

Drug, and Cosmetic Act was passed in 1938. Oversight was divided between the Food and Drug Administration and the Federal Trade Commission. (A blinding and a death from an eyeliner catastrophe had propelled Congress into action.)

The Food and Drug Administration watches over the use of certified dyes in the products, sees to it that the ingredients are listed on the packaging, and monitors any advertising statements that amount to "therapeutic claims" (which turn cosmetics into drugs). The latter are legal, but require documented proof of performance and safety.

The latest flurry of concern by the Food and Drug Administration arose in 1988 when the FDA felt that claims for "anti-aging" preparations had exceeded stated standards. The cosmetic producers had the choice of asking for drug approval or changing the language of their ads. The former is costly and time-consuming, so most of the companies opted for the latter, each following their own version of Harris O. Cutler's instructions to his corporation. (Cutler was division counsel of Olay products.) Words that could be used were:

Firms
Retexturizes
Smooths
Softens
Moisturizes
Promotes younger-looking skin

The following were abandoned and were now verboten:

Repairs skin
Maximizes oxygen uptake
Active biological ingredients
Speeds cell turnover
Strengthens skin's inner structure
Reverses the effect of age

The Federal Trade Commission concerns itself with false and misleading advertising and perceives itself as protecting both the consumer and the product's competitors. Given the enormous potential for damage claims, the major companies now invest as much care in quality control and product testing as any manufacturing group in the national economy.

Transgressions are miniscule in view of the size of the field. Indeed, cosmetics advertising not only sells the product, but would seem to be making a major contribution to the nation's sense of well-being. The purchasers of the product feel better using it, the models demonstrating its effectiveness fill the magazines and television screens with images of the most attractive of the nation's men and women,

1948

1969

The agency, Batten, Barton, Durstin & Osborne gave us the prize-winning line: "Which Twin has the Toni?" Home permanents for two dollars each were introduced following World War II, and the challenge was to assure the customer that she could actually get a beauty parlor equivalent herself; that nothing could go wrong; and that no one could tell the difference. The campaign achieved its purpose, sales boomed—and the idea of Toni parties actually was broadly embraced.

A technological innovation whose birth was assisted by the Delehanty, Kurnit & Gellner agency. In spite of the somewhat esoteric content of the copy, year-end research revealed that so many people had read every word of it—and remembered having done so—that it finished among the top recall ads of 1969.

One of advertising's most famous questions. It was created by Shirley Polykoff of Foote, Cone & Belding in 1955. Its original double entendre caused time-consuming concern within the agency, and then, once reluctantly approved, was refused by Life magazine's all-male managers. Polykoff convinced them they should poll the magazine's female staff and received a general endorsement for going with the ads. The campaign became an American classic, and the slogan was used for fifteen years.

1968

1986

1988

The first cosmetic ad we saw was selling musk in 1857 (see page 124). It tried to capture the reader's attention by showing two real live musk deer, the only ones in America. Coty and Jōvan here are still selling wild musk but are no longer interested in the cause, only the effect.

1987

A 1980s solution to the perpetual challenge, How do you explain how a perfume smells? The Calvin Klein ads present an inexplicable scene with unaccounted-for persons doing unknown things and leaving the whole image up to the viewer to do with it as he or she will. The suggestion of an erotic fantasy world peopled by the reader is supposed to imply that Obsession is equally beyond the realm of words or thoughts and only the customer can imagine what it may bring about. At least while the novelty lasted, it was very effective, taking a new and unknown brand of scent to the top of its market in a matter of months. The firm spent $17 million to launch Obsession, and it was selling $40 million of it within a year.

OPPOSITE:

A modern version of the 1898 "Parisian Rose" ad we saw on page 126.

and the tear-open perfume inserts leave our magazines and newsstands smelling like a perpetual Port Said Garden of Delight. Who could ask for more?

We thus come to the immortal words of Charles Revson of Revlon, Incorporated: "In the factory we make cosmetics; in the store we sell hope."

Nivea. For over seventy years, it's been appreciated by more women and men than any other moisturizer.

NIVEA Moisturizing Lotion

For Special Care of Your Skin

NIVEA Moisturizing Creme

Europe's Number One Moisturizer.

1986

This Saturday Afternoon,

Commencing at 2 o'clock P. M.,

A GRAND EXHIBITION OF SWIMMING AND DIVING

WILL TAKE PLACE AT

TERRACE BATHS, • • • • • ALAMEDA.

UNDER THE AUSPICES OF THE

Neptune Swimming and Boating Club,

OF SAN FRANCISCO.

ORDER OF CONTESTS:

1. Race for Boys under 16 years of age,............Gold Medal
2. Race for Amateurs who have never won a prize, 2 Gold Medals
3. Plain Diving, ...2 Gold Medals
4. Race for Amateurs who have won prizes,......2 Gold Medals
5. Fancy Diving,.......................................Gold Medal
6. Race for Professionals,..........................Cash Prize

MUSIC BY THE FIRST REGIMENT BAND.

1880

In 1880, travel for the ordinary man was pretty much limited to the excursion out to the edge of town. Nevertheless, the San Francisco Swimming Club was offering almost all the recreation one could hope for, and this ad surely achieved its purpose of getting the viewer up and off his front porch. (The quality of the wood engraving is impressive in itself.)

Faraway Places with Strange-Sounding Names

TRAVEL ADVERTISING is not intended to enrich the soul or push back the horizons of the sedentary American citizen. It is designed to make money. The way you make money in travel is to get the reader on his feet, out of the house, and on to someplace where you can convert his credit card into cash going into your account and out of his. In 1986, $1.1 billion was invested in such advertising, all of it trying to get the tourist up from his chair and on to the road. Of this $1.1 billion's worth of advertising, $625 million came from airlines, $127 million from cruise ship companies, $67 million from the cumulated states and the same amount from foreign countries. Thus nearly six times as much was spent touting *how* to get there as was spent glorifying what to see when you arrive.

Travel advertising may be the oldest form of paid space in American newspapers. The very earliest editions had announcements of where the stage/canalboat/ship was going and when it would leave. These appeared not only urging passage between towns, but on spur lines to vacation spots like Saratoga and White Sulphur Springs back in colonial times. George Washington took excursions to Berkeley Springs every year; Thomas Jefferson bought the already standing tourist cabins at the Natural Bridge in 1776 and installed several of his Monticello slaves to care for the overnight tourists. Printed announcements for these and similiar vacation spots appear in both Richmond and Williamsburg papers.

But mass travel didn't begin until after the Civil War and the development of the railroads. The travel merchant had exactly the same decisions to make in 1880 as he does today: how could he make his advertising money work best? Should he sell the excellence, safety, and convenience of his form of transport? Should he sell the marvels of some scenic or recreational attraction (and assume the only way the reader can get there is on the merchant's line)? Or should he sell the advantages of travel per se and hope the advertiser will simply get his share of the activity thus stirred up? The fashions in travel advertising kept swinging back and forth among these options, but oddly enough, rarely used more than any one theme at the same time. For a decade or so all travel ads would ring the changes on one accepted approach, and then abruptly everybody would be using another. Q. What should my travel ad look like? A. Let's see how everyone else is doing it.

The Excursion

The first travel ads after the Civil War were for a short trip just beyond the edge of town to the Chautauqua tent or the picnic pavilion where the band concert was to be held. The money to be made was on the food, rides, and intellectual improvement available. The ads were usually placed by the railroad or the interurban line—which also owned the park. The next step was for the railroad to examine its right-of-way to see if anything could be exploited: a lake, a mountain, a waterfall. The excursion had to be a one-day trip because nice singles didn't stay overnight, and married families with children could rarely afford it. The exception was the cottage at the beach or the cabin in the mountains, although these too had to be reached during the day with ample time to get to and from the station. Advertisements underlined the advantages: Boston hypochondriacs were told of the healthful benefits of the White Mountains, the Adirondacks, or the Thousand Islands. The White Mountain Railroad Line advertised "Safety and power . . . at the expense of speed, which is not sought." Walden Pond was perfect; Winnepesaukee was still a little far.

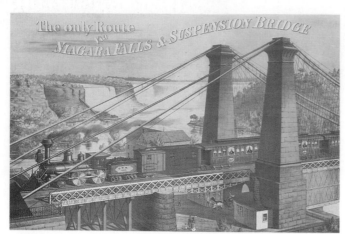

c. 1870

ABOVE:

As the trains got better, some of the natural wonders were within a long day's journey to nightfall. If you started at Albany or Cleveland or Pittsburgh, you could get to Niagara Falls by supper time and still get to bed at a respectable hour.

RIGHT:

It's 1885, and the Northern Pacific is urging delicate young ladies to come to Yellowstone Park. According to Oliver Jensen, who found this charming folder, "genteel Alice is staying at the Mammoth Hot Springs Hotel and writes a friend that she is still 'rubbing her eyes' at the wonders of the West. . . ." Small wonder—General Miles was chasing Geronimo with 1,500 men not too far away at the time, and the Battle of Wounded Knee was still five years ahead.

National Parks

The first national park, Yellowstone, was established in 1872, but it took more than ten years to get it ready for use and to get railroads close enough to deliver the people; but with it long-distance travel became attractive. Now travel was perceived as being educational, inspirational, and the right thing to do. The railroads pictured themselves as being responsible for making the opportunity available—and they quickly began advertising cross-country travel to increase the use of their passenger equipment. You only used a boxcar when there was something in it; passenger cars had to be sent whenever the timetable said the train ran whether there was anyone aboard or not. Advertising produced passengers who were the frosting on a cake that had to be baked anyhow.

The railroads, therefore, paid for most travel advertising up to World War I. Each line had its specialty. The Northern Pacific pushed Glacier National Park; the Southern extolled the Florida beaches; the Santa Fe not only claimed the Grand Canyon, but considered San Diego as its own. ("San Diego, that dreamy city of Mediterranean atmosphere and color, is terraced along the rim of a sheltered bay of surpassing beauty" according to one of its 1907 ads.) The Union Pacific, "The World's Pictorial Line," also claimed

1885

California farther north. As early as 1894, the U.P. was calling it "Our Italy—You Can Go to California in 67½ Hours" and enjoy the "Winter of Our Content." In very small print, this ad in *McClure's* explained that the sixty-seven-and-a-half hours were calculated from "Council Bluffs and Omaha."

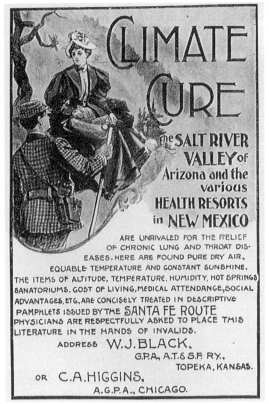

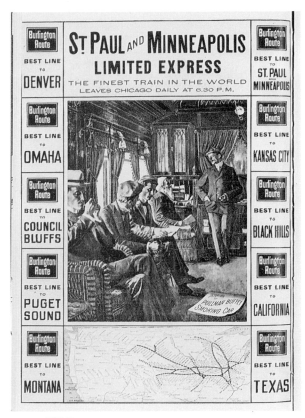

1888

This is a typical ad from McClure's magazine of 1888 (where all advertising copy was restricted firmly to the back of the book). In this case the Santa Fe Railroad is addressing persons with respiratory ills and their physicians about the very real health benefits of the desert Southwest.

1893

The preferred way to Florida, leaving New York every other day, and Boston every fourth day. The boat design was eclectic with a steam-driven screw propeller, square-rigged sails at the bow, and gaff-rigged at the stern. The company claimed theirs were the fastest passenger steamships flying the American flag.

1897

The Burlington Route is advertising where it goes around the edge of the ad; how it gets there is shown with an appealing view of the parlor car above and a route map below.

1898

Here the Frisco is selling vacations in the Ozarks, resulting in an unusual geographic orientation with the Midwest apparently pivoting on Eureka Springs, Arkansas—still a popular spa and watering place.

c. 1890

1900

1902

1903

OPPOSITE ABOVE LEFT:

It would be hard to get more into a travel ad than this: a lovely picture of the railroad's right of way, a beautiful woman obviously riding in comfort—and the route map precisely outlining her reclining chair.

OPPOSITE ABOVE RIGHT:

In 1900, the Delaware, Lackawanna & Western Railroad (the shortest line between New York and Buffalo) hired the famous copywriter Earnest Elmo Calkins to design a series of ads for the firm. The Lackawanna burned northern Pennsylvania anthracite coal instead of Virginia and West Virginia bituminous which poured forth clouds of sooty, black smoke. Anthracite burned comparatively clean.

Calkins decided to exploit this difference and hired an artist, Harry Stacy Benton, to create a spotless passenger, whom Calkins named Phoebe Snow (Phoebe, because he liked the poetic beat). Benton then hired one of the first female models, a Mrs. Marion E. Murray, and had her photographed in train cars, on loading platforms, and in waiting rooms, and then lifted elements of the pictures for his paintings of the lady and her friends.

The series was enormously successful and ran for years. The railroad put Phoebe Snow across its box cars and calendars, she got into vaudeville routines, and continued long after the line stopped running coal-fired engines—until the railroad itself expired in 1966.

OPPOSITE BELOW LEFT:

The Lackawanna Railroad is calling our attention to the delights of Lake Hopatcong (half-way between Paterson and the Delaware Water Gap) in New Jersey. The choice of model, however, seems to have lost something in the past eighty years. Can it be the flash of lingerie is supposed to draw our attention to the trademark?

OPPOSITE BELOW RIGHT:

The Missouri, Kansas, and Texas Railroad is promoting one of its vacation spots in this December 1903, Saturday Evening Post. The "Katy" nickname (from MKT, of course) was as common in the Midwest as the "Chessie" was for the Chesapeake and Ohio Railroad in the East.

ABOVE RIGHT:

This ad was run in House Beautiful magazine shortly before World War I broke out. It is an early example of targeting a fractional audience more likely to have the discretionary income needed to take around the world cruises.

RIGHT:

Here is straightforward travel copy spelling out every element of the appeal of the cruise. Berths could be booked at the nearest Navy recruiting office.

1912

1925

141

1925

Up to this point, travel advertising concentrated primarily on what company or device to use to get to the vacation spot. By the mid-1920s cars were sufficiently cheap and common and roads sufficiently improved that ordinary people could drive themselves to interesting places. At that point, the advertisers began to use the interesting place itself as the attraction and appeal. Here the famous John Held, Jr. (see page 167), captures the charm of Nantucket in, for him, an unusually literal way.

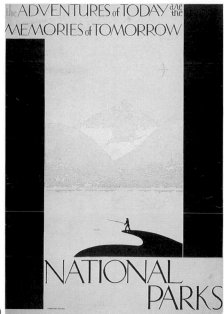

c. 1929

1929

ABOVE:

The federal government paralleled the railroads' new interest in "travel poster" promotion of the national parks. Here is a generalized, modish appeal instead of the traditional pine tree and shimmering lake.

RIGHT:

The Northern Pacific Railway is promoting the serenity of Mt. St. Helens in the traditional way of travel posters.

BELOW:

The Pennsylvania and the New York Central railroads competed with each other to bring out the most romantic calendar each year. Here three mighty engines wait at Chicago's LaSalle Street Station, eager to rush the Central's Twentieth Century Limited through the night to New York City.

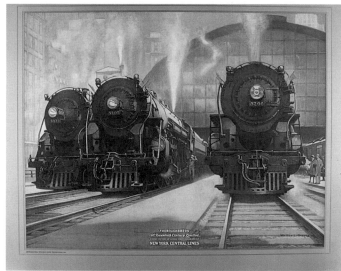

1927

RIGHT:

The years astride World War II were the last great days of American railroad travel. Railroad advertising filled the magazines with traditional ads, but business offices and public places were hung with dramatic posters and colorful calendars that set the railroads as a life apart.

c. 1941

c. 1965

After WW II, human railroad travel was steadily replaced by airplane travel. First domestic flying and then very rapidly, the invention of planes capable of easy trans-ocean flight put recreational travel into the air. Travel ads suddenly returned to the themes of the 1890s: the means of transport was as important as the destination. Braniff International reminds the viewer of how to get to South America; why to go is detailed in the fine print.

1962

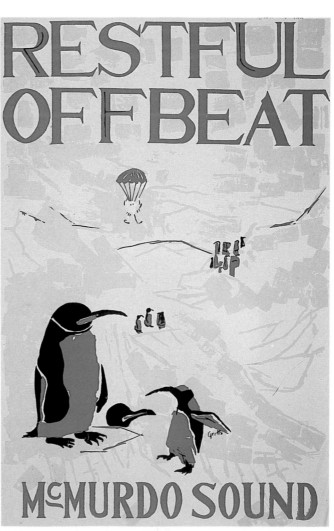

ABOVE:

Many advertising analysts believe that the 1960s was the Golden Age of American advertising. A strong case could be made with this as an almost perfect travel poster. It relies solely on the associations the viewer brings to the image, and eliminates the traditional thousand words.

RIGHT:

Where to go in South America is noted in this imaginative appeal for the attractions of the Antarctic ice shelf.

1962

This is the travel logo that taught many of the Baby Boomers to read their first printed words. The Holiday Inn "Great Sign" was designed in Memphis while the original Holiday Inn was being built in 1952. Holiday Inns were the earliest franchised motel chain which, with the coming Interstate Highway System, put the average person into his own travel program. The flashing yellow stars gradually appeared in almost every town in America, and the Holiday Inn Sign became one of the most recognizable commercial symbols in the country—until it abruptly disappeared in 1981.

When Hal Morgan set out to find what had happened to it, he learned that each one of the signs cost $35,000 to build, contained 426 bulbs and 836 feet of neon tubing. At the time they were retired, they were averaging $3,700 a year in electricity bills, with $2,400 worth of replacement bulbs demanded per sign, annually. In some communities the sign was burning up a substantial part of the yearly profits. They have all now been replaced with a quiet, remarkably unobtrusive, green sign which was deliberately designed to look like Interstate Highway directional graphics. But in the rationalizing process, they have clearly lost that highly identifiable, uniquely distinguishable, somewhat Vegas-like glitz of the founding inspiration.

El Al airlines makes its case with a simple line drawing—and a sense of humor. It was designed by Sid Myers for Doyle Dane Bernbach. (Going down a similar path, another of El Al's headlines read: "If You Liked the Book, You'll Love the Country.")

1952–1981

We've been in the travel business a long time.

1965

Following World War I, the dramatic appearance of the cheap automobile and ever-improving roads did not make the change in travel advertising that might be expected. The interurban to the local amusement park died under an assault from the family car and Sunday driving, but travel ads were still underwritten by railroads and steamship lines. It took long trips at considerable expense to justify advertising the service. Tourist cabins and roadside cafes were still mom-and-pop and locally owned. There were as yet no "chains," no "franchises" other than the gasoline companies. What expansion of ads there was came about from local development, cooperative promotion from communities like Miami Beach, Ft. Lauderdale, Long Beach, and Hollywood urging the tourists to come to see their attractions. Steamship lines and cruise ships expanded in the Twenties and Thirties, and even "ordinary people" began going to Europe to do the traditional Grand Tour. As a 1928 ad showing strollers on an upper deck said, "Crossing In The 'Acquitania' Carries As Much Prestige as Twenty Letters of Introduction. . . ."

All recreational travel shrivelled away during World War II, but with the return of peacetime in the 1950s, the travel themes that are still with us appeared. The money now came from airlines, hotel and motel chains, cruise companies.

What the ad said went right back to 1888. A modern travel ad tells us Why we should travel on a particular air or cruise line; or Why we should travel to a particular place; or simply Why we should travel . . . period. Only the machines and the joyous, recreating models have changed.

1976

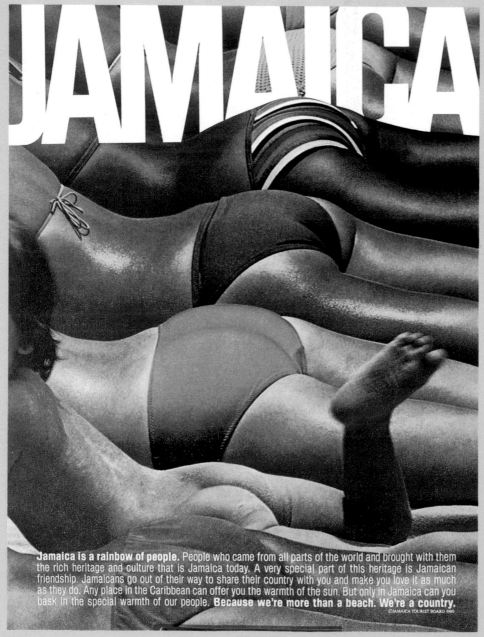

1980

"SOMEDAY"

we're going to see
the Old World castles. And
come back with enough memories
to last a lifetime.

What is your dream vacation? Someday a leisurely walk through history where kings and queens once strolled? Someday building castles in the sand on a faraway beach? Somedays have a way of turning into never. Yet, right now is the very best time to go. Your airline or travel agent can put you on a Boeing jetliner to most anywhere your someday may be. Often at discount fares. Good values that just might not be around next year. Or someday after that. ***BOEING***
Getting people together.

1982

147

The Homes That Never Serve Oatmeal

In the lowliest sections of our largest cities not one home in twelve serves oats. Among the homes of the highest types we breed, seven-eighths are oatmeal homes

Where People Don't Know

We have made a house-to-house canvass of the tenement districts, both of New York and Chicago.

We have gone to the homes where are bred the anemic, the incapable, the undeveloped. Where tuberculosis finds its ready prey. Where the average child is extremely nervous, and it shows at school the lack of concentration.

We have talked with the mothers who know the least about that which contributes to health and growth, to mental and physical power. To the ignorant, the careless, the unadvised.

We find in those sections that not one home in twelve serves oats in any form. Most of the stores supplying those sections scarcely sell oatmeal at all.

Where People Do Know

We have canvassed hundreds of homes of the educated, the prosperous, the competent—the homes of the leaders in every walk of life. We have talked with the mothers who know food values, or who are guided by physicians who know.

We find that oatmeal is a regular diet in seven out of eight of these homes. The percentage is even larger if we leave out the childless homes. We find that four-fifths of all college students come from these oatmeal homes.

We find that eight-tenths of all physicians serve oatmeal at home. We find, in one university, that 48 out of 50 of the leading professors regularly eat oatmeal.

We find that Boston consumes 22 times as much oatmeal per capita as do two certain states with lowest average intelligence.

What Does This Mean?

This doesn't mean that some can afford oats and others cannot. Quaker Oats—the finest oatmeal produced—costs but one-half cent per dish. And a pound of Quaker Oats supplies the nutrition of six loaves of bread.

It means that some know, and others don't know, the food needs of a child. Some know, and some don't know, what the food of youth means in a child's career.

Some know, and some don't know, that the highest authorities on foods for the young give the first rank to oatmeal.

Facts About Oats

Oats are far richer than all other cereals in proteids, organic phosphorus and lecithin.

Proteid is the body-builder, the energy-giving food. The average man at the average work uses up 3½ ounces of proteid per day.

Phosphorus is the most important element in the structure of the brain. Lecithin is the most important in the structure of the nerves and nerve centers.

Oats hold first place as a perfectly balanced food. It is the staple food of the world's hardiest race, famous for brain and brawn.

There is nothing else which compares with oats as a breakfast food for the young. Nothing else so well supplies the needs of the years of growth.

It is also a food of which one never tires—one of the most delicious foods in existence.

Quaker Oats

Just the Rich, Plump, Luscious Oats

By 62 siftings we pick out the richest, plumpest grains that grow for use in Quaker Oats. We get only ten pounds of such oats from a bushel. It is thus we secure that enticing flavor found only in Quaker Oats.

Millions of homes, almost the world over, have found this the best of the oat foods.

It has a larger sale than all others combined because children like it best.

Regular size package, 10c

Family size package for smaller cities and country trade, 25c.

The prices noted do not apply in the extreme West or South.

The Quaker Oats Company
CHICAGO

Look for the Quaker trade-mark on every package

1910

In this early Quaker Oats ad, the question was, Why buy oatmeal instead of corn or wheat? The ad explained (in 1910) that the company had "gone to the homes where are bred the anemic, the incapable, the undeveloped." It had talked to mothers, to "the ignorant, the careless, the unadvised," and it found "that not one home in twelve serves oats in any form."

However, when they "canvassed hundreds of homes of the educated, the prosperous, the competent—the homes of the leaders in every walk of life . . . we find that oatmeal is a regular diet in seven out of eight . . . four-fifths of all college students come from these oatmeal homes." Thus, Q.E.D. Irrefutable statistics. Surely no one could cavil with this approach.

Guilt, Shame, and Blame

EVERYONE AGREES that the first law of advertising is Get Their Attention. The next step, though, is Provoke Action. Get the customer to *do* something about your message. As long as the action is buying a *thing*, we can accept or reject it and forget the whole transaction. But there is a variety of advertising which makes the added move: If you don't buy what I'm selling *You'll Be Sorry!* Guilt. Make the customer feel bad. A marvelous way of moving from offering to action.

The result is the following gallery of shudders which amused and bemused the authors. Some must have been a mistake from the beginning, but others simply have become the victims of a change in accepted taste by the passage of time. And then there are a few which clearly were intended to provoke a "What!?? They can't be serious" from the outset.

The ironic aspect of this collection of eyebrow-raisers is that, thanks to their having pushed the Get Their Attention credo to the limit, the ads are now being reprinted a half century later, while all those other nice, respectable ones that were their peers have vanished into Forgotten Time. It does give one pause.

In any event, there follows a short album of panels which struck the authors as being unlikely and deserving of a wan smile, whether originally intended to or not.

1912

It should not surprise us that the most skillful practitioners of guilt as a motivation to buy have always been the insurance companies. Their case is, of course, reasonably valid albeit it reminds us all of the ever-present potential for disaster.

Here this widow has no skill but that from her needle, and "such skill is so poorly paid that poverty and privation stare her in the face."

To be sure the reader does not miss the point, The Travelers spelled it out: "No man has any excuse for subjecting his wife to such a future. Whatever he earns, a part of it should be used to guarantee her against it."

1916

Conspicuous Nose Pores — 1918

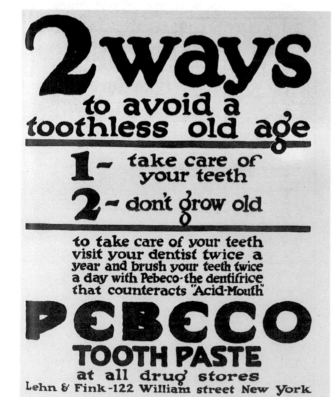

1918

RIGHT:

This ad is considered a classic among advertising historians, and is frequently included among The Hundred Greatest Advertisements collections. It was written by James Young for Odorono, the first major deodorant company. It so outraged some two hundred Ladies Home Journal subscribers that they cancelled their subscriptions—but the sales of deodorants increased 112 percent, and the approach was here to stay.

BELOW LEFT:

Four helpless women stalled on a double-track railroad crossing. Nowadays the image of a woman hand-cranking the car would be traumatic enough; in 1923 that was beside the point. Guilt was the theme. Would you want to have this situation on your conscience just because you were too cheap to buy a Philco?

BELOW RIGHT:

By 1925, the insurance companies had gotten even more skilled in describing the worst alternative, leaving every reader more threatened by guilt:

"Toil—toil—a merciless cycle of toil is all she knows. Daily the lines on that pitifully beautiful old face grow deeper. Daily those slender, needle-scarred fingers tremble more and more . . . A husband, a brother, a son has failed in his imperative duty."

There isn't a girl who can't have the irresistible, appealing loveliness of perfect daintiness

Within the Curve of a Woman's Arm
A frank discussion of a subject too often avoided

A woman's arm! Poets have sung of its grace; artists have painted its beauty.

It should be the daintiest, sweetest thing in the world. And yet, unfortunately, it isn't, always.

There's an old offender in this quest for perfect daintiness—an offender of which we ourselves may be ever so unconscious, but which is just as truly present.

Shall we discuss it frankly?

Many a woman who says, "No, I am never annoyed by perspiration," does not know the facts—does not realize how much sweeter and daintier she would be if she were *entirely* free from it.

Of course, we aren't to blame because nature has so made us that the perspiration glands under the arms are more active than anywhere else. Nor are we to blame because the perspiration which occurs under the arm does not evaporate as readily as from other parts of the body. The curve of the arm and the constant wearing of clothing have made normal evaporation there impossible.

Would you be absolutely sure of your daintiness?

It is the chemicals of the body, not uncleanliness, that cause odor. And even though there is no active perspiration—no apparent moisture—there may be under the arms an odor unnoticed by ourselves, but distinctly noticeable to others. For it is a physiological fact that persons troubled with perspiration odor seldom can detect it themselves.

Fastidious women who want to be absolutely sure of their daintiness have found that they could not trust to their own consciousness; they have felt the need of a toilet water which would insure them against any of this kind of underarm unpleasantness, either moisture or odor.

To meet this need, a physician formulated Odorono—a perfectly harmless and delightful toilet water. With particular women Odorono has become a toilet necessity which they use regularly two or three times a week.

So simple, so easy, so sure

No matter how much the perspiration glands may be excited by exertion, nervousness, or weather conditions, Odorono will keep your underarms always sweet and naturally dry. You then can dismiss all anxiety as to your freshness, your perfect daintiness.

The right time to use Odorono is at night before retiring. Pat it on the underarms with a bit of absorbent cotton, only two or three times a week. Then a little talcum, dusted on and you can forget all about that worst of all embarrassments—perspiration odor or moisture. Daily baths do not lessen the effect of Odorono at all.

Does excessive perspiration ruin your prettiest dresses?

Are you one of the many women who are troubled with excessive perspiration, which ruins all your prettiest blouses and dresses? To endure this condition is so unnecessary! Why, you need *never* spoil a dress with perspiration! For this severer trouble Odorono is just as effective as it is for the more subtle form of perspiration annoyance. Try it tonight and notice how exquisitely fresh and sweet you will feel.

If you are troubled in any unusual way or have had any difficulty in finding relief, let us help you solve your problem. We shall be so glad to do so. Address Ruth Miller, The Odorono Co., 719 Blair Avenue, Cincinnati, Ohio.

At all toilet counters in the United States and Canada, 60c and $1.00. Trial size, 30c. By mail postpaid if your dealer hasn't it.

Dr. Lewis B. Allyn, head of the famous Westfield Laboratories, Westfield, Massachusetts, says:

"Experimental and practical tests show that Odorono is harmless, economical and effective when employed as directed, and will injure neither the skin nor the health."

Address mail orders or requests as follows: For Canada to The Arthur Sales Co., 61 Adelaide St., East, Toronto, Ont. For France to The Agencie Americaine, 38 Avenue de l'Opéra, Paris. For Switzerland to The Agencie Américaine, 17 Boulevard Helvetique, Geneva. For England to The American Drug Supply Co., 6 Northumberland Ave., London, W. C. 2. For Mexico to M. E. Gerber & Cie, 2a Gante, 19, Mexico City. For U.S.A. to The Odorono Co., 719 Blair Avenue, Cincinnati, Ohio.

1919

3-Point Superiority

1. The Famous Diamond-Grid—the diagonally braced frame of a Philco plate. Both like a bridge. Can't twist—can't warp—can't short-circuit. Double lattice to lock active material (power-producing chemical) on the plates. Longer life. Higher efficiency.

2. The Philco Slotted Rubber Retainer—a slotted sheet of hard rubber. Retains the solids on the plates but gives free passage to the current and electrolyte. Prevents plate disintegration. Prolongs battery life 40 per cent.

3. The Quarter-Sawed Hardwood Separator—made only from choicest trees 1000 years old; quarter-sawed to produce alternating hard and soft grains. Hard grains for perfect insulation of plates. Soft grains for perfect circulation of acid and current, quick delivery of power. Another big reason why Philco is the battery for your car.

LOOK FOR THIS SIGN

of Philco Service. Over 1500 stations all over the United States. There is one near you. Write or address, if necessary.

PHILADELPHIA DIAMOND GRID BATTERY
With the PHILCO Slotted Retainer

Stop! Look! Think!
—and you'll get your Philco now

Safety demands the strongest, toughest, most powerful battery you can get—a battery that will stand by you in emergencies—that won't expose you to the embarrassments, humiliations and DANGERS of battery failure.

Thousands upon thousands of car owners today—in record-breaking numbers—are replacing their ordinary batteries with dependable, long-life, *super-powered* Philco Batteries.

They know the Philco Battery—with its tremendous power and staunch, rugged, shock-resisting strength—will whirl the stiffest engine—give them quick, sure-fire ignition—*get them off* at a touch of the starter.

The Philco Battery is guaranteed for two years—the longest and strongest guarantee ever placed on a battery of national reputation. But with its famous Diamond-Grid Plates, Slotted-Rubber Retainers, Quarter-Sawed Hardwood Separators and other time-tested features, the Philco Battery long outlasts its two-year guarantee.

Why continue taking chances on ordinary batteries? Why wait for an emergency to show you the absolute need for a dependable, power-packed Philco? Install a Philco NOW and be safe. It will cost you no more than just an ordinary battery.

RADIO DEALERS—Philco Dynamic Radio Storage Batteries are shipped to you charged but absolutely DRY. No acid slippage. No charging equipment. No batteries going bad in stock. Wire or write for details.

Philadelphia Storage Battery Company, Philadelphia

The famous Philco Slotted-Retainer Battery is the standard for electric passenger cars and trucks, mine locomotives and other high-powered, heavy-duty battery services.

PHILCO
SLOTTED RETAINER BATTERIES

with the famous shock-resisting Diamond-Grid Plates

1923

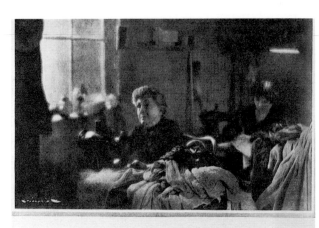

The little grey lady

Toil—toil—a merciless cycle of toil is all she knows. Daily the lines on that pitifully beautiful old face grow deeper. Daily those slender, needle-scarred fingers tremble more and more.

Someone is responsible for this—glaringly responsible. A husband, a brother, a son has failed in his imperative duty.

Because life insurance provides a way to give to old age the comforts and consideration it so richly deserves, this forlorn spectacle is less general today than in bygone days. May the time soon come when it will be completely obliterated!

THE PRUDENTIAL INSURANCE COMPANY *of* AMERICA
EDWARD D. DUFFIELD, *President*   HOME OFFICE, *Newark, N.J.*

1925

"SAFE AT HOME" yet

the door-knobs threaten them
with the danger of disease

BRIGHT eyes and happy greeting! Mothers have a satisfied feeling when they know their children are "safe at home," out of the danger of traffic and questionable companions. And yet we now know that even the most innocent-appearing objects may be fraught with the dangers of unnecessary illness to children who are "safe" within their own homes.

Health authorities tell us that disease germs are everywhere. Door-knobs, chair-arms, banisters—a hundred places around the home that big and little hands must touch daily—carry the germs of illness. 3,000,000 people in the United States are sick every day. And yet much of this illness is *preventable*.

A campaign to protect health

THROUGHOUT the country mothers, teachers, doctors, Health Officers, are uniting in a health-campaign to prevent unnecessary contagion, and safeguard health. The Health Officers of 365 cities, in a recent report, advocate as an important measure in this campaign *the regular use of a reliable disinfectant in all your weekly cleaning water.*

"Do you disinfect these important places?" ask the Health Officers

EVERYBODY, the Health Officers say, disinfects the garbage pail, drain pipes, toilet bowl. But do you also disinfect these other important danger-spots, door-jambs, chair-arms, tables, banisters, and telephone mouthpieces? Soap and water are not enough to destroy the germs on these surfaces. You must have a trustworthy disinfectant to drive germs out of your home.

"Lysol" Disinfectant is the standard disinfectant for this important weekly cleaning, the disinfectant used by physicians everywhere. Three times stronger than powerful carbolic acid, yet so carefully is it blended that in proper proportion it is not harsh for the most sensitive hands.

Use one tablespoonful to a quart of water. Its deodorant qualities and soapy nature help to clean as it disinfects.

Get "Lysol" at your druggists. The 16 ounce size is most economical. Be sure you get the genuine "Lysol."

MADE by LYSOL, INCORPORATED, a division of Lehn & Fink Products Company. Sole Distributors, Lehn & Fink, Inc., Bloomfield, N. J. Canadian Offices: 9 Davies Avenue, Toronto.

SEND FOR THIS *FREE "Lysol"* HEALTH LIBRARY

Three helpful, interesting volumes on keeping well: "Health Safeguards in the Home," "The Scientific Side of Youth and Beauty" and "When Baby Comes." You will enjoy reading and owning them. Send coupon for free set.

Disinfectant

LEHN & FINK, Inc., *Sole Distributors*, Dept. AB-4, Bloomfield, N. J.
Name
Street
City _____ State _____
(Please print name and address plainly)

1926

The ad copy here puts it clearly: "Health authorities tell us that disease germs are everywhere. Door-knobs, chair-arms, banisters—a hundred places around the home that big and little hands must touch daily—carry the germs of illness. 3,000,000 people in the United States are sick every day. And yet much of this illness is preventable.*" Preventable by simply wiping the "important danger spots" (door-jambs, tables, and telephone mouthpieces) with Lysol.*

This worker scorned Safety Goggles—

American Optical Company   Southbridge Mass USA

WELLSWORTH
PRODUCTS
for Better Eyesight

1925

But first you have to get their attention. A dramatic presentation of American Optical's story which seems questionable today but at a time before workman's compensation, Blue Cross, and Social Security, a stronger case could be made.

Do roaches spread cancer?

Read this

COCKROACH UNDER SUSPICION
AS CANCER CARRIER

TANGLEFOOT
FLY SPRAY
KILLS

AT GOOD STORES
EVERYWHERE

THE TANGLEFOOT COMPANY
GRAND RAPIDS, MICHIGAN

TANGLEFOOT SPRAY

1926

Is it any wonder the reading public was jumpy? The advertisers were introducing them to stresses they'd barely heard of yet.

The heating companies were running ads that said, "The house is full of poisonous gases . . . The strong become languid, inefficient . . . breathing baked, dry air . . . pneumonia and tuberculosis," and the bug spray people were shouting: "Cockroaches are under suspicion as carriers of cancer!"

1929

1930

Note the two dates: 1929 and 1930. The Depression has struck and the insurance company is not trying to sell new policies; it is trying to keep the old ones alive. By now they have abandoned the previous threatening copy, and have moved to a single sentence per ad with the damning point reduced to the pictures on the wall: "Mortgagee's Sale" and "Working Papers Issued Here."

1925

RIGHT:

This highly sophisticated artist has Tinea Trichophyton. "The tiny skin-cracks between his smaller toes are beginning to get on his sensitive, high-strung nerves to a serious extent . . ."; wholly avoidable, we are assured, had he used Absorbine, Jr.

"But why?" She had known Jarvis for a long time. When they announced their engagement it was no surprise to their friends.

"They had expected it.

"Then, as the plans for their marriage were well along, he came to her one day and told her the engagement would have to be broken.

"It came to her like a thunder-bolt out of a clear sky.

" 'But why?' she asked.

"He turned his head. It was something he could not bring himself to discuss."

The Listerine writer could, however. He explains that Listerine halts food fermentation in the mouth. It controls halitosis. If only she had known in time . . .

1930

Feel well *and* keep well *use* LISTERINE
AFTER SHAVING

1931

... often the only relief from toilet tissue illness

Doctors, Hospitals, Health Authorities approve **Scott Tissues** for Safety

1931

The man in the hospital bed was not using Listerine as an after-shave lotion. "Germs are uncertain things. On some people they seem to have little effect. On others they develop infection which, running a swift course, results in sickness and sometimes death. And these tiny germs often gain entrance through small wounds left by the razor." [Italics theirs.] Listerine would have killed the "germs within 15 seconds."

". . . Many of these cases are directly traceable to inferior toilet tissue. Harsh, chemically impure toilet tissue—made from reclaimed waste material." Others in this series of ads pointed out that "Strong acids, mercury, sand, chlorine—and even arsenic were found."

"Don't give pyorrhea a foothold. Remember that 4 out of 5 over the age of forty are claimed as its victims." Use Forhan's Toothpaste, and you'll have nothing to fear.

Every ad writer searches desperately for a way not only to get people to buy a unit of the product, but many units. (For years, Alka-Seltzer advertised "pop a tablet in a glass of water" until an ad man suggested they should pop two tablets in the glass, and increased the unit sale appreciably.)

Here we have an almost desperate attempt to sell more Dentyne gum. "Everyone in the family should chew Dentyne often. . . . It helps improve the mouth structure and strengthens the mouth muscles." The concept "think withered arm and then chew Dentyne" suggests they should have held one more ad conference on this one.

A graphic way to sell gauze bandage. Some advertising historians believe that the unusually harsh and threatening advertising that appeared during the Depression years came about, in major part, from the lack of color in ads. With ad budgets dramatically reduced (national advertising dropped nearly 70 percent in the early Thirties), color plates became a luxury and the endless black-and-white ads had to shout even louder to draw the reader's attention.

Another for the It Seemed Like A Good Idea At The Time Department.

"So badly burned were they that there was a thick crust of tissue on their faces through which their beards grew. It was quite impossible to use a blade to shave them.

"But the Schick Shaver glided gently and painlessly over the injured skin, removing the hair at the scarred surface." Well, yes, but . . .

This unusual piece of copy was discovered and preserved by Edgar Jones in his classic, Those Were the Good Old Days. *Things have gotten better no matter what people say.*

"She was a BEAUTIFUL WOMAN before her teeth ...went bad"

EVEN in our absence, even after we have left the room, our friends brood mournfully over the glories that have passed. She was—the *was—a* beautiful woman . . ."

The mouth is the most eloquent of human features, the seat of character. Any defect of mouth or teeth is sharply conspicuous. Actors who wish to look ugly or repulsive on the stage almost always blacken out one or more teeth. And when Nature really plays this trick upon either man or woman, Nature can be cruel indeed.

Do you know what causes lost teeth?

Lost teeth are a source of mental anguish. Even after they are skillfully replaced, the experience leaves a scar on the memory. How you dreaded the verdict, "Two in the front must come out." How you avoided acquaintances! How you

lost time from business! How the whole thing clouded your life for weeks!

Of course some teeth are lost through accident, but more than one-half the total losses of adult teeth are due to the condition known as pyorrhea. This disease is a great source of trouble for the dentist. Its treatment is long-drawn-out and usually painful. When it is a question of pyorrhea the modern dentist votes for *prevention* every time. And this means giving your dentist a chance to prevent by visiting him at least twice a year.

Cleanliness is only superficial

Your dentist will tell you that pyorrhea works *under the surface.* Its approach is silent. It may take years—five years, ten years—before it breaks out. That is why mere cleanliness, even *thorough* cleanliness, is not enough. One of the best-known names in all pyorrhea history is that of

Dr. R. J. Forhan, who spent 26 years in the study and treatment of pyorrhea. Thousands of practicing dentists, throughout the nation and abroad, are today using his special pyorrhea treatment, provided only for the use of the dental profession. For home use by the family, Dr. Forhan also perfected the toothpaste which bears his name. The active Forhan principle gives you an extra value, an added safeguard beyond a mere cleaning operation. Use it night and morning, on both teeth *and* gums, according to directions.

Do not wait for bleeding gums

Don't give pyorrhea a foothold. Remember that 4 out of 5 over the age of forty are claimed as its victims. So we repeat again: see your dentist and use Forhan's in between visits. Remember also, that Forhan's, judged simply as a *toothpaste* is the finest money can buy—pleasant, agreeable, long-lasting. Begin the use of Forhan's today. It's the double-duty toothpaste for teeth *and* gums. Look for the big, brown tube. Forhan Company, Inc., New York, N. Y. Forhan's, Ltd., 5te. Therese, P. Q.

SERIOUS THOUGHT ABOUT TEETH LEADS TO THE USE OF FORHAN'S

1932

LEARNING TO WRITE ... ALL OVER AGAIN

Tragedy!

The saddest tales, the dullest months can cause it—when infection finds a ready ally in carelessness.

So, in dressing the most trivial wound, make sure that the bandage you use is just as clean, just as safe as your own doctor would apply.

Don't take chances with a bandage of unknown make—even though the box is marked

"sterilized." It may not be worthy of your trust.

Even some "sterilized" bandages are apt to be sterilized only in an early manufacturing process. Later, in cutting and packing, they may pass through dirty hands and pick up dangerous germs.

To protect yourself and your loved ones against possible infection, use only the first-aid products of known and reputable concerns. Johnson & Johnson is one of them.

All Johnson & Johnson products that are marked sterilized—Red Cross cotton, gauze, bandage, etc.—are not only sterilized in the making. They are sterilized *again after they are put in the package.* After that, yours are the first hands to touch them.

Buy J & J Red Cross products with confidence—from your druggist. And if there is any doubt in your mind of your ability to care for a wound, consult your physician.

Don't risk infection...be safe with *Johnson-Johnson* **RED CROSS PRODUCTS**

1936

...LET THE MAN WITH THE WITHERED ARM WARN YOU
...chew delicious Dentyne often

For ten years the Indian fakir held his arm motionless, pointing toward Mecca. Now, through lack of exercise, his arm is withered . . . useless.

The mouth, too, needs exercise — regular vigorous chewing to make it work normally . . . to help keep the mouth and gums healthy . . . to keep the teeth clean and sound.

Dentyne, a special gum with an extra firmness, supplies the vigorous chewing we all need . . . in a pleasant way. Everyone in the family should chew Dentyne often . . . It helps improve the mouth structure

and strengthens the mouth muscles.

Many people chew Dentyne for mouth health, but even more chew it because of its spicy, delightful flavor. From the very first savory taste you will rejoice at having found so good a chewing gum. You'll enjoy its satisfying firmness — its smooth texture. Try Dentyne today and keep on chewing it for health and for pleasure.

Chew delicious

Dentyne

KEEPS THE MOUTH HEALTHY . KEEPS TEETH WHITE

1934

The survivors were shaved with *Schick Shavers*

MANY of the passengers and crew of the ill-fated "Hindenburg" whose faces were burned were shaved with Schick Shavers during their stay in the hospital.

So badly burned were they that there was a thick crust of tissue on their faces through which their beards grew. It was quite impossible to use a blade to shave them.

But the Schick Shaver glided gently and painlessly over the injured skin, removing the hair at the scarred surface.

MORE HOSPITALS ARE USING SCHICK SHAVERS

Each day's mail brings us stories of the use of Schick Shavers under extraordinary conditions. Men with skin troubles, patients confined to their beds, men with broken right arms or injured hands, blind men and those partially paralyzed—it is an amazing list and an overwhelming trib-

ute to the Schick Shaver which is changing the shaving habits of the world.

HOW MUCH BETTER FOR A NORMAL FACE!

The Schick Shaver, continuously and exclusively used, permits nature to discard the skin calloused and toughened by ordinary methods of shaving. In its place comes a new, more youthful-looking and softer skin easier to shave quickly and closely.

FIRST—AND STILL THE LEADER

Twenty years' thought and mechanical genius created the Schick *and the methods of making it.* We know of no mechanical shaver that shaves more quickly, more closely or with greater comfort. Six years' experience and a million-and-a-half users should convince you that Schick is the best and most economical way to shave with "no blades— no lather—no chance to cut yourself."

ASK A SCHICK DEALER TODAY

Any authorized Schick dealer will demonstrate the shaver, and show you how easily you can learn to shave either immediately or in the number of days necessary to bring your skin into perfect condition for Schick shaving.

SCHICK DRY SHAVER, INC., STAMFORD, CONN.
Western Distributor: Edises, Inc., San Francisco
In Canada: Henry Birks & Sons, Ltd., and other leading stores

SCHICK  SHAVER

1937

1895

Kenyon Cox (1856–1924)

The distinguished muralist is represented in this case with an ad to sell a magazine issue. The various "literary magazines"—Harper's, Atlantic, Scribner's—displayed monthly posters to announce each new issue, and the Parrishes, Penfields, and Pennells of the time were all represented in this device.

Art, Artists, and Illustrators

FROM THE VERY BEGINNING, advertising has told us how things ought to be. Without recognizing it, we have looked at it to tell us how "other people" or "everybody" or "those in the know" are decorating their homes, wearing their clothes, satisfying their wants. And the artists' role in this carves out a whole block of the territory as they teach us the visual aesthetics of the world around us.

The changing face of advertising has subtly taught us the currently acceptable rules of design, color, taste, and beauty. We have been astonishingly lucky in the quality of the artists who have shown us how things should look in this country. This chapter will try to note the individuals who have set our visual tastes for the past hundred years.

How did we get so fortunate? From the 1880s on, the advertisers very quickly went to the best of the art world for a variety of reasons. Getting a "name"—a "recognized" artist—to draw your ad was a subtle endorsement of the quality of your product. The eminently respectable artists who created *and signed* all those pictures of people washing with Ivory Soap wouldn't put their name on anything questionable. Norman Rockwell wouldn't lie to us. Andy Warhol surely had tried that vodka.

And the advertisers quickly learned that there should be a consistency in the way their ads looked so a Campbell's Soup ad or a General Motors ad should have a continuing, individual image all its own. The fastest way of achieving this was to use the same artist as long as he or she could keep coming up with new and interesting ways of decorating the product. For years McClelland Barclay's beautiful women introduced those beautiful bodies by Fisher, and Coles Phillips gave us those stunningly beautiful women in Holeproof Hosiery.

Posters First

Illustrations had been made on woodblocks all through the Civil War and the Gilded Age—literally blocks of wood that had been painted white on one polished side on which the artist had drawn the picture in pencil or ink. The wood was a fine-grained boxwood, cut across the grain of the tree, and since the tree didn't grow more than ten or twelve inches thick, a large picture had to be made up of many blocks bolted together. Once the artist had drawn his lines, an engraver carved away the white spaces, and for the portraits in *Harper's Weekly* and *Leslie's Illustrated*, the plate was signed by both the artist and the engraver, since the latter had such an impact on the way the shading was expressed by patterns of light and dark in ink.

The first illustrated ads appeared in the 1890s at just the time when the American art world was fascinated by the posters coming out of London and Vienna, soon to be followed by the Parisian designs of the Art Nouveau movement. The ads thus have the look of Beardsley and Lautrec, and are filled with clean, dark lines and near-silhouetted figures. When electroplating permitted multiple plates, the open spaces were filled in with wash and the striking ads of Edward Penfield and Jessie Willcox Smith begin to appear, bringing with them the new interest of the time in Japanese prints. (Penfield became art director at *Harper's* and extended his taste and influence among both the illustrators and the advertising directors linked to that magazine.) The creators of these early visual images were among the most skilled of American artists, and names like Frederic Remington, Maxfield Parrish, J.C. Leyendecker appeared equally as designers of magazine covers, literary posters, illustrators of magazine articles—and the designers of the better advertisements.

It should be noted that from the very beginning, being an illustrator or an advertising artist was extraordinarily profitable. The artists whose work is shown in this chapter were without exception very comfortably supported. Howard Pyle was educating such young artists as N.C. Wyeth, Jessie Smith, and Frank Schoonover at his school at Chadd's Ford, Pennsylvania, and as quickly as they got the skills, they received commissions that exceeded the annual salary of a college professor for each *single* ad or picture they drew. Three of the women artists lived together in a succession of castles they built on hundred-acre estates, and Jessie Willcox Smith was so generous with support to young artists that she was called "The Mint" by students in the Philadelphia area. The artists of the Twenties had town houses, country estates, and frequently villas in France, simultaneously. Remington was under contract to produce one painting a month for *Collier's* for a flat $1,000 (the equivalent of $22,000 today); Parrish got $1,250 a painting, and the average salary

1917

1918

1929

of the "name" illustrators exceeded $60,000 to $75,000 a year in their dollars, not ours. John Held bought 200 acres in Westport, Connecticut, built a huge house on it and brought in a Chinese cook and a full-time golf pro. Leyendecker's nearby, fourteen-room French chateau now houses a girls' school.

Having once learned to convert round objects into recognizable figures on a flat surface, the secret of success was to establish a consistent, appealing style. The great figure artists did this with astonishing success. There was a Gibson Girl, a Christy Girl, a Flagg Girl, a Petty Girl. A magazine would frequently select a few, continuing artists to do their covers, and thus the magazine would have a consistent look that could be quickly identified on the racks of newsstands—and the artist, when designing an ad, would be immediately recognizable as "that *Post* artist." J.C. Leyendecker and Norman Rockwell did hundreds of *Post* covers; Bradshaw Crandall did *Cosmopolitan* covers for twelve years in the Thirties and Forties, as did Harrison Fisher with *Women's Home Companion*. Jessie Willcox Smith produced *Good Housekeeping* covers for fifteen years.

Around 1890, the invention of photo-engraving appeared which permitted the reproduction of a gradation of tones of light and dark—halftones—as well as multiple-plate colors. Not only did this produce pictures that looked like paintings instead of hand-drawn pen and ink sketches, but they were

1902

Frederic Remington (1861–1909)
The great painter of western scenes (he was a Yale man actually) did a limited number of advertisements, but most of these were for Smith & Wesson revolvers, and his endorsement carried more than the usual authority for the product.

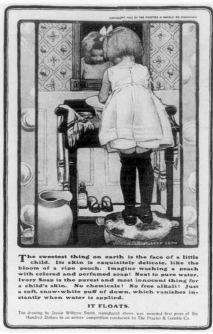

1902

Jessie Willcox Smith (1863–1935)
Smith studied under Eakins and Pyle, and was a part of the latter's famous class which included N.C. Wyeth and Frank Schoonover. By the time she started doing Ivory Soap and Kodak ads, she was already known as the person who set the nation's images for "The Child's Garden of Verses," "Evangeline," "Water Babies"—and over two hundred Good Housekeeping *covers.*

1918

Maxfield Parrish (1870–1966)
The king receives the stunning treasure of a Fisk non-skid tire in either cord or fabric construction. Parrish had a detailed style achieved by meticulous attention to textures that he painted in multiple layers of glaze like those used by the Renaissance masters. He had a woodworking shop in his studio where he built models of his columns and stages so he would get the shading and shadows just right. The result of all the exacting care was a photographic appearance that led many to believe he was pasting photographs on top of painted backgrounds.

1907

1944

N.C. Wyeth (1882–1945)
Now famous for being the father of Andrew and grandfather of Jamie Wyeth, in his day he did over 3,000 magazine illustrations, and set the images of Treasure Island, Tom Sawyer, *and* Robin Hood *for several generations of Americans. His Cream of Wheat boxes appeared in ads filled with cowboys and gold miners in much the way that The Marlboro Man lived in a consistent and continuing territory all his own. Nearly forty years later, Wyeth was still doing handsome advertisements, here an image selling Coca-Cola in Newfoundland.*

1897

Maxfield Parrish

Parrish painted a world of distant mountains, impossibly blue skies, and foregrounds filled with medieval characters out of fairy stories. At the height of his career, 1910–30, probably more American homes had more of his pictures cut from magazines and framed on living room walls than those of any other American painter. This poster for Century magazine, however, earned him only second prize in a national poster contest in 1898. Whoever won the first prize has eluded history.

1917

1919

J.C. Leyendecker (1874–1951)
Leyendecker had been painting for nearly twenty years when America joined WWI. By this time, his style was both established and well recognized. Norman Rockwell was just entering the trade and looked on Leyendecker as his role model. Their careers and productivity paralleled each other's for decades, each with a consistent, unique style. Oddly enough, Rockwell's models always looked like real people, and Leyendecker's always seemed to be paintings. Rockwell's faces and background became his trademark, while Leyendecker's identifying feature appeared to be the way he painted necks and cloth.

Howard Chandler Christy (1873–1952)
The famous Christy Girls were usually in the most up-to-date fashions, but in his several contributions to the war effort (WWI), they shared the costume with the Statue of Liberty. Christy's most famous assignment was the Signing of the U.S. Constitution canvas which now hangs in the Capitol in Washington. Christy spent two years researching all the faces (he could never locate three of them), and painted the huge picture in the Naval Gun Factory's sail loft. The canvas is 30 feet wide and 20 feet tall.

much cheaper to make. Woodblocks cost around $300 apiece, while halftones ran $20 for a picture the same size. Magazines thus exploded with pictures and by 1910 had permitted all forms of magazine printing to exploit the various styles of the artists.

For the first half century, there was no caste distinction between gallery and commercial artists, and the artist worked back and forth between the two. During this period, almost all advertising art was done by contract, directly between the agency or magazine and the artist. But by 1930, the strictures of the Depression forced both advertisers and publishers to tighten up and cut corners, and it became increasingly common to have an art department that turned out designs by salaried, in-house designers. The use of the "name" artists continued, but, as they ended their careers in the Forties and Fifties, they were not replaced.

Nowadays, while an advertiser will commission a major artist or illustrator to do a single ad, few are associated with a product over a long run. Bernard Fuchs, now a leading portraitist (he did the official pictures of Presidents Kennedy and Johnson), started his career working between the commercial and the fine-art fields, and he comments that it is no longer fashionable to establish a style and apply it to a continuing series of anything. He says, "Today editorial people look for the guy they know will do something he hasn't done before . . . if a job you do reverts to what you were doing two years ago then, I think, you're in trouble."

Let's look at some examples of the work from the great names who set the "feel" of fine advertising posters and magazine ads through the past one hundred years.

1922

J.C. Leyendecker

In 1899 he sold his first cover to the Saturday Evening Post, *and continued to provide successors with endless variety and charm for forty years. He created The Arrow Collar Man, who became such a convincing symbol that generations of college men followed every detail, and an equal number of college women sent in thousands of letters of loyalty and affection. He did the Arrow Man from 1907 to 1931, and painted fully-suited Hart, Schaffner and Marx models for almost as long.*

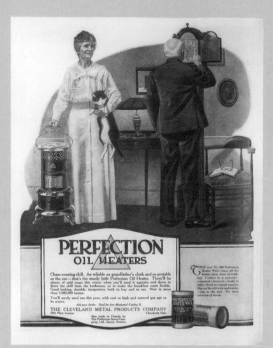

1917

1918

1929

AN ALBUM OF NORMAN ROCKWELL IN ADVERTISING

Norman Rockwell (1894–1979)
We know Norman Rockwell primarily for our memory images of his Saturday Evening Post covers (he did over three hundred), and his universal themes captured in his Four Freedoms, the Peace Corps, and integration posters. We must recall, however, that Rockwell was in perpetual demand for product advertising almost from the time he did his very first ad in the 1914 Official Boy Scout manual. (For this we must thank the H.J. Heinz Company; they and Rockwell urged us to embrace Heinz Baked Beans—"The Best Lunch for a Hike.") In the early years, Rockwell would paint a picture and the ad designer would put selling text below it, but before long (see his 1919 Grape-Nuts ad, page 65) Rockwell was designing the entire page. The art historian Walt Reed once got Rockwell to comment on his attitude toward advertising, and Rockwell said

1935

(in 1966) "[The advertising agency, which appeared in the 1920s] was a mixed blessing. To many illustrators, including myself, I feel that it was a corrupting one. The temptation of the big budgets took away the kind of integrity that earlier artists like Howard Pyle had brought to their work. One could easily become too busy or too dependent on the income from painting of one product after another to afford to take on more worthy projects, such as a mural or an important book."

Very quickly, the reading public learned to recognize Rockwell's style, and the variety and humor he would introduce in each scene, plus the integrity and very apparent love the artist had for the people he painted—all of these generated a sympathetic response from the viewer toward the advertised product. A Rockwell ad invariably interrupted the reader's "flipping the pages," and thus gave the advertiser a chance to make his case. And having Rockwell do your ad provided a subtle endorsement that the product must be honest and as advertised: surely Norman Rockwell would not lead you astray. Here are some samples from fifty years of Rockwell advertisements.

1942

From among representative Rockwell images, note the early genre paintings; one of his many posters supporting the World War II war effort; and the All-American symbols of dog, Santa, and kids for All-American Coke, Pepsi, and McDonalds (the last, cover art for a 1971 annual report). Note that toward the end of his career, his signature was getting larger than the product name.

   (The Mennen endorsement [opposite lower left] contains some interesting copy apart from the Rockwell link: The shaving soap does not just soften the beard, it provides "Dermutation"; you can test how rich the lather is by watching it support the metal top from the tube; and by sending in the coupon at the bottom, you will get two samples and the Mennen Company can tell how many people read the ad.)

1965

1971

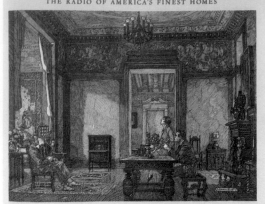

1925

FREED·EISEMANN
THE RADIO OF AMERICA'S FINEST HOMES

Now—in Radio, too, *Social Prestige* has been established

1926

This food without fibre
These gums without work!

1929

ABOVE LEFT:

Coles Phillips (1880–1927)

Some social historians credit Phillips with the invention of the pin-up girl. Working between WWI and the late Twenties, he created dozens of beautiful "modern" women, all startlingly displayed in carefully designed geometric frames, or surrounded by unusual fabrics and shadow pattern backgrounds. His pictures for Holeproof Hosiery were considered very daring at the time (see also page 72) and those he did for Community

Plate Silverware were among the first to introduce Art Deco principles to advertising design. Although his use of color was similarly innovative, he was able to make a simple black-and-white image almost equally arresting, as demonstrated here.

ABOVE MIDDLE:

Franklin Booth (1874–1948)

Booth always managed to give a sense of vast dignity and importance to his ads. Here he is selling the radio on the far wall; on page 213 he is selling Willys Overland sedans surrounded by knights in shining armor; and on page 66 he has created the Spires of Wellville. His artistic technique amazed his friends: he would take a piece of blank paper and start to draw his pictures from the center, working outward, completely finishing each inch square as he moved into the open space. Purpose? He didn't want to smudge anything he'd drawn.

ABOVE RIGHT:

Henry Raleigh (1880–1944)

Raleigh was known as the illustrator of sophisticated, high society fashion—he did all the stories of F. Scott Fitzgerald, William Faulkner, and the like—in the Saturday Evening Post. *When he designed ads, he carried with him the patina of Manhattan and Hollywood and gave the product a tacit endorsement. He did Maxwell House ads for nearly forty years (see page 101) always identifiable by his ink-sketch style overlaid with colored washes.*

BOOKS
MAKE the home

1930

LEFT:

Rockwell Kent (1882–1971)

Kent was well known as a wood engraver and lithographer before he got into advertising. He kept his dramatic style when he crossed into the commercial world and for years did classic ads for Steinway & Sons, Rolls Royce, and similar "upscale" accounts. The accompanying woodblock poster was done for an American Book Week publicity campaign.

1920

John Held, Jr. (1899–1958)
The illustrator who created the trademark of the Roaring
Twenties. He was both a social critic and a skilled artist whose
Held Flapper was as identifiable as the Gibson Girl. He
designed ads for Wanamaker's before going into satirical
cartooning, and after the joy of the Twenties was killed by the
Depression, he became an artist-in-residence at Harvard and the
University of Georgia.

George Petty (1894–   )
The Petty Girl was the Thirties' and Forties' version of the
Gibson Girl. Petty created her for Esquire magazine, and he
and she get the credit for the invention of the "center-fold"
publishing device. The Petty Girl was more approachable than
the Gibson Girl, and was created with an airbrush rather than
pen and India ink. Both shared proportions that were rarely
found in the regular population. (Among other elements,
anatomy teachers pointed out that their legs were one head
longer between ankle and hip than the models from which they
were drawn.)

1936

1929

McClelland Barclay (1891–1943)
McClelland Barclay was the painter of the beautiful people of
the post-Flapper period. His figures were always young, taking
part in sports, traveling, stylishly dressed—indeed the idea of his
generation was to dress and look like McClelland Barclay
models. His consistent style and "look" symbolized General
Motors "Bodies by Fisher" for many years.

McClelland Barclay
A startling shift in style from the delicate, chiffon-clothed
"Barclay women" to this WWII Barclay poster. Barclay was
lost at sea in 1943 when the Landing Ship Tank (LST) on
which he was sailing in the South Pacific Theater of War was
torpedoed and sunk.

1942

1941

James Thurber (1894–1961)
Thurber's gimlet eye detects the dreaded "gaposis" in this ad for Talon Fasteners. Thurber, a cartoonist, illustrator, and social satirist, worked mainly for The New Yorker *magazine, but his ads appeared everywhere.*

1937

Ansel Adams (1902–1984)
By 1937 Adams would already have started his series of dramatic western landscapes, and his high-contrast pictures of Yosemite were building in his files—but ads like this one for the Hawaiian Sugar Planters' Association were bringing in the money that would make the nature and conservation work possible.

Bernard Kliban (1935–   )
The illustrator Bernard Kliban is presently best known for his analysis of cats, but the titles of his many books reveal the breadth of his interests. Sample: Never Eat Anything Bigger Than Your Head . . . , Whack Your Porcupine . . . , Two Guys Foolin Around With the Moon . . . , *and* Luminous Animals.

Andy Warhol (1928–1987)
Warhol parodied the images of advertising—his Campbell Soup cans may have been as widely viewed as Campbell's own—but he also created advertising images as in this colorful design for Carillon Importers.

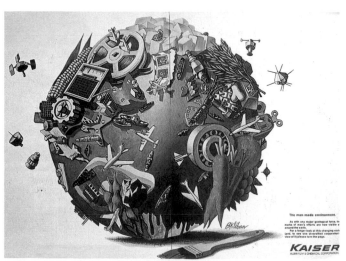

1970

1985

A pastiche is defined as a motif of art borrowed from a celebrated work or master. Herewith some pastiches that clearly lifted the tone of the advertising of their day . . .

1887

1918

Michael Angelo *conclusively proved on the ceiling of the Sistine Chapel that Adam was created* without *a beard. The J.B. Williams Celebrated Barbers' Soap could recapture that purity of chin a full one hundred years ago.*

Myron's Discobolus *modeling the Imperial "Drop Seat" Union Suit.*

LEFT:
Michelangelo's David "improved" by the addition of Levi's jeans in the manner of the day.

OPPOSITE ABOVE:
John Trumbull's Signing of the Declaration of Independence (with Independence Hall illuminated by eight Lightolier chandeliers). The ad was created by the famous graphic designer Herb Lubalin.

OPPOSITE BELOW LEFT:
The Levolor Company gives us a picture of the Fragonard original just in case we missed the point, but the similarities between the two models are indeed remarkable.

OPPOSITE BELOW RIGHT:
If you think this is one of the panels from Norman Rockwell's Four Freedoms, you will have brought great joy to the agency's art director who had that very thing in mind.

c. 1970

The American Way of Light. When the English, Dutch, French, Spanish first came to this country, they brought with them their own way of light. Now they're all at home in America. If you can afford an American antique—a Georgian chandelier, or Dutch lantern, or English oil lamp—by all means buy it. If you can't, you still don't have to do without. That's America. The Lightolier fixtures shown above are adaptations of American antiques—in design, materials and craftsmanship. But they cost much less. That's America, too. **LIGHTOLIER** New York, Chicago, Dallas, Los Angeles.

Lightolier distributors all over America can show you these and other handsome Lightolier fixtures. The listing is on p. 00.

c. 1979

**If it's really a painting by Fragonard, it says Fragonard.
If it's really a Micro Blind by Levolor, it says Levolor.**

Watch out for imitations. Make sure it's a signed original from the Levolor Micro Blind Collection. Slim, sleek, so very chic. In a rainbow of decorator colors. Featuring the exclusive Vogue™ Valance. At fine stores everywhere.

Lift a Levolor

© 1985 Levolor Lorentzen, Inc.

1986

AMERICA'S RIGHT TO TAPE: ONCE AGAIN, THEY'RE CHIPPING AWAY AT IT.

It started 20 years ago with the audio cassette. The big record companies didn't like it and couldn't sue the so-called for it.

Then 11 years ago some of the big Hollywood studios used to keep you from taping movies and programs off the TV. & took the Supreme Court to prevent the studios from preventing you from taping.

It's 1987. Do you feel that strong sense of déjà vu? You ought to. At this moment the recording industry is trying to get Congress to pass a law that would require all new digital audio tape recorders (DAT) to contain an anti-taping chip. That chip will prevent you from taping most new records, tapes and discs, as well as broadcasts.

These chips respond to a code in the music that will destroy the integrity and fidelity of music—even on playback.

This would be pretty awful by itself, but many see this as the first step in requiring anti-taping chips in all recorders—audio and video.

And to add injury to insult, there's talk of a hefty royalty tax on both recorders and blank tapes.

So there it is. Another example of the big record companies and Congress trying to muck around with your right to tape.

Now you can scream into your tape recorder. Or send the coupon to the Home Recording Rights Coalition.

We'll tell Congress you oppose any "chipping away" of your rights. Or call us toll free at 1-800-282-TAPE for more information (663-8595 in D.C.).

Send the coupon or call right away. So your rights won't be taken away.

HOME RECORDING RIGHTS COALITION
1-800-282-TAPE

Mail to:
the Home Recording Rights Coalition,
Box 33705, 2401 17th Street, N.W.,
Washington, D.C. 20037

Tell my representatives in Congress I oppose any bill banning digital audio-tape recorders (DAT) or requiring anti-taping chips.

Name
Address
City   State   Zip
Signature
Phone

1987

New Invented Washing-Mill,

Made by JOSIAH G. PIERSON—No. 10, White-Hall-Street, opposite the Government House.

THESE Machines will be warranted superior, in point of model, materials, and workmanship, to any yet introduced; they are attended with two and an half dollars more expence to the maker than those that have been heretofore introduced, which additional expence renders them durable, and more serviceable, notwithstanding they are sold from three to five dollars cheaper than the other kind, which will bring them from fifteen to seventeen dollars.

These machines render every kind of garment, sheet, table-linen, or any other article whiter and cleaner than any other mode yet found out: Yet it is entirely free from friction, and works by pressure only, and that in so equal and admirable a manner as not to wear the finest linen or muslin, and are even so easy as to wash bank bills without injury; so easy in the operation, that a child may work them with facility, and so expeditious as to wash the full quantity of linen, &c. put into them, at the rate of sixty shirts an hour.

DIRECTIONS.

SELECT that part of the clothes which you think will require the same time in washing; dip that part most soiled, such as the necks, wrists of shirts, &c. into warm water, and rub, at the same time, a little soap into the dirty places, as in the common mode of washing:— Then place six shirts on each side of the pressure in the mill—cut three ounces of soap into slices, and strew them among the articles already placed in the mill—pour two or three pails of hot water, sufficient to float the clothes, so as to cause them to turn in the mill with every rotation of the wheel, which may be made to revolve 60 times in a minute—continue the operation for the space of six or ten minutes, as the linen may require, and you will find the linen perfectly washed for the first time—let out a small quantity of the water, which afterwards replenish with boiling water and soap, and follow the same rule until all your clothes are washed the first time. Then examine every article washed once, and where you find any parts which may not be entirely clean, rub on such places a little soap.

To second them—put the same quantity of soap and boiling water as before mentioned into the same quantity of articles in the mill as before, and act with the mill as already mentioned, until you see they are clean, which will be in a very short time.

For calicoes and patches, boil the soap in the water, let it be perfectly cool before the articles are put in, and after they are washed lay them in cold hard water—but observe not to place a quantity of them together whilst they are wet: Be careful not to crowd the mill with any more articles than are directed. After the above operation is performed, you will find, that boiling of the clothes will be unnecessary, and a great saving of soap, firewood, labor, and wearing of the clothes.

N. B. The money must be paid on the delivery of the mill, and in case the mill should not prove to answer the above purpose, the money will be paid back on the return of the mill. The MANUFACTURER lives at No. 11, Albany Pier.

New-York, October 6, 1792.

T. GREENLEAF, print.

1792

The Croton Water rendered perfectly pure, and equal to Distilled Water.

JENNISON'S PATENT, 1846.
DIAPHRAGM FILTERS,
FOR PURIFYING WATER, AND OTHER LIQUIDS, WHILE UNDER PRESSURE.

This portable apparatus, not larger than a pint measure, can be readily, and without expense, attached to any hydrant or pipe conveying water, and will yield a steady stream of perfectly pure water, equal to one hundred gallons per hour, under the pressure of the Croton, more than enough for the culinary wants of the largest hotels. It separates with equal certainty and despatch all the animal, vegetable, and earthy matter found, despite of all possible precautions, in every distributing channel of the Croton and Schuylkill. They are also constructed for filtering water for manufacturing purposes.

The necessity of filtering the Croton Water, and the efficiency of the DIAPHRAGM FILTER, bears the endorsement of the following eminent Physicians and Chemists of the City of New York, by awarding to Mr. Jennison

A GOLD MEDAL AT THE RECENT FAIR OF 1846.

DR. LARDNER.
VALENTINE MOTT, M. D.
JOHN TORREY, M. D.
Prof. of Chemistry in the College of Physicians and Surgeons, N. Y.
ALEX. E. HOSACK, M. D.
JAMES R. CHILTON, M. D.
JOHN C. CHEESMAN, M. D.
A. GERALD HULL, M. D.
JAMES J. MAPES,
Professor of Chemistry.

JOHN W. FRANCIS, M. D.
JOHN W. DRAPER,
Professor of Chemistry at the University.
WILLARD PARKER, M. D.
JOHN F. GRAY, M. D.
J. KEARNY RODGERS, M. D.
JAS. A. WASHINGTON, M. D.
PROFESSOR HARE, Philadelphia.
JAMES A. COFFIN,
President of the Croton Commissioners.

Analysis of the Residuum of the Croton Water, by Dr. James R. Chilton.
"The dark green, muddy substance, separated from the Croton Water by Mr. Jennison's Filter, I find, by analysis, to consist of animal and vegetable matter, with the oxide of iron."

CORRECT DRAWINGS OF THE LIVING ANIMALCULES
CONTAINED IN GREAT ABUNDANCE IN THE CROTON WATER, AS CERTIFIED TO BY
DR. DYONISIUS LARDNER.

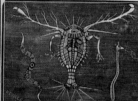

These FILTERS are highly ornamental, and will last for years, are not liable to get out of repair, or subject to damage from frost, and will prevent the pipes from bursting. They have the merit of cleansing themselves, and are also most admirably designed for filtering the Schuylkill, Mississippi, and all water under any degree of pressure. Persons desirous of examining the Filter, and understanding the principle of its operation, can call at No. where they are for sale and exhibition.

From the facilities in their manufacture, and the increasing demand, the proprietor is enabled to afford them at from $3 to $5 each.

Directions.

By the simple act of changing the Filter, end for end, and permitting the water to escape for a few seconds, it will be cleansed, which may be required three or four times a week, depending, however, on the quantity of water used, and the sediment contained. This act effectually secures the perfect operation of the instrument. At all times the first water that passes through the Filter should be permitted to escape for a few seconds, and the stream gradually diminished, by turning the faucet, until a steady and uniform flow of water is attained, when it will be found pure and clear as crystal.

WM. H. JENNISON,
For the Proprietor.
Manufactory 66 FRANKFORT STREET, N. Y.

1846

This is an almost perfect "new technology" ad, albeit it appeared in 1792. (The only thing it lacks is a picture.) It does everything a new invention ad should. It tells what the invention is, how it works, how it will improve the life and fortune of the user, and then gives detailed instructions on how to use it.

The second paragraph, for example, says: "These machines render every kind of garment, sheet, table-linen, or any other article whiter and cleaner than any other mode yet found out: Yet it is entirely free from friction, and works by pressure only, and that in so equal and admirable a manner as not to wear the finest linen or muslin, and are even so easy as to wash bank bills without injury: so easy in the operation, that a child may work them with facility, and so expeditious as to wash the full quantity of linen, &c. put into them, at the rate of sixty shirts an hour."

The machine itself worked with an up-and-down plunger; the back-and-forth action of present day washers did not appear until the Maytag family invented it in 1922.

They were complaining about New York City drinking water a hundred and fifty years ago— and making money from the problem. Here, an early water filter.

This excellent new technology ad adds the missing element: pictures (via two astonishingly effective wood engravings; note both the detail and the half-tones). By 1846, the microscopes were able to see the bacteria, but the scientific vocabulary had not yet determined the name for the "animaloules."

The Educator of New Technology

THERE IS GENERAL AGREEMENT that there are few things advertising does as well as introducing new inventions to the community. From the days of the sewing machine and the reaper to the hand-held calculator and ballpoint pen, it has done its job honestly and, even more surprisingly, with an astonishing restraint. In view of the typical ad writer's oversell, you will find the "first ads for . . ." remarkably temperate—almost understated.

As we saw with the unveiling of the Kodak, Gillette's safety razor, and the commercial airliner, a new technology ad should tell us four things:

What the invention is
How it works
What it will do for us
What we have to do to make it work

It might be interesting to test the "early ads" in this chapter against these requirements. How well and how fairly did they do their job?

It is also fashionable to charge advertisers with tricking us into new products that we don't really need, costing us money we don't really have. We have the suspicion that we've been getting along quite well without most of the things the sellers shove at us. It therefore might be equally amusing to check some of these early ads against the questions: Now that we've got this thing, are we really better off than we were before they produced it? Did the gadget really do what they said it would when they sprung it on us? And could we get along without it now?

The ads provoke another unrelated thought. In almost every case, what they are selling is going to cost more than what the invention would replace. The new product thus must be added on to current expenses. Where does the money come from to pay for all these things? We find the answer in two places.

First, the money for the purchase itself usually came through some form of installment payments, which was an idea that had begun as far back as the early sewing machines in the 1850s. (As Robert Atwan points out, an early Singer cost $125 when the average annual family income of the time was barely $500.) And then, second, the installments were paid off through the ever-rising standard of living of the American family. One of the endless arguments among economists is stirred up by this progression. You can either perceive this stream of new things that we "really must have" as driving us on to greater productivity, higher wages, and a more satisfying life-style; or you can see it as locking the average man into hopeless, despairing, never-resolved debt, and a perpetual sense of failure.

A footnote to the advertiser's unending list of new things that we really must have appears in the ads of the Depression times. We have noted how so many of the campaigns of the late Teens and the Thirties seemed to go for the throat—be unusually harsh, verging on the threatening and guilt-driven. It is clear that this links to "where is the money going to come from?" for all these new inventions. In the bad times, the average household's sliver of discretionary income got even thinner, and the more gracious campaigns of "wouldn't it be nice to have a . . . ?" slipped more easily into

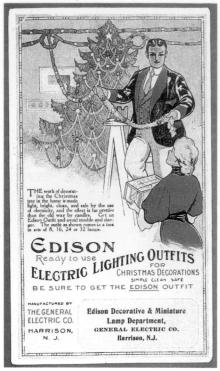

1890

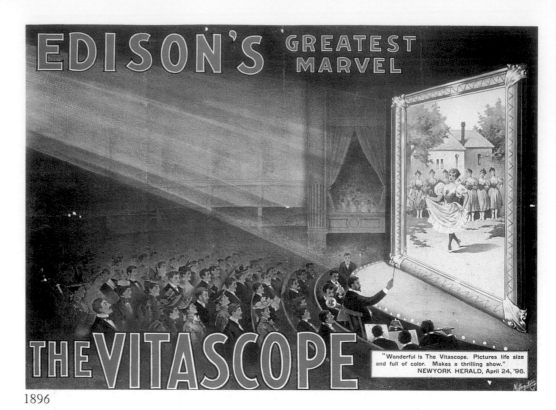

1896

Within three years of Edison's invention of the electric light, strings of colored Christmas bulbs were being sold (for the equivalent of a week's wages). As the copy says, "The work of decorating the Christmas tree . . . is made light, bright, clean, and safe by the use of electricity, and the effect is far prettier than the old way by candles."

In 1894, Thomas Edison invented the peepshow motion picture (the Kinetoscope, coin operated in a box), and in 1896 he came up with the Vitascope, which projected the peepshow images on a screen. This permitted many people to see them simultaneously, and, at least according to the ad, promptly filled the theater.

1855

1869

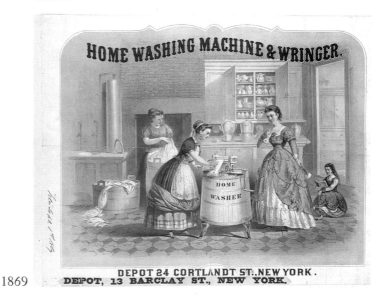

An 1855 ice box ad. The product had double doors for insulation, two spigots to drain out the melted ice water, and a hinged lid on top where you put the ice in. The ones they were selling fifty years later were very little different.

Here the product sits centered squarely in the advertisement. No descriptive copy. The picture tells all. Only the size of the lady's waist deserves comment.

"you've absolutely *got* to have this new whatever because. . . ."

But the majority of the products we see introduced here did free up time for the buyer, and when he claims a freedom from drudgery, the case is fair and we can agree with the ad writer. When he claims freedom of choice—what to do with the new time, however, the housewife has grounds for chal-

lenge: "It didn't work out the way they promised."

A 1917 *Saturday Evening Post* ad for Western Electric shows a fashionable young lady lassoing an electric iron, a toaster, a sewing machine, and a carpet sweeper. The caption reads: "The Servant Problem—Answered: Electrical Household Helps Tie the Servant to the Housewife." The copy asks, "Why are you having trouble in keeping a girl—

1899

This is an American classic. The Universal Food Chopper was not just a food processor, it was the first and overwhelmingly most popular food processor for nearly half a century. This was one of the earliest colored, half-tone ads, as well as being a popular, lithographed counter card. The product, hand-powered, was in almost every home, and not until Oster and Waring produced their blender-choppers, was there any real competition. The firm of Landers, Frary & Clark, manufacturers went on to produce a full line of home appliances with the company slogan of: "Serviceable Gifts for Sensible People."

1901

1903

The Edison required a machined screw to keep the needle in the track as it worked its way from one side of the cylinder to the other. The Victor simply followed the groove across the disc, but if jarred would gouge a damaging scratch. The Edison system prevented this.

Here the sound is so real the cat thinks there's a dog in there.

Centered in this ad is one of the most famous trademarks in the world. There really was a "Nipper," who lived in Bristol, England, and was owned by a landscape painter named Francis Barraud. Barraud had one of the cylinder-type phonographs, and whenever it was played, Nipper was fascinated by where the sound was coming from. Barraud painted the dog listening to the horn some time around 1895. The painter liked the result so well that he tried to sell it to one of the embryonic phonograph companies—without success until he reached the Gramophone Company, which thought it was splendid. Unfortunately the

1906

Already the struggle for high fidelity has begun. Here, years before its time, is stereophonic monophonic sound reproduction.

COMPETING TECHNOLOGIES—

So far as Americans are concerned, the phonograph was invented by Thomas Edison in 1877. It began the apparently endless series of competing entertainment inventions that are still costing us a fortune. It seems to take us years to make up our minds about (and then make obsolete) each successive breakthrough. Do we want 78, 45, or 33⅓ revolutions per minute? Do we want wire or tape? Do we want Beta or VHS? Do we want discs or cassettes, CDs or DAT? Mono, stereo, or quad? Edison got us started down this very costly selection-by-trial-and-error process.

His invention for capturing sound was based on a horn and a needle. You made the recording by singing down a conical horn with a diaphragm and a needle at the end. The needle was dragged around a tinfoil cylinder, where it made a "hill and dale" vertical groove. To play it back, you put a rounder needle in the groove and the original sound came back up the horn.

Edison soon got distracted from his phonograph by inventing the electric light and the electric distribution system for cities, and Alexander Graham Bell and a friend joined the field making cylinders of wax instead of foil. Edison (who came around to the wax after a decade or so) sold his machine under the name of the Edison Phonograph. Bell and friend sold theirs as a Columbia Phonograph, and a German by the name of Berliner began selling his as a Gramophone.

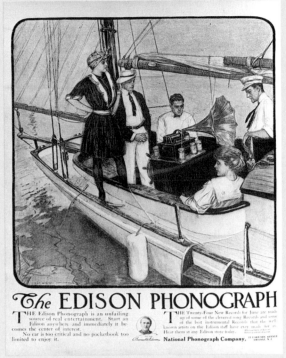

1908

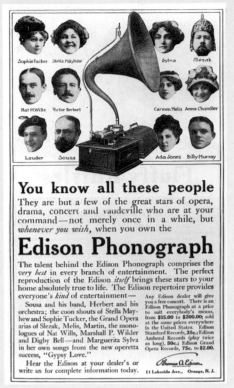

You know all these people

They are but a few of the great stars of opera, drama, concert and vaudeville who are at your command—not merely once in a while, but *whenever you wish*, when you own the

Edison Phonograph

The talent behind the Edison Phonograph comprises the *very best* in every branch of entertainment. The perfect reproduction of the Edison *itself* brings these stars to your home absolutely true to life. The Edison repertoire provides everyone's *kind* of entertainment—

Sousa and his band, Herbert and his orchestra; the coon shouts of Stella Mayhew and Sophie Tucker, the Grand Opera arias of Slezak, Melis, Martin, the monologues of Nat Wills, Marshall P. Wilder and Digby Bell—and Marguerita Sylva in her own songs from the new operetta success, "Gypsy Love."

Hear the Edison at your dealer's or write us for complete information today.

Any Edison dealer will give you a free concert. There is an Edison Phonograph at a price to suit everybody's means, from **$15.00 to $200.00;** sold at the same prices everywhere in the United States. Edison Standard Records, **35c.;** Edison Amberol Records (play twice as long), **50c.;** Edison Grand Opera Records, **75c. to $2.00.**

11 Lakeside Ave., Orange, N. J.

1912

company used flat records, not cylinders. The painter promptly repainted the machine and created the classic. It first appeared in the United States in 1902 and Nipper is now closing in on his first century.

ABOVE:

Top-of-the-line model: the Edison with Art Nouveau horn surrounded by the sophisticated elite of—Newport? Note 24 new Edison releases in June.

THE BEGINNING OF THE PHONOGRAPH

The Gramophone used the same cone and needle to record and reproduce the sound, but its disc was flat and the groove was cut from side to side, not up and down. The three forms battled one another from 1894 to 1929, when Edison finally gave up making cylinders.

The Gramophone went through various mergers and cross licenses and by 1900 had become the Victor Company and had acquired an English trademark of a dog listening to "His Master's Voice." In 1904, someone thought of putting recording on both sides of the disc, and in 1908 Columbia abandoned cylinders for the flat "records" which seemed to be winning the race.

The early ads we see here, then, involved a very complicated form of technological advertising. The ad had to explain what the new product did, what great satisfaction it offered, but at the same time it had to imply that everybody who was wise and sophisticated was using its particular format. A tacit understanding seemed to have been agreed upon that no one would criticize the opposing technologies nor, indeed, even mention them. Adverse comparisons were taboo.

We must recall that regardless of how the various competitors housed their machines, the sound was simply the sound of a needle scraping down a groove, amplified by the effect of a cheerleader's megaphone. Sound coming from an electric loudspeaker did not appear in private homes until the 1930s.

Although Victor was ultimately to win out, Edison advertised more than all his competitors combined. Each company had its "exclusive" artists, and each used signed endorsements. Victor was inordinately proud of its Sousa quote, and used it repeatedly. It read: "SOUSA, the March King, says: 'The Victor Talking Machine is all right.'"

This is the Columbia Grafonola "Favorite," the first Grafonola ever offered at its price or anywhere near it. We believe it is the best that can be constructed and sold at its price, or near it—the first instrument of the enclosed type offered at anything like its price, capable of all the tonal quality of the $200 instruments.

The 24 selections on the 12 double-disc records include the famous "Rigoletto" Quartette and also the splendid "Lucia" Sextette, for which two selections alone many talking machine owners have had to pay $13. Or your own selection of records will be supplied. (Record album extra, 10-inch, $1.50, 12-inch, $1.75.)

DEALERS WANTED—We intend to contract with over 1000 new dealers within two weeks. Columbia Distributors in every large city. Write to us for offer to dealers.

1912

The phonograph finally begins to look like it would for the next thirty years. The handle wound a clockwork, governor-controlled motor that would play two records before re-winding was needed. We are so conditioned to expect a loudspeaker where the sound comes out, that it requires an effort to recall that all the space behind the doors was an empty box through which you could hear the sound picked up by the diaphragm and needle.

Turn a Crank and the Copy's made on the

RAPID ROLLER COPIER

No preparation. No delay. No blurring. Copies everything that *will* copy. Gives you as many extra copies as you want. Booklet P tells the rest. *Send for it.*

YAWMAN & ERBE MFG. CO., Rochester, N. Y.
Makers of Card Index Outfits and Filing Cabinets of every description.

Branches: New York, Chicago, San Francisco

1901

"Rapid Roller Copier" clearly defines what the machine does, but even with the supporting cabinet cutaway, it is still not clear how it does it.

The predecessor to our shower spray on a hose was this shower spray from the walls. As complicated as this might appear, it was a standard fixture in the "better" apartment houses of New York and Chicago, and can still be seen in National Trust tour homes.

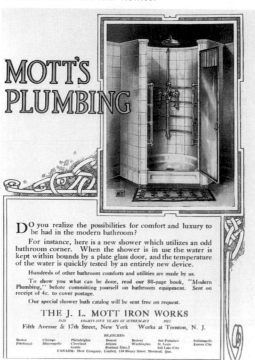

MOTT'S PLUMBING

D⁰ you realize the possibilities for comfort and luxury to be had in the modern bathroom?

For instance, here is a new shower which utilizes an odd bathroom corner. When the shower is in use the water is kept within bounds by a plate glass door, and the temperature of the water is quickly tested by an entirely new device.

Hundreds of other bathroom comforts and utilities are made by us.

To show you what can be done, read our 80-page book, "Modern Plumbing," before committing yourself on bathroom equipment. Sent on receipt of 4c. to cover postage.

Our special shower bath catalog will be sent free on request.

THE J. L. MOTT IRON WORKS

Fifth Avenue & 17th Street, New York   Works at Trenton, N. J.

1913

The first ad for the Hoover Vacuum Sweeper (or as the president, William H. Hoover, called it, "The Hoover Suction Sweeper"). The machine was invented by a janitor named James Murray Spangler who sold his first model to his cousin. His cousin's husband was William Hoover (a harness maker with money), who knew a good thing when he saw it. Hoover underwrote the enterprise, and became president—and Hoover believed in advertising.

This *Saturday Evening Post* ad is class "new technology." It describes what the gadget does, how you work it, and then says "We know this machine will satisfy you. It's only a question of getting you to try it." So Mr. Hoover offers to deliver it to you for free for ten days. "You pay no money . . ." but he is certain you'll be convinced. "The Hoover Suction Sweeper is as essential in household convenience as a sewing machine." Strangely enough the design appears to be a masterpiece of form following function. It looks more like a sweeper sucking up dirt than the present models do.

In only fifteen years, the machine has become so well known it need no longer be described, but its role in easing the pain of "the brave little woman" at home produces copy so awesome a modern critic would scarcely know where to start.

you darling!

1924

Sweeps and Dusts at the Same Time

Sweep With Electricity
10 Days' Free Trial

This little machine will instantly take all the dust and dirt from carpets, furniture and portières.

We want you to try it 10 days free—no money in advance.

It does exactly the same kind of work as the big vacuum machines some people hire at considerable expense—$10 to $50—to clean houses, hotels, churches, etc.

For less than one cent, and in 20 minutes, you can thoroughly clean any average room.

You don't have to take up rugs, or remove portières. The machine sucks all the dust and dirt right out of anything you touch it to. It pulls the dust off the floor up through the carpet.

It does all this easily and without any effort. It's easier than pushing a carpet sweeper and works twice as fast as any vacuum cleaner.

You simply attach the wire to an electric light socket, turn on the current and run the machine over the carpet. It sweeps and dusts at the same time. A child can do it, it's so easy.

You can throw ashes, sand, dust, flour, burnt matches, waste paper and similar dirt on the finest, deep, soft carpet, like thick moquette, stamp the dirt into the carpet and run the machine over it *once*.

Presto: all the dirt is gone. The carpet is as clean as new.

The machine has a brush like the kind in an ordinary carpet sweeper, which the motor rapidly revolves, sweeping up all the dust and dirt. A strong suction of air pulls the dust and dirt up from the carpet and deposits it into a dust-proof bag, attached to the handle.

There is nothing about the machine to get out of order. An electric motor, so simply made that it will last a lifetime, does the work. There are only four places to oil.

There are attachments for cleaning curtains, portières, pictures and books without taking them down. Nothing need be disturbed.

An attachment makes it possible to clean out the crevices around corners, under radiators, and places where even a broom won't reach.

The machine sucks the dirt right out of the most impossible places.

Removates Bed Clothes

It's great for cleaning and renovating bed clothes, including pillows and mattresses. Odors from sleeping and sick rooms are quickly removed.

An attachment furnishes a strong air pressure, similar to compressed air, powerful enough to blow dust and dirt through a pillow, comforter, quilt or mattress. The dead, dusty, foul air is driven out by the pressure of the sweet, fresh air from the machine.

Nothing could be more sanitary.

The Ten Day Free Trial

We know this machine will satisfy you. It's only a question of getting you to try it.

So if you will send your name and address we will deliver to you the Hoover Suction Sweeper, which you are to use ten days. If you don't like the machine we will send for it. You won't be inconvenienced in the least. You won't have to bother about even unpacking when the machine is delivered to you, and we will look after the packing if you don't want to keep it.

You pay no money until after you have used the machine 10 days and have decided to keep it.

This, of course, is not as cheap as a carpet sweeper, yet you would pay as much or more for a range, a kitchen cabinet or some other household article.

The Hoover Suction Sweeper is as essential in household convenience as a sewing machine.

We will take the risk of your keeping the sweeper. Send for it now. Requests for trial will be filled in the order received. We may not be able to fill all orders promptly if the demand is as great as we expect. So write at once.

To be sent if you don't care to write a Postal Card or a letter.

Electric Suction Sweeper Co., Dept. 11
New Berlin, Ohio

I would like to try the Hoover Suction Sweeper 10 days upon the Free Trial Offer you make. My address is

NAME

STREET

CITY   STATE

1909

Another year has slipped by since you last thought of giving her a Hoover.

But *she* has thought of it many times.

As cleaning days come and go she struggles resolutely with the only "tools" she has in her "workshop," your home.

And they are woefully inadequate, wasteful of time and strength.

As she wields her broom foot by foot across the dusty, dirty rugs her arms rebel and her back seems near to breaking.

Yet she tries to greet you with a smile when you come home at night.

In your heart you pay her tribute. "She's a brave little woman," you say.

But why put her courage to such an unfair test?

Why ask her to bear her burdens patiently when they can so easily be lifted?

The Hoover will save her strength.

The Hoover will speed her work.

The Hoover will safeguard her pride in a clean home.

You cannot afford to deny her these things for the small monthly payments which The Hoover costs.

Don't disappoint her again this Christmas.

Show her that you really do care, and throughout her lifetime your thoughtfulness will be ever in her mind.

The HOOVER
It BEATS.... as it Sweeps   as it Cleans

"His Only Rival"

The Lamp that Makes Electricity Do Triple Duty

EDISON MAZDA
BACKED BY MAZDA SERVICE

1917

Drudgery has Vanished
Since Electricity came into the home

GENERAL ELECTRIC COMPANY

1917

Why Have Two Standards of Efficiency?

Office Manager — Home Manager

YOUR wife—your *home* manager—is entitled to labor-saving equipment just as much as the manager of a business office, store or factory.

Take efficiency home with you. You are accustomed to every modern time and labor saver in *your* work. Your wife needs modern equipment, too. It will reduce housekeeping expense just as it cuts business costs. It will eliminate drudgery and tedious tasks in the home just as it does in business.

See what electricity will do! Carry the application home. Make the summer work easy to do and the hot weather easy to bear. Provide your wife with

Western Electric
Household Helps

The electric iron, the vacuum cleaner, the washing-machine, the portable electric sewing-machine, the electric dish washer, and the numerous other labor-saving conveniences, will put an end to the drudgery of housework—perhaps even replace one of your servants, and certainly make them more contented in their work.

And remember that when you invest in these devices you help your wife meet the rising cost of living, for, while most necessaries are increasing in price, the cost of current grows steadily less.

As a starter for a square deal to your wife and one single standard of efficiency, send today for a copy of our booklet, "Mrs. Bright's Way." Ask for No. 163-Q.

WESTERN ELECTRIC COMPANY
INCORPORATED
195 Broadway, New York City
Houses in All Principal Cities of the United States and Canada

Western Electric

1917

Edison's lightbulb introduced electricity to the city. Street lights, single bulbs hanging from apartment ceilings, multiple bulbs in private homes—but the reason that these elements were "wired" was to get the light they provided. By 1917 over half of all urban units had electricity; it then became the purpose of the electrical appliance manufacturers to explain to people that the wires would also run small machines that would make the ordinary person's life easier. Further, that these conveniences "cost only pennies" and need not be limited to the rich folks in the big house.

The lightbulb had essentially sold itself. The next steps took some assistance from the advertising professionals. Here, some examples. Note also the early recognition of the homemaker as a skilled professional.

even in getting one? Why do girls prefer working in a factory to working in homes?" The ad answers its own question: ". . . The most important reason is the unattractiveness of housework—the long hours—the dull, ceaseless drudgery. . . . The remedy is right at hand—in your electric light sockets." (Not in the wall plug, it will be noted. When the standing homes and apartments were "wired," wiring

meant a single wire hanging down in the center of the room. Wall plugs didn't appear for many years.)

But the loss of servants was very real. From 1900 to 1920, servants per thousand households fell from 98.9 to 58.0, as more women went into office and factory work, and then when the immigration quotas shrank so dramatically in the Twenties, domestics nearly disappeared for the middle class.

Listen to the best in radio

RIGHT in your own home, with a KENNEDY, you can hear the finest programs that have ever been offered to the public. Broadcasting attracts the headliners—and it is constantly improving in quality. The living voices of great speakers, the music of operas, bands, orchestras and soloists, can be heard with brilliant realism.

New heights have been attained in perfect reception on the KENNEDY, to equal the marvelous achievements in nationwide broadcasting. Every note and syllable comes in on the KENNEDY flawlessly clear, round, full and natural in tone. It is the instrument trained musicians approve.

KENNEDY prices—always moderate—are even lower this season.

Any KENNEDY dealer will gladly demonstrate the set you prefer in your home. Write for the nearest dealer's address, if you do not know where he is located.

THE COLIN B. KENNEDY COMPANY, *Saint Louis*

KENNEDY
The Royalty of Radio

1924

....and you shall have music wherever you go

A GAY BEACH. A cool swim. And a happy hour lazing on the sands in the sun, listening to music.

Or in the mountains. A clear evening. Tree shadows against the moonlight. And a fire of glowing embers just right to toast a marshmallow to a tender crust or burst the right jacket of a frankfurter. Ghost stories—and music. Music wherever you go—if you take along a portable Radiola.

On auto trips, it takes less room than a suitcase—and you can actually tune in while you speed along. But its chief joy is for the evenings. Tonight a campfire. To-morrow a dance—or a concert. A Broadway-full of programs travels with you.

Loop in the cover. Loudspeaker inside. Room in the back for the batteries. Small—complete—a real Radiola Super-Heterodyne. Portable—but with a dignified leather box, back home, that turns it into a living room set when the summer's fun is over!

RCA Radiola
MADE · BY · THE · MAKERS · OF · RADIOTRONS

RADIO · CORPORATION · OF · AMERICA · NEW YORK · CHICAGO · SAN FRANCISCO

1926

This Summer—Serve COLD Bottles Every 3 Seconds, This New Way

All Flavors Always Sorted—No Muss or Mix-Up
Just push a warm bottle IN and a cold one pops OUT!

Clears up to $675 a month

THE LIQUID CARBONIC COMPANY

1926

Make your Ice Box a Frigidaire

IT'S EASY. The cake of ice now in your refrigerator is replaced by the Frigidaire "frost coil," which is colder than ice and never melts. You enjoy, immediately, the full convenience of Frigidaire electric refrigeration.

Frigidaire maintains a constant, dry cold—keeps food fresh and wholesome in any weather—makes dainty ice cubes and delicious desserts for your table—saves the possible annoyance of outside ice supply—adds greatly to the convenience of housekeeping. And Frigidaire is not expensive. In many localities its operation costs less than ice.

There are thirty-two household models of Frigidaire—twelve complete with cabinet, and twenty designed for installation in the standard makes of refrigerators. One of these models will exactly fit your needs. There are also Frigidaire models for stores, factories, hospitals, schools and apartments.

Frigidaire—pioneer electric refrigeration—is backed by the General Motors Corporation and by a nation-wide organization of over 2400 trained sales and service representatives.

Write for the Frigidaire book, "Colder Than Ice." It gives complete information.

DELCO-LIGHT COMPANY, Subsidiary of General Motors Corporation, Dept. B-13, DAYTON, OHIO

Frigidaire
ELECTRIC REFRIGERATION

1925

OPPOSITE ABOVE LEFT:

When the first radios appeared, they were not only beautiful pieces of furniture (according to the ad, to be listened to when dressed in boiled shirt and smoking jacket), but they involved a multitude of dials that had to be delicately adjusted. Enormously satisfying, personal involvement.

OPPOSITE BELOW LEFT:

Thirty years before the invention of the refrigerated, coin-operated cold drink cabinet, the problem of storage and delivery had been effectively solved by the Liquid Bottle Cooler. The delivered bottle, dripping with icy water and thoroughly chilled, had sensual advantages over our present devices.

OPPOSITE ABOVE RIGHT:

Here RCA is introducing its portable radio. The price is high: $225 at a time when the average white-collar salary was still under a hundred dollars a month, but the copywriter's prose was even richer than the price tag.

OPPOSITE BELOW RIGHT:

In the early post-war years of "modernizing the American home," many of the new conveniences were designed to be installed in or on the traditional nineteenth-century device. There were wringers to be bolted on existing wash tubs, motors to be added to pedal sewing machines, and gas piping kits to be installed in wood and coal stoves and furnaces.

The first Frigidaire electric refrigerator units were sold as appliances to be inserted in your existing ice box. The slogan was "Colder than Ice"—and no melt water to empty when you put the cat out.

ABOVE RIGHT:

What we know as a "zipper" was actually invented in 1893, by a man named Whitcomb L. Judson. His design was a sort of hooks and eyes arrangement, and the slider opened and closed these—sometimes. Although it sold for a decade, it was notoriously unreliable.

During this time, a lawyer from Westinghouse had bought the patent, and hired a young engineer named Gideon Sunback to re-think it. Sunback did, lawyer Walker started over with a different firm name, and in 1913 the Hookless Fastener Co. began to produce the device we now know. It excited nobody until the Navy tried it on early flight suits, and in 1923 the Goodrich company put it on galoshes. (The latter declared you need only "zip it up," thus giving it its name. You will note that none of the early ads refer to a "zipper" on anything but the rubber shoes.) In 1926 the closer and trademark were simply "Hookless."

RIGHT:

Nearly thirty years after the introduction of its invention, the Hookless Fastener Co. was still trying to explain its innovation to the public. It had added "Talon" to the brand name, but was still showing all the places Talon fasteners could be used.

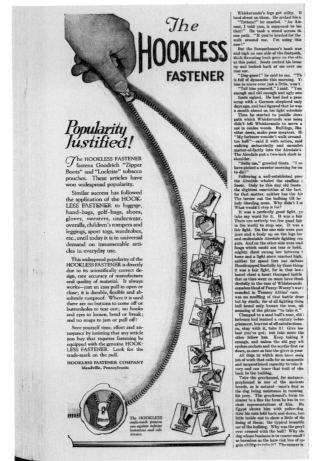

1926

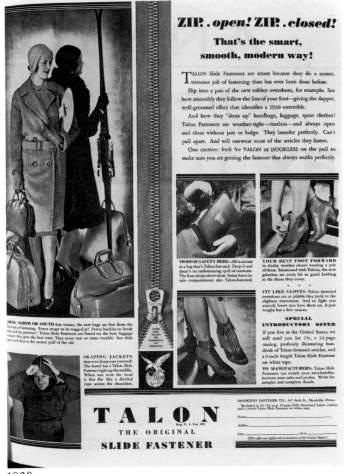

1930

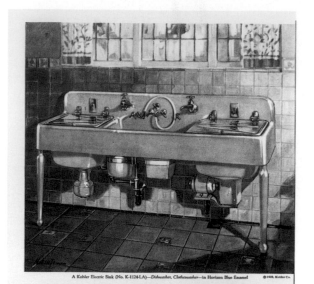

A Kohler Electric Sink (No. K-1124-LA)—Dishwasher, Clotheswasher—in Horizon Blue Enamel © 1928, Kohler Co.

See what a *modern* sink will do

Would you like to do the dishes by merely pressing a button, without so much as dipping a fingertip in water? You can, in the built-in electric dishwasher on the left.

Would you like to have an electric clothes-washer that is really convenient for the every-day light laundering of miscellaneous articles? You have it here on the right—a built-in washer that does not have to be trundled about; that fills and empties itself; that is never in the way when not in use.

But wait! This modern sink—this Kohler Electric Sink—does other things besides. It supplies hot, cold, or tempered water through either of its swinging spouts or through its rinsing hose. It holds water in its central well

—without a dishpan. It utilizes space beneath for the handy receptacles illustrated and described at the right.

Not content with being efficient, this wonderful sink brings grateful beauty to the kitchen—beauty of softly lustrous chromium-plated fittings: beauty of color. Like Kohler bath tubs, lavatories, and toilets, Kohler sinks offer you a choice of six colors—delicate, everlastingly permanent shades of blue, green, lavender, ivory, brown, and gray. *Color means Kohler. . . .*

Your own plumber can supply Kohler Plumbing Fixtures. The coupon in the corner will bring you many good reasons for asking him to be sure that he does.

KOHLER CO., Founded 1873, KOHLER, WIS.   Shipping Point, Sheboygan, Wis.   Branches in Principal Cities

KOHLER of KOHLER
Plumbing Fixtures

LOOK FOR THE KOHLER TRADE MARK ON EACH FIXTURE

1928

An amazing new way to make toast

You don't have to watch it—
—it comes out automatically
when it's done

Every piece perfect every time

It happens in the "best of regulated families" whenever toast is made. Everyone depends on everyone else to watch the toaster—with the result that everyone forgets until a thin column of smoke rises toward the ceiling.

Or the toast is made in the kitchen and arrives at the table either pale in color—scraped—stone cold —or dried out and hard.

Now an amazing new way of making toast has been perfected. You do not have to watch the bread after you put it into the toaster. You do not have to turn it. There is no danger of its burning. Yet every slice is done to perfection. An even golden-brown. Deliciously crisp. And so hot that the butter melts instantly.

Now—automatic toast

You've really never eaten toast quite so luscious as the new Toastmaster makes every time. And all you have to do is: 1. Drop a slice of bread into the oven slot. 2. Press down the two levers. This automatically turns on the current and sets the timing device. 3. Pop! Up comes the toast automatically when it's done, and the current is automatically turned off.

Both sides are toasted at the same time in an enclosed oven. Thus all the goodness and flavor of the bread are sealed in—the toast is always piping hot when served—and it is delivered to you twice as speedily as with the ordinary toaster which toasts each side of the bread singly.

At your dealer's—or order direct

The Toastmaster is a small brother of the big Toastmaster, used for years by famous restaurants, hotels and sandwich shops. It's a little beauty. Finished in flashing nickel, it makes an attractive piece for the server or dining table. So you can make toast right at the table the minute you want it.

See this novel toaster at your Electric Light Company, department store or electric dealer's. In case your dealer cannot supply you, send us a money order for $12.50. We will ship you a Toastmaster postage paid, on 30 days trial. Money back if it doesn't win you at once. Waters Genter Company, 231 No. Second Street, Minneapolis, Minn. Toastmasters are distributed in Great Britain through Hector C. Adam, Limited, Phoenix House, 19-23 Oxford Street, London, W. 1.

The TOASTMASTER

1927

THE ROXY, NEW YORK, LARGEST MOTION PICTURE HOUSE IN THE WORLD
Temperature and Humidity controlled by a Carrier System.

Manufactured Weather
keeps the theatregoer comfortable

MAGIC portals open wide to weary, heat-tormented men and women and children. Inside, the air is clean, cool, and fragrant. The theatregoer sinks into his seat sure of comfort. At last he is cool and no longer tortured by the worst torture of summer—excess humidity.

Every patron of a Carrier-equipped theatre, no matter where he sits, breathes only clean, pure, conditioned air. All the year round, Manufactured Weather plays its part for his health and comfort. In winter the cold, dry air is warmed and humidity added; in summer the hot, humid air is cooled and the excess humidity removed. Theatres all over the world have found that Carrier Manufactured Weather is often their greatest asset—not only the houses that seat thousands, but also those neighborhood theatres which cater only to hundreds; and the cost to make a patron comfortable amounts to less than one cent on each ticket.

Manufactured Weather has turned the theatrical summer slump—when receipts dwindled to the vanishing point—into a peak. The hotter the weather, the more patrons flock to the theatre where clean, cool air, freed of excess humidity, makes an oasis in the burning heat of the city. This is the spell cast by Manufactured Weather, the Carrier name for Scientific Air Conditioning.

Carrier Installations are versatile in application. The year round, a Carrier system maintains maximum comfort conditions in the House of Representatives in the Capitol at Washington. Other government buildings are prepared to install, or have already installed, similar systems. Department stores, hotels, business buildings and banking rooms are taking advantage of the comfort and health provided by Manufactured Weather. More than two hundred industries, including textiles, confectionery, tobacco, printing and lithography, rayons, ceramics, food products, paper, and pharmaceutics have found it profita-

ble to install Carrier Systems of Manufactured Weather to maintain the various temperature and humidity conditions best suited to different production problems. Many instances are on record where the entire cost of an installation has been more than paid for the first year by increase in production. Proper temperature and humidity conditions—winter and summer—have heightened the efficiency and morale of employees and decreased absences due to illness.

The temperature and humidity requirements of different industries vary widely. There are always new problems. Through the successful solution of these problems, Willis H. Carrier and

his associates have advanced the science of Air Conditioning to its present place of importance.

Where Carrier Systems are operating, they are making industry independent of outdoor weather and seasons—they make "Every day a good day."

THEATRES AIR CONDITIONED BY CARRIER

Paramount, New York   Mastbaum, Philadelphia
Paramount, Brooklyn   Olympia, Miami
State, Cleveland   Paramount, Paris
Stanley, Jersey City   Carlton, London
E. F. Albee, Cincinnati   El Encanto, Havana
                             and many others.

CARRIER ENGINEERING CORPORATION
NEWARK, NEW JERSEY

OFFICES: NEW YORK · PHILADELPHIA · BOSTON · CHICAGO · CLEVELAND
WASHINGTON · KANSAS CITY · LOS ANGELES

CARRIER ENGINEERING CO., LTD.   CARRIER LUFTTECHNISCHE GESELLSCHAFT

Manufactured Weather makes "Every day a good day"

1929

ABOVE:

The first announcement of the pop-up toaster for the home. There had been electric toasters since 1900, but they were little wire pyramids around a central heating core. You leaned the bread on the sides and hastily turned the slice around once the inner side was brown.

Toastmaster's breakthrough was heating both sides at the same time—and then turning off the electricity. The pop-up was icing on the cake.

Note that this initial ad is a model of new technology copy: it tells what the invention will do, how you get it to do it, and why you must have one. Complete with 1-2-3 how-to pictures.

ABOVE LEFT:

They've gone about as far as they can go. On the left is the dishwasher, in the center is the sink (with lift-out strainer), at the right is the washing machine. The two containers under the sink are swing-out holders for dishes on the left and garbage on the right. (The garbage disposal wouldn't appear for nearly two decades.)

LEFT:

The first air conditioning appeared as an experiment in a motion picture theater in 1922. It was an enormous success. Soon every major theater had to provide the service, and from 1925 to 1955 the summer ads across the land carried the phrase, "Relax in Air Conditioned Comfort." In many towns, the invention created the only space within the city limits that was pleasantly cool, and the chilled environment was worth more than the movie on the screen.

"What a lovely transparent wrapper!"

ON your next shopping trip, notice the variety of articles that are safeguarded for you with Cellophane. You have no doubt about them. Through this modern covering you can see for yourself what you buy.

Cellophane is the transparent, sanitary wrapping now used by a rapidly increasing number of leading manufacturers in various fields.

Remember: If it's something to eat, under Cellophane it is sure to be more appetizing. On any product, it is your assurance of protection, cleanliness—final evidence of exacting care.

You will find the Cellophane-wrapped packages at groceries, drug stores, department stores, almost every-

where. Choose them with confidence.

Du Pont Cellophane Co., Inc., Sales Offices: Two Park Avenue, New York City; Canadian Agents, Wm. B. Stewart & Sons, Limited, Toronto, Canada.

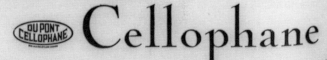

Cellophane

Cellophane is the registered trade mark of Du Pont Cellophane Company, Inc., to designate transparent cellulose sheets and films, developed from pure wood pulp (not a by-product)

1928

This advertising was too good. This is an early ad for the first clear packaging sheet (transparent cellulose) known as Cellophane. By the time the ads had developed the market, and the whole world knew and used Cellophane, Cellophane had become cellophane, the accepted generic name for any plastic wrapping film, and the DuPont company had lost the rights to its trademark.

The result was that the new electric appliances did not "keep the servants," but did help the housewife do cleaning and cooking jobs that her mother wouldn't even have attempted.

This continues to be true: even our grandmothers sent their dirty clothes to the "wash lady" and our mothers used a central laundry, usually with pickup and delivery service. In 1925 the average housewife spent 5.8 hours a week collecting, moving, and storing laundry. By 1964, a richer, better

1938

Since, by 1938, most radios sounded *the same, an enterprising ad man decided to shift the matter of brand choice to how you looked when you changed the station. The no squat, no stoop, no squint theme caught on, and was soon used in headlines, political speeches, and comedians' routines.*

The excuse for it all (a slight tilt to the face of the cabinet) also provided a large dial for tuning, a choice of short- and long-wave reception, and, as usual, required that you wear a tuxedo or party gown when listening.

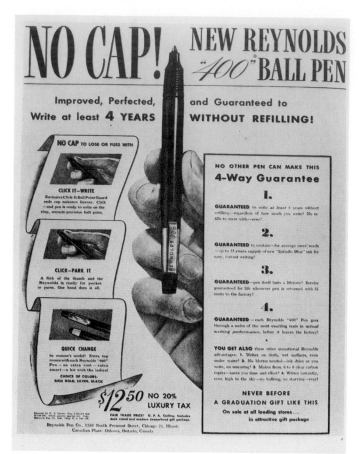

1946

The introduction of the ball point pen. Note that the primary selling strategy was how long it would go without filling. Only at the very end of the copy did they enumerate the other advantages: "1. Writes on cloth, wet surfaces, even under water! 2. No blotter needed—ink dries as you write, no smearing! 3. Makes from 6 to 8 clear carbon copies . . . 4. Writes instantly, even high in the sky—no balking, no starving—ever!" As time went on, the campaign shifted to the "Writes under water!" as the primary lead.

---

educated housewife spent 6.2 hours a week doing laundry because she had put an automatic washer in her basement and she had to do all the preparation and tending work herself. Ruth Schwartz Cowan, who has spent a good deal of time studying this phenomenon, is convinced that forty years of new inventions for "freeing the housewife" have cut down on the drudgery, but increased the time a woman spends on housework by 20 percent over her mother and even more over her grandmother. (Cowan makes a telling case that the invention of the automobile moved the time spent by the milkman delivering the milk, the grocer delivering groceries, the doctor making house calls directly into the housewife's limited time, leaving her to do all the work the merchants' men used to do—plus carrying the children all over the city for extra-curricular activities they used to get to by walking to the nearest school and playground.) Bottom line: the modern—usually working outside the home—

housewife spends more time cleaning more square feet of floors, doing more laundry more frequently, spends more time in food markets, and more time providing transportation than her mother did, regardless of what class she came from. The only time gain Cowan can find is in health care. Children get fewer diseases and get over what they do get faster than in mother's or grandmother's day.

As we look at the new technology ads, we must add one more factor to our understanding. These are national ads, sort of the headline for the product. Many got equal coverage at the local level—newspapers, radio, and later television. A new product demands education in many forms. A classic example was the introduction of frozen foods. General Foods bought Clarence Birdseye's rights and patents in 1929. It spent several years testing to find out which foods were most appropriate to the new idea; which could actually be frozen, which still tasted like fresh when they were

GARBAGE? WHAT'S GARBAGE?

Garbage nuisance ended by new kitchen appliance that shreds food waste and washes it down the drain.

Picture your home—rid forever of garbage.

Picture your family—safer, healthier because you've banished the garbage can, breeder of germs and disease.

Picture the ease, convenience and cleanliness—with all food waste disposed of *electrically*, right down the sink drain.

Make yours the most modern, most sanitary of kitchens. Install the amazing General Electric Disposall*—and forget you ever heard of garbage!

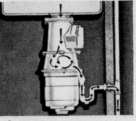

1. A simple appliance, hiding under and fitting most any sink. The Disposall has capacity enough for an average family's food waste from any one meal.

2. Once all food waste, even rinds and bones, is scraped into drain, you lock protecting sink drain cover. Clean, flushing water enters opening in cover!

3. Disposall starts automatically as cold water is turned on. Food waste is shredded into tiny particles, flushed into sewer or septic tank. The Disposall works with either sewer or septic tank.

4. Drains are kept clean by the Disposall's swirling action. Food waste that would have become garbage is disposed of—forgotten. This is the modern, easy, sanitary way!

5. We can hear you now, agreeing with other Disposall users who say: "It's one kitchen appliance I'd never give up." "So clean . . . so sanitary." "Great invention!"

DISPOSALL

DISPOSALL MEANS GOOD-BY TO GARBAGE AUTOMATICALLY!

*General Electric's registered trademark for its food-waste appliance.

For the perfect laborsaving combination, the Disposall can be teamed up with a General Electric Dishwasher in a complete Electric Sink! General Electric Company, Bridgeport 2, Conn.

GENERAL ⊕ ELECTRIC

1948

Here is an invention that was created fully developed at birth and has had almost no change since its appearance. General Electric's promotion has also been so effective that its registered trademark name "Disposall" has risked going generic from popular acceptance of its label for the device in general.

'Hello, Dorothy... *You're looking well!'*

1929

1949

1962

now anyone
can make
perfect copies
...on ordinary
paper... m. m. m. *magnifique!*

NEW XEROX® 914
OFFICE COPIER

No expensive copying paper needed	Up to 7 copies per minute!	What users say about the 914	If you spend $50 or more per month

1961

Experts agree. Xerox has come up with another miracle.

1986

prepared and served. General Foods next went to the Young & Rubicam ad agency to work up how to announce the innovation and how to explain how to use it. Once the campaign was laid out, the company and the agency selected Springfield, Massachusetts, as a test site and moved in.

The company offered freezer chests to grocery stores to hold the new product, and offered the product on consignment to twenty grocers to sell it. The agency got the local papers to run stories about the potential revolution in food habits, and distributed 16mm films to local service clubs for "how-to" programs. For the two-month test period, it took out newspaper ads pushing different frozen products: oysters, spring lamb, beef pot roast, and the expected series of vegetables. James Playsted Wood, who was involved in the initial presentation, recalls that there were problems. The freezer chests had to be upgraded, and the housewives stubbornly refused to "thaw before using," which caused much frustration on all sides. Preparation time thus exceeded that for simply opening a can, and the requirements for seasoning had to be slowly learned. Ultimately, however, the reduced waste, the time saved in preparation, and the year-round variety and availability of the foods won out, and almost ten years after the project started, the product became an accepted part of the family diet. Throughout the campaign, the advertising agency not only played a major role in the explanation and education aspects, but an equally im-

The 1961 ad above left is not the earliest ad for the Xerox machine. There was no print ad for the world-shaking invention for many months after the Haloid Corporation got all of the parts bundled together into a single box and put on the market as the now-famous 914.

When Haloid set out to advertise in the appropriate business and management magazines, the ad agency they had hired demurred. The agency urged that such an advanced technology should be shown only on television, and there be demonstrated not with words but with ACTION. Further, it should target not the business managers who would buy the machines, but the ordinary public who would use them.

George Lois recalls his first ad which showed a little girl coming into her father's office, taking some paper at his request and going over to the magic machine where she made copies quickly and with ease. The ad ran only once, whereupon competing copier manufacturers rushed to the FTC to have it pulled. Reason: they suspected a hoax.

Lois and his colleagues then restaged it under FTC oversight with a chimpanzee taking the paper, putting it under the flap, punching the button, scratching his armpit, and then trotting back with the copies to the same actor who had played the father before. Q.E.D.: The ad became folk history overnight.

Xerography is from the Greek "dry" and "writing." The 914 was from 9 × 14, the paper size the machine could copy. Note: "Xerox" as a verb meaning to duplicate is so threatened by the "generic" problem that the company runs ads in library journals reminding researchers "There Are Two R's in Xerox"—the second being the R in a circle for Registered Trademark.

William Hewlett and David Packard had been making measuring instruments since 1938 (they were the first corporation in Silicon Valley, which later grew up around them). In 1972, simply as another in their product line, they invented an "electric slide rule," the world's first handheld scientific calculator. It sold for $395 and was deliberately designed with lots of buttons to show all the things it could do. Two years later Texas Instruments got into the act, and between them the price has dropped steadily until the devices are now as common as wristwatches on campuses and in our laboratories. Here, one of the earliest announcements of the small wonder.

1973

1980

portant one in testing, probing, and experimenting to determine where the resistance to the innovation lay and what could be done about it. The pattern of presentation was finally repeated in communities all around the country.

But back to the inventions themselves. Here are some of the earliest ads for the new gadgets and the new technologies. Were they fair for what they were offering?—this was a major responsibility borne by the advertising profession. And are we better off for having said yes to their pleas and given the product a place in our lives? This was our responsibility, not the advertisers'.

Good technology advertising says dramatize what the product will do for the buyer, but how do you represent sound on a printed page? Many believe that it has never been done better than this. The ad was designed by Lars Anderson of Scali, McCabe, Sloves.

1900

Most of the money spent on early cigarette advertising went for premiums and picture cards inserted in the pack. Instead of the typical series of Foreign Landscapes, or Famous Statues, Buck Duke of the American Tobacco Company concentrated on a single series: Sporting Girls. The smoker had to collect 75 premium certificates, send them to Durham, and he received a deck of artistic pictures in return. This is "Study No. 10."

A Century of Cigarettes

BACK IN THE 1940s, Joseph C. Robert got preoccupied with a national anomaly. More money was being spent on advertising cigarettes than on any other product sold in America—yet there was more distress over smoking, more articles and sermons and newspaper texts were being focused on its elimination than on any other ill of his day. When did this resentment start? he asked himself. What precipitated it? Could the tobacco advertising have become so overwhelming—and so questionable—that it had brought the trouble on itself? So he started working backward down the history of tobacco to see where the hard sell had gone awry.

As he retreated through the years, he met a number of surprises. Cigarettes were much more recent than he had expected. They really only appeared in the 1880s, and, as late as 1910, they represented only a tiny fraction of the tobacco used in this country. Even cigars didn't really appear in any quantity until after the Civil War. For most of the first hundred years, "using tobacco" simply meant smoking a pipe or chewing plugs. And chewing was much more prevalent than would have been expected; as late as 1860, over half of all tobacco was used in the cased, tightly mashed, plug block form to be bitten off and chewed.

But having gotten back to early Federalist days, Robert discovered that he had barely scratched the surface in public outrage over the evils of the tobacco plant. Ultimately he reached the days of Rolfe and Pocahontas and their introduction of Jamestowne leaf to the high society of London. In 1604, King James I weighed in with as firm a statement as the Surgeon General's: James declared that the Virginia weed produced "a generall sluggishnesse, which makes us wallow in all sorts of idle delights." The use of the "precious stink" was a folly, an extravagance, a sin. The King declared it "A custome Lothsome to the eye, hatefull to the Nose, harmefull to the braine, daungerous to the Lungs, and in the blacke stinking fume thereof, nearest resembling the horrible Stigian smoke of the pit that is bottomelesse."

Having worked his way to the initial starting block, Robert concentrated on the early days of the tobacco trade and found that the Massachusetts General Court passed a law in 1634 against two or more persons "taking tobacco" together—either publicly or privately, and shortly thereafter the Connecticut Council put a similar anti-smoking statute into its legal code. Smoking and liquor were proscribed by the Methodist church at its first General Conference of 1792, and its abstention became a part of church doctrine. Tobacco was assaulted throughout the first half of the 1800s by almost all of the religious groups, and not until the Civil War did the criticism abate and cigars and chewing tobacco finally become acceptable for use by males of all classes. (Snuff was approved for women and for the aristocracy clear back to the Founding Fathers and Mothers.)

[Speaking of the Founding Fathers, Robert found an amusing footnote in the published works of William Byrd of Westover, Virginia Colony. One of Byrd's best sellers in England was a pamphlet called "A Discourse Concerning the Plague." Byrd owned 179,000 Virginia acres, most of which was in tobacco, so his objectivity may be somewhat in question but he declared in print, "In England [the plague] us'd formerly to make a visit about once in twenty or thirty years; but since the universal use of Tobacco, it has now been kept off above fifty four years." Smoking the leaves was good, but hanging them "about our clothes, and about our coaches" was even better. "We should hang bundles of it round our beds, and in the apartments wherein we most converse." This would presumably keep the plague at bay, and also help to move the crop off of those 179,000 acres. But note the vigor of the selling copy; George Washington Hill would have approved a hundred years later.]

James Robert traced the legal and religious strictures against the various forms of tobacco through nearly two centuries (taking him far earlier than they could be blamed on advertising), but reluctantly he came up against the core problem which he discovered in a quotation by G.L. Hemminger in the *Penn State Froth*, November 1915:

Tobacco is a dirty weed. I like it.
It satisfies no normal need. I like it.
It makes you thin, it makes you lean,
It takes the hair right off your bean.
It's the worst darn stuff I've ever seen.
  I like it.

The Cigarette Story in America

Tobacco had been grown in the colonies from the 1600s, and as the population moved west, they took the plants with them. The Carolinas, Virginia, and Maryland produced enough to make real profits on it, but Connecticut, Kentucky, Tennessee, and Missouri did almost as well. The leaf was grown in small plots, planted, transplanted, pruned, and ultimately cut and dried—all involving a great deal of hand labor. The product was twisted into hanks or pressed into cakes and sold within the local neighborhood or off pedlars' wagons.

Tobacco was tobacco just like sugar was sugar. Not until the 1850s was there such a thing as a "brand," but at the mid-century particular growers and manufacturers began branding (literally: hot iron on the ends of wooden packing boxes) with names they had thought up for their products. We still have panels marked with Cherry Ripe, Wedding Cake, Rock Candy, and Bouquet. These would have been "cased" tobaccos where the owner had soaked the leaves in flavored syrups which are still used and which produce the rich aromas traditionally found at fraternity meetings and in exclusive men's clubs. Other early brands were The People's Choice, Daniel Webster, and Lone Jack. These were made from strong tobaccos, un-flavored, and dried on poles in Southern barns. They caused severe "bite" to the roof of the mouth, and smoked hot. The chewing tobacco was given "binders" like honey to make the leaves stick together into the "plugs"; the hanks used for smoking were twisted tightly and when the smoker was ready to light a pipe, he would shave and shred the hank leaves into his pipe bowl with a pen knife or by twisting the ends between his fingers. By the outbreak of the Civil War, the sellers had designed little metal tabs the size of a thumbnail with a pointed spike on one end and the brand name on the other. These metal tabs were shoved into the hank or plug and bent down to identify the maker and the name of the tobacco.

With the discovery of gold and the resulting westward movement, pipe smoking receded and was replaced by cigars, and in the Civil War, the troops either smoked cigars or chewed plug tobacco. The cigars were handmade in urban factories where a center filler of small, shredded leaves was wrapped in a larger leaf as a binder, and then a thin, more attractive leaf was wound in a spiral around the outside to act as a final wrapper. The wrapper was started at the end that was to be lighted, but it completely surrounded the cigar as its only covering. In none of the products was the tobacco contained in any form of paper or foil to protect it against drying out.

Cigarettes and War

For some reason—certain historians attribute it simply to the ease of carrying the product—war has always advanced the use of *cigarettes*. The form was first discovered by the British during the Peninsular war where they met the Portuguese and Spanish smoking cigarros ("little cigars") of thin, shredded tobacco wrapped in paper. The British took these cigarros to the Crimean war where they met Turkish, highly aromatic tobaccos, and carried these home with them. By the 1880s, the Americans began buying English cigarettes—with their heavy overtones of the odor of burning straw, while by this time the English had discovered the much milder, sweeter Virginian tobacco. Thus, for the first forty years of the cigarette, American brands were heavily blended with Turkish, and the British cigarettes were almost pure American tobacco. Both versions were rolled by hand on stone tables, the paper being held together with flour paste. Before the end of the 1880s, a machine was invented for shaking the shredded tobacco into endless rolls of porous paper, which were then cut into the proper lengths by sharp knives. The cigarettes were still sufficiently loosely packed that they were sold in boxes to keep them straight and to keep the contents inside the paper.

Bull Durham Really Began It All

Through the closing years of the Civil War, Yankee soldiers occupying Virginia, Georgia, and the Carolinas became used to the lighter tobaccos of the South, and in particular a variety of "bright tobacco" processed by John Ruffin Green in Durham's Station, North Carolina. Green shredded his tobacco for pipe smoking, and sold it in small, cloth sacks with a picture of a bull on the side. At the close of the war, Green was delighted to receive letters from discharged soldiers all over the North, asking for that tobacco of his they had gotten during the campaigns against Gen. Johnston. In rapid succession, Green's product became known as Bull Durham tobacco, became nationally known, and stirred Green into major advertising. By the early 1880s he was spending $100,000 a year in country newspapers, $50,000 in metropolitan dailies, and giving out premiums (from coupons packed in the little sacks) of as much as $60,000 a year for clocks alone. By the mid-1880s, the Bull Durham factory was the largest tobacco processor in the world, employing over a thousand people in a single building.

About the same time, another North Carolina hamlet closer to the hills was also growing from the profits of tobacco: Winston, next door to the village of Salem, was becoming known for its chewing tobacco. While John Ruffin Green was making smoking tobacco, Pleasant Henderson Hanes was selling almost a million pounds of plug tobacco each year under the names of Missing Link, Man's Pride, and Greek Slave. Hanes got steadily richer until he sold out to the other Winston manufacturer, one Richard Joshua Reynolds. Hanes took the money he had made and went into the men's underwear business where he became even more famous making long johns, shorts, and ultimately knit hosiery. When we read that "Gentlemen Prefer Hanes," we are seeing the current form of the chewing tobacco fortune.

While the North Carolinians were becoming prosperous, the Virginians were also recovering from the Civil War, and in Richmond a surgeon who had served under Lee began to manufacture a chewing tobacco plug that could be shaved into pipe bowls. His name was Richard Archibald Patterson, he named his plug Lucky Strike, and tradition has it that the flavoring came from Dr. Patterson's homemade cough syrup.

Except for Bull Durham, tobacco advertising up to 1890 was still minimal, and almost all of the promotional money was spent on premiums. If you brought in enough of the little tin tags stuck in the chewing tobacco, or the paper tags hanging from the sack string on the pipe tobacco bags, you could get a pocket knife or a dinner pail absolutely free.

Bull Durham's saga rose to a remarkable climax at the time of World War I. Their ad not only tells the story, but is an incredible piece of copy. On May 4, 1918, the following full page appeared in the *Saturday Evening Post*:

ANNOUNCEMENT

Our Government has requested that we put at the disposal of the War Department our entire output of "BULL" DURHAM tobacco.

And we have complied—fully, gladly. For whatever the Government wants, whatever it needs, it must have from us and from you fully and with a generous heart.

We have been sending immense quantities of "Bull" to our men at the front, and at the same time trying to supply consumers at home. But now we are asked to give *all* our output:—36,000,000 sacks, 2,000,000 lbs., 100 carloads of "BULL" DURHAM every month.

This call means more than just huge figures to me and I know it will mean more than figures to the hundreds of thousands of men everywhere in the country who look upon that little muslin sack of good old "Bull" as a personal, everyday necessity.

But, if "Bull" is a necessity to you, here, in the peaceful pursuit of your daily life, how much greater its necessity to those splendid Americans who have gone to fight for *you*—to *win* this war for *you*.

I know that you will think of them as I do—only of them. I know there will not be a single complaint. I know that you will give up your share of "Bull", however long you have enjoyed it, however close it is to you, as you will give up anything you have if it is made clear to you that our forces over there need it.

That the Government has requested the whole output of "Bull", the night and day output of all of our factories, must make this absolute need clear to you.

And I know that you will not forget the little muslin sack—gone for the moment on its mission of hope and inspiration to our boys in the trenches.

"Bull" will come back, with ribbons of honor. Have no fear.

[Signed]
Percival S. Hill

The Duke of Duke University

Recall: Bull Durham was a loose, shredded tobacco which could be used either in pipe bowls or in roll-your-own cigarettes. Early in its rise, one of the Bull's smaller competitors back in Durham was James Buchanan Duke—Buck Duke—and his various sons from two marriages. The Dukes produced chewing and pipe tobacco, but after a few years realized that Bull Durham so dominated the market for these there was little room for anyone else. In 1881, the elder Duke decided to see if he could make any money on the newly invented, fully-fashioned, *pre*fabricated cigarette.

At this time, most cigarettes were made in New York by Russian immigrants who had learned the skill in the government tobacco factories of Kovno. Duke hired one of these rollers to come to North Carolina to train his own employees, and in a remarkably short time they were producing 2,500 to 3,000 hand-rolled cigarettes a day. Duke broke into the market by selling his cigarettes at half the usual cost. This generated so many orders that he was able to afford one of the earliest cigarette-making machines in America (invented by a neighboring Virginian), and by 1884 each *individual* machine was producing 120,000 cigarettes a day—at which point all the hand rollers were fired.

Duke's advertising man, Edward Featherston Small, discarded Duke's traditional Indian trademark and replaced all of the Duke trade cards, window posters, and counter displays with pictures of "Madame Rhea," an internationally known French actress of the time. This move drove the competition to include small, illustrated and numbered cards the size of the cigarette pack in their sliding boxes. The idea was to get the customer to seek a "complete set," thus urging the customer to stay with the brand and to buy generously and often. Duke promptly appropriated the competition's idea and raised it one. His set was entitled "Sporting Girls," and could only be secured by saving 75 certificates from as many packs and sending them to Durham.

In 1880, Duke was spending some $800,000 a year on

The earliest American cigarettes were heavily mixed with highly aromatic Turkish tobaccos, and Murad was the one most heavily advertised. As far as sales went (up to World War I), the three most popular brands were Liggett & Myer's Fatima, Lorillard's Zubelda, and American's Omar.

Lucky Strike was originally a chewing tobacco plug produced by Dr. Richard Archibald Patterson. Its flavor was rumored to be based on Dr. Patterson's homemade cough syrup. Around the turn of the century, the Doctor began shredding the plug tobacco into a pipe cut and selling it in a can. He could honestly advertise "less bite," since the industry had recently discovered a way to reduce the acids in the leaf and produce a milder smoke.

advertising. Most of it was dedicated not to increasing his own sales but simply to keeping his competitors at bay. This internal rivalry struck Duke (and his neighboring tobacco manufacturer friends) as wasteful, and they decided to combine their production. In 1890, five of the largest cigarette producers went together, divided up the capitalization and the markets, and became the American Tobacco Company. The combined companies controlled almost nine-tenths of the American cigarette production, plus a tenth of the pipe tobacco. Within twenty years, the American Tobacco Company dominated four-fifths of *all* aspects of tobacco production except for cigars.

The American Tobacco Company was soon hated by everyone from the farmers who grew the tobacco to the bankers who were frozen out of the industry by the trust's control of the capital. American cut prices to undersell competitors in even the smallest communities; with its immense capital it continued to upgrade its production with new and faster machines. It bought out opposition firms, skipped wholesalers and purchased supplies from individual planters (setting its own prices at will), created specific "fighting brands" to bankrupt opponents, and in general (in the words of the Supreme Court) did all the things the Sherman Anti-trust Act had been designed to prevent.

It took the government until 1911 to break up the company, splitting the cigarette operations among three of its constituent divisions: Liggett & Myers, P. Lorillard, and a new American Tobacco Company. The other big name in the trade was an independent outsider, Hanes's friend R.J. Reynolds, but Reynolds had always limited its production to pipe and chewing tobacco. Thus, when the World War I ballooned the use of cigarettes, Reynolds was left essentially without a modern product.

Up to this point, American cigarettes both tasted and smelled like "foreign" Turkish tobacco, and the most popular brand was Fatima by Liggett & Myers. Lorillard created Zubelda as a competitor, and American started Omar. Reynolds was looking for something that sounded equally Turkish, and came up with something he finally called Camel. The name was short, foreign, and recalled the scent of the desert. (They were actually made mostly of North Carolina bright flue-cured tobacco plus a highly flavored burley, but the company sprinkled in enough Turkish to make its burning fumes smell realistic even if the smoke had little taste of the imported flavor.)

The competitors were battling each other with a variety of premium gifts, so Reynolds decided to go against protocol and declared in large letters that its tobaccos were too costly to permit premiums, but they would, in return, guarantee the finest tobacco that money could buy. They set the price at the top of the market to give it an upscale feel and introduced the product in Cleveland, Ohio. The traditional advertising of the old-line companies was to display as many as a dozen of their brands in a "family" of products. The belief was that the smoker would have a loyalty to Lorillard, or a warm feeling to the many products of American. Reynolds limited its cigarettes to a single name, and began the saga with a teaser campaign: the first day the newspaper ads showed a single Camel behind the words, "The Camels are coming!" The next day the announcement was added that "Tomorrow there'll be more CAMELS in this town than in all Asia and Africa combined!" Finally the great moment arrived, the ads read "CAMEL CIGARETTES Are Here!" and Camels were on sale for the common man. The product was an immediate success. It later proved that the rich, saturated flavor of the burley leaves was more appealing than any other brand on the market. The foreign taste (and odor) of the Turkish became a sudden liability.

George Washington Hill, the head of the American Tobacco Company was taken completely by surprise by the camel attack. In no time, Camels had taken over the whole cigarette market, and Hill put his chemists to work to learn what made Camels so attractive and so different. The chemists pointed to the flavored burley. Hill bought as much burley as he could get his hands on and created a flavor even richer and sweeter than anything Reynolds had tried. It was so dense, in fact, that the leaf was soaked with the flavoring and the factory foremen had to run the leaves through wringers to get the moisture down so it did not stain the paper. Ultimately Hill had a product ready to mount an assault against the new Camels but he lacked the all-important name and logo.

Hill's new burley-flavored cigarettes were in fact withheld from the market for months while he searched through all the companies he had once owned during the "Trust days" when American Tobacco was buying up brands and breaking the competition. Hill was searching for a trademark he already owned that could be exhumed and he finally came on Dr. Patterson's cough syruped pipe tobacco which Patterson had called Lucky Strike. Patterson had meant it to connote the discovery of a vein of gold, but Hill seized the name, designed a bull's eye for the package to imply a hit on a target, and (after hearing someone describe the drying process used in the tobacco preparation) declared, "Lucky Strike, It's Toasted." In later years, the competition particularly resented this slogan, since *all* tobacco is dried or "toasted."

Hill did a test run in Buffalo, N.Y., found it to be good, and by 1917 Lucky Strike was on the market nationally. Hill supported his new product with the most expensive advertising campaign ever laid on the country up to that time.

The two powerhouses of Camel and Lucky Strike left Liggett & Myers without a competitive product. They took Hill's approach of looking for something they already owned, and selected a minor brand they had called Chesterfield. It had a simple, plain taste coming from Virginia and Maryland tobaccos—no exotic imports—and they mounted a major campaign stressing Chesterfield's aristocratic, smooth, and gentle flavor. The three brands—Camel, Lucky Strike, and Chesterfield—proceeded to dominate the cigarette market until after World War II.

1914

When the Camel pack was designed, it was first planned with the name spelled Kamel to make the product sound more exotic. The beast was modelled after a dromedary named "Old Joe" in the Barnum and Bailey menagerie which, fortuitously, was in a tent near Winston at the time. No one can charge the artist with taking liberties with the original image when he drew the trademark.

1915

R.J. Reynolds entered the cigarette contest by inventing a wholly new tobacco taste. Using American burley and flue-cured brights, it left the aromatic Turkish flavor behind, but being unsure how the new blend would go over, R.J.R. conducted a test run in Cleveland starting with a series of teaser ads in the local newspapers. The above announcement introduced Camel cigarettes to a waiting world. In five years it had 40 percent of the entire cigarette business.

1912

One of the earliest ads showing a "nice" woman in the same picture with a man smoking. Also possibly the first ad to hint that she herself might even be willing to smoke. The ad writer hastily covers himself by making it clear "No woman really wishes to be a man—still. . . ."

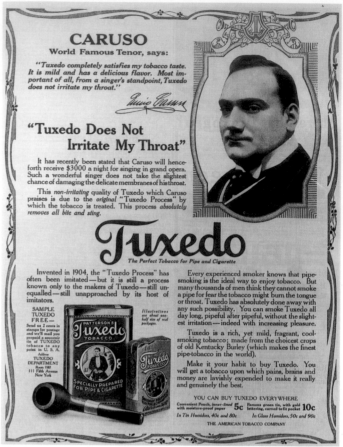

1914

Celebrity endorsements of tobacco started early. Here the opera star Enrico Caruso assures the customers that they have no need to worry about the effect of tobacco on their throats.

The Tobacconists Turn to Women

During the period between the wars, Camel held a firm grip on the mass male purchaser, and George Washington Hill could not open up the market share for his Lucky Strike. Hill increased his advertising until it broke all previous records (it never dropped below 20 percent of his total sales throughout his life), but the return on the investment was negligible. He then hired the advertising genius Albert J. Lasker and gave him carte blanche to do what was necessary to win the war. Lasker took Luckies (and cigarette advertising) off in a new direction.

Lasker decided not to fight for men who had already decided on their smoking brand, but to go after the 51 percent of the society thus far denied the pleasures of smoking. Women were to be Lucky Strike people.

The way to success was opened, of all sources, by Chesterfield. In 1926 it pasted across the nation's billboards a picture of a man and woman sitting beside a moonlit sea.

The man was lighting his cigarette and the woman was saying, "Blow some my way." At the time, outrage came over an innocent woman being seduced by the evils of nicotine. There was a blizzard of letters-to-the-editors and hundreds of sermons from pulpits, but rather than dropping the image, Liggett & Myers had the pair work their way through couches, porch swings, roadsters, and rumble seats, with the "Blow some my way" never changing. Pictures of women holding burning cigarettes (although not actually smoking them) followed shortly after. [The landmark "Blow some my way" billboard was designed by the Newell-Emmett agency; we regret we were unable to secure permission to reproduce the image.]

Lasker promptly drove Luckies through the breach in public taboos that Chesterfield had opened. He began by collecting endorsements from opera singers and movie stars, and his theme was that Luckies were actually good for you. The endorsements assured the reader that the cigarettes had in no way harmed their craft. "No Throat Irritation—No

1915

Bull Durham dominated the tobacco market from shortly after the Civil War to the outbreak of World War I. It was used in both pipes and the new, hand-rolled cigarettes. The tab on the draw-string was sent in for premium gifts, and, as can clearly be seen in the ad, it was equally at home on the farm and in the game rooms of the aristocracy.

1915

One of the earliest national ads about Camels, in which the maker educates the customer in a number of aspects of the new product. Note the first explanation of the use of the revenue stamp as a quality seal; this is believed to be the first attempt to sell cigarettes by the carton, not the pack; and note the continued use of "Turkish" tobaccos on the packaging, but (compared with the competitors) essentially eliminated from the smoking blend.

Cough." He proceeded to hammer slogans through the presses, repeating the same phrase over and over until it was recognized by the nation—and then starting over with a new one. A single ad would sometimes have as many as six catch phrases, and when the company began its radio show in 1928, the slogans were injected at the end of every song: "Lucky Strike Means Fine Tobacco" ultimately became simply "LS/MFT."

"Reach for a Lucky Instead of a Sweet."

"Be Happy, Go Lucky/Be Happy, Go Lucky Strike Today."

"So Round, So Firm, So Fully Packed, So Free and Easy on the Draw."

"Nature in the Raw is Seldom Mild" (Luckies, being "Toasted," avoided the unpleasant effects. "The Pillage of Paris," "Rape of the Sabines," and similar themes illustrated the primitive savagery—some of the images painted by N.C. Wyeth himself.)

"Lucky Strike Green Has Gone To War" (when Hill decided to change its package to white so it had the clean, antiseptic appeal of the white Chesterfield pack.)

The approach worked. Through the Thirties and Forties, Luckies and American Tobacco gradually overtook and passed Camels. As late as 1955, Lucky Strike led the field, but by then so many new brands had joined the race that "leading the field" meant only 33 percent of the market.

At this point the filter brands began to appear. They had been developed, not for health reasons, but were intended to appeal to women and thus simply to increase cigarette sales. It was hoped that the firm, protected end would resist lipstick adherence, and the filter pack would eliminate the shredding of the rolled tobacco and the staining of the mouthpiece end, which women found repellant. ("Don't you hate a soggy cigarette?" the ad writers asked.) The filter idea worked, but each of the competitors brought out their own

COME TO MARLBORO COUNTRY

The Marlboro campaign, believed by many advertising professionals to be Number One among the All-Time Greats, started in 1954 when Philip Morris moved an uninspired account to Leo Burnett in Chicago. By 1954, there were already six filter-tip cigarettes on the market. Marlboro then had a red paper "beauty tip" to camouflage lipstick, came in a white pack bearing the slogan, "Mild as May," and, not surprisingly, sold mostly to women. It held less than one quarter of one percent share of the cigarette market.

Burnett decided to go for the macho. The agency redesigned the pack to a flip-top box, changed the color to strong red and white, and chose the cowboy as the most effective shorthand symbol for the masculine image. (For the first ten years the cowboy always had a tattoo on the back of one hand.)

The original photographer of the series, Constantin Joffe, recalls that "the most successful Marlboro men were pilots, and do you know why? Because pilots seem to have a little wrinkle around the eyes."

At the time of this writing, the Marlboro series is the longest running modern campaign and has higher brand identification and recall than any other advertising theme in the marketplace. [We regret we were unable to secure permission to reproduce any of the Marlboro Man advertisements.]

brands immediately thereafter, and American's Pall Mall was unable to defend itself against Philip Morris' Marlboro and R.J. Reynold's Winston. ("Winston Tastes Good—Like a Cigarette Should" nearly unseated the reason of a generation of American English teachers; Winston also claimed that "It's what's up front that counts" to the delight of unnumbered college humor magazines.) By 1970 American was down to 19 percent of the total and in 1980 it sank to 11 percent. The company finally stopped the slide with its development of the low-tar Carlton, but the cigarette market was now vastly different from the days of George Washington Hill.

The Surgeon General's Report

Other than the generalized warnings of James I and the local minister, the average smoker had never been told of any specific threat to his or her health. For years the Girard Company had used doctors to sell their cigars. A full-page 1916 *Saturday Evening Post* ad shows the kindly (bearded, with pince-nez) doctor talking into a new, vertical telephone, and the copy reads:

THE DOCTOR SAYS "YES—GIVE THEM ALL GIRARDS"

Wise old Santa called him on the 'phone about it. And the doctor stands shoulder to shoulder with Santa, for the Girard cigar, because he knows it never robs the smoker of his mental efficiency or his physical well-being.

THE GIRARD CIGAR NEVER GETS ON YOUR NERVES.

When smokers switched to Philip Morris, "every case of irritation of nose and throat—due to smoking—either cleared up completely, or definitely improved." With Old Golds there was "Not a cough in a carload." Camels were good for your T-zone (taste and throat), and for years, Reynolds had used the slogan: "More doctors smoke Camels"; but in 1964 it became clear that maybe more doctors did, but not the Surgeon General of the United States.

The initial "Surgeon General's Report" spelled out for the first time over the imprimatur of the United States Public Health Service, the linkages between cigarette smoking and increased mortality rates. From the point of view of the advertising world, this resulted in first, the requirement that the words "Caution: Cigarette smoking may be hazardous to your health" must be printed on every pack and, second, the banning of all advertising of cigarettes on television. The latter forced a major shift of advertising revenues into magazines and newspapers, and ultimately the sponsorship of such sports events as the Virginia Slims tennis tournaments and the national challenger for the America's Cup. Needless to say, each contest carried the name of the sponsor proudly displayed in large letters.

The concern over cancer had many impacts on the tobacco trade, but one of the major ones was the search for ways of reducing the amount of tar in the cigarette without losing too much flavor or too much of the "kick" which smokers found attractive. Milder tobacco was grown, better filters were developed, the cigarette paper was made more porous, and chemical additives were created to replace the flavor that was withdrawn with the tar. The result of this activity was that while in 1976 low-tar cigarettes represented less than 17 percent of the total sold, by 1981 they constituted more than 60 percent, and over a hundred new brands were introduced—each of which had to be heavily advertised to break into the market and be recognized.

Yet it was becoming increasingly difficult to seize the public's attention for new tobacco products. *Reader's Digest, Good Housekeeping, Washington Monthly,* and *The New Yorker* refused to run any cigarette ads at any time (although some sources like *Parade* still received a fourth of their revenue from tobacco). But more money is still spent on cigarette advertising than any other product in America, though the *places* it can be spent are increasingly limited. At the time of this writing, the pressures from "secondary smoke" objectors—the non-smokers inhabiting the smoke-involved environment—are expected to result in greater restrictions than anything so far experienced.

Given the Health Concerns, What Do the Advertisers Have to Sell?

There seems to be no question that tobacco is addictive but at the same time, does "satisfy." Its calming effect, its tendency to "clear the mind and steady the hand," the general euphoria that smokers report, are not solely psychological. The advertisers take these effects and attempt to associate cigarette smoking with pleasant social experiences, good food, the completion of a task or the relief of tension. Handling the product has cosmetic uses—a pipe is supposed to make a man appear wise; a cigar implies a connoisseur of the finer things; a woman with a cigarette is perceived as in charge, sophisticated, urbane. And in the absence of Near Eastern worry beads, the various cigarette products provide something to do with the hands. The ad makers draw on all these perceptions to attract new devotees to their market.

One of the areas of bitterest resentment by the industry's critics is that of the manufacturers' apparent attempt to capture uncommitted teenage consumers. The critics deplore what they perceive as the exploitation of young people's desire to look wise and "with it," sophisticated and like their elders. The critics resent the advertisers' use of young adult models engaging in activities that appeal to the high school ages. The industry replies that their models simply reflect where the money now is—working singles and two-income families without children—and that the primary purpose of their advertising is to get current smokers to change their brands away from the enemy's packs and into their own.

Market Share

Whether this is true or not, there is no question that at the time of this writing, the number of cigarettes sold in America has been declining for nearly a decade. Mounting medical, political, and legal pressure has driven the industry to try less tar, denser filters, longer tubes, multiple flavors, discounts, and "smokeless" tobacco. The result has been a fragmentation of brands that must have George Washington Hill spinning in his grave.

Camel now controls only four percent of the total sales; Lucky Strike has one percent, and Chesterfield isn't even on the charts. The Top Twenty? "Top" is now defined by miniscule percentages. The well-known cigarette Virginia Slims, targeted at women buyers, controls only three percent of the market. Newport, whose ads dominate rapid transit, newspaper, and billboard space, controls four percent of the total. Only two brands rise above single-digit percentages: Marlboro with 24 percent, and Winston with 11. Media advertising for the top six peaked at $664 million in 1984 and has been shrinking steadily since. Again, at the time of this writing, "the battleground is now at the retail counter," according to an industry leader interviewed by *Business Week* magazine. The industry spokesman then proceeded to extol the marvelous marketing potential of better premiums and lower prices—precisely the two promotional devices used by the industry when cigarettes were introduced one hundred years ago.

So Are Cigarettes Finally Finished?

Hardly. The Surgeon General's report linking smoking to lung disease appeared in 1964. Warning labels were required on all cigarette packages beginning in 1965. Television stations were required to give equal time to anti-smoking messages in 1967. Tobacco ads were banned on television, and stronger warning labels were required in 1971. In 1983 the federal excise on cigarettes was doubled to 16 cents a pack. In 1985, even stronger labels were required. In 1988, the courts (for the first time) required a tobacco company to pay damages to a widower whose wife had died from lung cancer. Yet in 1988, the profit margin on a pack of cigarettes was the highest of all time, there were 50 million smokers left in the United States, and these spent $33.3 billion dollars on cigarettes. One hundred billion cigarettes were exported from the U.S. (up from 64 billion two years before), and a major investment house declared, "The industry is very healthy and doing very well." Does advertising work? It certainly has for the tobacco industry.

1874

We start the pilgrimage with a look at what was acceptable for public viewing in men's underpants. The ad was for shirts, but it demonstrates the going standards. All the elements are as would be expected except for the lady's fully developed bustle, and the expressions on the faces of the daughter and the cat.

Lingerie, Hosiery, and Underwear—
Selling the Package for the Form Divine

PITY THE POOR underwear manufacturer. His product is usually small. The variety of shapes in which his ware is sold is extremely limited, and respectable society is at best reluctant to see the product too explicitly shown. Hanging a slip from a rack, holding an empty stocking for an enumeration of its virtues, or displaying a pair of boxer shorts to energize sales leaves a great deal to be desired. About the best the maker can hope for is to seek a way for the person modeling his latest creation to do it in some eye-catching manner—without exceeding the limits of current convention. There follows here, then, an album of ads which tried to satisfy the challenges laid upon the products of lingerie, hosiery, and underwear. Each piece of merchandise acclaimed was, of course, trying to serve a higher cause: each was trying to encase the standard-issue, imperfect, American body with a package of comfort and style.

1888

This explains how the bustle in the picture opposite was achieved. This ad is from the Century Magazine *of January 1888. The bustle reached its greatest popularity about 1885 (before that the crinoline and hoop skirt of Civil War times had been fashionable), and the device disappeared about 1890.*

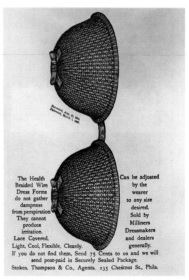

1885

While the bustle was carrying its supportive role below the waist, these wire "dress forms" were functioning above. The now-familiar brassiere was not invented until 1889 when the first one was designed by a Parisian coutourier named Herminie Cadolle. (The first American model was patented by Mary Jacob of Boston in 1914.) Until that time, braided wire forms such as these were distributed by manufacturers like Stokes, Thompson & Co., which sent them "post-paid in Securely Sealed Package[s]."

Redfern Corsets

1912

The corset followed the bustle and was designed to bend the woman into an S shape, as demonstrated by the Lily Langtreys and Lillian Russells of the time. Note that in this ad (right), much of what appears to be a ballroom gown is in fact the corset itself. The "ready-to-wear" model was designed to give a 21-inch waist. Anything that made this inappropriate required seamstress's modification and brought considerable embarrassment.

The S figure shown in the Worcester Corset drawing is demonstrated fully clothed in this Redfern Corset color ad (opposite) from the Advertising Supplement pages of House Beautiful, December 1912.

1903

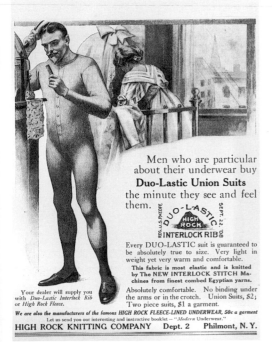

1910

This carefully groomed gentleman models the latest men's undergarments. We can assume that the figure is drawn, not photographed.

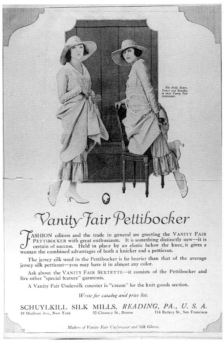

1917

The pettibocker. Here Yancsi and Roszika, the famous "Dolly Sisters," model a design that failed to stand the test of time.

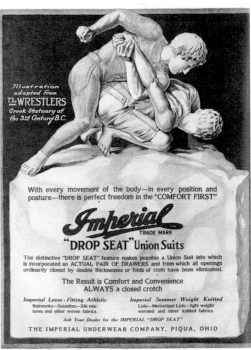

1918

Two styles of Union Suits modeled with impeccable (indeed aesthetically uplifting) taste.

1922

Exquisite!

IRON CLAD silk. Touch it. Feel it. The exquisite, fairylike beauty of Iron Clad silk hosiery, and the dreamy loveliness of the latest new shades are so tempting—so irresistibly captivating! Graceful feminine curves revealed in dainty silken hose as Iron Clads display a strangely elusive charm that only Iron Clad silk can give.

IRON CLAD No. 805—A glorious mixture of pure thread silk and artificial silk—13 inches of it, extending from the knee to an especially elastic mercerized top, 4-ply heel and toe, and silk splicing in the heel and double sole. Colors: Black, White, Cordovan Brown, Leather, Otter, French Nude, Mode, New Onyx, Jack Rabbit, Beige, Dawn, Russian Tan, Beaver, Rose Taupe, Gun Metal, Rosewood, Atmosphere.

IRON CLAD No. 809—Pure silk and artificial silk fashioned, with mercerized top and foot. Colors: Black, White, African Brown, Otter, Leather, New Onyx, Mode, Beige, French Nude, Russian Tan, Beaver, Silver Grey, Rose Taupe, Rosewood, Dawn. An Iron Clad guarantee of satisfactory service with every pair.

If your dealer cannot supply you with these two styles, send us your remittance ($1.60 for 805, and $1.50 for 809) and we'll supply you direct. State color desired and size (8 to 10½). We'll pay the postage.

COOPER, WELLS & CO.
232 Water Street, St. Joseph, Mich.
10th at N. Smith, Mich. and Ontario, Mo.

Iron Clad Hosiery

1925

New..
STYLE-KNITTED
SKIN-FITTED
PONIES by

MUNSING Wear

Light-weight yet warm. And very smart! And how smooth they fit beneath smooth frocks!

UNDIES must fit to perfection . . . the new tight-fitting clothes demand it! They must wear and wash and live a long and lovely life. Trim little, slim little Munsingwear "Ponies" . . . knit panties and vests . . . are styled for slim modern dresses and priced for this modern budget. Snug and warm for winter winds, in specially processed Munsingwear Rayon, in Silk, in Rayon-and-Cotton, and in Worsted-Cotton-and-Rayon. In a good store nearby. Munsingwear, Minneapolis.

UNDERWEAR · WATERWEAR
SLEEPING AND LOUNGING GARMENTS
HOSIERY · KNIT COATS · PULL-ONS
FOUNDATION GARMENTS

Munsingwear make all styles of smart undergarments in all types of fabrics, for men, women and children.

LET MUNSINGWEAR COVER YOU WITH SATISFACTION

1933

There's not much you can do with dramatizing a pair of black socks, but the famous illustrator Coles Phillips here has used all his skills to direct attention to the product. The background points to the center of interest, the fingers are pointed down, the legs are elongated to carry the line along, no human eyes are visible to distract the viewer, and even the hairline is pointed to those all-important stockings.

Here another artist tries the woman's version of Coles Phillips' solution. Everything points down. In 1925, women's stockings were knitted flat like a handkerchief or a sheet; they were cut to fit the shape of a woman's leg, and then sewn together up the back making the dark seam that men found attractive and women hated.

The art historians credit Coles Phillips' lingerie ads with creating the image for the American "pin-up." Here, by 1933, the technique has been embraced by other artists and is used to sell knit winter underwear. Munsingwear, made in Minnesota, had had early experience in knitting this warming product.

Smart style
...Fine fit
Wonderful wear...

This Munsingwear for men has everything. Garments styled to the minute . . . in fabric and flair . . . in color and cut . . . and offered in the widest variety of design and pattern for the young fellow . . . for the hale fellow . . . for the sedate business man. Smart Munsingwear! Knit to fit every curve and contour, or cut to hang with a freedom that never binds. Every model in every style is tailored in the fashion they've always been famous for . . . no creeping, no twisting, no bunching. Comfortable . . . cool! Fine fitting Munsingwear!

And, of course . . . the materials and the workmanship are just what you've always known them to be . . . and depend on it, they always will be. Wonderful wearing Munsingwear!

Munsingwear comes in every type of garment for every type of physique . . . or preference. Union-suits . . . knit and athletic . . . the popular shirts and shorts . . . or what will you have!

Woven fabrics, fancy fabrics, colors galore . . . there are garments in selected cotton yarns, in mercerized, and mixtures. And there are many models in the marvelous new Munsingwear Rayon . . . in white and in colors. Style . . . Fit . . . Wear . . . Munsingwear can give you just what you want . . . and just what you should have. See the Munsingwear Dealer.

MUNSINGWEAR, MINNEAPOLIS

MUNSING Wear

1929

A man's choice of underwear styles à la 1929.

WITH COMPLETE FREEDOM OF ACTION, PLAYTEX PANTY GIRDLE IS INVISIBLE UNDER ALL SUMMER CLOTHES

1949

Mark Twain had said that as a boy, the only way he found out what was going on under those hoop skirts was from the circus posters. A standard joke of the 1950s was that the only way a modern American boy was educated in these mysteries was from the National Geographic magazine and the Playtex ads. Playtex won The Best National Advertising Award of 1949 for the series including the above ad, many of which showed the models leaping over suitcases, sports equipment, and across ballet stages.

NO SEAMS TO WORRY ABOUT!

I'VE FALLEN FOR SEAMLESS STOCKINGS BY *Hanes*

HANES HOSIERY INC. · 350 FIFTH AVE., NEW YORK · $1.35 TO $1.95 AT LEADING STORES

1954

The hosiery manufacturers had been able to make stockings without seams for some time, but these "tube" hose did not fit tightly enough to be attractive, and sagged around the ankles. In the early Fifties, the knitters discovered how to heat-shape the Nylon invention of World War II, thus producing well-fit seamless hosiery. This is Hanes' imaginative ad to announce the innovation.

the Water Sports *just wear a smile and a Jantzen*

1965

Socks should lead an upright, yet colorful life.

1969

One of advertising's most famous slogans: "Just wear a smile and a Jantzen"—here demonstrated in a single cloth and a variety of styles.

BELOW LEFT:

The Maidenform Woman: the ad campaign that changed all the rules for advertising both men's and women's underwear. The first of the series appeared in 1949, and tradition has it that the ad designer had heard of psychological testing purporting that women had basic exhibitionist tendencies. As the years went by, the series increasingly infuriated feminists, but advertising research continually found it to be one of the most read, best remembered campaigns in all of advertising. While, as David Ogilvy said, if that's all you want, you can put a gorilla in a jock strap, it went one step further and sold Maidenform products at a breathtaking rate.

BELOW CENTER LEFT:

The aspect of the Maidenform ads that particularly outraged the women's movement was the picturing of the model in an environment with men—financial offices or architects' drafting rooms—so, in response to the criticism, the company shifted its images to women "in their own space," and solely in charge of their own destiny.

BELOW CENTER RIGHT:

Grandmothers get equal time under the new rules, and the copy gets longer, too. The model really is a banker in Sheboygan's First Interstate Bank, and the girls are her real-life grandchildren from Minneapolis.

Another imaginative solution to the question: How do you get the viewer to look at the socks?

LOOK YOUR BEST WHILE YOU WEAR YOUR LEAST.

JOCKEY

1976

While women's lingerie seems to generate more literary attention, the men's models appear to have every bit of parity when it comes to variety and style.

BELOW RIGHT:

An Eighties answer to: How do you get the reader to look at socks?

THE MAIDENFORM WOMAN. YOU NEVER KNOW WHERE SHE'LL TURN UP.

1980

The Maidenform Woman knows where she's going.

1986

JUST JOCKEY

1986

1986

fogal

for your legs only

1986

A modern version of the traditional dictum: don't show the eyes, don't give them anywhere to look except at the product.

Toys, Toys, Toys!

AT WHOLESALE AND RETAIL.

The Temple of Enchantment.

J. F. LOTTS,

97 HANOVER STREET,

Returns his thanks to the public for their patronage in years past, and respectfully solicits a continuance of favors. He invites all to call at his Store, 97 Hanover Street, where those possessing the most fastidious and refined tastes will be amply repaid for their inspection of his beautiful new assortment of

TOYS AND

FANCY GOODS!

New Goods Just Received from France and Germany.

Indestructable Birds for Infants, Zouave Caps, Seventh Regiment Hats, Pompoom Hats, Swords, Guns, Pop Guns, Fifes, Flutes, Whistles, Drums, American Flags of all sizes, and every description of Military Equipments.

New French CRY DOLLS!

Wax Dolls, Paris Dolls, beautiful China Dolls. China Dolls with Cloth Bodies, Kid Dolls, Cry Dolls, English Rag Dolls for Infants, Doll Bodies and Kid Arms, Dressed Dolls, and Dolls Dressed to order in splendid style.—NEW

ENGLISH TRUMPETS

Called the "*PRINCE OF WALES.*" New Toy—the OLD WINDMILL—turns one hour. Philadelphia Bugs, New Toy Fire Grates, Coal Scuttles, Cooking Stoves, Tin Kitchens, Porcelain Lined Ware, Plated Toy Spoons, Knives and Forks, Drumming Rabbits, Rabbits on Wheels, for Small Children. Wooly Dogs, Lambs, Rabbits, &c., &c.

PIANO FORTES,

From one octave to three, clasic chords, all sizes and prices. New style of Tea Sets, Dining Sets and Chamber Sets, just opened. New styles of Bureaus, Book Cases, Sets of Jewelry for Dolls, Doll Cribbs, Willow Wagons and Chaises, New Games for the Holidays, Dissected Pictures, Dissected Maps, Cube Blocks, Buildings, Blocks, Transparent Slates, Paint Boxes, German Game Balls, &c.

OUR PET ALPHABET ;

Combination Alphabet, Pictorial Alphabet, Hill's Alphabet, Painted in Oil Colors, Toy Books, Picture Books, Indistructable Books,

Chamber Furniture—Rich Sets of Parlor Furniture,

KITCHEN FURNITURE.

Every variety of MECHANICAL TOYS!

NEW AND SPLENDID MAGNETIC CHARIOT !

DRAWN BY SWANS !

Ducks, Fish, Swans, and every variety of Grocery Stores, Tool-Boxes, Children's Carriages, from $5.00 to $20. Rocking Horses, in great variety, from $2 to $14. Ladies' Leather Bags from 75 cents to $5.00. Port Monnaies, Money Bags, Card Cases, Hair Brushes, Writing Desks, China Vases, Cologne Bottles and every variety of China Ornaments, Reticules, Back Gammon Boards, &c.

FAIRS

Furnished with Goods at the shortest notice. All of the above named articles may be found at

J. F. Lotts, 97 Hanover Street,

Between Elm and Friend Streets, · · · BOSTON.

Great Stock of Toys for Girls and Boys, Can be found at Francis Lotts ; From parlor rig to Penny Gig, And little iron pots.	He sells Babes that speak, *yet do not eat,* And Birds that sweetly sing.
Great pussy Cats and long-tailed Rats, With many a curious thing.	So then good friends your ears do lend, While this I tell to you— Go where you will, see what you may, Lotts can show you something new.

Geo. B. Hamlin, Printer, 131 Hanover Street, (Opposite the Blackstone Bank,) Boston.

1860

Before they had pictures, they had type to attract attention. Here is a Boston toy shop ad that gives us a veritable circus of typefaces. (Recall, each of these would have been a complete font with multiple pieces of each letter.) The "J. F. Lotts" design is particularly imaginative with shaded tops like modern sunglasses.

The Face of Advertising

TWO QUESTIONS: Why is it that if you take this book, break it open at any page at random, you can guess the date of the ad you're looking at usually within a single decade? And second, Why is it that if you look at a thousand ads in your favorite magazine, 999 will look like all the rest, but that the one-thousandth is presented in a way that no one else has ever tried before (to be immediately copied, of course, in the next 999 succeeding)?

What are we seeing here? The answers seem to lie within a triangle of three forces: The first is the art style of the time. Whether it is Victorian, Art Deco, or the Psychedelic Sixties, the ad designer is working in the current, "very latest" artistic fashion of the moment. Why? Because it is new, attention getting, and proves that the advertiser, the agency, and the designer himself are avant-garde and sophisticated. The result is that advertising does more to educate the general public about new artistic styles than any other institution in our society. And as we will see in the ads illustrating this chapter, it educates in a surprisingly pure and skilled form.

Second, and less commendable, is the fact that almost no institution in our country is as prone to imitation—copycatting. At the time this is being written, a full third of all the perfume ads in this month's issue of the leading fashion magazine have a quiet pool of water, a single woman sitting in repose, tall poplar trees, and perspective lines leading dead center across a formal garden toward a distant blue sky (filled with small, white clouds, of course). James Cox reports that in a recent month he found ads declaring "All fiber is not created equal" (Metamucil), "All Calories Are Not Created Equal" (Campbell's Soup), "All Gold Is Not

Created Equal" (Visa), and "All cigarettes are not created equal" (Kool). Why? Lack of invention? Probably not. With ads so blindingly expensive, someone along the line carrying either authority or money probably said, "I want an ad just like that." Whoever had the last word went with what had worked for someone else.

But third, what about the Bernbachs and the Della Feminas and the Loises and the Wellses, who never seem to do anything anyone else has ever tried before? There seem to be some innovators who are simply unable to play variations on something anyone else has ever tried. Why doesn't everybody do it? Because there just aren't that many Bernbachs et cetera around; because the people who pay the bills are not that willing to look that different; and most important, because being different and innovative isn't enough. Innovation must be accompanied by a high (and rare) capacity for good taste, and an equally rare sensitivity about the reader/viewer's ability to understand the new design and respond to it.

We will glance at these two subjects in this chapter: ad dating and the mystical question of creativity.

What Dates an Ad?

First, simply the printing process itself and how the type is used. Type faces were the first element to date ads, because we had the different styles of type before we had pictures to put with the printed words. There are at least ten thousand identifiable (and named) type designs, and the contemporary graphics designer Herb Lubalin claimed that a good designer would have a working knowledge of about two thousand of these that he carried around in his head. He will

c. 1855

This is a fine example of a Victorian, lithographed ad—in this case selling an illuminating gas system. Victorian ads ran to great detail, fascination with new technology, and cutaway diagrams. The wonder of "what was happening behind the cover," was a sure-fire way of stopping the reader in ads for furnaces, hot water heaters, flush toilets, and Pullman cars.

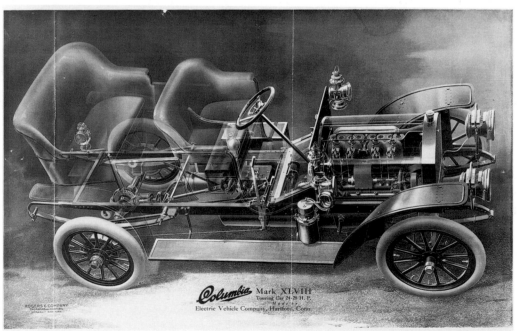

1907

An exceptionally explicit Edwardian cutaway for Columbia. The ad inadvertently records a famous firm's struggle to stay up with technological change. Columbia was the nation's largest maker of bicycles in the nineteenth century. When the automobile arrived, the company saw the handwriting on the wall and bet on the future of the electric machine. By 1907, it had recognized the failing future of that solution, and shifted to the internal-combustion gasoline engine instead. In this ad, however, while it has updated the product, it still has not updated the corporate name.

draw on them, said Lubalin, like an artist uses a palette of colors. Not only will the appearance of the type signal "colonial" Caslon or "modern" Futura, but the way the type is used is equally reflective of the changing fashion. Where are the margins? How much white space is there around the words? Is the ad neatly fenced in with a lined frame, or bled to the edges and run off the page? Is it black ink on white paper, or white letters dropped out of the black background?"

The Historical Sequence

Up to 1850, borders were ornamented, and white space was used generously to make the design interesting. Good ads were centered, balanced down the middle; type lines were flush on either side to make neat boxes of gray words. All paragraphs were justified at either margin.

Around 1840, sharp, fine-lined pictures begin to appear in the ads with the arrival of wood engravings. It took another decade or so to develop a cadre of engravers in the major cities but (especially with the huge increase in the numbers of illustrators to record the Civil War battles) the engravings became detailed, professional, and common. Illustrated ads followed the design still known as "Ayer No. 1" or "Layout A." N.W. Ayer of Philadelphia began using it in the 1870s, and Nelson likes to call them "picture window layouts." He notes it is still a favorite (top three-fifths of the ad filled with the picture; bold headline as a caption; bottom two-fifths filled with text in small type in one or two columns; with a logotype of the company signature somewhere around the base) and it can be found in such modern classics as the Bernbach Volkswagen ads. A standard example can be seen in the 1868 G.P. Rowell ad for its own advertising agency (see page 18). The hand-drawn wood (and then steel) engraving lasted up to the acceptance of the halftone photograph in the 1890s.

The Victorian Lithograph

With the mid-century invention of the limestone lithograph, advertising design came into its own. First the black-and-white and then the color lithograph were sublimely appropriate for Victorian taste. The Victorians apparently believed there was no such thing as too much detail, too much elaboration. "Cover every inch of the ad with something." The lithograph made everyone happy. The type designers no longer had to carve very detailed type faces: the lithographer could simply draw the fancy letters right into the ad. (Note the distorted perspective for J.J. Kromer's Upham Hair Dye, page 127, or the midnight romance produced by S.J. Patterson's wholesale coal, page 26.) While Victorian ads lacked restraint, most of them carried so much pictorial information that they brought the viewer as firmly to a stop as anything that would arrest our present-day page-turning.

A by-product of the stone lithograph was the chromo-lithograph invented by a German immigrant named Louis Prang. He developed a technique for what he called facsimiles of color paintings and began producing trade cards and window and counter cards that were astonishingly accurate reproductions of oil-paint originals. He did his pictures by drawing as many as thirty-two separate stones for slightly different colors that he built up with one printing after another until each end product was a more perfect color print than anyone had ever seen. (Examples of chromo-lithographs can be seen as the Goodyear rubber plantation, page 97, and the Singer Sewing Machine in Manila, page 102.) Prang got very rich with his printings—he did thousand-copy editions of Winslow Homer and Eastman Johnson paintings for the living room. He practically founded the Christmas and Valentine card business; and up to his death in 1909, plowed a great deal of money into the art education of the general public. We will return to Prang in a moment.

Art Nouveau

Art Nouveau arrived in the advertising world in the 1890s at roughly the same time the popular magazine was invented. Because of this timing, the average American's first introduction to the swirling cloth and drooping peacock feathers of Beardsley and Bradley was in magazine and poster ads. You had your choice of long-skirted ladies being wafted along on their latest safety-braked bicycles, or a newsstand flyer for the current issue of *Harper's* or *Atlantic Monthly* literary journals. The Columbia Cycle Company became so identified with Art Nouveau advertisements that Art Nouveau in turn became somewhat irrationally linked with transportation in general. An example of Art Nouveau's sweeping lines and solid blocks of color appears in the 1890s ad for Fisher Bodies (created back when Fisher built horse carriages instead of car fenders, page 224).

The reaction to the exaggerated line and fanciful backgrounds of Art Nouveau ads of course brought on its equal and opposite. In England the ads became much cleaner, and advertising drawings were cut down to single figures silhouetted against white backgrounds. In America, Louis Prang's influence rose. Prang had gotten so rich with his chromos that he spent his declining years putting art appreciation courses in grade schools, and producing colorful art textbooks for high school art and design classes. Prang's philosophy of art taught students to look at a colored object, break it down into flat, unshaded planes, and to get the effect of roundness by changing the tone of the paint. By reducing detail, these home town courses managed to clean up most of the Victorian complexity, and "Prang color" affected advertising design clear into the 1920s. The Heinz 57 apple butter jar and the butterflies, both on page 212, are painted just as Louis Prang told the class to do it.

(To this day, the effect of color on advertising is major. Research in 1988 found that color ads were 40 percent more effective than black and white; adding color to a black-and-white ad was supposed to attract 53 percent more readers than the same ad run solely in black and white. Incidentally, ads that run to the edge of a page—"bleed" pages without a margin—get one-tenth more readership than margined

1925

1926

1929

1929

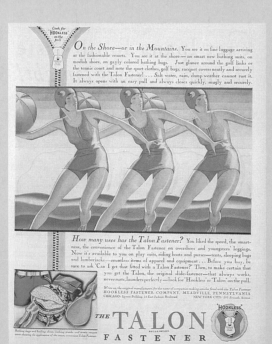

1928

1930

OPPOSITE ABOVE LEFT AND RIGHT:

One of the reactions to the detailed elaboration of Victorian ads was the simpler format of the Arts and Crafts School. A color printer, Louis Prang, introduced art courses into high schools across the country, printing and distributing free textbooks. His philosophy of reducing a picture or design to flat color planes became popular around World War I, and is evident in these two ads of the 1920s.

OPPOSITE MIDDLE LEFT AND RIGHT:

In the Twenties the illustrators continued with their attempts to simplify and suggest. While artists like Norman Rockwell and J.C. Leyendecker had drawn minutely detailed, realistic figures in the 1910s, by the 1920s they were in transition, stylizing and generalizing. Here are Leyendecker suggesting the collegian and Bradshaw Crandell vignetting the modern shopper. Note the new use of "loose" design in the A&P ad; the color sweeps the eye around the page and into the ad copy, off-center, at the base.

OPPOSITE BELOW LEFT:

Here is stronger Art Deco with its repeated patterns, parallel lines, and even more casually generalized design of the figures.

OPPOSITE BELOW RIGHT:

One of the last of the high art and style of the Twenties. This ad, although published in a million-copy run of the Saturday Evening Post, was printed in aluminum ink so the water, trucks, and picture frame flashed with a metallic gleam.

ABOVE RIGHT.

Art Deco arrived in the mid-Twenties with its smooth lines, furniture and housewares that could be mass produced, and its general simplification of forms. But the ad makers hated to abandon the romance of early images that tied modern inventions to mystic fairylands and dream worlds. The result was a series of ads for crystal-set radios with Arthurian castles in the background, pressed-steel furniture decorated with medieval tapestry designs, and automobiles somewhat inexplicably surrounded by turrets and armor as in this Franklin Booth pen-and-ink drawing for Willys Overland.

RIGHT:

Classic Art Deco and the look of the 1920s. Highly stylized figures, thin lines, sans-serif type, and Parisian architectural symbols.

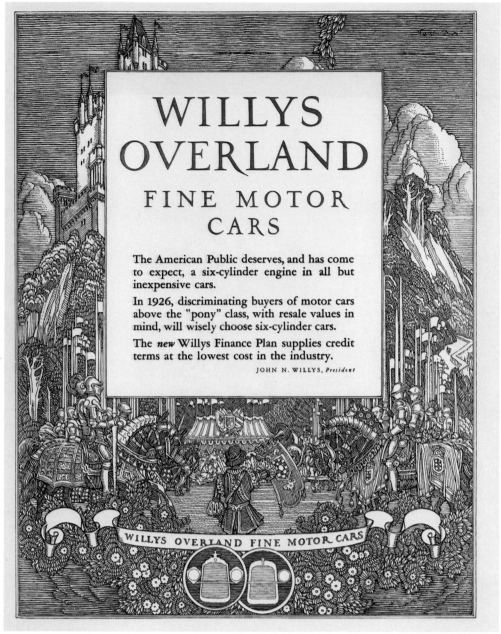

1926

1929

1934

What a difference a Depression makes. The high style and light touch of the late-Twenties art has disappeared into a frantic, almost desperate, attempt to seize the reader's attention and jam in every possible sales appeal in a single panel. The early Thirties seemed to have abandoned theme and restraint, and, lacking a link to any art style, appear to be more interested in reassuring the manufacturer that everything possible has been said, than catching the reader's eye and attention.

1934

pages regardless of being in color or black and white, and magazines charge one-tenth more, not because bled pages take more work in setting and printing, but because they get one-tenth more attention for the advertiser.)

Art Deco

The trend toward simplification continued into the Twenties and Thirties when Art Deco became the style of the leading advertising designers. Art Deco relied heavily on parallel lines, repeated (stylized) shapes, pastel colors, and a smooth, "clean" look. When it was created it was intended to look "modern," the "very latest" in design style. Interestingly, now seventy years later, it still symbolizes "modern" in graphic design.

Art Deco got its start in architecture where building edges were rounded like waterfalls, much shiny glass was used in walls and entrances, and such metal elements as elevator doors, banisters, and staircases were molded like cut clay and decorated with Aztec, Egyptian, and Indian designs. All of these elements appeared in advertisements, along with the Art Deco products themselves that had been designed for easy mass production (such as toasters, refrigerators, and tableware). The advertising designers became so enamored of the style that they produced some of the most beautiful ads ever drawn, but at this late date one senses they had almost forgotten that they were trying to sell something. The product often got smaller and the sales message so subordinated to the design that one can turn pages of the magazines of the Twenties without being conscious of the products at all.

The Mess of The Depression

So the inevitable backlash against the purity of Art Deco arrived at exactly the time the business world crashed and with it the "extra" money required for advertising. The ads of the Thirties are in appalling taste, the worst style in the two hundred years thus far experienced in the history of advertising. Multiple color plates almost disappeared, being much too expensive for the few companies still operating to afford. What advertising was purchased seemed to load copy from edge to edge, with great varieties of type shouting for attention. Drawn art nearly vanished (it being too costly to hire artists) and the few pictures that were used were mashed to one side or the other so the sales message could be spelled out in disordered detail.

The ads seemed to be without structure or centers of focus. They appear simply to reassure the account that the agency had put into the page as many possible selling themes as could be thought of without getting the type so small it would be ignored completely. The most generous explanation of a decade of graphic confusion is that it was the precursor of what is presently called a "circus" layout, characterized by such disorder and disarray that it stops the eye and challenges the reader to find something of interest in the design.

It is intriguing to speculate on how much of the clutter of

Depression ads stems from panic and how much from the change in how the ads were created. From the 1880s through the 1920s, it was traditional for agencies to rough "visualize" what they wanted an ad to look like, and then send the art director out on the open market to contract with a professional artist or photographer, who would create the visual art desired. The early New York Art Directors awards (which started in 1921 and are given annually) show the drawing or the photograph that won the prizes in the form in which it was created and brought to the agency in fulfillment of the contract. How the art work *actually* looked in the ad—frequently cropped or with copy type superimposed—is shown in postage stamp-sized pictures in the back of the volumes. Art and design were separate from the final print creation of the ad.

With the arrival of the Depression, the luxury of hiring a professional artist was abandoned, and the agencies set up their own art departments. Many of these were staffed by young, inexperienced and inexpensive commercial artists, and even more were essentially copy designers who knew text type better than art images. How much of the clutter is attributable to the still-learning, in-house artists is impossible to know.

Not until the middle of the Thirties was some order reestablished with single-theme, "slice of life," miniature "true confession" stories (usually of some domestic disaster) plus the use of comic strip continuities. The Forties continued the aesthetic confusion exacerbated by wartime shortages of paper for newspapers and magazines. Equal shortages in consumer products reduced what there was to sell, and there was major churning of personnel within the advertising agencies.

Nostalgia Time and the Fifties

Once World War II was over, there was an abundance of products, demand, advertising, and profits. The face of advertising went for normalcy, realistic representational art. The designs were comfortable; the corporate producers wanted to be associated with the good days before the War and the Depression. Figures were not stylized and images were not shocking. The product was shown in a peaceful, prosperous, un-stressed milieu.

But the ads did have a new element. They were much more deliberately targeted to specific strata of the buying public. The ads may have been realistic pictures, but what—and even more, who—was in the picture had changed. The ads now subtly chose certain income or interest groups dressed in a certain way, playing certain games, in certain environments. Where realistic art had traditionally been democratic—or least-common-denominator embracing as large a swatch of the buying population as possible—the post-war ads were much more selective. They provided images that implied either "just we relate to this product" or "if you want to be included with these kinds of people, you'd better buy this product." The images were in no way upper elite: they could just as easily

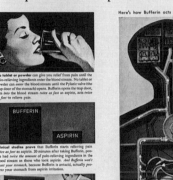

1950

Bufferin here uses the American fascination with cutaways to explain the way their new drug works. The circuit breakers in the brain pan are a nice touch. As cluttered as it may appear, the ad moves a great deal of information about a new product.

The format is "Ayer No. 1" and a far cry from the stylish ads of the late 1920s, but it is a classic example of 1950s advertising. Having struggled through twenty years of Depression and war, the reader wanted reassuring statements of how things should be. Home, kids, and small cats linked Squibb with stable reliability.

1951

OF TOIL

AND SIN

WITHIN
THIS VALE

THE BURMA-SHAVE SIGNS

From 1925 to 1963, no reflection on the "Face of American Advertising" could have been complete without thought of the 3,000 sets of Burma-Shave signs marching in cadence beside the highways of the nation.

The phenomenon began in southern Minnesota where the Odell family, father and sons, were out driving one Sunday and passed a series of signs nailed to scattered fenceposts. The signs simply said, gas, oil, eats, the name of the coming filling station, and a final one with an arrow on it showing how to get in to the pumps. What struck the Odells as noteworthy was that everyone in the car had read every sign, this in spite of the fact that they had failed to notice several dozen billboards they'd passed on the way to the series on the fenceposts. They decided to try the fencepost idea on their own shaving cream product.

It was nearly Fall, and the ground freezes early in Minnesota, so they had to work fast. They bought second-hand boards at Rose Brothers Wrecking Company, cut them into three-foot lengths, and hastily painted SHAVE THE MODERN WAY/ FINE FOR THE SKIN/DRUGGISTS HAVE IT/BURMA-SHAVE on the sets. They then rushed these out on Route 65 to Albert Lea, and on the road to Red Wing in the other direction.

From this straightforward beginning came a national phenomenon. The signs changed from prose to poetry, the area stretched out state by state in all directions, until they were ultimately in every jurisdiction except Arizona, Nevada, and New Mexico (too little traffic), and Massachusetts (roads so crooked there weren't enough stretches to stand six signs in a straight line).

The advertising historian Frank Rowsome was convinced that the reason everybody read the Burma-Shave jingles was that they were funny, and humor was so shockingly rare in the deadly serious days of Depression advertising. Rowsome believed that with Listerine, Lifebuoy, Absorbine, Jr., and Fleischmann's Yeast threatening the citizen with every ill in the physician's manual, any company who would push its product with DOES YOUR HUSBAND/MISBEHAVE/GRUNT AND GRUMBLE/RANT AND RAVE/SHOOT THE BRUTE SOME/BURMA-SHAVE or BEN/MET ANNA/ MADE A HIT/NEGLECTED BEARD/BEN-ANNA SPLIT/BURMA-SHAVE had to be admired.

The signs were set in such a way that at 35 miles an hour, it took three seconds to get from one board to the next—eighteen seconds total, or, as the advertising world noted despairingly, a lot more time than anyone advertising in the magazines or local paper could hope to hold the readers' attention. Alexander Woollcott claimed that it was as hard to read just one Burma-Shave sign as it was to eat just one salted peanut.

Rowsome was impressed with the way the pacing forced an unhurried tempo that built to the punch line: THE BEARDED LADY/TRIED A JAR/SHE'S NOW/A FAMOUS/MOVIE STAR/BURMA-SHAVE, or PITY ALL/ THE MIGHTY CAESARS/THEY PULLED/EACH WHISKER OUT/WITH TWEEZERS/BURMA-SHAVE. Rowsome noted that there was always someone in the family car who could read the signs backward as you met them in reverse on the other side of the road.

Burma-Shave could be had in either a jar or tube, but it came out like cold cream and was spread across the face with the fingers, not the traditional shaving brush. President Odell (who is also famous for having introduced the Chinese Ringneck pheasant into Minnesota), had barely gotten the cream invention accepted when the electric razor arrived and added to his competition. He himself created A SILKY CHEEK/ SHAVED SMOOTH/AND CLEAN/IS NOT OBTAINED/ WITH A MOWING MACHINE/BURMA-SHAVE.

The Odell family themselves wrote all of the early jingles, but by the end of the 1920s they were running dry, so they started an annual contest, offering $100 for any series accepted. They

BURMA SHAVE

BUT NOT YOUR CHIN

YOUR HEAD GROWS BALD

got thousands of submissions every year, and the Odells would take them all to their North Woods summer camp and spend their vacation reducing the heaps to the next year's couple of dozen. From this approach came such classics as HE HAD THE RING/HE HAD THE FLAT/BUT SHE FELT HIS CHIN/AND THAT/WAS THAT/BURMA-SHAVE, and BACHELOR'S QUARTERS/DOG ON THE RUG/ WHISKERS TO BLAME/NO ONE TO HUG/BURMA-SHAVE.

Rowsome ultimately worked his way into the Odell's confidence and finally discovered the ones that had been rejected as unfit for the national audience. We can scarcely wonder why: THE OTHER WOMAN/IN HIS LIFE/SAID "GO BACK HOME/AND SCRATCH YOUR WIFE" or MY MAN/ WON'T SHAVE/SEZ HAZEL HUZ/BUT I SHOULD WORRY/DORA'S DOES. The rest of the family seemed to have endorsed the following, but the President felt it did not meet the Company's high standards: LISTEN, BIRDS/ THESE SIGNS COST/MONEY/SO ROOST A WHILE/ BUT DON'T GET FUNNY/BURMA-SHAVE.

By the end of the 1930s, the Burma-Shave signs had become a universally recognized part of Americana, and the company shifted to public interest themes: PAST/SCHOOLHOUSES/ TAKE IT SLOW/LET THE LITTLE/SHAVERS GROW/ BURMA-SHAVE and HE SAW/THE TRAIN/AND TRIED TO DUCK IT/KICKED FIRST THE GAS/AND THEN THE BUCKET/BURMA-SHAVE. Rowsome noted that if the signs did no more than make people slow down to read them, they did some good. The company sensed this in 1955: SLOW DOWN, PA/SAKES ALIVE/MA MISSED SIGNS/FOUR/ AND FIVE/BURMA-SHAVE. A classic from this era was: DONT LOSE/YOUR HEAD/TO GAIN A MINUTE/YOU NEED YOUR HEAD/YOUR BRAINS ARE IN IT/ BURMA-SHAVE.

Farmers were given anywhere from five to fifty dollars a year rental, but most land owners were delighted to have one of the local series (it was a good way to direct visitors to their place), and the company would send out crews to replace and repair the signs all summer long. The series were pulled every two years, and new ones bolted onto the wood posts (steel poles corroded sooner). By the end, over five hundred jingles had been used.

Sales rose every year until 1947. Rowsome notes that that year the favorite jingle ran ALTHO/WE'VE SOLD/SIX MILLION OTHERS/WE STILL CAN'T SELL/THOSE COUGHDROP BROTHERS. There was a seven-year plateau, and then sales began to sink. Why? Super-highways. Even on country roads, people were driving too fast to read the words. And by the early 1960s (with the cost of the signs exceeding $200,000 a year), the family decided the jingles had outlived their usefulness. So, thirty-eight years after the start in Minneapolis, Burma-Shave sold out to Philip Morris, and became a division of its American Safety Razor Products. Philip Morris agreed with the family that the signs had had their day, and crews went out and removed every post, so nothing would fade before history's weather.

William Zinsser, the distinguished author of On Writing Well and long associated with Reader's Digest and the Book-of-the-Month Club, wrote a memorial article for the Saturday Evening Post, and the Advertising Club of New York erected a final set of the signs down the center island of Park Avenue. Frank Rowsome has, like the Oxford Shakespeare, brought together the entire canon, and preserved them arranged by year. The few of the signs that still exist are in museums—the boards here are in the Smithsonian Institution in Washington, D.C.; a second set hangs from the ceiling in the American Advertising Museum in Portland, Oregon; and a third is in the Ford Museum in Dearborn, Michigan.

Ugly is only skin-deep.

It may not be much to look at. But beneath that humble exterior beats an air-cooled engine. It won't boil over and ruin your piston rings. It won't freeze over and ruin your life. It's in the back of the car for better traction in snow and sand. And it will give you about 29 miles to a gallon of gas.

After a while you get to like so much about the VW you even get to like what it looks like.

You find that there's enough legroom for almost anybody's legs. Enough headroom for almost anybody's head. With a hat on it. Snug-fitting bucket seats. Doors that close so well you can hardly close them. (They're so airtight, it's better to open the window a crack first.)

Those plain unglamorous wheels are each suspended independently. So when a bump makes one wheel bounce, the bounce doesn't make the other wheel bump. It's things like that you pay the $1,585* for when you buy a VW. The ugliness doesn't add a thing to the cost of the car.

That's the beauty of it.

1962

We have placed a generous sample of the classic VW ads in the following chapter, but no survey of the Face of Advertising could be complete without an example of this series by Doyle Dane Bernbach. It is generally agreed that the change in the appearance of American ads brought about by DDB and David Ogilvy had a greater impact than any other source in the second half of the twentieth century. The VW ads, for example, made humor acceptable, flattered the reader that he was intelligent enough to learn by implication without having every point spelled out, and involved him in the dialogue with the advertiser. Both Bernbach and Ogilvy believed that each of their ads had to pass on specific information about the product. Simply announcing the existence of The New XXXX to keep the firm's name before the public was not enough.

Hathaway presents Antique Ivory — a color that never clashes

EVER noticed the marvelous color that ivory goes when it ages? It lies somewhere between cream and old gold. Very unobtrusive. Very soft. A perfect color for a shirt.

When Hathaway's experts were finally satisfied that an *Antique Ivory* dye could be made, we chose to present it on our famous all-cotton Batiste Oxford. You see the result above. A mellow color that refuses to clash with anything. Hathaway pioneered Batiste Oxford many heat-waves ago. This remarkable stuff retains the look and handle of top-grade Oxford but sheds nearly half the weight. It never feels steamy the way some summer shirtings do.

The shirt above costs about $7.50—long or short sleeves. See the full range of Hathaway Batiste Oxfords at the better stores. They're also in White and Bermuda Blue. For store names, write C. F. Hathaway, Waterville, Maine. Call OXford 7-5566 in New York.

Shirts in Antique Ivory stripes, about $7.50; solids, about $7.

1951

Hathaway had been making shirts since 1837, but few people had ever heard of them until David Ogilvy created this classic American ad campaign. The man in the eye patch was a displaced White Russian baron named George Wrangell. He made his living as a clothing model. There was nothing the matter with his eye; Ogilvy had simply bought a patch in a drugstore on the way to work to give the man "story appeal." Although the ads initially ran only in The New Yorker, in no time the figure became an up-scale folk hero, nationally recognized, and sales for Hathaway ballooned. The eye patch worked for nearly forty years, and is considered among the greatest ad ideas of all time.

---

be workingmen cheering a washtub full of iced beer; all-female patrons of a laundromat; or senior citizens at a family reunion. But the detailed, representational illustrations implied "folks like us like [the carefully drawn product.]"

The Far-Out Sixties and Seventies

So, of course, there had to be the reaction. Kids with kittens and the family washing the car in front of the nicely landscaped rambler tripped Op Art panels, Pop Art blowups of the product, Camp Art parodies, Psychedelic Art color riots, and Funky Art eclectic detail. Mondrian-like squares broke up the page. Anything to provide an excuse for color, variety, shock, and attention. Roy Paul Nelson called it the "What the Hell" style of the times.

Conclusion?

So is this where it's going to end? Have we finally distilled out true taste from long experience? Of course not. No one has the faintest idea of what will come next. The odds are equally high that the following fashion will be in Victorian stone lithographs or metal holograms. The Eighties tried pop-up inserts; peel-and-sniff perfume ads; and 3-D glasses the better to picture automobiles and computer terminals in the round. (The first paper pop-up of the Transamerica building that appeared in *Time* magazine took some 500 Mexican and Colombian workers to fold and glue. They assembled away for 17 weeks at a cost of over three million dollars. While the insert was one of the Della Femina

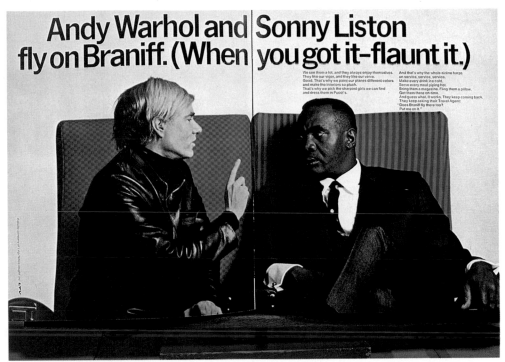

c. 1965

c. 1971

Another of the Sixties style of advertising, here expressed by the Jack Tinker & Associates agency. Again, the presumed intelligent reader is expected to make the connection between spicy, aromatic food and the need for Alka-Seltzer. Explicit explanatory text was not necessary.

The 1960s and 1970s were filled with enormously creative and idiosyncratic advertising innovators. Such personalities as George Lois, Carl Ally, Sam Scali, Mary Wells, Jerry Della Femina created whole new styles and genres which were immediately identifiable and have spawned whole schools of advertising forms.

This is a typical Lois ad: big pictures, big type, arresting images to stop the viewer and force him to read the small print. Lois loves to use celebrities; not to endorse a product but to create unlikely juxtapositions that seize the reader's attention. In this series for Braniff ("When You Got It—Flaunt It" is one of Lois' contributions to the American vocabulary) he paired Salvador Dali and Whitey Ford, Mickey Spillane and Marianne Moore, Hermione Gingold and George Raft as seatmates.

---

agency's greatest successes, it wiped out 35 percent of the Transamerica Corp.'s advertising budget for 1986. But it did get the readers' attention and did remind them of what the product was. *Time* later did a reader-awareness study and found that 97 percent of those queried recalled the ad.)

So Hire Me an Innovator

Again and again we have seen how some innovative individual has set a new style and image that the whole advertising profession copies until the reader/viewer is sick of it. The question of where do you find these innovators produces an interesting footnote to the creative process.

Edward Buxton, in trying to identify who on an agency's staff would prove to be the most useful, found: "Creative people are vain. According to psychologists and other people who studied them, the general view is that creative people have a stronger, more pronounced sense of self. Call it ego, pride of authorship, a larger-than-normal need for praise and approval. In any case successful creative people do indeed seem to have a need—often bordering on compulsion—to 'express themselves'—and to the largest and most appreciative audience possible. So be it—it is an integral part of their equipment. It can fuel a burning ambition—or cause untold misery. It usually does both."

Roy Paul Nelson, searching for a way to identify the creative person, concluded "The chances are that creative people are not pleased with the way things are." He quotes Burt Prelutsky's description of the "master griper": "A master griper is never put off by good news. A smile, he knows, is only a frown upside down. His motto is 'Every silver lining has a cloud.'"

Why does creativity make so much difference in advertising? Because the products today are all so nearly alike. Every idea has already been used. How can you possibly get anybody's attention for *your* paper towels, station wagon, airline discount? But there are techniques and, as always, they require choices.

The creative artist or copywriter or scriptwriter must first ask, Shall I focus on the product and try to sell it with some "news" about its contents or applications? This was the traditional approach, and as Pope says, "These were the campaigns of secret ingredients, greater horsepower, new formulas, brighter washdays."

The creator can next ask, Or should I go after a segment of the audience and shoot toward a likely buying group? The ads of the Sixties started this approach, and can be seen in the memorable layouts of Bernbach and Ogilvy. There is a special kind of person who wants to drive a stripped down,

1965–1979

While some designers were going back to the use of traditional typefaces, the period of the 1960s and 1970s contained some of the most skilled designers of new typefaces and one-of-a-kind logos. These were intended to catch the feel of the corporation or product represented yet still seize the attention of the reader on the run and remain in his memory to be recognized the next time the design was encountered. Here are a few examples from two of the most skilled of these graphic artists.

The Sound of Music logo was designed by Herb Lubalin to be used on record albums, motion picture theater posters, and newspaper ads, linking the many formats with a single product; the letter cube was a logo for a combined broadcast by the three networks involved.

The remaining designs are a sampling of logos coming from the pen of Lou Dorfsman, the legendary head of design for the Columbia Broadcasting System. Using only the standard letters of the traditional alphabet, he makes each design a unique, stand-alone image that identifies the company or product it represents.

1968–1980

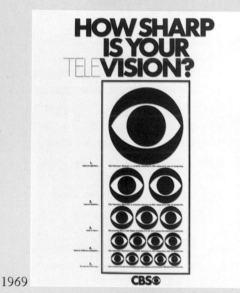

1969

In the shift from selling individual products to selling services and corporate bodies, this is one of Dorfsman's solutions to "how to sell the kinds of things the corporation does"—in this case, CBS' social consciousness.

1972

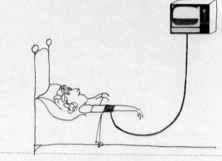

Some women can't live without it. Indeed, our daytime line-up is such a vital part of their lives that the 9 most popular programs are all ours. Of our 16 daytime programs, 12 are in the Top 15. The ladies have taken us to their hearts.
CBS Television Network

1963

Dorfsman spent forty years exploring variations on the theme of the CBS eye. He had inherited the symbol from his mentor, William Golden, but he took it to heights that Golden had never dreamed. He used it on the sides of CBS buildings, cuff links, automobiles and vans, on paper cups, stationery, matchbooks, and decades of CBS magazine and newspaper ads. Here, one of the latter from the New York Times.

Another Dorfsman layout directed at similar purposes as the previous image, but treated with a lighter touch. Dorfsman got Toni Ungerer to draw the illustration; the copy is set in CBS Didot, a seventeenth-century type style selected by Dorfsman (with a Dorfsman-designed sans serif) to be the two basic fonts for all CBS graphics.

Modess.... *because*

1966

This was an unusually effective ad campaign in the Sixties selling the Modess brand of sanitary napkins. At a time when print descriptions of personal products were tightly circumscribed, Modess presented a long series of high-fashion models wearing couturier gowns in ads carrying only two words of copy: "Modess because . . ." The viewer was expected to supply the rest based on the product's long-standing reputation for quality. Cynics in the advertising profession claimed that the company's ad writers, given the copy restrictions of the time, simply could never figure out what to say.

Mitsouko a perfume by Guerlain

1966

This is a stylish solution to the How do you sell perfume? problem. Arresting, off-balance layout; exotic, beautiful woman; crisp, colorful image of the unusual Mitsouko bottle; and a black border on each side which is bound to contrast dramatically with neighboring ads. This stunning design received the Gold Medal Award from the New York Art Director's Club. The art director was Gennaro Andreozzi for the Gilbert Advertising Agency.

---

functional VW bug; one with a palate for fine wines and Dijon mustard who uses Schweppes in his drinks. Should I describe my product as an accepted ornament of a special kind of life, or a guarantee of a certain kind of experience for a limited, select kind of consumer?

Or should I side-step the issue completely? Tell nothing about the product, make no mention of price or quality or use, but simply suggest life-style? Coke is it! The Heartbeat of America. Pepsi Generation. Three persons in evening clothes wrestling on a Scandinavian couch in front of a Greek statue. Oddly enough, all of the above options seem to sell products quite efficiently.

Ultimately the creator will settle on a core idea, the central selling concept. He then proceeds through the next series of questions: What point do I wish to make? What is my target audience (students, mothers of young children, doctors, Yuppies)? What do I want my viewer to do? Buy now? Simply love Chevrolet until she's ready to buy a car? Move his money out of CDs into bonds? Feel benevolent about Weyerhauser and AT&T so if they ever get cross-wise with the Forest Service or the Anti-trust Division, they'll at least listen to our side of the argument?

John Caples said to be effective you must appeal to the reader's self-interest. What's in it for me? Give the reader some news; something she hasn't heard about yet. Stir up his curiosity. Get him involved. And then proceed. Shirley Polykoff said, "Creativity has always been just a knack or talent for expressing a single idea or simple concept in a fresh arresting new way—what I call 'thinking it out square,' then saying it with flair."

Meeting the needs
of international agribusiness
takes a bank that's involved
from the ground up.

Bank of America. A major force in agriculture all over the world.
Bank of America understands agribusiness. For 75 years we've been a part of the enormous agriculture industry of California. Today our involvement has spread around the world.

From production loans to dockside financing to leases, no other bank has played a more active role in California's agriculture than Bank of America. In fact, we're the leading bank in the United States in loans to farmers. And our loans to agribusinesses around the world

approach $3 billion.

In Asia and Africa, Europe, Latin America, North America and the Middle East, our experience with the unique problems facing agribusiness makes us a leading resource upon which to draw.

We cover agribusiness from production to processing to distribution.
Crop and livestock producers, food processors, distributors and exporters. Family-owned companies, cooperatives, large multi-national conglomerates and governmental

agencies. Bank of America has served them all. And from them we've learned just about everything there is to know about helping agribusiness companies grow and thrive.

To serve our international clients where they do business, Bank of America has created a network of in-place Global Account Officers who specialize in the specific needs of agribusiness in the region where they're stationed. They understand the problems facing agribusiness in both developed and developing countries. Whether you need financing for crop and livestock production, pro-

cessing and distribution, or import and export, Bank of America's on-the-spot presence means you'll have a close working relationship, responsive to your individual situation.

Our commitment to international agribusiness is growing.
At Bank of America, our ability to draw upon up-to-date technology and data plus the market contacts we've made over the years have made us a recognized leader in agribusiness finance. And we're committed to using this worldwide network of resources and expertise to help agri-

businesses prosper. Through our agribusiness specialists, you can tap our resources to structure funding or to supply financial advisory services.

From drought to foreign exchange, the problems facing international agribusinesses can be unpredictable, even beyond control. But your banking relationship must

be one upon which you can rely. So let us put our experience and world-wide network to work for you. Look to the bank that understands agriculture from the ground up.

Look to the Leader.™

BANK OF AMERICA

1983

This is "Ayer No. 1" format taken to its modern extreme. With offset or laser printing, current color work is pushing the limits of perfection. The brilliance and the subtle gradations of color have become still another clue dating an ad, while the traditional half-tone is disappearing before our eyes.

OPPOSITE ABOVE LEFT:

Both the cat and the format have come a long way from the Squibb kitten of 1951. The photo was by Barry Seidman, for the Tolson and Company advertising agency. The cat's eyes are as arresting as a shocking headline.

OPPOSITE ABOVE RIGHT:

What dates an ad? A saddening answer is this example, linked to the AIDS epidemic. This was the first ad for this product ever directed to a female audience (thus breaking a longtime publishing taboo), and appeared in Cosmopolitan *magazine. It was developed by the Bloom Agency of New York for the manufacturer, Mentor Corporation.*

OPPOSITE BELOW:

How do you distinguish your ad from the dozens surrounding it? In the 1980s, the designers tried dramatic variations on flat print—Toyota cars provided 3-D glasses, Salem cigarettes inserted party poppers, Absolut vodka gave us microchips playing Christmas carols and snowflakes floating in plastic pillows.

Children's pop-ups appeared as a cartoon Camel, a paper Apple II computer, and here the one that started it all, Jerry Della Femina's Transamerica building. Readers' recall was nearly total, and, as Della Femina declared, "It's not just an ad but a happening."

It all sounds marvelously easy, and in the hands of the experts, it may be. But regrettably, as Jugenheimer and White remind us, it does not take into consideration the negative review by the account executive because he *knows* the client doesn't like that sort of thing; or the research department head who *knows* the ad doesn't fit the market as they've analyzed it; or the client himself who *knows* you'll never sell anything that way, and anyway his son at college won't like it.

How does anything successful ever get done? Maybe the

answer is in George Lois's reflection on his forty years in the trade: ". . . I plunged into the mediocrity of the commercial world and got myself a reputation as the *enfant terrible* of the advertising world. I'm sure I deserved it, and I'm just as sure that without fighting for my work every second of my life, my work would be just as dull and uninspired as most of the so-called communications in the world (the bland leading the bland). To produce work I could be proud of, I've had to shove, push, cajole, persuade, wheedle, exaggerate, flatter, manipulate, be obnoxious, occasionally lie, and always *sell*."

1984

1986

1986

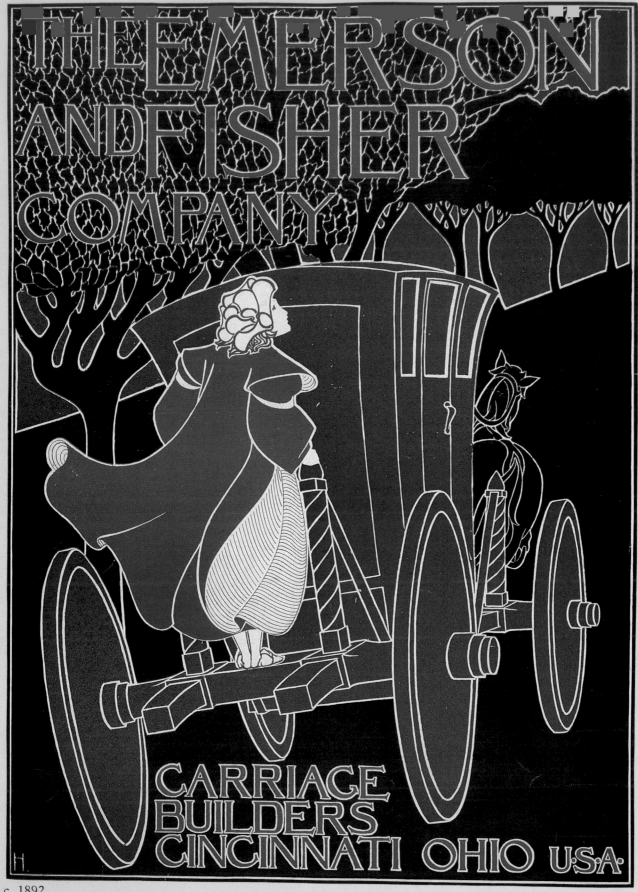

THE EMERSON AND FISHER COMPANY

CARRIAGE BUILDERS CINCINNATI OHIO U·S·A·

c. 1892

At the start of the auto age, personal, wheeled transportation was by carriage and bicycle. The carriage trade advertised little, but the cycle companies flooded the new magazines with flowing pictures of cyclists—mostly female—effortlessly pedaling through the open country without mud, sand, or bumps. Here is a rare carriage ad in the contemporary cycle style advertising the product of the Fisher family. Grandfather Fisher had made carriages in Germany; Father Fisher made them in Cincinnati; and the six sons would form the Fisher Body Company in 1908 in Norwalk, Ohio.

The Automobile

WHEN THEY ADVERTISED wagons, they said "We Make Wagons" or "Studebaker has been making wagons for fifty years." They made no attempt to say what the wagon would do or why the Studebaker was the best one for *you*. When they advertised carriages, they showed silhouettes of all kinds of two- or four-wheeled vehicles and said, "We'll make what you want" or "Fisher Makes Twenty-five Kinds of Carriages for the Trade." Never an explanation of why one was better than another or why there were that many different shapes. When they advertised bicycles (and there was a lot of that going on when the automobile suddenly appeared—ten million of the two-wheelers had been built by 1895), they said, "See the Beautiful World on Your Columbia Cycle" or "Life is more fun on a Peerless." Absolutely no mention of how it worked in sand, mud, ruts, and tall grass. So how do you sell a horseless carriage?

The first automobile was built in America in 1893, when the Duryea brothers of Springfield, Massachusetts, put a one-cylinder, four-horsepower engine under the seat of a standard buggy and started the revolution. The Duryeas created the first auto ad in 1894, and added an illustration to it in 1895. They weren't quite sure what to call the contraption that they'd built, so they tried three names and in so doing symbolized the first twenty years of the auto. The beginnings were to be a steady series of choices among possibilities: What *kind* of wagon would you use to carry the engine? Should the engine be steam, electric, or gasoline? How would you start the thing? How would you stop it? How should you steer it? Tiller or wheel? Throttle on the wheel or the dash or the floor? Brakes on the wheels or the chain or the drive shaft? Steel wheels or wooden? Spokes or discs? Solid tires or balloon? And how would you advertise what you'd built to your customers?

The answer to the last question was easy, Henry Ford said, don't waste money on print. The kind of person who would buy a car would have to see it to want it. So for the first few years, all the manufacturers put their promotional money into public races. The first race in America was sponsored by the *Chicago Times-Herald* on Thanksgiving Day, 1895. Six cars managed to get to the starting line (in a heavy snow), and they took off down the 54-mile race course toward Evanston. Two of the machines were electric, three were German gasoline auto cars, and the Duryea boys had their "auto wagon." Ten hours and 23 minutes later, two vehicles managed to get back. Three of the cars had broken down, one had run into a horse and hack, and one driver had succumbed to the cold. The Duryea came in first, and one of the Benz electrics came in second—one hour later.

That race got enormous (free) newspaper coverage, and magazine reporting of the French and English experiments in automaking got good treatment in *Scientific American* and similar magazines, so by 1896 dozens of backyard mechanics were trying to build something that would make a carriage go without a horse. Henry Ford put one together in his parents' shed, Ransom Olds hung his engine under a stylish buggy and drove it from Lansing to Detroit. In September, Alexander Winton got his solution to the puzzle to run around Cleveland. By 1899 over 2,000 mechanics were involved in putting individual motors together in almost that many different ways.

1904

THE HORSELESS AGE.

Duryea Motor Wagon Company,

SPRINGFIELD, MASS.

MANUFACTURERS OF

Motor
Wagons,
Motors, and

"1896 MODEL"

Automobile
Vehicles
of all kinds.

1896

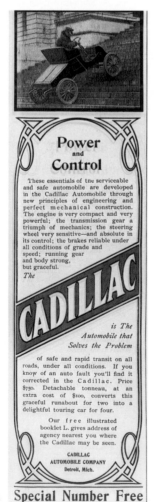

1903 Special Number Free

The first illustrated ad for an automobile ever printed. The same copy had appeared some six months earlier, but without the picture. Note the chassis is simply a buggy without the horse shafts. Nobody knew what to call their products yet, so the Motor Wagon label is as good as any and better than most.

Ransom Eli Olds had been experimenting with both gasoline and steam in the 1890s, but in 1901 he settled on a three-horsepower gasoline engine and produced the first commercially successful production model made in America. He sold 425 the first year, 2,500 in 1902, 4,000 in 1903, and 5,000 in 1904 (when the above ad appeared). His success stimulated literally dozens of other mechanics to try it. 1904 was the last year anyone used a tiller instead of a steering wheel, and engines were taken out from under the seat and put up where the horse used to be since that's where the customer expected the power to come from. Olds had a bad fire in 1901 and was forced to buy components from other machinists to fill his orders (up until then all the parts had been machined within the owner's own shop), and the device proved so efficient that others copied his technique, thus laying the basis for the coming invention of the assembly line.

Not surprisingly, all the early automakers had been manufacturing something else before the gasoline engine arrived. White, the truck maker, had been making sewing machines; Peerless had been making washing machines; Pierce of Pierce-Arrow had been making birdcages. Henry M. Leland, father of the Cadillac, had been a machine tool maker. (The car was named after the French explorer who founded Detroit in 1701.) Leland's Cadillac was an exceptional machine from the start, and was built throughout from standardized parts. In a day of hand-fitted machining, this claim so challenged the English that in 1908 their Royal Automobile Club bought three of the cars,

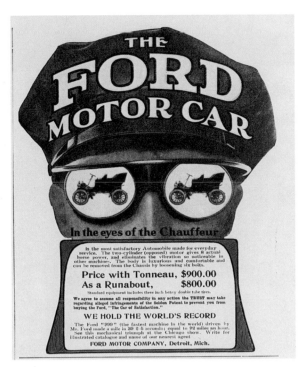

1904

1905

disassembled them all to loose parts and reassembled them, deliberately using parts for each from the other two. The three then ran so perfectly on a 500-mile test, that the Club awarded Cadillac the Dewar Trophy. The ad shows a 1903 Cadillac charging up the steps of the Wayne County Courthouse.

ABOVE LEFT:

Henry Ford was a racing driver and a self-taught mechanic who founded his company in June of 1903. This ad ran eight months later, and Ford was already making money. The early cars were all toys of the very rich, and at this stage of Ford's thinking, he assumed the car would be driven by the family chauffeur. In 1904, a middle-class employee averaged $2 a day, so the Runabout would have cost the "average man" his total wages for four-hundred days of work.

ABOVE RIGHT:

In the beginning, Goodyear Tires were solid rubber and proud of it. The tread was deep cuts into the "endless" rubber, leaving islands or cleats to seize the road.

RIGHT:

Most of the automakers ran ads showing women driving their cars with ease (most with even less determination than this lady in her Franklin), and photographs of the time all show women drivers. The major element that women found daunting was the hand crank. Not until Leland and Cadillac invented the electric starter in 1911, was there any way of starting the car other than by turning the crankshaft, by hand, hard enough to compress the gasoline fumes and get the spark to ignite a piston. It frequently took many spins to fire, and then when the engine took over, it frequently spun the crank, breaking knuckles, thumbs, and occasionally arms. Equally, if a car was not firmly braked, it could drive over the starter with devastating results. Leland got his company inventor, Charles F. Kettering, to produce the electric, battery-operated self-starter for the benefit of both sexes.

1907

1908

Henry Ford's earliest cars were conceived for the luxury trade, but in 1908 he announced his design for a People's Car. He claimed it would get you there and get you back. It had four cylinders, sat very high above the road for maximum clearance, was simple to operate, and got thirty miles to the gallon. You gave it gas by moving a lever on the steering wheel. As assembly line production cut costs, Ford reduced its selling price to an

1909

astonishing $290 for a fully equipped model in 1926. He sold 15 million units and at one time, one half of all cars in the world were Model-T's.

ABOVE:

Henry Ford did not believe in selling his cars with beautiful women leaning against the tonneau. His ads were long copy, straightforward, telling the prospective buyer chapter and verse about what the product

1912

would provide. Footnote: the Model-T was the first car to put the steering wheel on the left side, as noted above.

ABOVE:

Right up to our own time, the tire manufacturers have been unable to make up their minds on the most efficient tread design. Firestone's 1912 solution has a straightforward feel about it: just mold "Non Skid" right into the rubber.

1914

John and Horace Dodge had been machinists making engines on order for Olds and Cadillac and in 1914 decided to go into business for themselves. This is both their first car and their first ad. The car proved to be unusually reliable, and in three years was the third largest seller in the country.

1915

No acrophobe he, but let's hope he set the brakes. In 1915, he would have had brakes only on the rear wheels, activated by cables from the pedal to the drums. And these worked only while someone's foot was on the pedal. You set the car with the hand brake, a cable-linked caliper that seized the drive shaft—nothing held the wheels directly. Four-wheel cable brakes wouldn't appear until 1924, but four-wheel hydraulic brakes followed soon after.

1916

An early example of an aberration in auto advertising design which has afflicted auto artists for decades. Cars get longer and higher, while their owners get smaller and more petite. In the coming days of 1950s and 1960s "dream" and "muscle" cars, it was estimated that auto ads exaggerated the length of the chassis by almost 25 percent—even when the picture was a photograph! The above shows a 1916 Mitchell in all its glory.

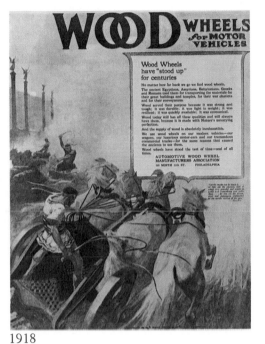

1917

1918

1924

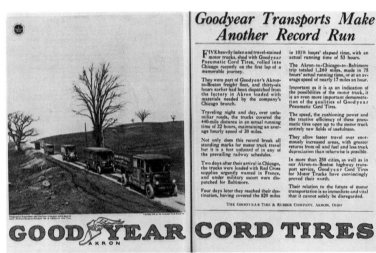

1917

1918

1912

1916

In 1912, there were twenty companies making electric cars, and 33,842 of the cars were registered in the U.S. They were quiet, responsive, very reliable, clean, and a favorite of women drivers for city use. They had a range of 40–50 miles (you had to be back in the garage for a recharge at the end of that loop), and, until World War I, most of the manufacturers were located in New England. For the first decade of the century, many believed the ultimate future for personal transportation would be electric. Note that this stylish ad (left) was created by Coles Phillips, later to be known for his hosiery and lingerie pictures.

On the right is another Coles Phillips model using fingertip controls on her 1916 Overland, revealing one of the first of the engineers' endless experimentation with ways of shifting gears.

Ransom Olds was the first to produce a commercial model and put it up for sale, guaranteeing each one to look like the others in the shop. His machine was reliable, it had three horsepower and a curved dash that looked slightly like a sleigh, and it inspired Gus Edwards to write, "In My Merry Oldsmobile." More free publicity.

Olds sold 425 of these in 1901, 2,500 in 1902, 4,000 in 1903, and 5,000 in 1904. The very first year he had a major accident in his shop, which in turn had a major impact on the industry yet to come. By 1901 there were several dozen companies selling cars and all of them guaranteed that every element of their machines was made in their own shop under careful, personal control. Olds' machine was getting good press plus word of mouth support and his orders were accumulating—at which point a fire broke out and destroyed both his inventory and his lathes. Determined not to lose the orders, Olds decided to farm out contracts for various elements of his car—made to his specifications—and the resulting parts not only came back cheaper and faster than he could have made them, but permitted all the orders to be filled essentially "simultaneously" instead of sequentially. The component technique was quickly taken up by Olds' competitors and the device began the diversification of production that created Detroit as an automaking center. It also created the environment which made Henry Ford's assembly line possible in 1914.

The promotional public races multiplied. Henry Ford hired a flamboyant cyclist by the name of Barney Oldfield to drive Ford's red "999" racer, and all three did well on the tracks. The annual Vanderbilt Cup was established; a track was built in Indianapolis. In 1901 the first of many endurance runs was set to go from New York to Buffalo (75 cars entered); and Charles J. Glidden, a wealthy New Englander,

organized the Glidden Tours which ran from New York to St. Louis.

What kind of car were they driving? The pioneers were still trying to decide. The New England mechanics believed the way of the future was steam. It was cheap, reliable, accelerated smoothly, and the technology was well developed. Twenty-six in the Buffalo race were steam cars. The first automobile to be used at the White House (for President Taft) was a steamer. In 1906 a Stanley steam car went 127.88 mph on the track at Daytona Beach, Florida, but for cross-country runs above 50 mph, the boiler simply could not produce steam as quickly as the engine required it.

Electric cars were even more reliable, shifted even more smoothly, and steadily gained in popularity until 1912, when there were 20 companies selling their brands, and nearly 34,000 electric cars were registered. They worked fine in town, but they had to be back in the garage to be recharged after 40 or 50 miles, and they really could only cruise at 30 mph.

So the gasoline car (mostly centered in Michigan and around the Great Lakes) won out chiefly because of the open country road. The gas engine was "cranky," unreliable, constantly breaking down, and murderously hard to start, but it could handle primitive roads and go a long way from home.

The various things that went wrong with the cars got fixed a part at a time. The period of adjustment was not easy. Makers of wooden wheels fought the steel spoke producers. Hand horns resisted electric "warning signals." Reliable acetylene head- and tail-lights fought erratic electric lights. But once Charles Kettering had invented the electric self-starter for Cadillac, and General Motors had perfected the installment plan, there was little further resistance, and the

THE FINAL WORD IN A CAR
—for the man whose word is final

THE PRESIDENT, a Studebaker Big Six Custom Sedan, is built to do justice to men identified with successful business achievement—and christened The President to symbolize the leadership of its owners!

The long, low-swung lineaments of its custom body are a joy to behold—while the interior, luxuriously upholstered with broadlace trim, is replete with every nicety and novelty of custom treatment and appointments.

Equipped with disc wheels and four-wheel brakes—with the silvered figure of Atalanta above its radiator, prophetic symbol of the quiet Studebaker L-head motor, which recently smashed all transcontinental records—New York to San Francisco in 86 hours and 20 minutes!

By all means, see The President!

Equipment: No-draft ventilating windshield, nickel-plated bumper and bumperettes, Watson Stabilators, engine heat indicator and gasoline gauge on the dash, coincidental lock, oil filter and air purifier, automatic windshield cleaner, automatic spark control, double rear-view mirror, clock, arm rests, toggle grips; dome light, automatically turned on when right rear door is opened; and two-beam aëero headlights, controlled from steering wheel; furnished in broadcloth upholstery with ebony lacquer body; or mohair upholstery with body finished in Croatin green lacquer.

THE PRESIDENT
A Big Six Custom Sedan *(for seven)*

$2245

Standard Six Custom Sedan . $1385
Big Six Custom Brougham . . $1985

Prices f.o.b. factory, including 4-wheel brakes, disc wheels and equipment listed

S · T · U · D · E · B · A · K · E · R

1926

As the poet decreed: "Build thee more stately mansions, O my soul." Studebaker was the distinguished successor to the Studebaker wagon firm which had been the nation's largest carriage maker back to the days of the Oregon and Santa Fe trails. Note that by 1926 the argument over wooden vs. wire wheels had been resolved by steel disks.

1916

1925

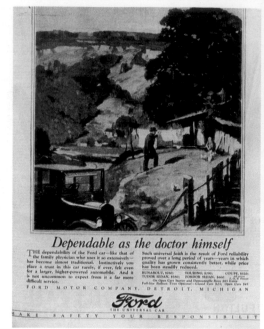

1925

Accessory ads pressed hard on danger and guilt. You owed it to your loved ones to add the devices that would protect the passengers. Cadillac was the first to offer electric lights and Ford put them on the Model-T at the end of 1914. Electric warning signals came somewhat later—note that no one knew they were supposed to be called horns.

1925, and the accessory ads are still terrifying the customer. It is hard to know whether early wrecks really were so dramatic, or only the artists' re-creations were, but when a brake or battery or headlight ad showed the dangers of failing to buy their product, a "totalled" car was totally totalled.

ABOVE RIGHT:

This ad has two historic elements: the first purchasers of a car in a town were "the rich folks" who bought the early automobiles as

playthings; the second purchasers (actually starting around 1915) were the doctors. The sound of a car at night or off the highway would bring people on to the porch to "see what's wrong" since it was almost always the doctor on a house call. The second notable thing about this ad is that it is the first Ford advertisement after the original pure text ads announcing the machine in 1908 and 1909. Ford did not believe in print ads, and only the costly campaigns of Chevrolet in the early Twenties drove him to defend his product.

---

primitive predecessors disappeared from the scene.

By 1915, what was to be known as "the car" was fairly stabilized and the ways of advertising it changed. The first problem for the ad makers was to overcome the savage disappearance of companies, factories, and brands. In our own time we have seen well-established computer companies evaporate leaving "orphan" machines behind. In the automobile world, over 1,500 name companies had produced branded cars up to 1925. By the end of 1926, only 44 were still in business, and that was down to 15 by the Great Crash in 1929. Thus, one of the continuing themes of early automobile advertising was the reliability of the company.

The second target of the early advertisers was who the car was built for. The early machines were essentially adult toys. You really didn't *use* them for anything. Next they became the device the rich folks took the family to church in, and finally they were the way the doctor got to the farm on the house call. At this point the manufacturers put a closed body on the frame and began to sell the machine to the father to drive the family around town in. They put wide, solid tires on the chain-driven wheel, and called it a truck. Different companies created specialized truck bodies to carry things on the frame.

This was where the automobile was when World War I broke out, and like all our wars, the experience had a major impact on transportation. A generation of young men drove their first car as an ambulance or a supply truck in Europe, and the wife or girlfriend at home learned to drive at the urging of the ads "to go to the Red Cross and volunteer meetings." The problem of turning a cold engine fast enough to get compression and fire usually required a man to jerk the crank, but by the war electric starters on the new cars permitted women to start the machine. (In the early days, a lot of men had to ask for help, too.) The ads began to show more women driving the cars than men.

The third shift in auto advertising hung on price. By the time the car manufacturer had solved its various problems the average price was around $2,800 stripped, running up to the expensive models at $8,000 to $10,000. The average clerk or craftsman made $2.41 a day (note a *day*, not an hour) and something was going to have to give if the car was to be sold to anyone except the boss. Henry Ford declared that he was going to make The Universal Car for the common man, and he did: the Model-T. He designed the almost perfect car for the time, invented the highly efficient assembly line to produce it, and began paying his mechanics

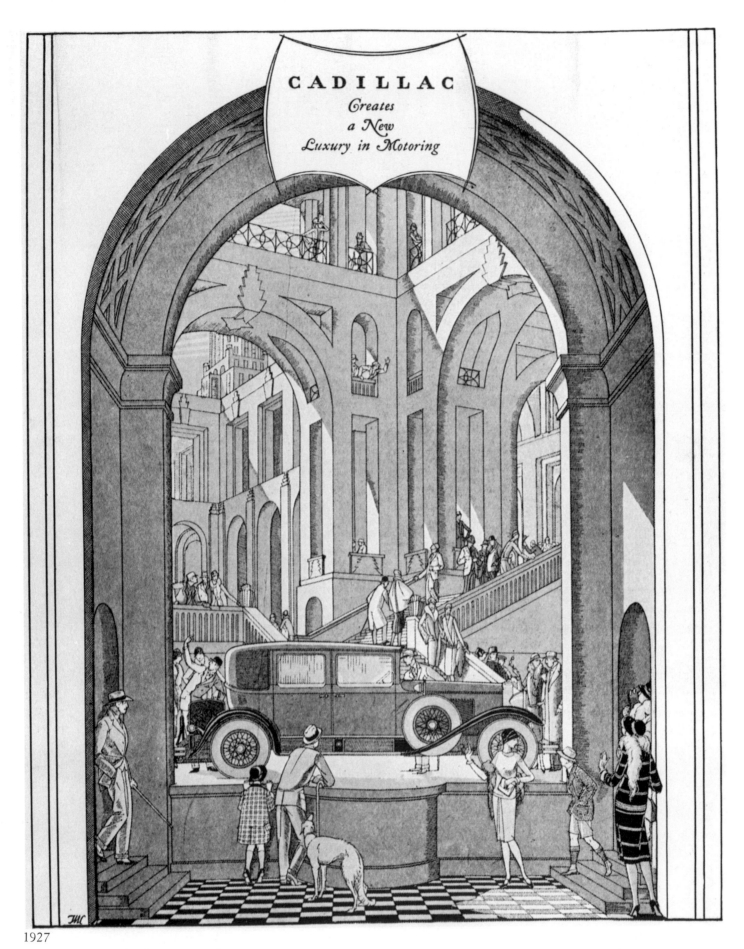

CADILLAC
*Creates
a New
Luxury in Motoring*

1927

How it would have looked if Piranesi had owned a Cadillac. By 1927, Cadillac was sufficiently recognized for its excellence and the quality of its product that seven words were sufficient copy to achieve its purpose. This ad, by Thomas M. Cleland, received an award from Harvard for its "Effective use of illustration." Cleland also drew Piranesian arches for Rolls-Royce ads, and sold Locomobiles by re-creating Pompeiian frescoes and mosaics around the company logo.

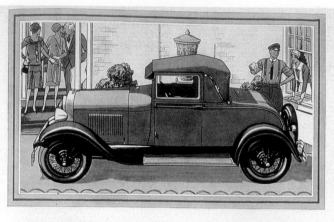

Everything *you want or need in* A Modern Automobile

EVERYTHING you want or need in a modern automobile is brought to you at a low price in the new Ford . . . beauty of line and color—steel body—speed of 55 to 65 miles an hour—mechanical, internal expanding-shoe type four-wheel brakes to balance this speed and to provide the safety demanded by present-day motoring conditions—flashing pick-up and ease of control that put a new joy in motoring—power for any hill because of a remarkably efficient engine which develops 40-brake-horse-power at only 2200 revolutions a minute —new transverse springs and four Houdaille hydraulic shock absorbers for easy-riding comfort—the economy of 20 to 30 miles on a gallon of gasoline, depending on your speed—three-quarter irreversible steering gear—reliability and low cost of up-keep.

Check over these features and you will find that not one essential thing that you require of a motor car is omitted from this list.

Yet the completeness of the new Ford goes farther even than this. It extends to every least little detail of finish and appointment and to the equipment which is standard on the car.

This includes speedometer, ammeter, gasoline gage on instrument panel, electric windshield wiper on closed cars, five steel-spoke wheels, four 30 x 4.50 balloon tires, dash light, mirror, combination stop and tail light, oil indicator rod, theft-proof coincidental ignition lock, high-pressure grease gun lubrication, and Triplex shatter-proof glass windshield.

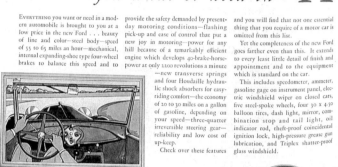

The sturdy strength and sweeping lines of the new Ford are shown in this view from the driver's seat. Windshields in all the new Ford cars are made of Triplex shatter-proof glass—an important safety feature.

1928

All Ford cars have roomy interiors, wide, deeply-cushioned seats, rich upholstery, and are finished in a variety of beautiful two-tone color harmonies.

Five years ago—three years ago—one year ago—it would have been impossible to produce such a really fine car at such a low price. It is possible today only because of the development of new machines, new manufacturing methods and new production economies that are as remarkable as the car itself.

The Ford Motor Company did not set out to make a new car at a certain figure. It decided on the kind of car it wanted to make and then found ways to build it at the lowest possible price. Every purchaser shares the benefits of the Ford policy of selling at a small margin of profit, of owning or controlling the source of raw materials and of constantly giving greater and greater value without greatly increased cost.

As Henry Ford himself has said: "We make our own steel—we make our own glass—we mine our own coal. But we do not charge a profit on any of these items or from these operations. Our only profit is on the automobile we sell."

When you know the joy of driving the new Ford—when you see its outstanding performance under all conditions—you will know that it is not just a new automobile—not just a new model—but the advanced expression of a wholly new idea in modern, economical transportation.

Proudly at home in any company is the new Ford Tudor Sedan. Distinguished by its low trim lines and the quiet good taste of every detail of finish and appointment.

FORD MOTOR COMPANY
Detroit, Michigan

LEFT:

In 1927 Chevrolet created an Art and Color Division to concentrate on style and color. That year they had introduced the chrome around the radiator, the painted wheel discs, and a variety of colors from their Duco enamel locker. For the first time, a General Motors product sold more than Ford. By the above 1928 model, it was the nation's choice for a basic car.

ABOVE:

Ford's Model-A, now in pursuit of the Chevrolet.

1928

$5.00 a day minimum. Ford wanted to force other employers to enrich the worker to a point where they would have enough discretionary income left over to be able to afford a car. All three devices worked beyond anyone's expectations.

The Model-T itself was a four-passenger, four-door model without a top. (Not until 1923 were over half of American cars supporting a closed body.) The Model-T got 30 miles to the gallon, had two forward speeds and one reverse, and was so high that it would roll over almost any "road" in America. Jane and Michael Stern report a dying man with only one request: bury me in my Model-T; he claimed he had never yet been in a hole where his Ford couldn't pull him out. Henry said you could have it in any

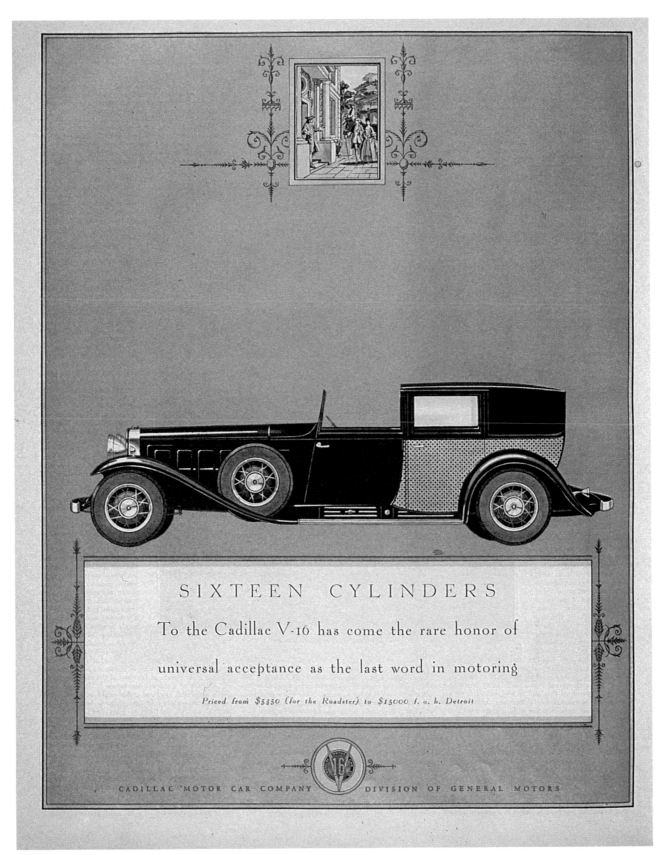

SIXTEEN CYLINDERS

To the Cadillac V-16 has come the rare honor of

universal acceptance as the last word in motoring

Priced from $5350 (for the Roadster) to $15000 f. o. b. Detroit

CADILLAC MOTOR CAR COMPANY · DIVISION OF GENERAL MOTORS

1930

It is hard to believe that they really built cars that looked like this, but, from 1925 to 1930, about five percent of the American auto product was for the great marque cars. Stephen Sears says "they were the grandest, most glorious automobiles that have ever traveled the American road." Richard Burns Carson called the period the age of the Olympian cars. Even the names are carved in marble: the Duesenberg Model J, Chrysler's Imperial, the Cunningham, Pierce-Arrow, Packard, the 2,900 American Rolls-Royces built in Springfield, Massachusetts. Half of the firms died in the Depression, and none of the models survived the Crash.

THE NEW FORD CAR

An announcement of unusual importance to every automobile owner

by
HENRY
FORD

Henry Ford

FORD MOTOR COMPANY
Detroit, Michigan

1927

The pioneering Model-T had outlived its purpose. The high wheels, designed for ruts, mud, and sand, were inappropriate for brick and graded highways. The "any color you want so long as it's black," was losing sales to General Motors' Duco palette. Speed was now more important than simplicity. So Ford invented the Model-A. The contract to announce the revolution was given to N.W. Ayer of Philadelphia, and George Cecil was assigned the copywriting task. Cecil wrote five ads (to be run sequentially) mimicking Henry Ford's well-known style. When all was ready, son Edsel Ford took the train to Philadelphia and read the copy. According to Julian Watkins (who probably was there), Edsel said, "I think they will do all right. I have one change I'd like to suggest. In one of the advertisements I see you use the word perfect. I think it would be better to say correct. Nothing is perfect." The campaign went forward; Edsel had approved an initial outlay of $1.5 million.

color you wanted so long as it was black, and its top speed was 50 mph down hill.

Part of Ford's promise had been to produce a car cheap enough for anyone to afford. The method was to have the components built by specialized technicians who could do the best job at the least cost, and then have these elements brought to the line to be assembled by less expensive, semi-skilled laborers. The result was that when he got everything going as he had planned, he had Model-Ts coming off the line every 24 seconds. He rolled 300,000 out in 1914, 500,000 in 1915, and the price dropped from $850 at the outset, to $440 in 1915, and down to $290 in 1925. This was retail, bought and driven away by the customer. The car had gone from being a luxury toy to a household necessity.

Henry Ford had firm ideas about advertising his car. He did rather little of it, and when he did the copy was personally approved within his precise guidelines. As he declared in a 1912 *Saturday Evening Post* ad:

What is it that is selling 75,000 Ford cars in 1912? Is it unusually clever advertising?

NO! Ford advertising never attempts to be "clever"— never aims at the spectacular—never dallies with the English language—merely states the facts of the case so that he who runs may read, and, reading, stop running and buy a FORD. Yet that is not the big factor.

Is it unusually clever dealers? No! Ford dealers rank at the top—are all wideawake, keen, obliging, proud of the car and the good name of [the] firm. But there are many clever dealers trying to sell other automobiles.

WHAT IS IT?

Nothing but this—*the guarantee of accomplishment*. . . . Satisfied buyers are the backbone of the Ford success.

The Competition

The Ford Model-T was a hard act to follow. It was so popular that by 1920 over one half of all the cars in the world were Model-Ts. The other half was divided among several dozen other brands, and by the Twenties they had figured out that their only hope of survival was to build models that would appeal to specific levels of income and styles of life. They became so successful at this that Sinclair Lewis could declare in his 1922 novel *Babbitt*, "In the city of Zenith, in the barbarous twentieth century, a family's motor indicated its social rank as precisely as the grades of the peerage determined the rank of an English family."

This came as a great disappointment to Henry Ford. He had genuinely believed that quality and reliability plus low cost would keep his customers loyal and buying Fords forever. The competition—General Motors in particular—figured out how to negate this commitment. GM got its allied company, DuPont, to invent a complete palette of colored lacquers which they called Duco. Starting with Chevrolet, General Motors began offering marvelously colored body styles with lushly trimmed interiors, in a deliberately rising caste system of cars. You bought your first Chevrolet with your first job, and then through the years rewarded yourself and impressed your neighbors as you "traded up" through Pontiac, Oldsmobile, Buick, and (for a limited few) Cadillac. The automobile advertisements fostered this life style by glorifying each annual change of model, describing each technological advance, and in general making the current owner dissatisfied with whatever he or she owned at the moment.

WELCOME STRANGER!

SOMETHING has happened to the car . . . perhaps it's only a flat tire . . . Maybe you've skidded off the road, and the rear wheels are slipping in the mud. Possibly it's only a broken battery-cable . . . Whatever the reason—when your car is stalled—your first thought is to get help. Who to call? What is needed?—are questions that leap into your mind. But if you are a member of your local A. A. A. motor club these disturbing thoughts are answered by your membership card! For all you need to do is 'phone the nearest club (A. A. A. is usually the first name listed in the telephone book), and an emergency service car, manned by skillful, courteous mechanics, and equipped to make all road-side repairs, will come speeding to your assistance wherever you happen to be. Your wife, your daughter, or any member

of your family, is entitled to all the benefits of your membership. You join the local A. A. A. motor club in your own town, but your membership protects you in the United States and Canada, and in every territory, where A. A. A. clubs are located. There are 1075 A. A. A. clubs, and when you belong to one, you belong to all. The cost is approximately one cent per club year.

The A. A. A. emergency road service is but one of the many advantages a membership will bring you. Your A. A. A. club will arrange any motor trip you care to take—

IT PAYS TO BELONG

This emblem, registered U. S. Patent Office, can be used only by motor clubs affiliated with the American Automobile Association.

furnish accurate, up-to-the-minute information about road conditions and detours all the way—provide you with maps, motor logs and make reservations for you at the best hotels. Furnish you with a list of tourist camps and places of scenic or historic interest. Give you free legal advice if you need it—and will arrange all the details if you should want to take your car abroad.

Don't deprive yourself any longer of the benefits of membership in an A. A. A. motor club. If you do not know the location of the nearest affiliated club, write direct to the American Automobile Association, Pennsylvania Avenue at 17th Street, Washington, D. C., today for a list of clubs, and booklets containing complete information.

THRU YOUR LOCAL
A. A. A. MOTOR CLUB

AMERICAN AUTOMOBILE ASSOCIATION
WORLD'S LARGEST FEDERATION OF MOTOR VEHICLE OWNERS—ORGANIZED 1902

1928

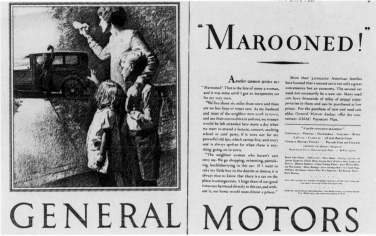

1929

GM goes for guilt to sell America on owning two cars. You owe it to your wife, marooned at home. Note that the corporation has put its General Motors Acceptance Corporation in place to help with the installment loan, reminds us that the second car need not be new ("many used cars have thousands of miles of unused transportation in them"), and, with its nine brands, has "A car for every purse and purpose."

Both Ford and GM were convinced that they had to sell the woman, not the man. Ford in particular talked to the woman and believed that though she was not interested in the "nuts and bolts," it was she who determined how the money was to be spent. The smaller brands believed equally strongly in this (the Stutz Bearcat roadster was always targeted solely at the women), and the luxurious Jordan used prose that sounded like blank verse to capture the feminine allegiance. Example: the car is the Jordan Playboy, the year is 1923, and the illustration shows a single girl in scarf and cloche, driving a roadster with the top down alongside a galloping cowboy. The text:

Somewhere west of Laramie there's a broncho-busting, steer-roping girl who knows what I'm talking about.
She can tell what a sassy pony, that's a cross between greased lightning and the place where it hits, can do with eleven hundred pounds of steel and action when he's going high, wide and handsome.
The truth is—the Playboy was built for her.
Built for the lass whose face is brown with the sun when the day is done of revel and romp and race.
She loves the cross of the wild and the tame.
There's a savor of links about that car—of laughter and lilt and light—a hint of old loves—and saddle and quirt.
It's a brawny thing—yet a graceful thing for the sweep o' the Avenue.

Step into the Playboy when the hour grows dull with things gone dead and stale.
Then start for the land of real living with the spirit of the lass who rides, lean and rangy, into the red horizon of a Wyoming twilight.
JORDAN

Most of the advertising stressed appearance, but through the Twenties the automobiles were in fact improving in performance as well, and some of this was included in the smaller print of the copy. Duesenberg introduced four-wheel hydraulic brakes in 1920; the first hardtop appeared in 1922 (the Essex); and Dodge introduced the first all-steel body in 1923. Power windshield wipers also arrived in 1923; hydraulic shock absorbers in 1925; safety glass (developed in England) appeared in windshields in 1928; and ever increasing power and number of pistons grew until Cadillac brought out its V-16 engine in 1929.

And there is one school of thought that believes what really killed the Model-T was the advent of decent roads. Once each layer of government assumed responsibility for grading the country road, graveling the state road, and bricking the inter-city highway, there was no longer either a need or an excuse for the Model-T. Under great pressure from his son Edsel, Henry Ford abandoned the T in 1927 and brought out the Model-A to play catch-up to the Chevrolet. In only three model years through the next thirty did Ford succeed in overtaking the enemy.

1934

Again "Look at All Three"— and may the Best car Win!

WALTER P. CHRYSLER

makes a Frank Statement to Buyers of Low-priced Cars

A SHORT time ago I introduced a new Plymouth Six. Today we reach the time of year when *other* manufacturers are telling you about new models.

I want to take this occasion to say again, "Look at All Three low-priced cars . . . *and may the best car win!*"

We believe in that method of buying. We practice it ourselves. And in these times we have no right to ask for your business unless we earn it on a fair, point-by-point comparison.

● ● ●

The new Plymouth is a Six . . . with patented Floating Power engine mountings.

I have said before that no car without Floating Power is really up-to-date. I hope you will have a Plymouth dealer give you a ride in this new Six . . . to *prove* that there isn't a trace of vibration . . . to *feel* what a difference Floating Power does make. The Plymouth is a *full-sized* automobile. People like that today . . . because they

want to ride in comfort. Get out your ruler . . . or better yet, get into the car. See how you can stretch your legs in this BIG automobile!

And what about Safety . . . your own . . . your wife's . . . your children's? That's something *you* never forget in this age of crowded highways and high speeds. We didn't forget it either.

That's why we used safety-steel bodies . . . hydraulic four-wheel brakes . . . safety-glass windshields . . . every single safety feature our engineers could devise!

And of course you're thinking about *economy*. We all are. In this new Six, our engineers have surpassed themselves in making gasoline . . . oil . . . tires *go further*.

It's a *good-looking* automobile . . . a car your friends will admire. Its new design also cuts down wind-resistance, giving you more speed and even greater mileage on gasoline.

Severe tests in sand pits . . . on jagged mountain roads . . . in long endurance

runs . . . prove that the new Plym[outh] *stand up* . . . no matter how you look into these things for you— Plymouth Six do its own talkin[g]

make this clear: *we welcome critical buying!* Look at All Three . . . *ride* in All Three. Get down "under the paint" and behind the upholstery. And may the best car win!

IT'S A SIX AT $60 LESS THAN LAST YEAR

Business Coupe $495 . . . Rumble Seat Coupe $545 . . . Four-Door Sedan $575 . . . Convertible Coupe $595 . . . All prices F. O. B. factory. Low delivered prices. Convenient time-payments. On all models—Floating Power Engine Mountings, hydraulic brakes, free wheeling, full-sized safety-steel bodies, safety-glass windshield, easy-shift transmission with "silent second," rigid-X double-drop frame, Oilite squeak-proof springs. Closed cars wired for Philco-Transitone Radio. Optional — Automatic Clutch $8 . . . Duplate Safety Plate Glass Windows—Coupe $10, Sedan $16.50.

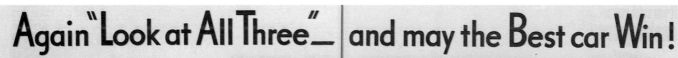
IT'S A SIX WITH FLOATING POWER

PLYMOUTH SIX IS SOLD B[Y]   DESOTO, DODGE AND CHRYSLER DEALERS EVERYWHERE

1933

With the Depression, auto advertising changed dramatically. Color disappeared, and the accounts seemed to feel that they had to crush everything they knew about a product into a single frame. The very clutter seemed to symbolize the fear and tension of the period. Auto production dropped by 75 percent, and whole companies and dealerships disappeared throughout the industry.

Here Chrysler uses the "Look at All Three" and buy-the-best theme which Lee Iacocca was to use fifty years later when he salvaged the same firm from near-bankruptcy in the Eighties.

The car that revolutionized automobile styling. The keynote of the Thirties was "streamlining"—the look of the airplane. The Chrysler and DeSoto "Airflow" sedans not only looked like they'd come from the wind tunnel on the outside, but actually were equally innovative inside. The engine and dash were moved forward, the rear seat came forward (off the rear axle for the first time), headlamps disappeared into fenders, spare tires into the trunk, and running boards began to shrink and then disappear. The price of progress was a severe loss of visibility that worsened all through the decade, and the boxy silhouette killed the long hoods and upright bodies of the Twenties. The streamlining spread to everything else: corners were smoothed on typewriters, refrigerators, tea kettles, and wristwatches. Indeed, nothing was too small or too large (right below) to be streamlined.

1934

The Depression Again

The Depression struck the automobile scene in a strange way. Production plunged by 75 percent. In 1932, fewer than 25 percent of the cars made only three years before were manufactured and of these, even fewer were sold. But the gasoline consumed in 1932 fell off only 4 percent from the Twenties' high. The car was no luxury; even with a fourth of the country's workers unemployed, the wheels seemed to receive high priority for what little money anybody had.

One of the leading devices for getting federal relief money into communities was the roads and highways program, so that "make work" produced thousands of miles of upgraded highways and farm-to-market roads, and by the end of the Thirties, the nation's road network was vastly improved as paths for the car. Through the Depression years, highway travel became one of the cheapest forms of recreation, and inter-city trucking grew steadily. The effect on the face of the nation was a mixed blessing. Phil Patton discovered that in the early Thirties, one 48-mile strip of U.S.1 had 3,000 buildings tied directly to the highway slab, and there was a

1935

Nothing

could be finer

LINCOLN CONTINENTAL CABRIOLET FOR 1946

Lincoln DIVISION OF FORD MOTOR COMPANY

1946

World War II brought an abrupt stop to the production of civilian cars, and Detroit shifted to tanks, Jeeps, and 6×6 field trucks. Four years later, with the war won in Europe but still unresolved in the Pacific, GM started to remind the anticipated returning veteran of what he'd been fighting for: big, new cars. This was the start of fender skirts, huge bumpers, and tail fins.

Ford, too, tried to give the returning veteran "cars like they used to be," and this 1946 Lincoln Continental went all the way back to the Twenties for its silhouette, even taking the tire back out of the trunk.

gas station every 895 feet. The 47 miles between Newark and Trenton had 700 businesses with road access sitting among 472 billboards.

The Dream Cars of the Fifties and Sixties

World War II brought the production of civilian cars to an abrupt stop in 1942; but when the tanks and military trucks were in turn pulled off the assembly line in 1946, the automotive scene was paradisiacal for the industry. Through the war years civilians had been working steadily plus overtime, and they had built up fat bank accounts with little to spend the money on. Returning soldiers were given discharge allotments and cashed the war bonds that had been deducted from their service pay, and between ten years of Depression and five years of war, a huge thirst for new and exciting cars had accumulated. Detroit set out to satisfy this demand with ever larger, more chrome-laden, and ever more powerful machines. From 1946 to 1966 was the time of the dream cars.

The theme of the time was Long, Low, and Powerful. The first fender fin was put on a Cadillac in 1948, and these grew to huge, sharp, lethal spears by the 1959 model. (Jerry Flint called the tail fin "a pretty touch gone absolutely wild—like a fifty-foot woman.")

The advertising themes of the time were two-fold:

First, each new, annual model must be dramatically different from the one before, so the present would be manifestly outmoded. The new car customer had to be made dissatisfied and frustrated with his old car by the annual Fall revelation of "The All-New . . . Whatever." It should be noted that the idea of planned obsolescence was not precisely accurate. The car companies and dealers wanted the newest car to be demanded, but for the first time there was a huge used-car market through which the autos would be sold once, twice, three times. Obsolescence in outside metal could be fostered, but "there's a lot more transportation left in that baby" required that the engine itself last through several owners. Before the war, the senior male or female of the household owned the car. After the war, thousands of teenagers who accumulated money with part-time jobs came into the market for the re-cycled autos.

This layering of the buyers produced the second advertising theme: Cars were to be personal expressions of the psyche of the owner. Thus, motivational psychology bloomed, and cars were seen as mistresses, workhorses, weapons, plumes to be flaunted, or bait for sexual conquest. This perception resulted in an endless variety of styles: hardtops, convertibles, two- and four-door sedans, station wagons, four-wheel-drive off-road units, and on and on.

The Muscle Car

One of the most spectacular of the personal cars was the category known as muscle cars. These not only looked aggressive, they came with phenomenal engines. (Even the Edsel's version had a 6.7-liter engine producing 345 horsepower.) It is hard to remember that gasoline was so cheap that no one ever mentioned fuel efficiency. At less than twenty-five cents per gallon, who noticed? Throughout the Sixties, the major cars that everybody's father drove got barely ten miles to the gallon.

The dramatic ads announcing each year's new addition to the line not only portrayed colorful (and frequently exaggerated) views of the car, but each year there was a new series of headlines shouted across the latest art work. Ads from the period reveal such creative copy as:

"Hands off the grab bar, Charlie, you're tearing out the dash!" [1964 Pontiac 421 starting up]

"Separates the men from the toys." [1970 Chevrolet Camaro Z28]

"New Mercury Cyclone. Password for action. We made it hot. You can make it scream." [429 V-8; 1970]

"A word or two to the competition: You lose." [1969 Chevrolet Camaro]

"Sedate it ain't." [1966 Olds 442]

"I wouldn't stand in the middle of the page if I were you . . . It's a Pontiac GTO!" [1964 model coming straight at the reader]

"A flying machine for people who can't stand heights." [1965 Pontiac 2 + 2]

"These Super Torque FORD engines climb hills like a homesick Swiss yodeler. One is available with 425 horsepower (a few more than the average private plane). Try *total performance* on your local Matterhorn." [1963]

"After a few moments of respectful silence, you may turn the page." [Picture of a 1969 Pontiac GTO]

The "GTO" model name (a Sixties equivalent of "Model-T" or "Model-A") stood for Gran Turismo Omologato, and represented the advertising world's application of the motivational psychologists' theories. Jane and Michael Stern called them "identity kits" for the owners, and collected them into categories. For the person with time and leisure, you could have the resorts: Riviera, Bel Air, Malibu, Newport, and Monaco. For heavy-footed drivers, you could have auto race tracks: Bonneville, LeMans, GTO, and Grand Prix. And for the truly assertive, you could ride a Marauder, a Challenger, or a Charger; a Barracuda, a Cutlass, a Cobra, or a Stingray.

Too Much

By 1965, the auto manufacturers had gone too far. The two-toned behemoths (John Keats called them insolent chariots), were clumsy, an insult to the eye, and as energy costs started to rise, an insult to the pocket book. Consumer groups began to attack their safety record, environmentalists their pollutants, and owners grew resentful of their unreliability.

The Magic Touch of Tomorrow!

The *look* of success! The *feel* of success! The *power* of success!
They come to you in a dramatically beautiful, dynamically powered
new Dodge that introduces the ease and safety of push-button driving
—the Magic Touch of Tomorrow! It is a truly great value.

New '56 DODGE

VALUE LEADER OF THE FORWARD LOOK

1955

DRAMATIC EDSEL STYLING is here to stay
—bringing new distinction to American motoring

In one short year, the fresh and original individuality of Edsel styling
has become a familiar part of everyday American life. Today, everyone
recognizes the distinctive Edsel. And everyone who's driven an Edsel
knows that Edsel *features* are out in front, too. Exclusive Teletouch Drive
that lets you shift by a touch at the steering-wheel hub, Edsel's high-
economy engines, new self-adjusting brakes and comfort-shaped contour

seats are the biggest advances in years. Why not enjoy all these wonde
features—and drive the car with the advanced design—right now!? E
cially since there's less than fifty dollars difference between the magnifi
new Edsel and V-8's in the Low-Priced Three!* See your Edsel De
about it this week.

EDSEL DIVISION • FORD MOTOR COMPA

Less than fifty dollars difference between Edsel and V-8's in the Low-Priced Three

1958

ABOVE:

*The Fifties were the days of motivational research that started
the "you are what you drive" philosophy of advertising and
body styling. Convertibles were perceived as a man's mistress,
and sedans as the home and living room. The hardtop design
was intended to secure the best of both worlds. Chrome was
hung all over the car to imply modernity and luxury (the 1958
Buick topped out with forty-four pounds of trim), and the
upswept tail fins of the time were described by psychiatrists as
"feminine" and "invitations to copulate." Note the lady
changing gears with her fingertips, taking us right back to Coles
Phillips' model of 1916 (see page 230).*

ABOVE RIGHT:

*The Edsel was created because Ford needed a "middle car" for
increasingly prosperous Ford customers "to move up to." Lewis
Crusoe, an executive at Ford, was quoted as saying, "We have
been growing customers for General Motors"—Pontiac and
Oldsmobile owners. The horsecollar grille came about because
GM grilles went back and forth horizontally like a mouthful of
teeth, so the Ford designers thought if they did one vertically, it
would "stand out." In fact it did; endless jokes were made about
it, some even printable, but all making the design laughable
from the start. Inside there were pushbutton gear shifts (on the
steering wheel), pushbuttons to open the trunk, to work the
wipers, to run up the antenna, and to turn on the lights. They
made 63,110 Edsels in 1958, 44,891 in 1959, and 2,846 in
1960. It sold poorly from the beginning, in spite of massive
publicity and promotional stunts.*

So everyone began to "downsize." The cars grew smaller
and more efficient. For the first time in decades, the advertising discussed what the car would do for *you*, rather than
saying "this is the new X-X, and therefore you will want to
buy it."

The Japanese recognized the American makers' vul-
nerabilities and rushed in with their smaller, more reliable,
and more gasoline-sparing designs. Doyle Dane Bernbach
took advantage of all of these elements when the agency
created the enormously effective Volkswagen ad campaign.
Each ad demonstrated a single, different appeal. By the time
the series had run its course, it was sure to have touched at
least one of the motorist's dissatisfactions with his own
present vehicle. By the time the campaign crested, VW
hoped to have suggested an "endless" number of ways it was
superior to its competitors and therefore to be desired. The
campaign prided itself on "an honest car honestly described." The novelty of the idea attracted astonishing attention, but almost no one tried to copy the approach.

The Eighties

In spite of nearly a hundred years of practice and testing, by
the end of the 1980s, advertising the American automobile
still had no particular rules or conventions. Beautiful women
still leaned against the hoods, the backdrops still implied
wealth and leisure. The cars themselves had become more
rational and appealing, but the devices for selling them
seemed even less precise than in the first decades of the
invention. With the Volkswagen Bug gone, no one was

The Rolls-Royce Silver Cloud—$13,995

"At 60 miles an hour the loudest noise in this new Rolls-Royce comes from the electric clock"

What __makes__ Rolls-Royce the best car in the world? "There is really no magic about it—it is merely patient attention to detail," says an eminent Rolls-Royce engineer.

1. "At 60 miles an hour the loudest noise comes from the electric clock," reports the Technical Editor of THE MOTOR. Three mufflers tune out sound frequencies—acoustically.

2. Every Rolls-Royce engine is run for seven hours at full throttle before installation, and each car is test-driven for hundreds of miles over varying road surfaces.

3. The Rolls-Royce is designed as an *owner-driven* car. It is eighteen inches shorter than the largest domestic cars.

4. The car has power steering, power brakes and automatic gear-shift. It is very easy to drive and to park. No chauffeur required.

5. The finished car spends a week in the final test-shop, being fine-tuned. Here it is subjected to 98 separate ordeals. For example, the engineers use a *stethoscope* to listen for axle-whine.

6. The Rolls-Royce is guaranteed for three years. With a new network of dealers and parts-depots from Coast to Coast, service is no problem.

7. The Rolls-Royce radiator has never changed, except that when Sir Henry Royce died in 1933 the monogram RR was changed from red to black.

8. The coachwork is given five coats of primer paint, and hand rubbed between each coat, before *nine* coats of finishing paint go on.

9. By moving a switch on the steering column, you can adjust the shock-absorbers to suit road conditions.

10. A picnic table, veneered in French walnut, slides out from under the dash. Two more swing out behind the front seats.

11. You can get such optional extras as an Espresso coffee-making machine, a dictating machine, a bed, hot and cold water for washing, an electric razor or a telephone.

12. There are three separate systems of power brakes, two hydraulic and one mechanical. Damage to one will not affect the others. The Rolls-Royce is a very *safe* car—and also a very *lively* car. It cruises serenely at eighty-five. Top speed is in excess of 100 m.p.h.

13. The Bentley is made by Rolls-Royce. Except for the radiators, they are identical motor cars, manufactured by the same engineers in the same works. People who feel diffident about driving a Rolls-Royce can buy a Bentley.

PRICE. The Rolls-Royce illustrated in this advertisement—f.o.b. principal ports of entry—costs **$13,995.**

If you would like the rewarding experience of driving a Rolls-Royce or Bentley, write or telephone to one of the dealers listed on opposite page. Rolls-Royce Inc., 10 Rockefeller Plaza, New York 20, N. Y. CIrcle 5-1144.

1963

The Sixties gave us "dream" cars, "personal" cars, and one of the all-time great advertisements: David Ogilvy's Rolls-Royce electric clock. The styles of the first half of the decade had such an overload of bulk and chrome that they became parodies of themselves; the second half had dozens of designs for fractional parts of the auto-buying public. Rolls-Royce was no part of any of either of these trends, but a totally conservative company that had been developing since the nineteenth century. The famous clock ad ran in only two newspapers and two magazines for a total cost of $25,000, but it has gone down in advertising history. It is a classic example of long copy that treats the reader as being intelligent enough to understand it (and rich enough to be able to afford the product should he decide to buy).

Think small.

WILLIAM BERNBACH AND THE VOLKSWAGEN
BUG: AN ALBUM

This, one of the most famous ad campaigns in American advertising history, started in 1959. Volkswagen was already selling tens of thousands of cars in the U.S., without any form of a national ad program. But at this point, the company decided to try general advertising and wanted the most imaginative agency in America. They were told that at the time that was Doyle Dane Bernbach, and they gave them the account.

In 1959, the auto theme was chrome-covered dream cars, and the agency's first inclination was to design a campaign that came down hard on American figures selling the car to an American audience. The initial feeling that there was still too much "foreign" about a German car; still not far enough from WW II. One of the DDB design team remembers "I thought we should shoot Suzy Parker next to the car" and "talk with a midwestern accent," but the agency sent a team to the German factory to get the feel of the product.

For three weeks they followed the production line step by step and interviewed hundreds of workers. What struck the Americans the most was the incredible quality control—components and whole cars being rejected for defects that an American dealer would not have corrected even if a new owner complained about them.

The DDB team came home and reported; Bernbach himself discarded all the past sketches and recommendations, and decreed that the theme would be "an honest car promoted with honesty." Art director Helmut Krone and copywriter Julian Koenig proceeded to design a campaign so strong that in the ensuing decade it went through ten sequential design teams without the slightest diminution of theme or reader interest.

The campaign was built on selling a single advantage of the car in each panel. The picture was kept simple, the copy was short, factual, and straightforward. Each ad gave a specific reason why the car was good, and the artwork was held to "honest" black and white regardless of how slick the magazine it was to be published in.

The Volkswagen Beetle was designed by Ferdinand Porsche of the luxury car fame—he had created, among other high-end classics, the Mercedes SS sports models. He had long wanted to design an affordable "people's car," and in 1927 began it on the drawing board. In 1933, he got Adolph Hitler interested in the project, but in 1937, when the first cars were supposed to come off the line, Hitler shifted the factory to the production of German "jeeps" and amphibious personnel carriers, and the People's Car was indefinitely postponed. During the post-war Allied occupation, the British got the bombed-out factory going again as an anti-unemployment program, and the first Beetles finally appeared at the end of 1945.

The occupying British army then tried to sell the factory to one of the British or American car companies, but one after another examined the factory and the automobile and decided it had no future. Finally, a General Motors–trained German took over the operation, and between 1950 and 1970 production rose from 19,000 cars per year to 1.6 million.

The innovative Doyle Dane Bernbach campaign had a major part in the export portion of this success. Possibly the most astonishing thing about the campaign was that while it had an enormous readership—people stopped at the ads and read every word and were able to recall the illustration and the point months after the publication—NO AUTOMOBILE COMPANY HAS COPIED THE APPROACH TO THIS DAY. No one examines his product and explains what it does, how it compares with its competitors, why its unique features specifically make it drive better, more reliably, more economically, or why the reader should buy it, as Volkswagen did time after time. It should be noted, too, that the ads assumed that the reader was intelligent, and could recognize a joke when the ad attempted to be funny. In an industry that follows winning ideas like a herd of reindeer, the fact that (while Volkswagen ads can still be described decades after their appearance) no one else has tried to copy the approach, may be the most unusual aspect of the Volkswagen experience.

After we paint the car we paint the paint.

You should see what we do to a Volkswagen even before we paint it.

We bathe it in steam, we bathe it in alkali, we bathe it in phosphate. Then we bathe it in a neutralizing solution.

If it got any cleaner, there wouldn't be much left to paint.

Then we dunk the whole thing into a vat of slate gray primer until every square inch of metal is covered. Inside and out.

Only one domestic car maker does this. And his cars sell for 3 or 4 times as much as a Volkswagen.

(We think that the best way to make an economy car is expensively.)

After the dunking, we bake it and sand it by hand.

Then we paint it.

Then we bake it again, and sand it again by hand.

Then we paint it again.

And bake it again.

And sand it again by hand.

So after 3 times, you'd think we wouldn't bother to paint it again and bake it again. Right? Wrong.

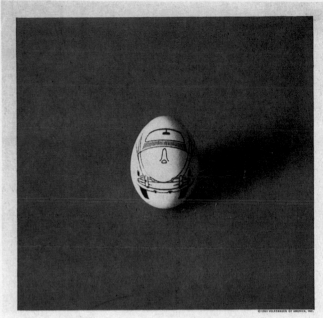

Some shapes are hard to improve on.

Ask any hen.

You just can't design a more functional shape for an egg.

And we figure the same is true of the Volkswagen Sedan.

Don't think we haven't tried. (As a matter of fact, the VW's been changed nearly 3,000 times.)

But we can't improve our basic design.

Like the egg, it's the right kind of package for what goes inside.

So that's where most of our energy goes.

To get more power without using more gas. To put synchromesh on first gear. To improve the heater. That kind of thing.

As a result, our package carries four adults, and their luggage, at about 32 miles to a gallon of regular gas and 40,000 miles to a set of tires.

We've made a few external changes, of course. Such as push-button doorknobs.

Which is one up on the egg.

Dealer Name

Dealer Ad—600 lines
This advertisement prepared by **DOYLE DANE BERNBACH**, Inc. for
VOLKSWAGEN—Job No. VWSP-2248

Volkswagen's unique construction keeps moisture out.

For years there have been rumors about floating Volkswagens.

Why not?

The bottom of the Volkswagen isn't like ordinary car bottoms. A sheet of flat steel runs underneath the car, sealing the bottom fore and aft.

That's not done to make a bad boat out of it, just a better car. The sealed bottom protects a VW from water, dirt and salt. All the nasty things on the road that eventually eat up a car.

The top part of a Volkswagen is also very seaworthy. It's practically airtight. So airtight that it's hard to close the door without rolling down the window just a little bit.

But there's still one thing to keep in mind if you own a Volkswagen. Even if it could definitely float, it couldn't float indefinitely.

So drive around the big puddles. Especially if they're big enough to have a name.

A Volkswagen, obviously.

It's easy to spot a Volkswagen.

Even with enough snow on it to hide the beetle shape.

It's the one that keeps moving.

A Volkswagen will even go up icy hills when other cars won't go at all because we put the engine in the back. It gives the rear wheels much better traction.

That's half the problem.

But the engine can't just be there. It has to keep working.

So we cool the VW engine with air, not water. There's no need for anti-freeze, no chance of the block cracking. (No possibility of boiling over in summer, either.) And there's no draining. No flushing. No rust.

You can park a VW outdoors in sub-zero weather or dig it out of a snowbank; it's ready to roll as soon as you turn the key.

If you happen to live where ice and snow are no problem, don't think you can't judge the VW's extra-ordinary abilities.

Just try it in sand or mud.

Goldilocks and the two Bears.

The Bear on the right is a stock Belvedere GTX.

That is to say it carries the standard 440 cu. in. V-8, which, aside from being the biggest GT engine in the world, generates 375 hp. and 480 lbs.-ft. of torque through a fast-shifting TorqueFlite automatic and the recommended 3.23-to-1 rear axle.

Said Bear also carries a heavy-duty suspension—including beefed-up torsion bars, ball joints, front stabilizer bar, shocks and rear springs—along with bigger brakes, low-restriction exhausts, a pit-stop gas filler, chromed valve covers, Red Streak tires, wide rims, hood scoops and bucket seats. And this is the *standard* Bear, mind you.

The Bear on the left is also a stock GTX—with a heavy-duty 4-speed gearbox—and a few extra-cost options, including the famed Hemi, with 426 cu. in. and 490 lbs.-ft. of torque. It also has our super-duty Sure-Grip differential; not to mention racing stripes and front disc brakes.

So what's the moral? Simply that GTX is one very tempting bowl of porridge. In one form, even Goldilocks can drive it (although you'll recall Goldilocks was a highly adventuresome kind of female). In another form, it's strictly for the "Move over, honey, and let a man drive" set. You know the story: there's bound to be one that's just right. After all, we're out to win you over. '67 Belvedere GTX. ♥

Plymouth ⬥ CHRYSLER

1967

Dodge ⬥ CHRYSLER

Mother warned me...

that there would be men like you driving cars like that. Do you really think you can get to me with that long, low, tough machine you just rolled up in? Ha! If you think a girl with real values is impressed by your air conditioning and stereo . . . a 440 Magnum, whatever that is . . . well—it takes more than cushy bucket seats to make me flip. Charger R/T SE. Sounds like alphabet soup. Frankly, I'm attracted to you because you have a very intelligent face. My name's Julia.

Join the fun . . . catch
Dodge *fever*

1969

Other cars with the Chevelle SS 396 would hold still long enough for them to catch up.

Other cars with the 1970 SS 396 hadn't added those 25 more horses to boost its standard V8 to 350 hp.

Other cars with the SS 396 didn't offer a 4-speed or a 3-range Turbo Hydra-matic transmission.

Induction Hood.

And other cars with the stock SS 396 didn't give you power disc brakes, heeled-up suspension, F70 x 14 white-lettered wide ovals and 7"-wide spot wheels.

Aren't you glad other cars don't have anything to say about it?

On the move. CHEVROLET

Chevelle SS 396. Other cars wish we'd keep it this way.

1970

Nobody's Pussycat.

Of all the sports cars available to you, this is the one—the ultimate car.

Because it offers what the others can't offer: the Jaguar V-12 engine.

And that changes the discussion from what a sports car can do to how well it can do it.

That's what the Jaguar E-type V-12 is all about. How well it glides from zero to idle. How well it accelerates out of a pack and into the clear. Even how well it behaves in downtown traffic or quitting time before a holiday weekend.

In a word, the Jaguar V-12 is smooth. It's smooth going up the eight floors zero and it's smooth going from cruising speed to passing speed. It's ever smooth waiting for the light to change.

Because, from an engineering viewpoint, the Jaguar V-12 is in perfect balance. Since its 5.3 litres of capacity are divided by twelve—not eight or six—the forces are spread more evenly over the crankshaft by delivering smaller but more frequent pulses of power.

What is the effect like? Well, it's something like a turbine. And it's something like an express elevator. But it's not exactly like anything else. That's why you have to drive a Jaguar E-type V-12 before you decide on anybody else's sports car.

Since it is a Jaguar, it has independent front and rear suspension with "anti-dive" control. Power-assisted rack and pinion steering. Power-assisted disc brakes on all four wheels—ventilated to the front. A four-speed manual is standard, an automatic is optional.

So see the Jaguar E-type V-12. It's the only production V-12 sports car in town. And that makes it unusual to state.

For your dealer's name and for information about overseas delivery, call (800) 447-4700. In Illinois, call (800) 322-4400. Calls are toll free.

BRITISH LEYLAND MOTORS INC., LEONIA, N.J. 07605

Jaguar ⬥ BRITISH LEYLAND

1974

Can you spot the Buick in this picture?

BUICK REGAL. If you picked the dark green car in the background, you're right. It's a 1953 Buick Roadmaster, portholes and all.

If you picked the rakish, low-slung one in the foreground, you'd be right again. It's a Buick, too. A 1976 Buick Regal Coupe. The only mid-size American car powered by a V-6 engine. And a Buick V-6 at that.

The point is simply this. Back in 1953,

when gasoline was 25 cents a gallon, Buick built comfortable, solid, well-constructed automobiles.

Today, we still do.

But in addition, we ask them to be something the Buicks of old never really had to be: Efficient.

That's why the Buick in the foreground, while it still contains a core of pure Buick luxury, is also equipped with a score of

devices to help it operate more efficiently in this day and age.

There's a 22-gallon fuel tank for added range between fuel stops.

There are steel-belted radial tires and High-Energy Ignition. Both are standard; both contribute to efficient operation.

There's a trim 112" wheelbase, so it's easy to thread through traffic.

And there's seating for six. After all, if it wasn't roomy and comfortable inside, it just wouldn't be a Buick, would it?

BUICK *Dedicated to the Free Spirit in just about everyone.*

1975

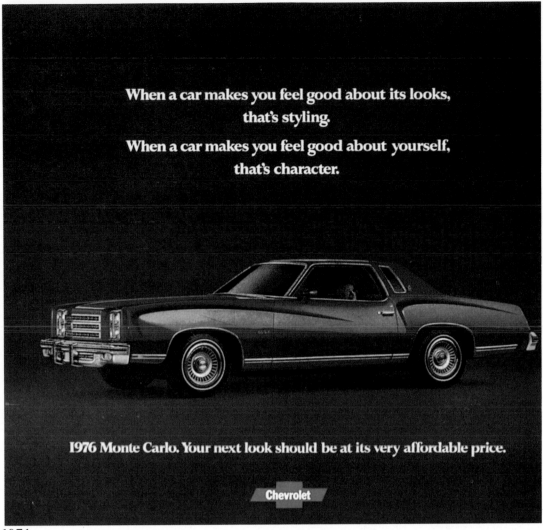

When a car makes you feel good about its looks,
that's styling.

When a car makes you feel good about yourself,
that's character.

1976 Monte Carlo. Your next look should be at its very affordable price.

Chevrolet

1976

OPPOSITE ABOVE LEFT:
This is the ultimate "personal" car approach, a single ad aimed at two kinds of male buyers. It provides one attractive model to capture male attention, and then copy offering a single body style but two forms of "muscle" to match the psyche of the man.

OPPOSITE ABOVE RIGHT:
Sixties automobile copy accepted as a given that power cars were prime bait to attract beautiful women, and vice-versa.

OPPOSITE MIDDLE LEFT:
Since it has always been difficult to represent the smooth surge of power of a running automobile in a print ad, Chevrolet here has caught the feel of a "muscle" car without moving it forward on the ground.

OPPOSITE MIDDLE RIGHT:
Ad copy for the luxury level.

OPPOSITE:
The Buick fender holes appeared in 1949, and on their advent they each had a tiny light bulb which went on and off to match the spark plug firing sequence. The lights disappeared with the 1950 model, but the holes lasted thirty more years.

ABOVE:
In the Seventies ads, no car could be too long or too low.

enumerating the nuts-and-bolts of the cars; no one was describing why their machine was new or better or different. The advertiser was simply saying it was. There was little comparison copy, and with the wind tunnel carving almost all cars into the same shape, there was even less difference in the art work. In 1904, the Oldsmobile was urging the customers to buy it mainly because it was an Oldsmobile. By the final decade of the century, ninety percent of the car ads were using the same theme.

Coda

The trouble with that cavil is that it implies there is a right way to sell automobiles if only someone would use it. But test it: What would it take *in an ad* to get your husband to abandon the brand of car he is driving, and go out to buy something completely different? What would it take to get your boss to abandon that shiny model she is driving, and purchase an entirely different car from a different company? When you last changed brands, was it a print ad that did it? TV commercial? Or something quite different? The solution is not as simple as it sounds.

At the close of 1987, Rolls-Royce ran an ad in *Architectural Digest* that consisted of a peel-and-sniff strip giving off the smell of the leather upholstery in a standard Rolls interior. The auto advertisers may figure it out yet.

1891

Our current joy and ecstatic delight over a new detergent are simply a part of a long-established advertising tradition—here expressed a century ago.

Gender Change

WOMEN AND ADVERTISING. A centuries-old love affair—which in our time has become more of a field of combat. The argument seems most unlikely. If ever there was an occupation committed to offending no one it has been advertising, yet here the ad makers have managed to outrage their favorite clientele and to threaten the very purpose of their being. How did the agencies get into this situation? Let's see.

Women and the Advertisers for the First 150 Years

From the very first, advertising has recognized that the customer who mattered most was female. For decades the statisticians have reported that 80 percent of all retail purchases are made by women. (By 1988, it had risen to 85 percent.) As early as the 1880s the professional advertising literature consistently referred to their audience as "she," and "she" is still used for the customer in conversations along Madison Avenue today.

Not only does the woman control the actual spending of the husband's money in the overwhelming number of married households, but the number of women receiving income for their own work has grown steadily since the beginning of this century until it is now well over 50 percent. And this is neither pin nor egg money. In 1988, 54 percent of all Americans with annual incomes over $100,000 are women.

Both the advertising agencies and the magazines have explicitly declared the importance of women to advertising from the 1890s to date. "Never underestimate the power of a woman" was proclaimed by the *Ladies Home Journal* for years, and we have seen N.W. Ayer's view of "The Supreme Court," page 39. There is little doubt that the advertisers have loved their female audience, but did the writers really know what they were talking about when they created their ads for women?

Professor Roland Marchand of the University of California, Davis, explored this question in detail, and found the following:

Who actually wrote the ads intended to appeal to the women? Men. Then was it really men who were telling women what they thought the women wanted to hear and who created the images of the women in the ads? Pretty much. In 1928, for example, Marchand found that the staffing of the 20 largest ad agencies amounted to a ratio of only one woman to ten men above the secretarial level. But, surprisingly, this was the highest ratio of women to men of any American business category except for publishing and department store retailing. The salaries for women, incidentally, were unusually good. The wages for the women at N.W. Ayer and Son, for example, put them in the top five percent of all personal income in the U.S. at the time. (As is always the case with averages, there were certain situations that needed to be footnoted like that of the J. Walter Thompson Agency where the ratio of one woman to ten men held precisely, but did not reflect the role of the president's wife who many believed ran the company. Helen Lansdowne Resor had herself been a nationally known copywriter before Stanley Resor married her.)

Marchand found that the women of the various agencies had been explicitly hired to cover the "women's viewpoint." George Batten's agency advertised in 1927 that it recognized that "women talked only among themselves about such things as garter runs, the color of a chair that got on one's nerves, the way straps of underthings fell off one's shoulders, and the problems of a kitchen sink placed too low. . . . A thousand and one intimacies she gives to you and your advertising." Another agency declared that "The proper study of mankind is *man* . . . but the proper study of markets is *woman*."

When it came to "style," only women had the sensitivity

1882

to recognize it. Women possessed "a sixth sense for what is stylish, for what is good, for what is beautiful." And, of course, here we meet the problem that later was to distress the women's movement, the matter of stereotypes. "All women respond to style, fashion." "Women are the preservers of beauty and culture in an industrial society."

Were the mostly male advertisers simply reflecting women as the women saw themselves, or were they telling women what they should be and do and *how* they should see themselves? In the Twenties and Thirties there were many ads for new labor-saving devices and services, and in these the women were urged to give up the time-consuming and "drudgery" aspects of labor in the home so they had "more time to devote to their children" or more "companionship with their children." Researchers who have examined hundreds of ads of the period found "Children" was the most acceptable way to invest the time saved, followed by "Friends." Clubs, reading, golf, and going to the theater, followed in that order. "Going to the motion pictures" never appeared in any ad addressed to the homemaker (it was an unacceptable waste of time), nor did part-time work, or civic affairs. Marchand, who limited his study to the period up to World War II, concluded that the ads were indeed mostly written by men who chose for the women acceptable uses of time that would make the women "better wives and mothers."

The present authors noted a corollary to the situation described above. During the first half of the 1900s, the ad writers accepted the concept of a *division of labor*. Within this division, men and women were equal. Men ran the offices or worked at the factory; women created the home as a retreat from the stresses of the man's world and built a nest in which to nurture the children. And within these rules of the game, the advertisers felt free to challenge the woman to re-examine her traditional role.

Examples: Throughout 1917 and 1918, *The Delineator* magazine ran ads showing such images as the man behind his desk and the woman setting a table with crystal and candles. The headline asked, Whose Job Is The Harder? The answer maintained it was "the housewife's." She had to be an expert in purchasing, education, personnel management, and so on, while the husband could simply concentrate on his single task.

In 1920, Libby's food gave us The Woman Who Never Went Out. "What happened when she realized there was more in the world than the view from her kitchen window?" The copy explained:

It hurt—that sudden flash of seeing herself as others must see her. A drudge—that's what she was. One of the army of women past whom the world whirls gaily, while they grow older and more faded and colorless. Till finally one morning they wake up and realize that their chance to play has slipped away forever.

GEE!! I WISH I WERE A MAN

I'd JOIN The NAVY

Howard Chandler Christy

BE A MAN AND DO IT
UNITED STATES NAVY
RECRUITING STATION

1917

U·S·NAVY

OVER THERE

1918

Will you help the Women of France?

SAVE WHEAT

They are struggling against starvation and trying to feed not only themselves and children: but their husbands and sons who are fighting in the trenches

UNITED STATES FOOD ADMINISTRATION

1918

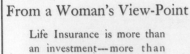

1902

Here the Prudential is noting the woman's point of view, but the copy is directed to the man whose protection he is "in duty bound to provide."

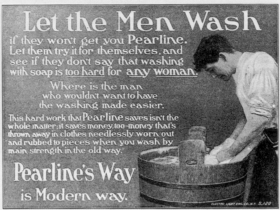

1903

The sight of a man doing the washing was expected to be an attention grabber. Pearline's Modern Way referred to softer soap; the washboard was as modern as the technology had become.

1910

She who ran a typewriter was still called an operator in 1910, but the image of the working woman as a typist was already established. As late as 1958, most working women shown in advertisements were secretarial.

1908

Note the caption: "A man's voice, anyhow." This would bring the manufacturer a blizzard of outraged letters today. The open box of bonbons wouldn't help much either.

1910

"You men who have no wives or sisters to darn for you will find genuine Holeproof Hose to be the softest, most comfortable . . ." et cetera. The insured part refers to the company's guarantee that six pairs will not wear out for six months, and in view of the owners' inability to solve their holey problems, it is a good thing.

1914

Totally disarmed (she has dropped her broom), the master of the house has her completely under his control. This ad could be used for a "what's wrong with this picture?" discussion in a modern women's seminar.

The Mothers of the Race

"I will tell my story," a young woman wrote, "the story of a business woman and her car.

GENERAL MOTORS

1924

Following a testimonial letter, this ad declares: "This young business woman is one of thousands of women who have written about their automobiles. Most of them are mothers. They say that the car has pushed back the horizon of a mother's world; baby legs no longer measure the extent of her travels.

"Wherever there are roads she can go with her children, her neighborhood is as broad as the miles that can be covered between the dawn and the dark."

Often a bridesmaid but never a bride

EDNA'S case was really a pathetic one. Like every woman, her primary ambition was to marry. Most of the girls of her set were married—or about to be. Yet not one possessed more grace or charm or loveliness than she.

And as her birthdays crept gradually toward that tragic thirty-mark, marriage seemed farther from her life than ever.

She was often a bridesmaid but never a bride.

1925

SHE WANTS NO CLERKS... to tell her what to buy...

A nation-wide vogue in shopping that leaves women free to choose for themselves

PIGGLY WIGGLY STORES

1928

MEN DO CRY

THERE ARE some things that move a man to tears. You seldom see him cry, because he does it quietly, and often to himself. I have known of men who have been so shocked and chagrined by a sudden realization of property loss that they cried.

The American Insurance Group
Newark   New Jersey

1939

One of the classic advertising slogans, "Often A Bridesmaid, But Never A Bride," was written by an ad writer named Milton Feasley. He started his copy by drawing on a universal truth about women (as perceived by males in 1925):

"Edna's case was really a pathetic one. Like every woman, her primary ambition was to marry . . . And as her birthdays crept gradually toward that tragic thirty-mark, marriage seemed farther from her life than ever.

"She was often a bridesmaid but never a bride."

Piggly Wiggly, the first major supermarket chain, explains the advantages of cans on open shelves out in front of the counter: "Take what you please from the shelves at Piggly Wiggly. Just read the price tags and help yourself." "The woman of today wants to choose for herself when she buys foods." ". . . you compare values, you reach your own decisions purely on merit, uninfluenced by salesmen." ". . . self-reliant as never before, sweeping aside old barriers, winning new freedom."

While in later years a man who cries would have been credited with sensitivity, in this 1939 ad he was tearing over "a sudden realization of property loss . . ." and inadequate insurance.

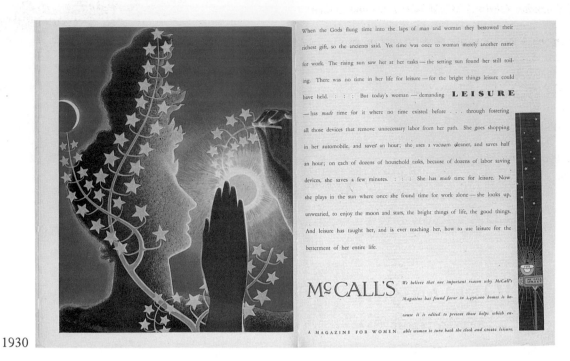

1930

In classic Art Deco, McCall's salutes the newly acquired leisure of the homemaker, and promises to help her spend the free time wisely.

1942

Rosie the Riveter, symbol of the American woman on the production line making the armaments the nation needed to win World War II. Once she had gotten the job done, the place of women in America would never be the same.

1942

Here is the World War II equivalent of Charles Dana Gibson's Girl of World War I.

"I'd rather be with them— than waiting for them"

Good soldiers... THE **WAC**

1944

Libby explained that "she had allowed her housekeeping to absorb not only all her time but her interest and vivacity." It was time to relegate her "housekeeping chores" to the level they deserved. Using Libby's pre-prepared canned meats was, of course, an aid in achieving this end.

For several years in the Twenties the American Laundry Machine Company ran monthly "Send It To The Laundry" ads, which urged the housewife to flee the washtub and ironing board in order to do all sorts of enriching activities. One ad asked if the woman shown looking wistfully through the multi-mullioned window was "Nightingale or canary?" and then filled the whole page with a letter from Madame Fried Hempel, "Famous prima donna of the Metropolitan Opera Company," who urged the housewife to break out of her cage and soar—going to the local opera, among other things. Giving the dirty clothes to the local laundry would provide the time required. Another of the series showed the son "hanging out on street corners" and "going with the gang." His mother started sending the clothes out to the laundry "And now she is the 'best girl' of the big boy! A *real* pal—a sharer of joys and sorrows—a 'good fellow' whose house rings with the gay laughter of the boys . . . the hours she 'found' for her youngster have grown into golden years!"

A *Saturday Evening Post* A&P ad of 1928 asked, "Do wives think differently today?" and answered, "Changing habits prove they do. . . ." The artwork is a four-color painting of three women and a girl on the porch talking among themselves, and the copy reads,

> How different is the new order that has been ushered in. Today, your wife finds opportunity to vary her interests . . . to be a companion to your children . . . to study closer your welfare. She has won a new freedom in her daily life.
>
> What has brought about this change? Your wife will tell you . . . thinking differently . . . thinking of housekeeping in much the same terms as you think of your business position . . . discarding time-worn ideas and old-fashioned methods in favor of a new-day efficiency in home management.

(This approach was hardly new. A vacuum cleaner company ad from 1909 shows the man looking crossly over the caption "The Man always wonders why some way of cleaning can't be found without tormenting him with choking clouds of dust." The saddened wife is shown over the caption, "The Woman thinks she is performing praiseworthy and necessary work in an unavoidable manner." The solution at the bottom calls a broom "a relic of barbarism, a mockery and a farce," and the Husband is shown now vacuuming the drapes.)

But so far as we can know from this distance, up to World War II the female consumer either accepted or agreed with the way she was pictured in ads. The man carried on aggressive business in "the real world," and she provided a safe and comfortable haven for him to return to for solace, where she nurtured the children to make them both proud.

The War Changed All That

Once again, American society came out of a war—World War II—with all the rules changed. With the men gone for four years, the women had to do everything—work on the production lines, run the offices, *and* run the home and care for the children all by themselves. And there was little doubt in their minds that they had done it just as well as the men had, and probably better.

In the immediate years after the war, the status quo antebellum was tacitly accepted, but this did not last long. By the mid-Fifties, with politics, foreign affairs, wages, hours, and a multitude of other norms being challenged, advertising began to attract its critics. The first came from the ethnic minorities. To the art directors' surprise, all those pictures of Aunt Jemima, the Frito Bandito, and Mama Mia began to draw furious letters from representatives of the minorities so caricatured. (The agencies could not claim even a fraction of in-house understanding in this area. While they could point to a ten-percent female representation on their personnel lists, Daniel Pope could identify only 92 Jews out of 5,000 men listed in Who's Who in Advertising, and almost no Italian or Polish names appeared on the staff lists of agency annual reports. Pictures of the staffs in trade journals and these same annual reports showed no blacks at all.) But it was the women's movement, starting soon after Betty Friedan's 1963 *The Feminine Mystique*, that caught advertising with a full broadside.

Before any social engagement

What she *really* wanted was Children

LISTERINE ENDS HALITOSIS

1931

It means so much to a woman
...the fact that you remembered!

GIVE Whitman's CHOCOLATES...IT'S THE THOUGHTFUL THING TO DO!

1939

For the
HEAD OF THE HOUSE
..and her
HUSBAND

The Convertible Feature .. one of 16 major improvements

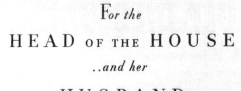

The New Grand Prize
EUREKA De Luxe
VACUUM CLEANER

1931

Why Life's SWANDERFUL when you have a Baby

The baby's daffy over you.

The husband kisses you. And kisses you.

The house sparkles at you.

Baby-mild for Everything SWAN IS PURE AS FINE CASTILES

1945

AN ALBUM OF GENDER ADS

For decades, the advertising world had thought it was telling its female audience what it wanted to hear—and then the women's movement arrived and the advertisers found themselves raked from every side. Betty Friedan charged them with creating a limited world for women and then endlessly propagandizing the woman into believing that she had no choice other than to be a better housekeeper, a better mother, and a more loving, caring wife. Others among the

1951

1962

1968

1971

feminist. *feminists expressed their resentment over advertising's condescension toward women, their stereotyping of the housewife as being emotional, shallow, preoccupied with fashion, cosmetics, and getting the attention of men. The advertisers maintained they had done no such thing, and even if they had, it was what their audience wanted to hear. Here is a sample of the kinds of images that had raised their critics' ire.*

The phone company wants
more installers like Alana MacFarlane.

Alana MacFarlane is a 20-year-old
from San Rafael, California. She's one
of our first women telephone installers.
She won't be the last.
We also have several hundred male
telephone operators. And a policy that
there are no all-male or all-female jobs
at the phone company.
We want the men and women of the
telephone company to do what they want
to do, and do best.
For example, Alana likes working
outdoors. "I don't go for office routine,"
she said. "But as an installer, I get plenty
of variety and a chance to move around."
Some people like to work with their
hands, or, like Alana, get a kick out of
working 20 feet up in the air.
Others like to drive trucks. Some
we're helping to develop into good
managers.
Today, when openings exist, local
Bell Companies are offering applicants
and present employees some jobs they
may never have thought about before. We
want to help all advance to the best of
their abilities.
AT&T and your local Bell Company
are equal opportunity employers.

1974

LEFT:
It's a decade after Betty Friedan's The Feminine Mystique, *and the advertising industry has learned its lesson. Here AT&T is stoutly declaring, "There are no all-male or all-female jobs at the phone company."*

OPPOSITE ABOVE LEFT:
One of the last traditional decades-old ad themes.

OPPOSITE ABOVE RIGHT:
By the mid-Eighties, the feminist successes had gone from an era of "New Frontiers for Women," to "Superwoman" who could do everything, to a point of fatigue if not exhaustion. Both the advertisers' research and the women's movement itself began to search for the real truths of the new liberated age. What have we learned? Here the Ladies Home Journal, *which has been fighting for women's equality for nearly a century, gathers the symbols of the options.*

OPPOSITE BELOW LEFT AND RIGHT:
Two imaginative uses of pedal symbols to represent female parity and the new options available to women.

What the Feminists Were Mad About

The feminists pointed out how enormously important advertising was to the way the American people saw themselves. We had been taught to look at ads to see how to dress, what to eat, how our houses and our cars should appear—and in the case of women, what women should do and how they should act. They saw advertising as limiting the lifestyle of women, perpetuating the care of the children, decorating the home, making life easy for the husband as the final goal of the woman's life and the ultimate high wall around her creative opportunities. Friedan believed that having pictured women in this role, the advertisers either deliberately or inadvertently created images of women to fit that idea or keep them in their place.

Others in the women's movement followed with increasing resentment over advertising's repeated use of women as either sex objects or brainless housewives wildly excited about a detergent or a new decaffeinated coffee. They resented the implication that women were preoccupied with cosmetics, style, fashion, and attracting men. And throughout, they accused advertising of trying to sell the idea in a thousand subtle ways that woman's place was in the home.

The managers of the advertising agencies were initially astonished. They had thought that they had been giving women what they wanted. They were sure that the "average woman" either was neutral or disagreed with the movement's views, and at first, they dismissed the criticisms as the views of a strident, unrepresentative minority.

But the criticism would not go away. The feminists mounted confrontations with the agencies themselves, fos-

tered revolts within agencies, covered subway ads with "This ad insults women" stickers, and distributed "Plastic Pig" awards to companies who portrayed women in a denigrating manner. The industry finally recognized they had indeed been insensitive to the problem, and asked the women precisely where had they erred, and what should they do about it?

Chapter and Verse about the Industry's Errors

The critics were eager to tell them. They described numerous areas of concern.

There were the ads of Function Ranking. Here the person shown *doing something*—teaching tennis, taping an ankle, leading a pack train—was always a man. The women in the pictures were *watching* a man do something. When the men and women were doing something together, the man was always feeding the woman candies, a bite of food at an expensive meal, the woman was never doing anything to the man.

There were the ads demonstrating the Ritual of Subordination. The women were lying on beds, lying on carpets, lying on couches. Men were never shown doing these things. As Erving Goffman explained in his "Gender Advertisements" manual, "Beds and floors provide places in social situations where incumbent persons will be lower than anyone sitting on a chair or standing. Floors also are associated with the less clean, less pure, less exalted parts of a room—for example, the place to keep dogs, baskets of soiled clothes, street footwear, and the like. And a recumbent position is one from which physical defence of oneself can least well be initiated and therefore one which renders one very dependent on the benignness of the surround." (Goff-

1971

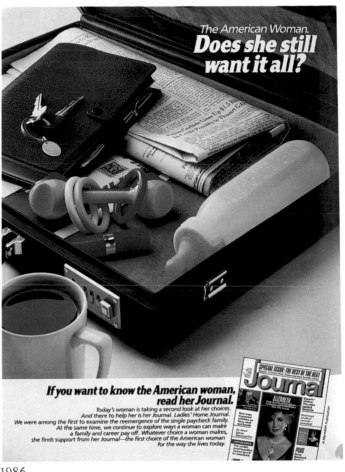

1986

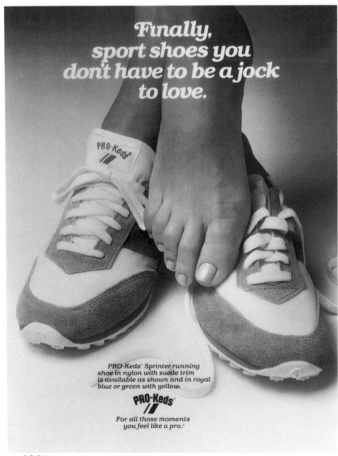

c. 1981

1986

When I grow up
a rich man will
fall in love with me
and marry me
and take care of me.

At Girls Clubs, girls learn that fantasies don't come true
except in fairy tales. But the dream of becoming a doctor
or teacher or even a Supreme Court justice does. Interests
they may have felt too helpless to pursue are explored in
career awareness programs. Remedial classes make it
possible for them to continue their education. And the
problems that can permanently sidetrack a girl, teenage
pregnancy and drugs, are confronted. Girls Club members learn that it doesn't matter where a girl comes from,
as long as she knows where she's going.

To help girls help themselves, contact us.

GCA GIRLS CLUBS OF AMERICA, INC.
205 LEXINGTON AVENUE, NEW YORK, NEW YORK 10016

1987

man demonstrated his case with 508 reproduced and analyzed recent ads.)

A corollary was described by Marchand. Research
showed that in the traditional living room scene of parents
and children, the man clearly dominated. "Out of 88 family
circle tableaux in which only a single chair or sofa seat is
occupied, the husband claims the right to the seat in 65. In
51 of these instances, the wife perches accommodatingly on
the arm of the chair or sofa, usually balancing herself by
putting her arm lightly around her husband's shoulders. In
14 instances, she stands behind him diffidently bending or
looking over his shoulder. Interestingly in 19 of the 28
contrary examples, in which the man balances on the arm of
his wife's chair or stands nearby, the tableau advertised
either a radio or a phonograph. Apparently in the presence of
culturally uplifting music, the woman more often gained the
right of reposed concentration while the more tech-
nologically inclined man stood prepared to change the records or adjust the radio dials."

Another study collected ads with people on staircases or
porch steps. The man was always on a lower step and the
woman above him, thus demonstrating the man on the lower
step is "dominant" since he would have had to select his
position before the woman sat down.

A different study showed another example of domination
in which ads for Raleigh's cigarettes, Bermuda travel, Sea-
gram's Gin, et cetera showed women smiling, but the men
were simply "relaxed." The researchers recommended that

this could be corrected by making the men smile, and the
women look "either remote or detached."

Goffman also studied ads in which two persons were
shown, one with their arm around the other's shoulders. Art
directors were urged to avoid this form of denigration because, "The 'shoulder hold' is an asymmetrical configuration
more or less requiring that the person holding be taller than
the person held, and that the held person accept direction
and constraint. Typically the arrangement seems to be
dyadically irreversible. When employed by a cross-sexed
adult pair, the sign seems to be taken to indicate sexually-
potential proprietaryship."

Alice Courtney and Thomas Whipple's *Sex Stereotyping
in Advertising* pointed out that a broader criticism was the
constant division of women into working women or non-
working women. All working women appeared to be secretaries; any home-based activity was considered non-
working. The research studies praised ads showing women
buying cars and houses, and criticized ones showing them
buying "trivial things" like cosmetics and cleaning products.

Ultimately, the advertising industry began to produce
working manuals or checklists on how to deal with the
gender issue in the creation of an ad. One of the most
popular of these was the following prepared by a consultive
panel of the National Advertising Review Board:

Am I implying in my promotional campaign that
creative, athletic and mind-enriching toys and games
are not for girls as much as for boys? Does my ad, for
example, imply that dolls are for girls and chemistry
sets are for boys, and that neither could ever become
interested in the other category?

Are sexual stereotypes perpetuated in my ad? That
is, does it portray women as weak, silly, and over-
emotional? Or does it picture both sexes as intelligent,
physically able, and attractive?

Are the women portrayed in my ad stupid? For
example, am I reinforcing the "dumb blonde" cliche?
Does my ad portray women who are unable to balance
their checkbooks? Women who are unable to manage a
household without the help of outside experts, particularly male ones?

Does my ad use belittling language? For example,
"gal friday" or "lady professor?" Or "her kitchen" but
"his car?" Or "women's chatter" but "men's
discussion?"

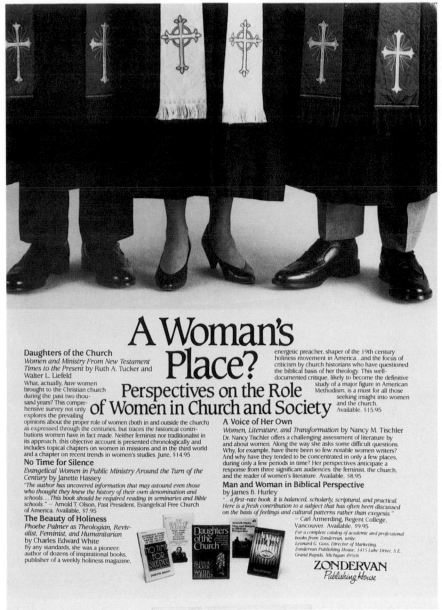

1987

Does my ad make use of contemptuous phrases? Such as "the weaker sex," "the little woman," "the ball and chain," or "the war department"?

Do my ads consistently show women waiting on men? Even in occupational situations, for example, are women nurses or secretaries serving coffee, etc. to male bosses or colleagues? And never vice versa?

Is there a gratuitous message in my ads that a woman's most important role in life is a supportive one, to cater to and coddle men and children? Is it a "big deal" when the reverse is shown, that is, very unusual and special—something for which the woman must show gratitude?"

An additional checklist by the National Advertising Review Board contained such admonitions as:

Are sexual stereotypes perpetuated in my ads? Do they portray women as weak, silly, and over-emotional?

Are the women portrayed in my ads stupid?

Do my ads portray women as ecstatically happy over household cleanliness or deeply distressed because of their failure to achieve near-perfection in household tasks?

Do my ads show women as fearful of not being attractive, of not being able to keep their husbands or lovers, fearful of in-law disapproval?

Does my copy promise unrealistic psychological rewards for using the product?

Did the Industry Really Pay Any Attention to this Concern with Gender?

It did indeed.

Research studies of ad model symbols showed that in 1958, most "working women" were shown as secretaries. In 1970, most were entertainers; in 1972 most were simply "decorative objects." Then the indexes began to change. By

1976 the women began to look "professional" in business and managerial roles extolling headache remedies in offices. "Power-dressed" women began to appear in suits and laboratory uniforms selling credit cards, cosmetics, and frozen dinners, and women engaged in sports were shown not as doing it for recreation, but as part of hard driving competition. Oddly enough, up to the mid-1970s men were usually shown as business leaders, military men, or sports figures. After the mid-1970s, Courtney and Whipple found the majority of the men were shown in "non-working roles." For example, in 1978, 54 percent of the men were shown in "decorative roles" only.

Barbara Lippert believes the turning point came with the 1973 Charlie perfume campaign which showed a "confident young model in a pantsuit, striding resolutely alone." Following this came so many female models engaged in traditionally male-oriented activities that the race car driver whipping off the helmet to let a headful of flowing curls fall into place, quickly became a cliché.

By the late 1960s, New Frontiers for Women had become Superwoman. Tracy Lynn credits this ratcheting up to the Virginia Slims' "You've come a long way, Baby" series, shortly followed by the cosmetic ads that showed a hard-driving woman in the corporate scene by day and a softly glamorous seductress by night. With women entering all the professions by the late 1970s—more single women from divorces and late marriages, more women independently working for higher salaries—the ads not only showed the professional women in the art work, but the sales pitch was increasingly directed at the women themselves to buy securities, buy cars and houses, and take out insurance.

Then the Inevitable Reaction

By the late 1980s the pendulum was starting to swing back. Women who were actually working in the corporate scene began to feed back irritation with the new treatment. Some resented the "need to live up to the new image"; some said the ads "did not look believable"; others said the commercials of the women striding through offices with men taking down dictation behind them "insulted our intelligence" and were "just another synthetic cliché." (The studies that revealed these responses also drew reactions to the overall "condescension" of advertising in general, and the "increased tendency to advertise things that shouldn't be discussed in public.")

Some believed the gender criticism had achieved its purpose. Yankelovich, Skelly and White found that "women now feel that it's OK to dress up and wear evening clothes. It's not seen as inconsistent." Lippert felt that "women want the basic changes that have come about since the early 1970s but they want romance, too." Suzanne Gordon identified more resentment: ". . . what has happened to reformist feminism in the past decade is perhaps the most dramatic example of capitalism's genius at defusing protest by winning the protesters over to the very values and institutions they once attacked."

But there was an overt, possibly costly backlash building from two specific quarters. The women who actually preferred or placed a higher value on the home and care of the children not only felt left out, but resented the implied value judgments. Some product research found the choice of which of the oft-denigrated cleansers and washing detergents to buy actually related to the role played by the model of the homemaker shown in the ads. "Which of the ads look like me? I'll buy that one. She's doing what I do." The impact of the stylish working woman shown preparing haute cuisine frozen foods was so strong that housewives were avoiding that particular brand "because those foods are for women who work."

And then there was the anti-male problem. To get the woman up, the ads had put the man down, and a slow-burning resentment was seen to be growing. Raised consciousness had finally eliminated the dumb blonde and the clinging flower as an object needing to have the product explained to her—whereupon the ads began using the male as the incompetent and the butt of jokes. No one worried; decades had made him a sufficiently strong figure his image could take it. But the conceit went on too long. Men's Rights, Inc. began the traditional analysis of print and video ads and began to compile lists. Claiming to have scanned and categorized "thousands of ads," they found men were "the objects of rejection, anger and violence 100 percent of the time."

It was the man who stupidly awakened his wife for comfort and a cold pill; the man who was so clumsy the tennis ball bounced off his head; the near-naked and oiled model demonstrating knit shorts in a pose that would have outraged the feminists were the genders reversed.

Warren Farrell believes that the trend demonstrated that women now view men either as "success objects" or "jerk objects." David Rose, president of the National Congress for Men, was distressed that the trend went beyond just being funny or getting even for past slights. He believes that the most destructive images involved fathers, and "the portrayal of dads being inept affects some important aspects of our lives." Jennifer Foote, a *Newsweek* editor, elaborated his concern that "the government and the judiciary, especially in divorce, still treat men as though they are incompetent parents."

So Is There a Solution Here?

Not yet nor not easily. Foote thinks that "the new sexism may reflect nothing so much as the ad world's never-ending search for novelty," and she quotes with approval the conclusions of Al Ries, a market strategist. Says Ries, "There is tremendous pressure inside the [advertising] industry to shock. It gets to the point where they'll sacrifice everything to get attention." But many observers of the field believe that the balance board that now has the male one down, is not likely to come back up for some time. The female was down so long.

SHE'S VERY CHARLIE.

Charlie

REVLON

1988

The Charlie perfume woman had been one of the earliest (in 1973) to show a confident working woman striding purposefully through a male world. The ad here was refused by the New York Times *for being sexist and "in poor taste," but eleven women's magazines accepted and ran it and the publisher of* Ms. *called it "light-hearted." "It's kind of fun to see a couple where the man is not the tall, powerful one," she explained. The ad still "works" and the image was still being run in 1988.*

Niagara Falls will be Destroyed

Unless those who care to do as **President Roosevelt** suggests assist promptly in a movement to restrain a few citizens of the United States and Canada who are now rapidly diverting the water for the production of commercial power.

The American Civic Association

has succeeded in bringing the threatened desecration to the attention of the whole country. Its effort has awakened the United States Government. It has now in its hands the threads of a movement which will certainly save the Falls if they are worked into a solid cable by the necessary funds to twist them together.

Organized self-interest, endeavoring to destroy for the profit of a few this natural wonder which belongs to all of us, must be met by **organized unselfishness.** A campaign of investigation, education, and organization has been begun to ascertain the exact facts in respect to the Niagara grab, to present them to the whole country, and to propose such individual and united action as shall seal this great scenic glory forever from desecration.

President Roosevelt, a life member of the American Civic Association, has urged its officers to continue the work of awakening the country to the imminent danger to Niagara, and to thus sustain his action and that required of Congress.

The American Civic Association exists solely for the purpose of making and keeping America beautiful and clean for all its people. It can only continue its organized work as it is supported by those who believe that Niagara should be saved, and civic righteousness stimulated in all directions.

This is an Appeal for Help

The international character of the Niagara-salvation campaign, opposed by intrenched corporate interests, entails large expenditures, which must increase if the work is to be continued and invigorated. Fifty dollars or more pays for a Life Membership, and two hundred Life Memberships received within four weeks would almost positively assure the success of the Niagara-salvation effort. Contributions of $25 and $10 and $5 count up rapidly. Annual membership is but $2, and the important Niagara and general literature of the Association, forming a constant stream of helpful experiences and suggestions, is sent to all members.

AMERICAN CIVIC ASSOCIATION
North American Building, Philadelphia

J. HORACE MCFARLAND, President
GEORGE FOSTER PEABODY,
FRANKLIN MACVEAGH, } Vice-Presidents
JAMES D. PHELAN,
ROBERT C. OGDEN, Chairman Advisory Committee
CLINTON ROGERS WOODRUFF, Secretary

I enclose.........to help save Niagara Falls and to aid in the general work of the American Civic Association.

Name....................................

Address..................................

To American Civic Association, Philadelphia

1906

A Great Wrong!
SEE HOW ONE YEAR OF FACTORY LIFE AGES LITTLE GIRLS

Little Ola, eight years old when she went to work in a Georgia cotton mill. The sun shining in her face causes a slight frown, but she has rosy cheeks and a childlike expression.

This is another picture of little Ola one year after she began work in the cotton mill. Her childhood has gone forever. How much was it worth to the mill, to society, to her?

Our National Disgrace

Two million children in this country are at work, while other children play or go to school. Two million children sacrificed to greed! Here is the record. Read it.

10,000 Boys from 9 to 13 years old work in the Coal Breakers.

7,500 Children work in Glass Factories. Hundreds of them work ALL NIGHT.

60,000 little Children toil in Southern Cotton Mills. Little girls 8 years old work through a TWELVE-HOUR NIGHT.

Little Messenger Boys are ruined by NIGHT calls at Houses of Vice.

"*The truth is, these child victims are working for us. They are working for me. They are working for you.*"—HON. CHARLES P. NEILL, United States Commissioner of Labor.

The National Child Labor Committee is a purely philanthropic organization formed to secure and enforce legislation that will stamp out this enormous evil. We are struggling to save millions of children from the stunted bodies and blighted minds caused by industrial slavery. You can help us by becoming a member of the Committee and lending your influence to the enactment of necessary laws in your own State.

$2 will make you an associate member; $25 a sustaining member and $100 a guarantor. This money will all be expended in saving little boys and girls from a life of ignorance and misery. Put your shoulder to the wheel and help us all you can. The cause is a noble one. If *your* boy were at work in a coal mine, or a glass factory, or the cotton mills, *you* would be grateful to those who were trying to save him. Others will now be grateful to you.

Detach the coupon now—before you turn this page—and become at least an associate member. Your $2 may save a little boy or girl from industrial slavery.

DETACH, SIGN AND RETURN

MEMBERSHIP ENROLLMENT

I take pleasure in contributing $............to the work of the National Child Labor Committee. Please enroll me as { An Associate Member.
{ A Sustaining Member.
{ A Guarantor.

Name ....

Address ....

Make all checks or orders payable to the National Child Labor Committee, 287 Fourth Avenue, New York City.

National Child Labor Committee
287 Fourth Ave., New York City.   Century Building, Atlanta, Ga.

OFFICERS:
Felix Adler, *Chairman*   Samuel McCune Lindsay,
Homer Folks,   *Secretary*
          Vice-Chairman   A. J. McKelway } *Assistant*
V. Everit Macy, *Treasurer*   Owen R. Lovejoy } *Secretaries*

1906

Spies *and* Lies

German agents are everywhere, eager to gather scraps of news about our men, our ships, our munitions. It is still possible to get such information through to Germany, where thousands of these fragments—often individually harmless—are patiently pieced together into a whole which spells death to American soldiers and danger to American homes.

But while the enemy is most industrious in trying to collect information, and his systems elaborate, he is *not* superhuman—indeed he is often very stupid, and would fail to get what he wants were it not deliberately handed to him by the carelessness of loyal Americans.

Do not discuss in public, or with strangers, any news of troop and transport movements, or bits of gossip as to our military preparations, which come into your possession.

Do not permit your friends in service to tell you—or write you—"inside" facts about where they are, what they are doing and seeing.

Do not become a tool of the Hun by passing on the malicious, disheartening rumors which he so eagerly sows. Remember he asks no better service than to have you spread his lies of disasters to our soldiers and sailors, gross scandals in the Red Cross, cruelties, neglect and wholesale executions in our camps, drunkenness and vice in the Expeditionary Force, and other tales certain to disturb American patriots and to bring anxiety and grief to American parents.

And do not wait until you catch someone putting a bomb under a factory. Report the man who spreads pessimistic stories, divulges—or seeks—confidential military information, cries for peace, or belittles our efforts to win the war.

Send the names of such persons, even if they are in uniform, to the Department of Justice, Washington. Give all the details you can, with names of witnesses if possible—show the Hun that we can beat him at his own game of collecting scattered information and putting it to work. The fact that you made the report will not become public.

You are in contact with the enemy *today*, just as truly as if you faced him across No Man's Land. In your hands are two powerful weapons with which to meet him—discretion and vigilance. *Use them.*

COMMITTEE ON PUBLIC INFORMATION
8 JACKSON PLACE, WASHINGTON, D. C.

George Creel, *Chairman*
The Secretary of State
The Secretary of War
The Secretary of the Navy

Contributed through Division of Advertising

United States Gov't Comm. on Public Information

1918

Causes—Advertising
in the Service of the Community

WE WILL CLOSE this book with a look at the fine art of advertising causes—advertising campaigns that tried to persuade the distracted viewer that he or she should care about some intangible condition and then, even harder, DO something about it. The product here is intangible in that what is being sold cannot be acquired, taken home, or used. Doing something about it now requires that the reader change his concerns or priorities or change the way he spends his time or his money. This is the area in which advertising lays its cynicism aside, and tries to improve the community in a non-material way.

And it isn't easy. David Ogilvy says, "Advocacy advertising is not a job for beginners." But there is a tradition of it within the profession.

The first to use advertising for community action was the government itself: recruiting ads. Announcements for musters and parades were placed in the local press by the local authorities, and the space was made available, free, by the publishers. During the Civil War, the government sold bonds via newspaper advertisements which were placed throughout the North, and 1) the space was given free, plus 2) the device was so effective that the national bond sales have been credited with demonstrating "what advertising could do" and resulted in the first national ad campaigns of baking powder, soap, and railroad travel.

The first non-governmental issue ads appeared after the turn of the century. In 1906, the American Civic Association *bought* pages in national magazines to apprise the public of the threat to Niagara Falls by the power industry.

(Electric companies hoped to exploit the difference between the water level above and below the falls to turn generator turbines. Concerned citizens feared that all the water would be diverted, leaving only a dribble flowing over the lip. Surprisingly, that was exactly what the companies planned. Public pressure forced complicated scheduling that drew off only half of the water flow during daylight hours, and up to three-quarters at night—an arrangement that still holds today.)

At roughly the same time, ads were run to dramatize the outrages of child labor. The National Child Labor Committee was chaired by Felix Adler, the early welfare leader, who saw to it that his board always contained a substantial number of newspaper publishers, and the child labor ads were placed free, as a public service, by local papers.

This mix of paid and free issue advertising has continued to our own time. Nowadays whether the media charge or not usually depends on the tax status of the organization seeking the ad space or time. If the ad or program is directed toward specific, potential legislation, the media will normally charge a special, nonprofit institution rate. If the cause is still at the point of simply raising public consciousness and concern about the issue, the media normally make the space or the air time available without charge. Again Ogilvy gives his usual crisp advice, noting that when a group is seeking to raise money through advertising, "it is rare for any advertisement, however powerful, to bring in enough direct contributions to pay for the cost of the space." He believes, however, that "What advertising *can* do, is to 'sensitize' the market,

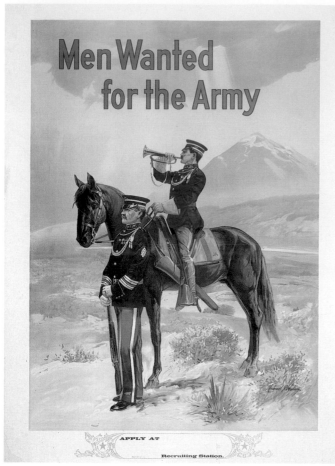

1914

1918

1918

1918

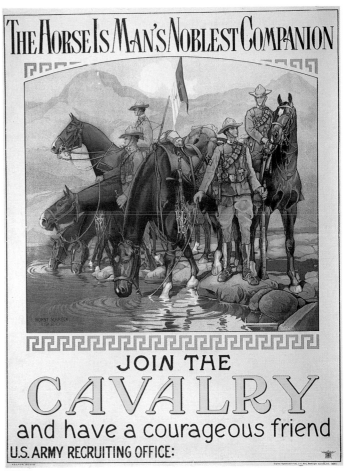

1920

thus making it easier to raise money by more personal methods of solicitation. It is difficult to persuade people to give money to a charity unless they know something about it."

When the U.S. was drawn into World War I in 1917, the government hastily created a Federal Committee of Public Information to tell the public what was needed to win the war and to dramatize the reasons for "why we fight." Within the Committee, a "Division of Pictorial Publicity" was formed by the artist Charles Dana Gibson, who pulled in the leading illustrators of the time. At a weekly meeting at Keens Chop House on 36th Street in New York, Gibson passed out requested images and ads to his friends sitting around one of the circular tables at the back of the restaurant. James Montgomery Flagg drew the assignment for "Uncle Sam Needs You" at one of these lunches. Hundreds of other images which have become a part of the national memory developed from the gathering of this group. All of the art work was contributed free; the posters were printed free; and the ads were run without charge in the newspapers and magazines of the day.

After the war, the tradition of making free space available for good causes continued. The public issues of the Twenties were mostly of a public health nature, while the Depression days of the Thirties brought out the need to aid victims of the drought and Dust Bowl. Other campaigns of this period included pleas to cooperate with public reclamation projects, and programs to explain and generate support for

WPA and PWA work projects, the NRA economic recovery efforts, and the park work of the CCC.

The "Ad Council"

When America got into World War II, the various offices of war information immediately re-created the poster and ad programs that had worked so well in World War I.

The War Advertising Council was founded in 1942 and rushed into action selling war bonds. As the war progressed, the Council produced campaigns promoting internal security, rationing, housing solutions, collecting metal waste, protection against venereal disease, and so on. Ultimately more than a hundred public service series were developed, the ad copy work all being donated. The business and advertising community considered it their contribution to the war effort.

The whole program worked so well that those involved were reluctant to see it disbanded once peace was secured. Therefore, at the close of the war, a new Advertising Council was set up as a "private, nonprofit corporation supported entirely by American business, including the advertising and communications industries."

The Council started its peacetime career aiding causes for which there was already a general consensus, and it dedicated most of its efforts simply keeping the topics in the public's eye. During this period the electorate was introduced to such familiar themes as Register and Vote, Prevent Forest Fires, and Buy U.S. Savings Bonds. The ad cam-

1918

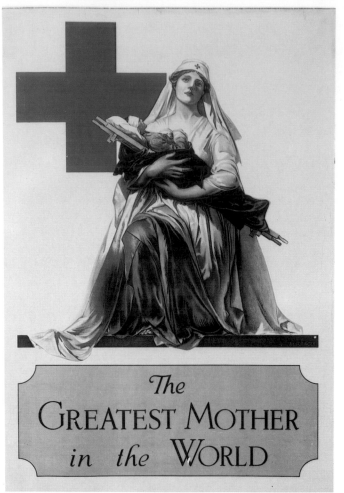

The
GREATEST MOTHER
in the WORLD

1918

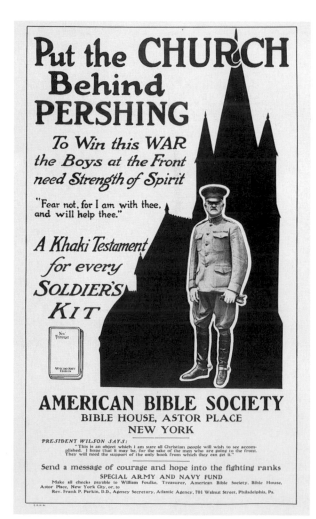

1918

paigns were done tastefully (if not innovatively), and the slogans became a part of the national vocabulary:

Give to the College of Your Choice
Take a Bite Out of Crime
Peace Corps—The Toughest Job You'll Ever Love
United Way—Thanks to You It Works for All of Us.

Smokey the Bear and his "Only You Can Prevent Forest Fires" almost became synonymous with the Ad Council, but it became one of those campaigns that got to be more complicated than anyone expected. After hanging guilt on millions of readers for years that they alone were the cause of the destruction of our forests, it first began to seep into the readers' consciousness that maybe it wasn't they alone but someone else, and then the Forest Service suddenly confused everyone by deciding that a few forest fires every so often really were healthy to the trees. At the time of this writing, the rule in the national parks is that if the fire was started by lightning, "let it burn." It will kill the wood borers, weed out the stunting sucker trees, and strengthen the large timber. Only if people or park buildings are threatened, is it to be extinguished. While millions who had been told that only they could prevent fires found at least one source of social guilt had been lifted, they felt somewhat

1918

1932

distressed at having been threatened for so long and so often.

As is always the case with public issue advertising, it is very difficult to determine how much of a successful campaign can be credited to the advertising about it and how much to a host of other factors. In the case of Smokey, the Council reports proudly that forest fires have been cut in half since The Bear appeared. The United Negro College Fund increased its receipts from $11 million to $30 million in the early years of the Ad Council's care.

In the 1960s, when there was so much resentment against traditional institutions in general, the Ad Council began to collect its share. Critics charged that the Council only took on causes that were already won. Another complaint was that too often the campaigns (if not the issues themselves) were too superficial to justify the effort and space the Council devoted to them. These attacks resulted in several new approaches.

First, the Council committed itself to sharper-edged causes. Second, more public institutions themselves went into advertising (the American Lung Association, Greenpeace, Sierra Club), and third, many of the agencies of the federal government began buying space and running their own campaigns. The Post Office started buying ads to explain how to use its service in 1973; the armed services went into multi-million-dollar campaigns for recruiting; and

1935

1942

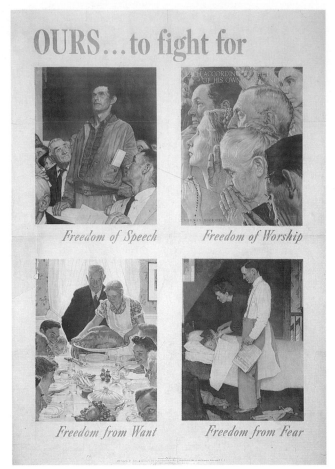

1943

1943

1944

who has a better right to oppose the war?

to send contributions and for information, write:
student mobilization committee to end the war in vietnam.
857 broadway, new york city 10003, (212) 675-8465

1969

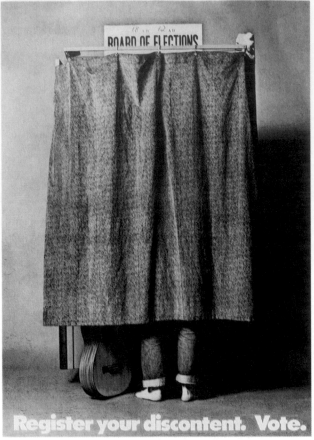

1972

1970

the Immigration Service began to put the latest rules and regulations before the foreign community via national advertising.

The Ad Council soon regained its approval from its advertising and business supporters, and it now uses over $800 million worth of donated time and space each year.

Like so many public institutions, the Council walks a narrow line, trying to avoid criticism from the government on one side and the public on the other.

To maintain its effectiveness over the long term, it avoids any governmental subsidy and it tiptoes around anything that looks like lobbying for specific legislation. At the same time, it tries to pursue campaigns of service "to the nation at large, avoiding regional, sectarian, or special interest drives of all kinds." With so many interested parties, Solomon himself would be pressed to bring this off without criticism.

Just as with the World War I experience when the very finest artists and illustrators of the nation contributed their skills to the good causes, in our own time many of the most striking of the public issue images come from our most creative photographers and designers. The Red Cross symbol, "The Greatest Mother in the World," was produced by Courtland N. Smith and A.E. Foringer, and is as familiar to the British as it is to Americans. *The Four Freedoms* by Norman Rockwell showed his picturization of the Churchill/Roosevelt wartime goals. The *Years of Dust* was drawn by Ben Shahn. The image of the Vietnam veteran was by the fashion photographer Richard Avedon. The Viet

Nam Moratorium poster was drawn by John Schreider. The anti-smoking theme was expressed by the then-teenage role model Brooke Shields. "Not everyone who drives drunk dies," was by Sal DeVito and Jamie Seltzer. "Till death or drinking do them part," was designed by Howard Benson and Barry Biederman. The body bag was created by Bob Barrie and Mike Lescarbeau; "The cost of living high" by Demaine, Vickers and Associates; and the Narcotics Anonymous image by Goldberg/Marchesano. Finally, the image for AIDS research was created by Annie Liebovitz with the help of nine of the nation's most famous models with their children.

The demand for media support has become breathtaking. In 1987, the Columbia Broadcasting System alone received 5,500 requests for public service announcements, complete with pre-prepared storyboards, written copy, and taped presentations. CBS chose among these and ultimately ran some 17,000 spots during the year in support of the various causes they represented.

Here are examples of some of the early antecedents of our public issue advertising plus some current parallels in the printed form. Note the skilled and subtle ways in which the advertising community now brings social problems to the community's attention, and note how it involves us in the need to *do* something about these concerns. Here the modern techniques of advertising and visual communication are demonstrated at their very best.

1981

1970

1972

1980

1981

1986

Jim just met his neighbor's son.

Tom was a normal teenager. B average, steady girl, part-time job at the bookstore. And a $100-a-day habit that led him to pry open Jim's living room window last night.

Jim was a normal guy, too. Until he killed a burglar who turned out to be a kid. His neighbor's kid.

Too often, this is how America fights drugs in the home. No plan. No thought. Just a quick reaction followed by an eternity of regret.

Wake up to the drug problem in your community before the problem wakes you up. Contribute time or money to the organizations that fight abuse and addiction among children and adults. Stay in close touch with family and friends so you can catch the problems before they hit home.

Prepared as a public service by Demaine, Vickers and Associates. Photography by Fred Kligman.

Fight the cost of living high.

1986

Today Bob started in on his son's college education.

If you're putting drugs ahead of everything else in your life— your family, your friends, your career—you've got a problem. Take the first step towards solving it. Call Narcotics Anonymous 338-7989, or the National Drug Abuse Hotline, 1-800-COCAINE.

Created as a public service by Goldberg/Marchesano and Associates Inc.

1986

For the future of our children...
Support the American Foundation for AIDS Research. We do.

SEND CONTRIBUTIONS TO: AMERICAN FOUNDATION FOR AIDS RESEARCH, BOX C, NEW YORK, NEW YORK 10116

Models:
Ariane
Christie Brinkley
Kelly Emberg
Cindy Harrell
Beverly Johnson
Andie MacDowell
Paulina
Julianne Phillips
Joan Severance

Photographer:
Annie Leibovitz

Sponsor:
Kenneth Cole

1986

275

ACKNOWLEDGMENTS

The work plan of this book was as follows: we first did the research on the topic and determined what facts and analysis we wished to include. Searching through materials in the Library of Congress, we then selected the ads we needed to present the visual image of the history covered. The captions were next written to explain the significance of the pictured ads, and finally we wrote the text essays to provide a matrix for tying the pictures of each chapter together. The result of this work plan was to make the *pictures*—the ads—all-important. Thus we cannot overstate our indebtedness to the many people who searched company and agency files to find us reproducible images and give us permission to use the ads we selected. We cannot identify the over one hundred individuals so involved, but the presence of the pictures reveals the corporate support that the people represented.

It should be made clear that in no instance did a company make any suggestions as to what images should be used, but once we had identified (and sent photocopies of the advertisements we wanted), such corporations as Coca-Cola, Procter & Gamble, Levi Strauss, Jantzen, and Ford went to generous extremes to support us in our project.

A great many of the historical plates came out of the Library of Congress files, and we are equally grateful for the patience of the staffs of such units as the Collections Management Division, the Prints and Photographs Division, and the Photoduplication Service of the Library. We want to express special thanks to Frank Evina of the Copyright Office for his help with historical deposit materials. Similarly, we want to express our appreciation for the enthusiastic assistance we were given by the staff of the Duncan Library of the Alexandria Public Library, and our thanks to the librarians at the Queen Street Library, Alexandria, for their equally professional assistance. All of the above granted us a great deal more time and help than any individual patron has a right to request.

Two highly skilled readers examined the full manuscript and, while they should not be held responsible for any errors in fact or judgment, they made the completed book a far better piece of work than it would have been without them: Dana Pratt, Publishing Officer of the Library of Congress, read it as a longtime university press editor and publisher; and Paul Conrad, Executive Director of the Pacific Northwest Newspaper Association, read it as a media attorney. Two advertising agency directors read it in detail, and their vigorous and incisive comments were both supportive and enhancing. For professional reasons, they requested to be left anonymous. We are in debt to all four of these advisors, as well as to the many specialists who examined parts of the manuscript at our request.

This book would never have seen the light of day without the patience and persistence of many members of the staff of Harry N. Abrams, Inc. We want especially to express our thanks and appreciation to Barbara Lyons and Neil Ryder Hoos, whose job it was to deal with the nearly 600 images in the book and obtain permission from their creators to use them; and to Dirk Luykx, who brought sensitivity and skill to the task of assembling the pictures, text, and captions into an attractive and readable package; to Edith Pavese, our long-time editor at Abrams, we want to convey our warmest thanks for her continued support and encouragement throughout the duration of this project.

C.G. and H.D.
Washington, D.C., 1988

SOURCES AND SUGGESTIONS FOR FURTHER INFORMATION

We have listed below some of the best sources for general background reading on the subjects of this book. The volumes mentioned will be those we found to give the most information in the fewest number of words, were written the most attractively, and were most likely to be available in the general reader's home community. Specialists, candidates for doctoral dissertations, and researchers seeking more specific studies on narrower topics will find these listed in the comprehensive Bibliography beginning on page 281. The full bibliographic treatment (including publishers and dates of publication) for the "further reading" suggestions below will also be found in the Bibliography.

CHAPTERS ONE AND TWO: A Short History of Advertising in America

If you have time to read only one volume, we would recommend Daniel Pope's *The Making of Modern Advertising* (1983). He moves an astonishing amount of information in a graceful manner, and his conclusions are more convincing than anyone else's trying to determine what really mattered—and what it all really means—across the history of American advertising.

If you are looking for reproductions of historic advertisements, there are three fine volumes: *Edsels, Luckies and Frigidaires* by Robert Atwan, Donald McQuade, and John W. Wright (1979); *Advertising: Reflections of a Century* by Bryan Holme (1982); and *They Laughed When I Sat Down* by Frank R. Rowsome (1959). The above are essentially the *only* extant volumes that attempt to cover more than an individual decade or so of advertising history, but there are a few good studies that focus on specific ten- or twenty-year periods. Roland Marchand concentrates on the 1920s and 1930s in *Advertising the American Dream* (1985). The 1960s are explored by Larry Dobrow in *When Advertising Tried Harder: The Sixties, The Golden Age of American Advertising* (1984), and in *The New Advertising; The Great Campaigns from Avis to Volkswagen* by Robert Glatzer (1970).

As Dobrow points out in despair, the advertising profession has had an astonishingly cavalier attitude toward its past history and traditions. There has been only a single full-dress history of the profession, and that is by Frank Presbrey, *The History and Development of Advertising* written in 1929. This volume was reprinted in facsimile form by Greenwood Press in 1968, so it is more likely to be available in your local library than might appear.

Both Dobrow and we had a surprisingly difficult time finding reproducible copies of the ads we wanted and securing permission to run those we had. We are particularly grateful, therefore, for the ones that do appear in this book, and the agencies and corporations that made them available in response to our requests. Few advertisers keep scrapbooks or file copies of past campaigns; buyouts and mergers have wiped out corporate records; and—surprisingly— the rather recent trend for photographic models to control reproduction rights, limits further use of some of the most memorable campaigns.

The generally barren scene of past records and files seems finally to be coming to an end with a new concern over advertising's past. The lay audience has taken a renewed interest in old ads via the nostalgia and American folk history movements, and the professional and research communities are initiating new centers of advertising preservation and study.

The recently opened American Advertising Museum in Portland, Oregon, has public displays, a growing advertising library, and has custody of a large number of privately donated advertising collections. At the time of this writing, the Smithsonian Institution has announced a forthcoming Center for Advertising History in its National Museum of American History. The Smithsonian has had extensive materials on file as an element of its Collection of Business Americana (Pepsi-Cola materials and the 400,000-piece N.W. Ayer archive in particular), and these will be enlarged. Marlboro and Alka-Seltzer have donated materials, and the Institution has been compiling oral histories of various ad campaigns since 1984. The new Center will concentrate on post–World War II advertising activities, and (differing from the American Advertising Museum) will be available only to scholars and researchers.

The 125-year-old J. Walter Thompson Agency was for years the major exception to the "nobody keeps old ads" school, and in fact had a full-time, in-house archivist for decades. The carefully preserved materials were given to Duke University in 1988 and they will now be available to researchers, thereby opening yet another new source of research data. The New York Art Directors Club is building a retrospective file, and the Prints and Photographs Division of the Library of Congress has recently expanded its examples of early advertising as it drew in early deposits from turn-of-the-century Copyright Office records. All of the above provide dramatically enlarged new sources for advertising historical research in the coming 1990s.

Although this book is primarily a history of American advertising over the past two centuries, some readers may wish to pursue the actual mechanics of advertising in the 1980s—how advertising campaigns developed, and how you chose between the competing media. For this how-to approach, we would suggest two titles, which are included in the Bibliography: Donald W. Jugenheimer and Gordon W. White's *Basic Advertising* (1980), and Courtland L. Bovee and William F. Arens' *Contemporary Advertising* (1982). In addition, two excellent, fully-developed, scholarly guides to the industry are C.H Sandage, Vernon Fryburger, and Kim Rotzoll's *Advertising Theory and Practice* (1983), and Louis Kaufman's *Essentials of Advertising* (1980).

In addition, all of the biographical works and reminiscences in the full Bibliography reflect the various authors' views on their industry and "how advertising works."

CHAPTER THREE: Cereals, Soap, and Sex

There are two fine volumes on the story of Procter & Gamble. Alfred Lief's *It Floats: The Story of Procter & Gamble* (1958) is as good as the next for the early history, but Oscar Schisgall's *Eyes on Tomorrow: The Evolution of*

Procter & Gamble (1981) brings the story further along. Two volumes that are sketchier but both surprising and amusing are Lawrence Wright's *Clean and Decent: The History of the Bath and Loo* (1980), and a promotional pamphlet that was sent to every local library in the country, *A Tale of Soap and Water* by Grace T. Hallock (1937). The source of the latter was the Cleanliness Institute, a trade association for all the soap companies before soap was as universally employed as now.

The early cereal wars are described in charming detail in Gerald Carson's *Cornflake Crusade* (1957), one of the classics of American commercial history. A rather surprising biography of C.W. Post, Nettie L. Major's *C.W. Post—The Hour and The Man* (1963) has the disadvantage of being an "official biography" approved by the family, but has the advantage of revealing a great deal of anecdotal material that only the family knew. The latter appears to have been remarkably objective about its earlier generations.

The primary monographic treatment of Elliott White Springs is his own iconoclastic volume (which apparently appeared only as a frequently reissued and updated paperback) called *Clothes Make the Man* (1955).

The business press provided frequent contemporary reports on his advertising campaigns and his managerial style; the most useful ones are: "Playboy of the Textile World," *Fortune*, January 1950:66 + , "Textile Tempest," *Time*, July 26, 1948:72 + , and "Elliott Springs," *Newsweek*, Oct. 26, 1959:107 + .

The John Trytten quotation appears in *Sales Management*, May 28, 1973:36 + . The Prudence Glynn quotation comes from her *Skin to Skin* (1982). This whole volume is a delight and provides the historical context for the continuing vigor of sex in advertising. The philosophical content is developed with humor in Robert Atwan, Donald McQuade, and John Wright's *Edsels, Luckies and Frigidaires* (1979) (see their chapter on sex starting on page 325).

The studies discussing ad and brand recall when linked to nudity are described in the *Journal of Advertising Research*, April 1972:15 + and February 1978:47 (as well as numerous textbooks cited in the full Bibliography); The Rice Council ad is reproduced in the same journal, October–November 1982:53 + .

CHAPTER FOUR: The Great Names Go Back So Far

The quickest sources for information on company histories and trademark data are: Hal Morgan's *Symbols of America* (1986), a colorful, well-written compilation; *Everybody's Business, An Almanac* edited by Milton Moskowitz, Michael Katz, and Robert Levering (1982), which is, as the editors themselves subtitle the volume, *The Irreverent Guide to Corporate America*; and Ronald Hambleton's *The Branding of America* (1987), similar to Morgan but with longer essays and fewer entries. A young people's version of this sort of thing is *What's In a Name: Famous Brand Names* by Oren Arnold (1979). The comprehensive, formal reference book for industrial history is the annual publication *Moody's Industrial Manual.*

A modern survey of like products and trademarks is *I'll Buy That: 50 Small Wonders and Big Deals that Revolutionized the Lives of Consumers* by the editors of *Consumer Reports* (1986).

More fully developed histories of individual brands and firms are included in the Bibliography.

CHAPTER FIVE: The Hard Ones—How Do You Sell A . . . ?

The most detailed biography of George Eastman is Carl W. Ackerman's *George Eastman* (1930), which traces the early years of Kodak in detail. *George Eastman and the Early Photographers* by Brian Coe (1973) is well illustrated (Coe was curator of the Kodak Museum), and three of the basic surveys of advertising mentioned above (Presbrey, Rowsome, and Pope) all explore Eastman's role in industrial and consumer product advertising. James Playsted Wood's *The Story of Advertising* (1958) also examines Eastman's philosophy and techniques for promotion.

The best biography of King C. Gillette is *King C. Gillette: The Man and His Wonderful Shaving Device* by Russell B. Adams, Jr. (1978), which contains a fully developed recounting of the invention. A short version appears in *Look Sharp! Feel Sharp! Be Sharp! Gillette Safety Razor Company Fifty Years 1901–1951* by J.P. Spang, Jr. (1951), who was the president of the firm for many years. The Ford Tri-motor story is told interestingly and in detail in David Weiss's *The Saga of the Tin Goose* (1971). An earlier book by Douglas J. Ingells, *Tin Goose: The Fabulous Ford Trimotor* (1968), includes some rare photographs of the planes from the Ford Archives.

The astonishing attempt to identify all the original purchasers of the two hundred planes and their ultimate fate appears in *The Ford Story: A Pictorial History of the Ford Tri-motor, 1927–1957* by William L. Larkins (1957). This is also a gold mine for model builders since it provides "blueprints" of the various Tri-motors and their sequential modifications.

An analysis of Henry Ford's role in the acquisition and abandonment of the design appears in the classic Ford biography by Allan Nevins, the second volume, *Ford: Expansion and Challenge, 1915–1933* (1957).

CHAPTER SIX: Cosmetics—How to Attract the Opposite Sex

Two of the more readable volumes on the history of cosmetics are: Fenja Gunn's *The Artificial Face* (1973), and the earlier *A History of Cosmetics in America* by Gilbert Vail (1947). The critical consumer's point of view can be found in Toni Stabile's *Everything You Want to Know About Cosmetics* (1984), and the earlier *More Than Skin Deep* by

Mary Catherine Phillips (1948). Reflections on advertising techniques in the cosmetic fields usually appear in volumes on high fashion and style; the researcher will find that, except for professional trade journals, there has been surprisingly little published material about the cosmetics industry in general.

CHAPTER NINE: Art, Artists, and Illustrators

For the interested reader, there are two excellent books on American illustrators which include material on their role in advertising: Susan E. Meyer's *America's Great Illustrators* (1978), and Walt and Roger Reed's *The Illustrator in America, 1880–1980* (1984). Reed's *Great American Illustrators* limits itself to the top 76, and is able to provide more and larger illustrations.

For someone researching the topic, complete books on most of the leading individual artists (Rockwell, Parrish, Leyendecker, Smith, Held, Phillips, Flagg, Remington, Wyeth, etc.) can be found in the Bibliography that follows.

CHAPTER TEN: The Educator of New Technology

You will find the various stories of the early advertising experiences of the new inventions in the histories of each, the encyclopedias, and many of the biographies of the early advertising "founding fathers" all detailed in the Bibliography. The interesting insight about time and "time-saving inventions" comes from Ruth Schwartz Cowan's "Less Work for Mother?," which appeared in *American Heritage*, v. 38, September–October 1987. The story of marketing Birdseye and frozen foods is spelled out in James Playsted Wood's *This Is Advertising* (1968).

CHAPTER ELEVEN: A Century of Cigarettes

As the distress over the environmental and health aspects of smoking has grown, there have been many books on the topic of tobacco but relatively few exploring the techniques of advertising the product. The best (of those that are likely to be available in most communities) are:

Joseph C. Robert's *The Story of Tobacco in America* (1967); Nannie May Tilley's monumental history of *The R.J. Reynolds Tobacco Company* (1985); Susan Wagner's *Cigarette Country: Tobacco in American History and Politics* (1971); and Peter Taylor's more critical *The Smoke Ring: Tobacco, Money, and International Politics* (1984). E.S. Turner's *The Shocking History of Advertising!* (1953) is full of dry comments and amusing anecdotes about the early tobacco years and, although it is now aging in years, it is not in wisdom.

An unlikely source of graphics relating to early tobacco advertising appears in *Cigarette Pack Art* by Chris Mullen (1979). Although of British origin, it does an equally good job on American brands up to World War II. Mr. Mullen generously gave us permission to use several examples of his original photography and plates for this book, but we were unable to secure releases from the companies whose products were involved. Indeed it will be noticed that the illustrations for this chapter stop abruptly with 1915, the last year in which advertisements are in the public domain. We had selected some two dozen examples of tobacco advertising from 1916 to 1988, but we were unable to secure permission to reproduce any of those sought.

Because so many of the traditions of American advertising are linked to the early tobacco campaigns, all of the basic works mentioned in Chapter One—Pope, Rowsome, Atwan, Presbrey—discuss tobacco in the years up to the mid-1900s.

CHAPTER THIRTEEN: The Face of Advertising

Although advertising is only a part of its treatment, one of the best general surveys of printing and page design appears in Clarence Hornung and Fridolf Johnson's *200 Years of American Graphic Art* (1976). Miles Tinker's *Legibility of Print* (1963) is a much broader handbook of how to use type effectively than the title might suggest.

If one has time for only a single "how-to" book on designing advertisements, we would suggest Roy Paul Nelson's *The Design of Advertising* (1985). It was both the most useful as a manual, and the most interesting for his views on the *philosophy* of art and advertising. Wendell C. Crow's *Communication Graphics* (1986) is also excellent as an instructional volume, and is useful in offering choices of how best to move a message to an audience—whether it is advertising or any other means of passing images and facts.

The many personal formulas for successful advertising appear in the individual biographies listed in the Bibliography. Dobrow's and Glatzer's examination of the 1960s style mentioned in Chapters One and Two above is appropriate here, as well as George Lois and Bill Pitts' *The Art of Advertising* (1977).

Much of the material on the Burma-Shave signs is drawn from Frank Rowsome's amusing *The Verse by the Side of the Road: The Story of Burma Shave Signs and Jingles* (1965), which contains the complete canon of all known Burma-Shave series, as supplied to Rowsome by the Odell family

itself. This has recently been re-issued by Publishers Choice (Huntington Station, N.Y.).

The question of "creativity" has been best explored by Edward Buxton in *Creative People At Work* (1975), and *Promise Them Anything: The Inside Story of the Madison Avenue Power Struggle* (1972).

CHAPTER FOURTEEN: The Automobile

There are some excellent sources both for information about the automobile in America and the advertising of it. Jane and Michael Stern's *Auto Ads* (1978) is charming social history. E. John DeWaard's *Fins and Chrome* (1982) is a picture book; Jerry Flint's *The Dream Machines* (1976) is a thoughtful discussion of the 1946 to 1965 period; while Mitch Frumkin's *Muscle Car Mania* (1981) concentrates on the 1964–74 decade.

The Volkswagen Saga is well illustrated in *Is The Bug Dead?* by Alfredo Marcantonio, David Abbott, and John O'Driscoll (1983), and Robert Glatzer's *The New Advertising* (1970) contains additional data about the personalities involved.

Finally, the "Automobile" essays in each of the major encyclopedias are research writing at its best. Roger Huntington and David L. Lewis did the *Collier's* article; Kenneth William Purdy and John Bill Rae, the *Encyclopaedia Britannica* piece; and Dennis Simanaitis of *Road and Track* wrote the *Americana* study.

CHAPTER FIFTEEN: Gender Change

Two general texts give the best overall coverage of the treatment of gender in advertising: Roland Marchand's *Advertising the American Dream* (1985); and C.H. Sandage, Vernon Fryburger, and Kim Rotzoll's *Advertising Theory and Practice* (1983). Marchand concentrates on the 1930s and 1940s; Sandage *et al* discusses practices as of the 1980s.

The argument between the feminists and the advertisers is described in *Sex Stereotyping in Advertising* by Alice E. Courtney and Thomas W. Whipple (1983), and Erving Goffman's *Gender Advertisements* (1976). The trade publication *Adweek* does an annual essay on "Women in Advertising" which attempts to chart the yearly developments in this on-going area of change.

BIBLIOGRAPHY

The materials noted below are those that sat on our desks at one time or another in the course of our writing this book. Normally any work referred to in the text would have received a bibliographic footnote on the same page as the reference, but such scholarly format was impossible to fit around the multi-shaped ad plates throughout the volume; thus the full bibliographic information appears in this appendix instead. It should be emphasized that this list makes no attempt at being a comprehensive bibliography of advertising. For such compilations, please see the detailed professional bibliographies noted at the end of this listing.

BOOKS

Aaker, David. *Viewers Perceptions of Prime Time Television Advertising.* Cambridge, Mass.: Marketing Science Institute, 1981.

Aaker, David A., and John G. Myers. *Advertising Management.* 2d ed. Englewood Cliffs, N.J.: Prentice-Hall, 1978.

Ackerman, Carl. *George Eastman.* Boston: Houghton Mifflin, 1930.

Adams, Russell B. *King C. Gillette: The Man and His Wonderful Shaving Device.* Boston: Little, Brown, 1978.

Advertising Age Yearbook. Chicago: Crain. 1981, 1982, 1983.

Advertising Arts and Crafts, v. I and II. New York: Lee and Kirby, 1924.

Advertising: Today, Yesterday, Tomorrow. New York: McGraw-Hill, 1963.

Allen, Douglas and Douglas Allen, Jr. *N.C. Wyeth: The Collected Paintings, Illustrations, and Murals.* New York: Crown, 1972.

Allen, Oliver E. *The Airline Builders.* Alexandria, Va.: Time-Life Books, 1981.

American Heritage. *The American Heritage History of the Automobile in America.* New York: American Heritage, 1977.

Andrist, Ralph. *American Century: One Hundred Years of Changing Life Styles in America.* New York: American Heritage, 1972.

Angelucci, Enzo. *The Automobile from Steam to Gasoline.* New York: McGraw-Hill, 1974.

Annenberg, Maurice. *Advertising 3000 B.C.—1900 A.D.: A Not Too Serious Compilation.* Washington, D.C.: Maran Printing Services, 1969.

Annual of Advertising and Editorial Art and Design. New York: The New York Art Directors Club, Yearbook, 1921+.

Arlen, Michael. *Thirty Seconds.* New York: Farrar, Straus & Giroux, 1980.

Arnold, Oren. *What's in a Name?: Famous Brand Names.* New York: Julian Messner, 1979.

Atwan, Robert, Donald McQuade, and John Wright. *Edsels, Luckies and Frigidaires: Advertising the American Way.* New York: Delacorte Press, 1979.

Baker, Stephen. *Visual Persuasion.* New York: McGraw-Hill, 1961.

Banta, Martha. *Imaging American Women: Idea and Ideals in Cultural History.* New York: Columbia University Press, 1987.

Barker, Raymond F. *Marketing Research.* Reston, Va.: Reston, 1983.

Barmash, Isadore. *The World is Full of It.* New York: Delacorte Press, 1974.

Barnicoat, John. *A Concise History of Posters, 1870–1970.* New York: Abrams, 1972.

Barnouw, Erik. *The Sponsor: Notes on a Modern Potentate.* New York: Oxford University Press, 1978.

———. *Tube of Plenty: The Evolution of American Television.* New York: Oxford University Press, 1975.

Bates, Charles Austin. *Short Talks on Advertising.* New York: Press of Charles Austin Bates, 1889.

Bell, Daniel. *The Coming of Post-Industrial Society, 1973.* Beverly Hills: Sage Publications, 1981.

Berman, Ronald. *Advertising and Social Change.* Beverly Hills: Sayre Publications, 1981.

Bernays, Edward L. *The Later Years: Public Relations Insights, 1956–1986.* New York: H&M Publishers, 1986.

Bernstein, Sid. *This Makes Sense to Me.* Chicago: Crain Books, 1976.

Blake, Peter. *God's Own Junkyard.* New York: Holt, Rinehart & Winston, 1979.

Block, Maurice E. and others. *The American Personality: The Artist-Illustrator of Life in the United States 1860–1950.* Los Angeles: The Grunwald Center for the Graphic Arts, University of California, 1976.

Bockus, H. William. *Advertising Graphics.* 3d ed. New York: Macmillan, 1979.

Bolen, William H. *Advertising.* New York: John Wiley, 1984.

Bond, David. *The Guinness Guide to 20th Century Fashion.* Enfield, Eng.: Guinness Superlatives Limited, 1981.

Booth-Clibborn, Edward, and Daniele Baroni. *The Language of Graphics.* New York: Abrams, 1980.

Bovee, Courtland L., and William F. Arens. *Contemporary Advertising.* Homewood, Ill.: Richard Irwin, 1982.

Braznell, William. *California's Finest: The History of Del Monte Corporation and the Del Monte Brand.* San Francisco: Del Monte Corp., 1982.

Brooklyn Institute of Arts and Sciences. *A Century of American Illustration.* New York: 1972.

Brower, Charlie. *Me and Other Advertising Geniuses.* New York: Doubleday, 1974.

Brozen, Yale, ed. *Advertising and Society.* New York: New York University Press, 1974.

Bryan, Joseph. *The World's Greatest Showman: The Life of P.T. Barnum.* New York: Random House, 1956.

Buechner, Thomas S. *Norman Rockwell, Artist and Illustrator.* New York: Abrams, 1970.

Burnett, Leo. *Best Read Ads, 1969.* Mamaroneck, N.Y.: Daniel Starch and Staff, 1970.

Burton, Jean. *Lydia Pinkham is Her Name.* New York: Farrar, Straus, 1949.

Burton, Philip Ward. *Cases in Advertising.* Columbus, Oh.: Grid, 1981.

Busch, H. Ted and Terry Landek. *The Making of a Television Commercial.* New York: Macmillan, 1980.

Buxton, Edward. *Creative People at Work.* New York: Executive Communications, 1975.

———. *Promise Them Anything: The Inside Story of the Madison Avenue Power Struggle.* New York: Stein and Day, 1972.

Cahn, William. *Out of the Cracker Barrel: From Ani-*

mal Crackers to ZuZu's. New York: Simon & Schuster, 1969.

Calkins, Earnest Elmo. *And Hearing Not.* New York: Scribners, 1946.

Campbell, Hannah. *Why Did They Name It?* New York: Ace Publications, 1964.

Caples, John. *How to Make Your Advertising Make Money.* Englewood Cliffs, N.J.: Prentice-Hall, 1983.

————. *Tested Advertising Methods.* Englewood Cliffs, N.J.: Prentice-Hall, 1975. (Foreword by David Ogilvy).

Carson, Gerald. *Cornflake Crusade.* New York: Rinehart, 1957.

————. *One for a Man; Two for a Horse: A Pictorial History, Grave and Comic of Patent Medicines.* New York: Doubleday, 1961.

Cassucci, Piero. *Classic Cars.* Chicago: Rand McNally, 1981.

Castleman, Harry. *Watching TV.* New York: McGraw-Hill, 1982.

Century Magazine. Advertising Supplements. Nov. 1890–April 1891; May–Oct. 1892; Nov. 1892–April 1893; Dec. 1897–April 1898.

Chamberlain, John. *The Enterprising Americans: A Business History of the United States, 1963.* New York: Harper & Row, 1963.

Chandler, Alfred D. *The Visible Hand.* Cambridge, Mass.: Harvard University Press, 1977.

Chester, Giraud. *Television and Radio.* New York: Appleton-Century, 1971.

Christy, Joe. *High Adventure: The First 75 Years of Civil Aviation.* Blue Ridge, Pa.: Tab Books, 1985.

Claus, Karen E. *The Sign User's Guide.* Palo Alto, Calif.: Institute of Signage Research, 1978.

Cochran, Thomas C. *Social Change in America.* New York: Harper & Row, 1972.

Coe, Brian. *George Eastman and the Early Photographers.* London: Priory Press, 1973.

Cohen, Daniel. *The Last Hundred Years — Household Technology.* New York: M. Evans and Co., 1982.

Cone, Fairfax M. *With All Its Faults: A Candid Account of Forty Years in Advertising.* Boston: Little, Brown, 1969.

————. *The Blue Streak: Some Observations, Mostly About Advertising.* Chicago: Crain Communications, 1973.

Corn, Joseph J. *The Winged Gospel: America's Romance with Aviation, 1900–1950.* New York: Oxford University Press, 1983.

Courtney, Alice E. and Thomas W. Whipple. *Sex Stereotyping in Advertising.* New York: Lexington Books, 1983.

Crow, Wendell C. *Communication Graphics.* Englewood Cliffs, N.J.: Prentice-Hall, 1986.

Cummings, Bart. *The Benevolent Dictators: Interviews with Advertising Greats.* Chicago: Crain Communications, 1984.

Day, John. *The Bosch Book of the Motor Car.* London: Collins, 1976.

DeWaard, E. John. *Fins and Chrome.* New York: Crescent Books, 1982.

DeWeese, Truman. *Book on Advertising.* New York: The System Co., 1906.

Delaware Art Museum. *The Golden Age of American Illustration, 1880–1914.* Wilmington: Wilmington Society of the Fine Arts, 1982.

Della Femina, Jerry. *From Those Wonderful Folks Who Gave You Pearl Harbor: Front-Line Dispatches from the Advertising War.* New York: Simon & Schuster, 1970.

Diamant, Lincoln. *Television's Classic Commercials: The Golden Years, 1948–1958.* New York: Hastings House, 1971.

Dibacco, Thomas V. *Made in the U.S.A.: The History of American Business.* New York: Harper & Row, 1987.

Dichter, Ernest. *Psychology of Everyday Living.* New York: Barnes & Noble, 1947.

————. *Strategy of Desire.* Garden City, N.Y.: Dou-

bleday, 1960.

Dobrow, Larry. *When Advertising Tried Harder: The Sixties, The Golden Age of American Advertising.* New York: Friendly Press, 1984.

Donahue, Bud. *The Language of Layout.* Englewood Cliffs, N.J.: Prentice-Hall, 1978.

Douglas, Ann. *The Feminization of American Culture.* New York: Knopf, 1977.

Doyle Dane Bernbach, Inc. *Sex on the Airwaves.* New York: 1978.

Eicoff, Alvin. *Or Your Money Back.* New York: Crown, 1982.

Evans, Jacob A. *Selling and Promoting Radio and Television.* New York: Printer's Ink, 1954.

Ewen, Stuart. *Captains of Consciousness: Advertising and the Social Roots of the Consumer Culture.* New York: McGraw-Hill, 1976.

Farrell, Warren. *The Liberated Man.* New York: Random House, 1974.

Fasteau, Marc. *The Male Machine.* New York: McGraw-Hill, 1974.

Felton, Charles J. *Layout Printing and Design.* St. Petersburg, Fla.: 1970.

Flesch, Rudolph. *The Art of Plain Talk.* New York: Collier Macmillan, 1962.

Flexner, Stuart B. *I Hear America Talking.* New York: Van Nostrand Reinhold, 1976.

Flint, Jerry. *The Dream Machine: The Golden Age of American Automobiles, 1946–1965.* New York: New York Times Quadrangle Books, 1976.

Flower, Raymond. *100 Years on the Road: A Social History of the Car.* New York: McGraw-Hill, 1981.

Foster, Eugene S. *Understanding Broadcasting.* 2d ed. New York: Addison, Wesley, 1982.

Foster, G. Allen. *Advertising: Ancient Marketplace to Television.* New York: Criterion Books, 1967.

Fox, Richard W., ed. *The Culture of Consumption.* New York: Pantheon Books, 1983.

Fox, Stephen. *The Mirror Makers; A History of American Advertising and its Creators.* New York: Vintage, 1985.

Frazier, Gregory and Beverly Frazier. *The Bath Book.* San Francisco: Troubador Press, 1972.

Freeman, Larry. *Victorian Posters.* New York: American Life Foundation, 1969.

Frumkin, Mitch. *Muscle Car Mania: An Advertising Collection, 1964–1974.* Osceola, Wisc.: Motorbooks International, 1981.

————. *Son of Muscle Car Mania: More Ads, 1962–74.* Osceola, Wisc.: Motorbooks International, 1982.

Furnas, J.C. *The Americans: A Social History of the United States, 1587–1914.* New York: Putnam, 1969.

————. *Great Times: An Informal Social History of the United States, 1914–1929.* New York: Putnam, 1974.

Galanoy, Terry. *Down the Tube.* Chicago: Henry Regnery, 1970.

Gallo, Max. *The Poster in History.* New York: McGraw-Hill, 1974.

Gentry, Curt. *The Vulnerable Americans.* New York: Doubleday, 1966.

Glatzer, Robert. *The New Advertising: The Great Campaigns from Avis to Volkswagen.* Secaucus, N.J.: Citadel Press, 1970.

Gluck, Felix. *Modern Publicity, 1978.* New York: Van Nostrand Reinhold, 1978.

Glynn, Prudence. *Skin to Skin.* New York: Oxford University Press, 1982.

Goffman, Erving. *Gender Advertisements.* New York: Harper & Row, 1976.

Golden, Cipe Pineles, Kurt Weihs, and Robert Strunsky. *The Visual Craft of William Golden.* New York: Braziller, 1962.

Goldsborough. *Great Railroad Paintings.* New York: Peacock Press, Bantam, 1976.

Gottschall, Edward M. and Arthur Hawkins, eds. *Advertising Directions.* New York: Art Directors Book Co., 1959.

Grayson, Melvin J. *Forty-two Million a Day: The Story of Nabisco Brands.* East Hanover, N.J.: Nabisco Brands, 1986.

Groome, Harry C. *This Is Advertising.* Philadelphia: Ayer Press, 1975.

Grossinger, Tania. *The Book of Gadgets.* New York: McKay, 1974.

Gunn, Fenja. *The Artificial Face: A History of Cosmetics.* London: Hippocrene Books, 1973.

Gunther, John. *Taken at the Flood: The Story of Albert D. Lasker.* New York: Harper & Row, 1960.

Guptill, Arthur L. *Norman Rockwell—Illustrator.* New York: Watson-Guptill, 1946.

Haller, John S. *The Physician and Sexuality in Victorian America.* New York: Norton, 1974.

Hallock, Grace T. *A Tale of Soap and Water.* New York: Cleanliness Institute, 1937.

Hammond, Dorothy. *Collectible Advertising.* Des Moines: Wallace Homestead, 1974.

Harmon, Jim. *The Great Radio Heroes.* New York: Doubleday, 1967.

Harris, Neil. *Humbug: The Art of P.T. Barnum.* Boston: Little, Brown, 1973.

Harvard University. *First Five Years: Harvard Advertising Awards, 1924–1928.* New York: McGraw-Hill, 1930.

Harvard University. Graduate School of Business Administration. Harvard Advertising Awards, 1929, 1930.

Haserick, Peter H. *Frederic Remington.* New York: Abrams, 1973.

Heighton, Elizabeth J. *Advertising in the Broadcast Media.* Belmont, Cal.: Woodsworth, 1976.

Heimann, Robert K. *Tobacco and Americans.* New York: McGraw-Hill, 1960.

Held, John, Jr. *The Most of John Held, Jr.* Brattleboro, Vt.: Stephen Greene Press, 1972.

Henderson, Sally, and Robert Landau. *Billboard Art.* San Francisco: Chronicle Books, 1980.

Hess, Dick, and Marion Muller. *Dorfsman and CBS.* New York: American Showcase, 1987.

Higgins, Denis. *The Art of Writing Advertising.* Chicago: Advertising Publications, 1965.

Hodgson, Godfrey. *America in Our Time.* Garden City, N.Y.: Doubleday, 1976.

Holme, Bryan. *Advertising: Reflections of a Century.* New York: Viking, 1982.

Hopkins, Claude C. *My Life in Advertising.* Chicago: Crain Books, 1966.

————. *Scientific Advertising.* New York: Crown, 1966.

Horn, Marilyn J. *The Second Skin.* Boston: Houghton Mifflin, 1981.

Hornung, Clarence P. *Handbook of Early Advertising Art.* New York: Dover, 1953, 1956. 3d ed.

————, and Fridolf Johnson. *Two Hundred Years of American Graphic Art.* New York: Braziller, 1976.

Houck, John W., ed. *Outdoor Advertising: History and Regulation.* Notre Dame, Ind.: University of Notre Dame Press, 1969.

Hower, Ralph M. *The History of an Advertising Agency.* Rev. ed. Cambridge, Mass.: Harvard University Press, 1949.

Hunt, Robert. *The Advertising Parade: An Anthology of Good Advertisements Published in 1928.* New York: Harper, 1930.

Hutchinson, Harold F. *The Poster: An Illustrated History from 1860.* New York: Viking, 1968.

Ingells, Douglas J. *Tin Goose: The Fabulous Ford Trimotor.* Tallbrook, Cal.: Aero Publishers, 1968.

Inglis, Fred. *The Imagery of Power: A Critique of Advertising.* London: Heinemann, 1972.

International Advertising Association. *Controversy Advertising, How Advertisers Present Points of View in Public Affairs.* New York: Hastings House, 1977.

Jenkins, Reese V. *Images and Enterprises.* Baltimore: Johns Hopkins University Press, 1975.

Jensen, Oliver. *The American Heritage History of Railroads in America.* New York: Crown, 1975.

Johnson, J. Douglas. *Advertising Today.* Chicago: Science Research Associates, 1978.

Jones, Edgar R. *Those Were the Good Old Days: A Sumptuous Collection of Advertisements* . . . New York: Simon & Schuster, 1979.

Jugenheimer, Donald W. and Gordon W. White. *Basic Advertising.* Columbus, Oh.: Grid, 1980.

Kanter, Rosabeth M. *Men and Women of the Corporation.* New York: Basic Books, 1977.

Katz, Judith A. *The Ad Game: A Complete Guide to Careers in Advertising, Marketing, and Related Areas.* New York: Barnes and Noble, 1984.

Kaufman, Louis. *Essentials of Advertising.* New York: Harcourt, Brace, Jovanovich, 1980.

Keady, Carolyn. *American Posters of the Turn of the Century.* New York: St. Martins, 1975.

Kelly, Charles J., Jr. *The Sky's the Limit.* New York: Arno Press, 1972 (c. 1963).

Kennett, Lee. *The Gun in America.* Westport, Conn.: Greenwood Press, 1975.

Key, Wilson Bryan. *Subliminal Seduction: Ad Media's Manipulation of a Not So Innocent America.* Englewood Cliffs, N.J.: Prentice-Hall, 1973.

————. *Media Sexploitation.* Englewood Cliffs, N.J.: Prentice-Hall, 1976.

Kleinman, Philip. *Advertising Inside Out.* London: W.H. Allen, 1972.

Kurtz, Bruce. *Spots: The Popular Art of American Television Commercials.* New York: Arts Communications, 1977.

Langholz Leymore, Varda. *Hidden Myth: Structure and Symbolism in Advertising.* New York: Basic Books, 1975.

Larkins, William L. *The Ford Story: A Pictorial History of the Ford Tri-motor, 1927–1957.* Wichita: Robert R. Longo Co., 1957.

Lasker, Albert D. *The Lasker Story as He Told It.* Chicago: Advertising Publications, 1963.

Levine, Harris. *Good-bye to All That.* New York: McGraw-Hill, 1970.

Lief, Alfred. *It Floats: The Story of Procter and Gamble.* New York: Rinehart, 1958.

Lifshey, Earl. *The Housewares Story.* Chicago: National Housewares Manufacturers Assn., 1973.

Lois, George and Bill Pitts. *The Art of Advertising.* New York: Abrams, 1977.

Luck, David J., and others. *Marketing Research.* 5th ed. Englewood Cliffs, N.J.: Prentice-Hall, 1978.

Ludwig, Coy. *Maxfield Parrish.* New York: Watson-Guptill, 1973.

Lyons, John. *Guts: Advertising From the Inside Out.* New York: AMACON, 1987.

Maas, Jane. *Adventures of an Advertising Woman.* New York: St. Martins, 1986.

MacDonald, J. Fred. *Don't Touch That Dial!: Radio Programming in American Life, 1920–60.* Chicago: Nelson-Hall, 1979.

McLuhan, Marshall. *The Mechanical Bride: Folklore of Industrial Man.* New York: Vanguard Press, 1951.

————. *Understanding Media.* New York: McGraw-Hill, 1964.

McGann, Anthony J., and J. Thomas Russell. *Advertising Media: A Managerial Approach.* Homewood, Ill.: Richard D. Irwin, 1981.

McMahan, Harry Wayne. *Communication and Persuasion: A Hard Look at Successful TV Commercials.* Baja California, Mex.: Stephens Press, 1981.

Major, Nettie L. *C.W. Post — The Hour and The Man.* Washington, D.C.: Judd and Detweiler, 1963.

Mandell, Maurice I. *Advertising.* 4th ed. Englewood Cliffs, N.J.: Prentice-Hall, 1984.

Marcantonio, Alfredo, David Abbott, and John O'Driscoll. *Is The Bug Dead? The Great Beetle Ad Campaign.* New York: Stewart, Tabori, and Chang, 1983.

Marchand, Roland. *Advertising the American Dream.* Berkeley: University of California Press, 1985.

Margolin, Victor. *American Poster Renaissance: The Great Age of American Poster Design, 1890–1900.* New York: Watson-Guptill, 1975.

Margolin, Victor, Ira Brichta, and Vivian Brichta. *The Promise and the Product: 200 Years of American Advertising Posters.* New York: Macmillan, 1979.

Margolius, Sidney. *The Innocent Consumer vs. The Exploiters.* New York: Trident Press, 1967.

Marquette, Arthur F. *Brands, Trademarks and Good Will: The Story of the Quaker Oats Company.* New York: McGraw-Hill, 1967.

Marin, Allan, ed. *Fifty Years of Advertising As Seen Through the Eyes of Advertising Age, 1930–1980.* Chicago: Crain Communications, 1980.

Mayer, Martin. *Madison Avenue, USA.* New York: Harper & Row, 1958.

Meyer, Susan E. *America's Great Illustrators.* New York: Abrams, 1978.

————. *James Montgomery Flagg.* New York: Watson-Guptill, 1974.

Moline, Mary. *Norman Rockwell Encyclopedia.* Indianapolis: Curtis, 1979.

Moody's Industrial Manual. New York: Moody's Investor Service, 1988.

Morgan, Hal. *Symbols of America.* New York: Viking, 1986.

Mott, John Luther. *A History of American Magazines.* Cambridge, Mass.: Harvard University Press, 1938–1968.

Mullen, Chris. *Cigarette Pack Art.* London: Galley Press, 1979.

Muller-Brockman, Josef. *The Graphic Designer and His Design Problems.* New York: Hastings House, 1983.

Nelson, Roy Paul. *The Design of Advertising.* Fifth ed. Dubuque, Ia.: Wm. C. Brown Pubs., 1985.

Nevins, Allan and Frank Ernest Hill. *Ford: Expansion and Challenge, 1915–1933.* New York: Scribners, 1957.

Nylen, David W. *Advertising: Planning, Implementation and Control.* Cincinnati: South-Western, 1986.

Ogilvy, David. *Confessions of an Advertising Man.* New York: Atheneum, 1963.

————. *Ogilvy on Advertising.* New York: Crown, 1983.

Oliver, Robert E. *Advertising.* New York: McGraw-Hill, 1969.

O'Toole, John E. *Making Ads.* New York: Foote, Cone and Belding, 1976.

Packard, Vance. *The Hidden Persuaders, 1957.* New York: David McKay, 1957.

Palmer, Carl J. *A History of the Soda Fountain Industry.* Chicago: Soda Fountain Manufacturers Assoc., 1947.

Parson, Frank Alvah. *The Art Appeal in Display Advertising.* New York: Harper, 1921.

Patterson, William D., ed. *America: Miracle at Work: The Best Public Interest Advertising of 1952 Based on the First Annual Saturday Review Awards for Distinguished Advertising in the Public Interest.* New York: Prentice-Hall, 1953.

Patti, Charles H., and John H. Murphy. *Advertising Management.* New York: John Wiley, 1978.

Patton, Phil. *Open Road: A Celebration of the American Highway.* New York: Simon & Schuster, 1986.

Phillips, Coles. *A Young Man's Fancy.* Indianapolis: Bobbs-Merrill, 1912.

Phillips, Mary Catherine. *More Than Skin Deep.* New York: Richard R. Smith, 1948.

Pitz, Henry C. *200 Years of American Illustration.* New York: Random House, 1977.

Pleuthner, Willard A., ed. *460 Secrets of Advertising Experts.* New York: Thomas Nelson, 1961.

Polykoff, Shirley. *Does She . . . Or Doesn't She? — And How She Did It.* Garden City, N.Y.: Doubleday, 1970.

Pope, Daniel. *The Making of Modern Advertising.* New York: Basic Books, 1983.

Poppe, Fred C. *The 100 Greatest Corporate and Industrial Ads.* New York: Van Nostrand Reinhold, 1983.

Porter, Michael. *Competitive Strategy.* New York: Free Press, 1980.

Postum Cereal Company. *A Trip Through Postumville,*

Where Grape-Nuts [etc.] Are Made. Battle Creek: 1920.

Potter, David. *History and American Society, 1973.* New York: Oxford University Press, 1973.

Powell, William J. *Pillsbury Best: A Company History from 1869.* Pillsbury, 1985.

Presbrey, Frank Spencer. *The History and Development of Advertising.* New York: Doubleday, 1929. Reprinted by Greenwood Press, 1968.

Preston, Ivan L. *The Great American Blow Up: Puffery in Advertising and Selling.* Madison: University of Wisconsin Press, 1975.

Price, Jonathan. *The Best Thing on TV: Commercials.* New York: Viking, 1978.

Printer's Ink. *Advertising: Today/Yesterday/Tomorrow.* New York: McGraw-Hill, 1963.

————. *Fifty Years 1888–1938.* (No. 33 in *The History of Advertising: 40 Major Books in Facsimile.* Ed. by Henry Assael. New York: Garland Pub. Co.)

Rae, John. *The American Automobile: A Brief History.* Chicago: University of Chicago Press, 1965.

Reader, William J. *Fifty Years of Unilever, 1930–1980.* London: Heinemann, 1980.

Reed, Walt. *Great American Illustrators.* New York: Abbeville Press, 1979.

Reed, Walt and Roger Reed. *The Illustrator in America, 1880–1980: A Century of Illustration.* New York: The Society of Illustrators, 1984.

Reeves, Rosser. *Reality in Advertising.* New York: Knopf, 1961.

Rennert, Jack. *One Hundred Years of Bicycle Posters.* New York: Harper, 1973.

Ritchie, Carson I. A. *Food in Civilization: How History Has Been Affected by Human Tastes.* New York: Beaufort Books, 1981.

Robert, Joseph C. *The Story of Tobacco in America.* Chapel Hill: University of North Carolina Press, 1967.

Roberts, Peter. *Any Color So Long As It's Black: The First Fifty Years of Automobile Advertising.* New York: William Morrow, 1976.

Rogers, Edward J. *Getting Hired.* Englewood Cliffs, N.J.: Prentice-Hall, 1982.

Roman, Kenneth and Jane Maas. *How to Advertise.* New York: St. Martins Press, 1976.

Roman, Kenneth and Joel Raphaelson. *Writing That Works.* New York: Harper & Row, 1981.

Ross, Ishbel. *Taste in America: An Illustrated History, 1967.* New York: Crowell, 1967.

Roth, Laszlo. *Display Design.* New York: Prentice-Hall, 1983.

Rotzoll, Kim B., James E. Haefner, and Charles H. Sandage. *Advertising in Contemporary Society: Perspectives Toward Understanding.* Columbus, Oh.: Grid, 1976.

Rowsome, Frank. *They Laughed When I Sat Down: An Informal History of Advertising in Words and Pictures.* New York: McGraw-Hill, 1959.

————. *Think Small: The Story of Those Volkswagen Ads.* Brattleboro, Vt: Stephen Greene Press, 1970.

————. *The Verse by the Side of the Road: The Story of Burma Shave Signs and Jingles.* Brattleboro, Vt: Stephen Greene Press, 1965.

Samstag, Nicholas. *How Business is Bamboozled by the Ad-Boys.* New York: James H. Heineman, 1966.

Sandage, C. H., Vernon Fryburger, and Kim Rotzoll. *Advertising Theory and Practice.* Homewood, Ill: Richard D. Irwin, 1983. (11th ed.)

Sarnoff, Dorothy. *Speech Can Change Your Life.* New York: Doubleday, 1970.

Schau, Michael. *"All-American Girl": The Art of Coles Phillips.* New York: Watson-Guptill, 1975.

————. *J.C. Leyendecker.* New York: Watson-Guptill, 1974.

Schisgall, Oscar. *Eyes on Tomorrow: The Evolution of Procter & Gamble.* Chicago: J. G. Ferguson, 1981.

Schnessel, S. Michael. *Jessie Willcox Smith.* London: Studio Vista, 1977.

Schofeld, Perry. *100 Top Copywriters and Their Favorite Ads.* New York: Printer's Ink, 1954.

Schrank, Jeffrey. *Deception Detection*. Boston: Beacon Press, 1975.

Schudson, Michael. *Advertising, The Uneasy Persuasion: Its Dubious Impact on American Society*. New York: Basic Books, 1984.

Schultz, Don E., Dennis Martin, and William P. Brown. *Strategic Advertising Campaigns*. 2d ed. Chicago: Crain Books, 1984.

Schuwer, Phillipe. *History of Advertising*. London: Leisure Arts, 1967.

Schwarz, Theodore. *The Successful Promoter*. Chicago: Henry Regnery, 1976.

Schwimmer, Walter. *What Have You Done For Me Lately?* New York: Citadel, 1957.

Scott, Walter Dill. *The Psychology of Advertising*. Boston: Small, Maynard and Co., 1902.

Scull, Penrose. *From Peddlers to Merchant Princes: A History of Selling in America*. Chicago: Follett, 1967.

Seldin, Joseph J. *The Golden Fleece: Selling the Good Life to Americans*. New York: Macmillan, 1963.

Sell, DeWitt E. *Handguns Americana*. Alhambra, Calif.: Borden, 1972.

Settel, Irving. *A Pictorial History of Radio*. New York: Grossett and Dunlop, 1967.

————. *A Pictorial History of Television*. 2d ed. New York: Frederick Ungar, 1983.

Sissors, Jack Z., and E. Reynold Petray. *Advertising Media Planning*. 2d ed. Chicago: Crain Books, 1982.

Sklar, Robert. *Movie-Made America*. New York: Random House, 1975.

Snyder, Gertrude and Alan Peckolick. *Herb Lubalin: Art Director, Graphic Designer and Typographer*. New York: American Showcase, 1985.

Sobel, Robert. *The Manipulators: America in the Media Age*. Garden City, N.Y.: Anchor, 1976.

Sobieszek, Robert A. *The Art of Persuasion: A History of Advertising Photography*. New York: Abrams, 1988.

Smith, Cynthia S. *How to Get Big Results from a Small Advertising Budget*. New York: Hawthorn Books, 1973.

Southern Creativity Annual, The 1973. Ashland, Ky.: Century Communications, 1973.

Spang, J. P. *Look Sharp! Feel Sharp! Be Sharp!: Gillette Safety Razor Company Fifty Years 1901–1951*. New York: The Newcomen Society in North America, 1951.

Spero, Robert. *The Duping of the American Voter: Dishonesty and Deception in Presidential Television Advertising*. New York: Lippincott & Crowell, 1980.

Springs, Elliott. *Clothes Make the Man*. New York: Empyrean Press, 1955.

Stabile, Toni. *Everything You Want to Know About Cosmetics*. New York: Dodd, Mead, 1984.

Starch, Daniel. *300 Effective Advertisements, Selected on the Basis of 5,000,000 Inquiries Received From 3,500 Magazines and Newspaper Advertisements of 163 Firms*. New York: Starch, 1931.

Stern, Jane and Michael. *Auto Ads*. New York: Random House, David Obst Books, 1978.

Stoltz, Donald Robert, Marshall Louis Stoltz, and William B. Earle. *The Advertising World of Norman Rockwell*. New York: Madison Square Press, 1985.

Stone, Bob. *Successful Direct Marketing Methods*. Chicago: Crain Books, 1979.

Sutphen, Dick. *The Mad Old Ads*. Minneapolis: Dick Sutphen Studio, 1966.

Switkin, Abraham. *Ads: Design and Make Your Own*. New York: Van Nostrand Reinhold, 1981.

Taylor, Peter. *The Smoke Ring: Tobacco, Money, and International Politics*. New York: Pantheon, 1984.

Tierney, Patricia E. *Ladies of the Avenue*. New York: Bartholomew House, 1971.

Tilley, Nannie May. *The R.J. Reynolds Tobacco Company*. Chapel Hill: University of North Carolina Press, 1985.

Tinker, Miles A. *Legibility of Print*. Ames, Ia: Iowa State University Press, 1963.

Turner, E. S. *The Shocking History of Advertising!* New York: Dutton, 1953.

Ulanoff, Stanley M. *Advertising in America*. New York: Hastings House, 1977.

U.S. Committee on Public Information. Division of Advertising. Government war advertising. Washington, D.C.: U.S. Govt. Printing Office, 1918.

Uslan, Michael and Bruce Solomon. *The TV Commercial Trivia Quiz Book*. New York: Arbor House, 1985.

Vail, Gilbert. *A History of Cosmetics in America*. New York: The Toilet Goods Association, 1947.

Vries, Leonard de, and Ilonka Van Amstel, comp. *The Wonderful World of American Advertisements, 1865–1900*. Chicago: Follett, 1972.

Wademan, Victor. *Risk-free Advertising: How to Come Close to It*. New York: John Wiley, 1977.

Wainwright, Charles A. *Television Commercials: How to Create Successful TV Advertising*. New York: Hastings House, 1970.

Wagner, Susan. *Cigarette Country: Tobacco in American History and Politics*. New York: Praeger, 1971.

Watkins, Julian Lewis. *The 100 Greatest Advertisements: Who Wrote Them and What They Did*. New York: Moore, 1949.

Watson, Ernest W. *Forty Illustrators: And How They Work*. New York: Watson-Guptill, 1946.

Watters, Pat. *Coca-Cola: An Illustrated History*. New York: Doubleday, 1978.

Weilbacher, William M. *Advertising*. New York: Macmillan, 1984. 3d ed.

————. *Cases in Advertising*. New York: Macmillan, 1981.

Weiss, David Ansel. *The Saga of the Tin Goose: The Plane that Revolutionized American Civil Aviation*. New York: Crown, 1971.

Weisberger, Bernard A. *The American Heritage History of the American People*. New York: American Heritage, 1971.

Whelan, Elizabeth M. *A Smoking Gun: How the Tobacco Industry Gets Away with Murder*. Philadelphia: George F. Stickley, 1984.

White, Gordon. *John Caples: Adman*. Chicago: Crain Books, 1977.

White, Hooper. *How to Produce an Effective TV Commercial*. Chicago: Crain Books, 1981.

Wiebe, Robert. *The Search for Order*. New York: Hill and Wang, 1966.

Wilk, Max. *The Golden Age of Television*. New York: Delacorte, 1976.

Wilson, Charles. *The History of Unilever*. New York: Praeger, 1968.

Winters, Karen Cole. *Your Career in Advertising*. New York: Arco, 1980.

Wise, David Burgess, and others. *The Automobile in The First Century*. New York: Greenwich House, 1983.

Wood, James Playsted. *The Story of Advertising*. New York: Ronald Press, 1958.

————. *This Is Advertising*. New York: Crown, 1968.

Wright, John S. *Advertising's Role in Society*. St. Paul: West, 1974.

Wright, Lawrence. *Clean and Decent: The History of the Bath and Loo*. London: Routledge and Kegan Paul, 1980.

SERIALS
[Articles cited in text]

Atherton, Lewis E. "The pioneer merchant in mid-America." *University of Missouri Studies*, vol. 14, no. 2 (1 April 1939).

Cowan, Ruth Schwartz. "Less work for mother?" *American Heritage*, v. 38, Sept-Oct 1987.

"How it was in advertising, 1776–1976." *Advertising Age*, 19 April 1976.

Norris, Vincent P. "Advertising history — according to the textbooks." *Journal of Advertising*, vol. 9, no. 3 (1980).

(Sex appeal in advertising.) *Journal of Advertising*, vol. 22, no. 5, Oct/Nov 1982.

Ticer, Scott. "Where there's smoke, there's trouble." *Business Week*, 18 January 1988.

General sources for current reporting of advertising:
Advertising Age
Adweek
Broadcasting
Journal of Advertising
Madison Ave.

BIBLIOGRAPHIES ABOUT ADVERTISING

Advertising Research Foundation. Sources of published advertising research. New York: 1960.

Blum, Eleanor. *Basic Books in the Mass Media*. Urbana: University of Illinois Press, 1980.

Halpern, George Martin. *Bibliography for Graphic Arts and Advertising Technology*. New Hyde Park, N.Y.: Nonpareil Assoc., 1968.

J. Walter Thompson Company. *Advertising: An Annotated Bibliography*. London: National Book League, 1972.

Corkindale, David. *Advertising Effectiveness Bibliography*. Cranfield, Eng: Cranfield School of Management, 1975.

Courtney, Alice E. *Sex Stereotyping in Advertising*. Cambridge, Mass: Marketing Science Institute, 1980.

Goehlert, Robert. *Political and Social Advertising*. Montecello, Ill: Vance Bibliographies, 1985.

Lipstein, Benjamin. *Evaluating Advertising*. New York: Advertising Research Foundation, 1978.

Meringoff, Laurene. *Children and Advertising*. New York: Children's Advertising Review Unit, National Advertising Division, Council of Better Business Bureaus, 1980.

Pollay, Richard W., ed. *Information Sources in Advertising History*. Westport, Conn: Greenwood Press, 1979.

CREDITS

Photograph Credits

The authors and publisher wish to thank the manufacturers and advertising agencies and others who permitted the reproduction of ads in their possession and who supplied the necessary photographs. We also wish to thank Jonathan Wallen, who photographed many of the ads from their original sources. Additional permissions are gratefully acknowledged below. In all cases, the publisher has made every effort to contact all copyright holders. Should there be any oversight, we would be happy to update our information.

Numbers refer to pages on which the illustrations appear. t = top, b = bottom, l = left, r = right, m = middle row, c = center illustration within a row.

American Automobile Association (A.A.A.), 237tl. Absolut Vodka: Carillon Importers, Ltd., 168br. AIDS Research ("For the Future of our Children"): Kenneth Cole Productions, Inc., 275b. Aluminum Company of America (ALCOA), 212br. American Airlines, Inc./DDB Needham Worldwide, 257bl. American Lung Association, 273. Anti-Drug Campaign: Demaine, Vickers & Associates, 275. The Arrow Company, 44, 45t, 84, 85, 163. AT&T/Bell: AT&T Archives, 87, 258tl. Bank of America National Trust & Savings/Ketchum Advertising, 222. P.T. Barnum: Museum of the City of New York, 17. Betty Crocker: General Mills, Inc., 40. Black and Decker, 86b. The Boeing Company/Cole & Weber, 147. Bon Ami: Faultless Starch, 86tl and tr. Braniff Airlines, Inc., 144t and bl, 129tr. Breck: Shulton, Inc., U.S.A., 41. Bufferin: Bristol-Myers Squibb Company, 125tr. Buick Motor Division of General Motors, 246b. Burlington: Kayser-Roth Hosiery, Inc., 206tr and br. Burma Shave: Collection of Advertising History, Archives Center, 216, 217; photo inset: LIFE Magazine © Time, Inc. Magazine Company, photo by Joe Schershel, 217. Cadillac: Reprinted with the expressed permission of Cadillac Motor Car Division of General Motors, 233, 235. Campbell Soup Company, 88. CBS Television Network, 43, 220. Chevrolet Motor Division of General Motors, 234bl, 246ml, 247. Chrysler Corporation (Dodge, Chrysler, Plymouth, De Soto), 229tr, 238b, 239t, 242tl, 246tl and tr. Clairol, 133. The Coca-Cola Company, 29, 89, 90tr, ml, mr, br, 91, 92, 93, 94, 95, 160r, 164r. Colgate-Palmolive Company, 130. Coty Musk, 134tl. Dentyne Company, 155bl. Du Pont Company, 183. Eaton Corporation, 259bl. Edison Christmas Lights: Gotham Book Mart, New York, 174tl. El Al Israel Airlines, 145br. Eureka Vacuum Cleaners, 256bl. Fogal: Media Consulting, Zurich, 207. Ford: From the Collections of the Henry Ford Museum and Greenfield Village, 277tl, 228tl and tc, 232tr, 234t, 236tl, 242tr. General Electric Appliances, Louisville, Kentucky, 8, 185. General Motors Corporation, 237tr, 253t. The Gillette Company, 114, 115. Girls Clubs of America, Inc., 260. Goodyear Tire and Rubber Company, 97b, 214bl, 229br. Hanes Hosiery, Inc., 204. Hathaway: C.F. Hathaway, a Warnaco, Inc. Company, 218tr. H.J. Heinz Company, 212tl. Hewlett-Packard Company, 188tl. Hires Root Beer: Courtesy of the Procter and Gamble Company, 93tr and bl, 98. Home Recording Rights Coalition/Soghigian & Macuga, 171br. Hoover Company, 178br. ITT Corporation, 274mr. Ivory: Procter and Gamble Company, 48, 50, 52, 53, 55, 71tr. Jamaica Tourist Board, 146b. Jantzen, Inc., 167bl, 206tl. Jockey International Company, Kenosha, Wisconsin, 206m and bc. Johnson & Johnson Company, 155tr. Jordache Enterprises, Inc., 47. Jōvan Musk: Beecham Cosmetics, Inc., 134tr. Kaiser: Reprinted by permission of Kaiser Aluminum & Chemical Corporation, 168bl. Keds: Stride Rite Corporation/Young & Rubicam, Inc., 259bl. Kellogg Company, 60mr and bl, 61, 62tl, 63, 252br. Kodak: Eastman Kodak Company, 108, 110, 111, 112. Kohler Company, 182tl. Kraft General Foods, Collection, 64, 65, 66, 67br, 101br. © *Ladies' Home Journal,* 1986, 259tr. Lady Remington: Remington Products, Inc., 133tr. Levolor: Levolor Lorentzen, Inc./MullerJordanWeiss, Inc., 171bl. Levis:

Levi Strauss & Company, 100, 170. Lightolier, Inc., 171t. Lintas: Campbell Ewald Company ("Secret of Advertising"), 46bl. Listerine, 154tl, 256tl. Lysol, 152. Maidenform, Inc., 81, 206bc. Maxell Corporation of America/Scali, McCabe, Sloves, New York, 189. *McCall's* Magazine, 254tl. McDonald's Corporation, 165br. McGraw-Hill Publications Co./Fuller, Smith & Ross, 45b. Mentor Condom: Mentor Corporation/Bloom Agency, New York, 233tr. Mitsouko: Guerlaine, Inc., 221tr. Modess, 221tl. Morton Salt: Division of Morton Thiokol, Inc., 37tr. Movado Watch Corporation, 223tl. Munsingwear, Inc., 70, 203tr and bl. Narcotics Anonymous: Goldberg/Marchesano & Associates, Inc., 275tr. National Archives, Washington, D.C.: Air Mail, 119; Look Why Freeze, 141b; Save Wheat, 251b; We Can Do It, 254bl. National Museum of American History, Smithsonian Institution, Washington, D.C., Photograph Archives: Camels, 195tr; Cracker Jacks, 96tr; Grove's Tasteless Chill Tonic, 6; Quaker Cereal, 57, 59, 126br, 148; Sweet Heart of the Corn, collection of Business Americana, photo by Joe Goulait, 62. NIKE, Inc., 11. Nivea: Beiersdorf, Inc., Norwalk, Connecticut, 135. Obsession: Calvin Klein, 134bl. Oldsmobile Motor Division of General Motors, 238t. J.C. Penney, 37br. Pepsi: Pepsi and Pepsi-Cola are registered Trademarks of PepsiCo Inc. (Norman Rockwell Santa Claus art used with permission of PepsiCo Inc.), 165bl. Playtex Apparel, Inc., 203br. Polaroid: Polaroid Corporate Archives, 186bl and br. Prudential Life Insurance: Reprinted with permission by the Prudential Life Insurance Company of America, Inc., 9, 151br, 153tl and tr. Revlon, 132tl and tr. Rice Council, 80. Norman Rockwell: Estate of Norman Rockwell/Thomas Rockwell: Black Cat Hosiery, 164ml; Coke, 164r; Four Freedoms, 270tr; Grape Nuts (photo courtesy of the Norman Rockwell Museum at Stockbridge, Mass.), 65; McDonald's, 165br; Mennen, 164bl; Pepsi, 165bl; Perfection Oil Heaters, 164tl; Sears-Roebuck, 36; Shredded Wheat (photo courtesy of the Norman Rockwell Museum at Stockbridge, Mass.), 68b; Soldier with Gun, 165t. Schick, 155br. Schlitz: Stroh Brewery Company, 257tl. Scott Paper Company, 154b. Scripps Howard: United Media, 186tl. Sears, Roebuck and Co., 36. Smith Brothers: F & F Laboratories, Inc., 103. Springmaid: Springs Industries, Inc., 75, 76, 77, 78. Squibb: C.E.R. Squibb & Sons, Inc., 215br. Student Mobilization Committee: copyright Richard Avedon 1969. All rights reserved, 271. Sunkist Growers, Inc., 131. Talon, 46, 168tr, 181tr and br, 212bl. Toni: The Gillette Company/Edelman Public Relations, 133tl. Transamerica Corporation, 223b. United Way of America, 274tl. Volkswagen United States, Inc./DDB Needham Worldwide, 10, 46tl, 218tl, 244, 245. Johnny Walker: Courtesy of Schieffelen and Somerset Company, 259tl. Whitman's Chocolates, 106l, 256tl. Wrigley's: William Wrigley Jr. Company, 106tr and br, 107. Xerox, 187tl and tr. Zondervan Corporation ("A Woman's Place?"), 261.

The broadsides on pages 12, 14, 15, 16, 172, and 208 are from the Rare Book and Special Collections Division of the Library of Congress.

Text Credits

Grateful acknowledgment is made for permission to quote from the following works:

Creative People at Work, 1975, by Edward Buxton. *Skin to Skin* by Prudence Glynn, Oxford University Press. *Gender Advertisements* by Erving Goffman. Copyright © 1976 by Erving Goffman. Reprinted by permission of Harper & Row, Publishers, Inc. *Advertising: The American Dream* by R. Marchand, 1985, University of California Press. National Advertising Review Board. *The Verse by the Side of the Road: The Story of the Burma-Shave Signs and Jingles* by Frank Rowsome, Jr. Copyright © 1965 by Frank Rowsome, Jr. Published by The Stephen Greene Press. Reprinted by permission of Penguin Books USA, Inc.

Printed and bound in Japan